POPULATION HISTORY OF WESTERN U.S. CITIES AND TOWNS, 1850–1990

RILEY MOFFAT

The Scarecrow Press, Inc.
Lanham, Md., and London

SCARECROW PRESS, INC.

Published in the United States of America
by Scarecrow Press, Inc.
4720 Boston Way
Lanham, Maryland 20706

4 Pleydell Gardens, Folkestone
Kent CT20 2DN, England

British Cataloguing-in-Publication Information Available

Library of Congress Cataloging-in-Publication Data

Moffat, Riley Moore
Population history of western U.S. cities and towns, 1850–1990 / by Riley Moffat.
P. Cm.
Includes bibliographical references.
1. West (U.S.)—Population—History. 2. Cities and towns—West (U.S.)—History.
3. Texas—Population—History. 4. Cities and towns—Texas—History. I. Title.
HB3525.W38M64   1996   304.6'0978—dc20   96–14583   CIP

ISBN 0–8108–3033–7 (cloth : alk. paper)

⊖™ The paper used in this publication meets the minimum requirements of
American National Standard for Information Sciences—Permanence of
Paper for Printed Library Materials, ANSI Z39.48–1984.
Manufactured in the United States of America.

This compilation is dedicated to my family who have tolerated my population collecting for the past thirty years. Thanks for being patient, guys.

CONTENTS

ACKNOWLEDGEMENTS

Over the past ten years that I have been working to put this data into publishable form a number of individuals and institutions have been very generous with their time and resources. None of this would have been possibe without the support of Brigham Young University's Harold B. Lee Library and Brigham Young University-Hawaii Campus in the form of professional development grants. I have enjoyed working with several great individuals who have lent their clerical and technical skills to help whip this material into shape. They include Bonnie Percival, Joela Craven, Diane King, Rose Meno, Travis Lund, Kim McAvoy, and especially Don Christensen, Wesley Wong, Sidney Ngai, Denny Denfield, and Sara Clemons. Mahalo nui loa.

INTRODUCTION

As a university reference librarian with background and experience in geography, history, business, and planning, I noticed a gap in reference sources dealing with historical population figures, Students and faculty researchers were wanting to see the long term population history of a community which would reflect the ebbs and flows of its development and may help identify current and future trends. Gazetteers and atlases tended to only show current information. Publications of the U.S. Bureau of the Census would sometimes include comparative data from the previous one or two censuses but no farther. Researchers then had to plow through volume after volume of older census data to construct these histories. In an attempt to fill this gap John Andriot compiled and published *Population Abstract of the United States*, which only covered 2,000 cities with a current population of over 10,000 and only went back as far as the city was incorporated. Obviously there are many more communities, and their history goes back beyond the point at which they were incorporated.

Geographically this volume covers the western United States from Texas to North Dakota on west. This tended to be the "permanent " Indian frontier beyond which settlement was discouraged until the middle of the nineteenth century. However, "manifest destiny" and the Gold Rush broke this barrier, and settlers flooded in. The U.S. Bureau of the Census began counting people beginning in 1850 as the West came into U.S. possession and settlers began moving in.

The primary source for this compilation was the population figures published by the U.S. Bureau of the Census. Their decennial census of population data by minor civil divisions gives the population of all incorporated cities and towns as well as unincorporated 'census designated places' of over 1,000 since 1950. When an unincorporated community had at least 100 people it could incorporate itself with city limits and be separately enumerated in the censuses. Most communities would wait until they were much larger; politics and economics played a key role in determining when a community would incorporate. With set city limits census enumerators could hope to identify a precise population figure for the community.

Another published source was the various state and territorial censuses. some states and territories felt the U.S. Bureau of the Census' decennial census of population did not occur often enough so they conducted their own censuses, often midway between the federal censuses in the years ending in "5." These censuses are identified in Dubester and in Schulze. Where these published censuses list cities, towns, and other minor civil divisions they have been included. But there are many more communities than just those incorporated and provide a population history for all communities that had at least 200 people at some point in their history - a size, I felt, that would tend to engender a sense of community and be large enough to begin to include some of the services and accouterments normally associated with an emerging town. Citations to state, territorial, or special census are give at the end of each state list.

Population figures for unincorporated communities are of course estimates since there are no definable city limits. Since 1950 the Bureau of the Census has provided reliable estimates for certain "census designated places" of over 1,000. Besides the Census Bureau's figures for "census designated places" the primary authority for the population of unincorporated places was the *Rand McNally Commercial Atlas and Marketing Guide* published annually since 1876. I relied on the edition for the years ending in "2" so that data from the federal decennial censuses could be utilized where possible. Rand McNally has been the most consistent and reliable estimator over the last century. They use the term 'central built-up section of a community' in defining the population of an unincorporated place. Rand McNally surveys postmasters, chambers of commerce, planning officials, and municipal officials in estimating the population of a place. Traditionally a good way was by the number of patrons a post office served.

Estimates are still only guesses. If Rand McNally did not consistently follow up on a town or the town did not respond to Rand McNally's query then an estimate may have appeared in print years after it ceased to be relevant. While the figures for the incorporated places should be complete there undoubtedly are other sources of varying quality that I'm not aware of that could be used to fill in some of the gaps for the unincorporated places. The quest to find and examine these possible sources will continue. Where local history researchers disagree with the estimates for unincorporated places remember that they are taken from contemporary sources using varying methods for arriving at those figures and are given as found.

Other issues that impact this compilation include the fact that a few communities have changed their names. Unless this was noted in the census schedules it may not be noted here. If I found that a community was know by more than one name in its history I have included both names separated by a slash, and if there is more than one community with the same name in a state I have put the name of the county of each community in parenthesis. Growing cities would sometimes annex neighboring communities as they grew. This is usually seen as an abrupt halt in a growing population trend. And of course some communities declined and are possibly abandoned.

Another good source that I used whenever I found one was the R.L. Polk state directories. They include a good contemporary description of each community in the state being surveyed, including population, and list prominent businesses and services. They were especially helpful in identifying which places really were communities with commerce and services and which places may only have been rural neighborhoods or railroad stops.

BIBLIOGRAPHY

Dubester, Henry J. State Censuses: An Annotated Bibliography of Censuses of Population Taken After the Year 1790 by State and Territories of the United States. New York: B. Franklin, 1969.

Rand McNally Commercial Atlas and Marketing Guide. Chicago: Rand McNally, 1876- (annual).

Schulze, Suzanne. Population Information in Nineteenth Century Census Volumes. Phoenix: Oryx Press, 1983.

Sealock, Richard B., Margaret M. Sealock, and Margaret S. Powell. Bibliography of Place-Name Literature: United States and Canada. 3rd ed. Chicago: American Library Association, 1982.

U.S. Bureau of the Census. A Century of Population Growth: From the First Census of the United States to the Twelfth 1790-1900. Washington: GPO, 1909.

U.S. Bureau of the Census. Historical Statisitics of the United States: Colonial Times to 1970. Bicentennial Edition. 2 vols. Washington: GPO, 1975.

POPULATION HISTORY OF ALASKA CITIES AND TOWNS 1880-1990

COMMUNITY	1990	1980	1970	1960	1950	1940	1930	1920	1910	1900	1890	1880
Adak	4633	3315										
Atognak				190	158	197	298	308	318	307	409	339
Akhiok	77	105	115	84	72			94	106	165	43	
Akiachak	400	438	312	229	179	156	228	150	165			
Akiak	285	198	184	187	168	209						
Akolmiut		641	526									
Akutan	589	169	101	107	86	80	71	66				
Alakanuk	544	522	414	278	140	61						
Aleknagik	185	154	128	181	153	78						
Alitak							86	215			420	
Allakaket	170	163	174	115	79	105	85					
Ambler	311	192	176	70								
Anaktuvuk Pass	259	203	99	35								
Anchorage	226338	173017	48081	44237	11254	3495	2277	1856				
Anchor Point	866	226	102	171								
Anderson	628	517	362									
Angoon	638	465	400	395	425	342	319	114				420
Aniak	540	341	205	308	142	122						
Annette	43	139	337	302								
Anvik	82	114	83	120	95	110	79	140	151	166	191	
Arctic	96	111		110								
Atmautluak	200	219										
Atqasuk	216	107										
Auke									218	261	324	
Aurora			1100	293								
Barrow	3469	2207	2104	1314	95	363	330	322	446			
Bayview							342	342				
Beaver	103	66	101	101			103	82				
Belkofski							123	129	147	147	185	
Bethel	4674	3576	2416	1258	654	376	278	221				
Big Delta	400	285										
Big Horn	360											
Birchwood			1219									
Brevig Mission	198	138	123				262					
Brook												
Buckland	318	177	104	87	108	115	104	52				
Butte	2039	988	448	559								
Candle				103	105	119	85	91	204			
Cantwell	147	89										
Cape Pole			123									

POPULATION HISTORY OF ALASKA CITIES AND TOWNS 1880-1990

COMMUNITY	1990	1980	1970	1960	1950	1940	1930	1920	1910	1900	1890	1880
Cape Smythe									314			
Carmel									381	381	189	
Chalkyitsik	90	100										
Chatanika			130						193			
Chauthbaluk		105			30	106						
Chefornak	320	230	146	133	106							
Chena			146					50	185			
Chevak	598	466	387	315	230							
Chickaloon							28	290				
Chignik	188	178	117				518	518	566			
Chitina	49	42		31	92	176	116	171				
Chuathbaluk	97	105										
Chugiak			489	585								
Circle	73	81		41	83	98	50	96	144	242		
Clarks Point	60	79	95	138	128	22	25					
Clover Pass	451		231	169								
Coffman Cove	180	200										
Cold Bay	148	192	256					225				
College	800	4083	3000	1755	424	234	61					
Cooper Landing	243	116										
Copper Center	213		206	151			80	71	91			
Cordova	2110	1879	1164	1128	1165	938	980	955	1152			
Council					41	48	109	109	289			
Craig	1260	527	272	273	374	505	231	212				
Crooked Creek	106	108										
Deadhorse	26	64										
Deering	157	150	85	95	174	230	183	73	100			
Delta Junction	652	945	703									
Dillingham	2017	1563	914	424	577	278	85	36				
Diomede		139	163	88	103							
Dome										135		
Douglas				1042	699	522	593	919	1722	825	402	
Dyea							54	98	261	261		
Eagle	168	110	36	92	55	73	78	60	178	383		
Eagle River			2437									
Edna Bay			112	135								
Eek	254	228	186	200	141	170	119	119				
Egegik	122	75	148	150			86	83				
Eielson AFB	5251	5232										
Eklutna						159	158					

POPULATION HISTORY OF ALASKA CITIES AND TOWNS 1880-1990

COMMUNITY	1990	1980	1970	1960	1950	1940	1930	1920	1910	1900	1890	1880
Ekwok	77	77	103	106	131	68	40					
Elim	264	211	174	145	154	100	97	162				
Emmonak	642	567	439		67	42						
English Bay	158	124										
Ester	147	70	264	81	74	218	320	320	213			
Eyak/Meakerville	172	47	349			365	366	320	222	222		
Fairbanks	30843	22645	14771	13311	5771	3455	2101	1155	3541			
False Pass	68	70										
Fire Lake			475									
Flat					95	146	124	158				
Fort Davis									180			
Fort Egbert									198			
Fort Gibbon							181					
Fort Liseum							153		162			
Fort Seward							186		255			
Fortuna Ledge/Marshall	273	262	176	166	95	91	329	329				
Fort Yukon	580	619	448	701	446	274	304	319	321	156	109	
Fox	275	123										
Galena	833	765	581	261	176	44	67					
Gambell	525	445	372	358	309	296	250	48	221			
Girdwood			144									
Glennallen	451	511	363	169								
Golovin	127	87	117	59	94	116	135	217	158	185		
Goodnews Bay/Mumtrak	241	168	218	154	100	48						
Graehl			349						198			
Grayling	208	209	139									
Gustavus	258	98		107								
Haines	1238	993	463	392	338	357	344	314	445	85		
Healy	487	334										
Heering Cove	99		114	126								
Holy Cross	277	241	199	256	157	226	337	142				
Homer	3660	2209	1083	1247	307	325						
Hoonah	795	680	748	686	563	716	514	402	462	447	438	
Hooper Bay	845	627	490	460	307	299	209	44				
Hope	161	103							200			
Houston	697	370	69									
Howkan												
Hughes	54	73			65	32	45	45				
Huslia	207	188	159	168	49							
Hydaburg	384	298	214	251	353	348	319	346				

POPULATION HISTORY OF ALASKA CITIES AND TOWNS 1880-1990

COMMUNITY	1990	1980	1970	1960	1950	1940	1930	1920	1910	1900	1890	1880
Hyder	99	77		32	30	72	254	237				
Iditarod								50				
Igagik									203			
Igloo							113		141			
Ikogmute									166			
Iliama	94	94		110			100	66	121			
Johnston			365									
Juneau	26751	19528	13556	6797	5956	5729	4043	3058	1644	1864	1253	
Kachemak	365	403	76									
Kake	700	555	448	455	376	419	386	387	232			
Kaktovik	224	165	123	120								
Kalifonsky	285	92										
Kalskag	130		122	147	121	140	137		141			
Kaltag	240	247	206	165	54	113	177	89	165			
Kanakanak												
Karluck	71	96		129	144	189	192	99	549	470	1123	302
Kasaan	54	25		36	47	85	112	126	129			
Kasigluk	300	342		244								
Kasilof	383	201							159			
Katalla									188			
Kenai	6327	4324	3533	778	321	303	286	332	250	290	264	44
Kennecott							217	494	208			
Kesuna												
Ketchikan	8263	7198	6994	6483	5305	4695	3796	2458	1613	459	40	
Kiana	385	345	278	253	181	167	115	98				
Killishoo								256	351	172	79	
Kinak						26	192	429	269			
King Cove	451	460	283	290	162	135						
King Salmon	696	545	202	227			42					
Kipnuk	470	371	325	221								
Kivalina		241	188	142	117	98	99	87				
Klawock	722	318	213	251	404	455	437	19	241	131	287	
Klukwan	129	135	103	112	91	97	97	167	245		236	261
Knakatnuk					38	31			145			
Kobuk	69	62		54								
Kodiak	6365	4756	3798	2628	1710	864	442	374	438	341	495	
Kodiak Station	2025	1370										
Kagiung				100					533			
Koliganak	181	117	142									
Kongiganak	294	239	190									

POPULATION HISTORY OF ALASKA CITIES AND TOWNS 1880-1990

COMMUNITY	1990	1980	1970	1960	1950	1940	1930	1920	1910	1900	1890	1880
Koserefsky									231			
Kotlik	461	293	228	57	44	35		83				
Kotzebue	2751	2054	1696	1290	623	372	291	230	193			
Koyuk	231	188	122	129	134	100	110					
Koyukuk	126	98	124	128	79	106	143	124	121			
Kwethluk	558	454	408	325	242	186						
Kwigillingok	278	354	148	344								
Larsen Bay	147	168	109									
Latouche						40	339	505				
Lemeta			1318	1227								
Levelock	105	79										
Little Diomede	178	139					101	101				
Livengood	75	75		40	153	22	131	131				
Long							20	617			200	
Loring							84	84	168	168		
Lower Kalskag	291	246	183	122	88							
McCarthy	25	35			49	49	115	127				
McGrath	528	355	279	241	175	138	112	90				
Manokotak	385	294	214	149	120							
Mutanuska							330	330				
Mekoryuk	177	160	249	242	156							
Metlakatla	1407	1056	1050	798	817	674	466	574	602	465	823	
Miller House							225					
Minto	218	153	168	161								
Moose Creek	610	510										
Mountain Point	396											
Mountain Village	674	583	459	372	221	128	76	136				
Naknek	575	318	419	300				111	166			
Napakiak	318	262	318	249	135	113	173	173	179			
Naparegarak			259	190								
Napaskiak	328	244	188	154	121	67						
Nenana	393	470	382	286	242	231	291	634	190			
Newhalen	160	87	88	63	48	55						
New Stuyahok	391	331	216	145	88							
Newtok	125	131	114	129	69							
Nightmute	153	119	127	257	27	78						
Nikishka	2743	1109										
Nikolai	109	91	112	85	88							
Ninilchik	456	341	134	169								
Noatak	333	273	293	275	326	336	212	164	121			

POPULATION HISTORY OF ALASKA CITIES AND TOWNS 1880-1990

COMMUNITY	1990	1980	1970	1960	1950	1940	1930	1920	1910	1900	1890	1880
Nome	3500	2301	2357	2316	1870	1559	1213	852	2600	12488		
Nondalton	178	173	184	205	103	82	24	69				
Noorvik	531	492	462	384	248	211	198	281				
North Pole	1456	724	265	615								
Northway	123	73		196								
Nuchek									144			
Nuiqsut	354	208										
Nulato	359	350	308	283	176	113	204	258	230	281	118	168
Nunapitchuk	378	299										
Nunivak				327		225	191	189	127			
Nushagak									74	324	368	
Old Harbor	284	340	290	193	121	109	84	54				
Olness							214	215				
Ophir					68	84	19	22	122			
Orea									141			
Ouzinkie	209	173	160	214	177	253	168					
Palmer	2866	2141	1140	1181	890	150		96				
Pelican	222	180	133	135	180	48						
Peninsula Point	175		175									
Perryville	108	111		111	72	45	93	85				
Petersburg	3207	2821	2042	1502	1619	1323	1252	879	585			
Peter Creek			340									
Pilot Station	463	325	290	219	52	39	87	145				
Pitkas Point	135	88										
Platinum	64	55		43	72	45						
Point Hope/Taigara	639	464	386	264	257	139	141	243	623	301		
Point Lay	139	68		49								
Poorman							217	217				
Port Alexander	119	86				87	107	36				
Port Graham	166	161	107	139			47	47				
Port Heiden	119	92	75	74			51	30				
Port Higgins			189									
Port Lions	222	215	227									
Purdhoe Bay	47	50										
Quinhagak	501	412	340	228	194	224	230	193	111	201		
Rampart	68	50			94	106	103	121				
Richmond												110
Ruby	170	197	145	179	132	138	132	128	119			
Russian Mission	246	169	147	102	55	34	54	90	143	211		
St. George	138	158	163	264			138	138				

POPULATION HISTORY OF ALASKA CITIES AND TOWNS 1880-1990

COMMUNITY	1990	1980	1970	1960	1950	1940	1930	1920	1910	1900	1890	1880
St. Marys	441	382	384	225	135	142	147	371	415			109
St. Michael	295	239	207	205	157		247	212	201	857	101	298
St. Paul	763	551	450	378	359	299						
Salamatof	999	334										
Salcha	354	319										
Sand Lake			4168									
Sand Point	878	625	360	254	107	99	69	60				
Savoonga	519	491	364	299	249	209	139					
Saxman	369	273	135	153	167	111	112	103	154	142		
Scammon Bay	411	250	166	115	103	88						
Scow Bay	250		238									
Selawik	596	361	429	348	273	239	227	274				
Seldovia	316	479	437	460	437	410	379	258	173	149	99	75
Seward	2699	1843	1587	1891	2114	949	835	652	534			
Shageluk	139	131	167	155	100	92	88	130				
Shakan									118			
Shaktoolik	178	164	151	187	127	128	104	73				
Sheldon Point	109	103	125	125	43							
Shemya Station	600			124								
Shishmaref	456	394	267	217	194	257	223	131				
Shouing									336			
Shungnak	223	202	165	135	141	193	145	95	210			
Sillitmute									242			
Sitka	8588	7803	6109	3237	1985	1987	1056	1175	1039	1396	1190	989
Skagway	692	768	675	659	758	634	492	494	872	3117		
Sleetmute	106	107	109	122			133					
Soldotna	3482	2320	1202	332	200							
South Bjerremark	450		402	231								
South Naknek	136	145	154	142								
Spenard			22500	9074	2108							
Stebbins	400	331	231	158	115	98						
Sterling	3802	919										
Stevens	102	96		102			48	103	100			
Sulzer							226	226				
Sumdum									137			
Sunrise							52	48	130			
Susitna				42					233			
Sutton	308	182		162								
Talkeetna	250	264	182	76	106	136	89	70				
Tanacross	106	117		102								

POPULATION HISTORY OF ALASKA CITIES AND TOWNS 1880-1990

COMMUNITY	1990	1980	1970	1960	1950	1940	1930	1920	1910	1900	1890	1880
Tanana	345	388	406	349	228	170	185	213	398	186	203	
Tatitlek	119	68	111				70		156			
Teller	151	212	220	217	160	118	76	121	125			
Tenakee Springs	94	138	93	109	140	188	210	174	126			
Tetlin	87	107	114	122								
Thane				82	81	66	68	421				
Thorne Bay	569	377	443									
Tofty								225				
Togiak	613	470	383	220	108		225					
Tok	935	589	214	129			71					
Toksook Bay	420	333	257									
Totem Park	580		450									
Trapper Creek	296											
Treadwell							16	325	1222	522		
Tuluksak	358	236	195	137	116	88	96	73				
Tuntutuliak	300	216	158	145								
Tununak	316	298	274	183								
Two Rivers	453	359										
Tyonek	154	239	232	187			78	58	107			
Uganik									155			
Unalakleet	714	623	574	469	329	261	285	247	241	175		
Ugashik							84		348			
Unalaska	3089	1322	342	218	173	298	226	299	281	428	317	
Unga				43	107	152	150	313	108	175	159	185
Upper Kalskag	172	129										
Usibelli	300		102									
Valdez	4068	3079	1005	555	554	529	442	466	810	315		
Venetie	182	132	112	107								
Wainwright	492	405	315	253	227	341	197	99				
Wales	161	133	131	128	141	193	170	136	337	396		
Ward Cove	270		105									
Wasilla	4028	1559	300	112	97	96	51	118				
White Mountain	180	125	87	151	129	199	205	198				
Whittier	243	198		809	627							
Willow	285	139	130									
Wiseman							58	175				
Wrangell	2479	2184	2029	1315	1263	1325	948	821	743	868	316	106
Yakutat	534	449	190	230	298	292	265	165	271	247	308	

POPULATION HISTORY OF ARIZONA CITIES AND TOWNS 1850-1990

COMMUNITY	1850	1860	1864	1870	1880	1884	1890	1900	1910	1920	1930	1940	1950	1960	1970	1980	1990
Aguila									100	119		175	147	250	450	600	600
Ajo									50	2336	4571	3049	5817	7049	5881	5189	2919
Alpine									35	84	165	200	250	900	300	500	950
Apache Junction													200	900	2390	9935	18100
Arivaca		61			200	200	236	170	170	170	150	250	120	152	165	170	400
Arizona City								170							400	1117	800
Ashfork						75			517	571	894	999	675	750	800	600	400
Aubrey					250												
Avondale/Coldwater											400	500	2505	6151	6304	8168	16169
Bagdad											275	275	800	1462	2079	2331	1858
Bapchule												150	150	100	150	380	380
Benson					150	700	348	450	1035	825	925	962	1440	2494	2839	4190	3824
Big Bug						100											
Bisbee						600	1535	6000	9019	9205	8023	5853	3801	9914	8328	7154	6288
Black Canyon														150	400	600	850
Bouse									200	200	100	100	100	150	150	450	600
Bowie									200	415	250	400	600	500	500	600	700
Brigham City					191												
Buckeye									375	420	1077	1305	1932	2286	2599	3434	5038
Bullhead City													350	500	1500	5000	21951
Bylas											500	285	636	750	1125	1175	1219
Cameron										63	63			100	150	500	493
Camp Bowie			74	400	184												
Camp Crittenden				215													
Camp Goodwin				200													
Camp Grant				340	243	500	498	450			76	57	150	150			
Camp Verde				174	310	700	175	280	169	182	240	458	550	600	900	3824	6243
Carefree															350	986	1666
Casa Blanca																500	500
Casa Grande					243	500	328	357	357	948	1351	1545	4181	8311	10536	14971	19082
Cashion											200	200	200	500	2705	3014	3014
Catalina															200	2749	4864
Catalina Foothills															1200	1500	1470
Cave Creek								40	100	113	175	175	250	450	500	1589	2925
Central								51	250	315	290	290	290	200	200	250	300
Central Heights												69	750	2486	2289	1500	1500
Chambers													150	200	250	400	400
Chandler										1013	1378	1239	3799	9531	13763	29673	90533
Charleston					350	350											
Chinle											65	140	150	400	500	2815	5059

POPULATION HISTORY OF ARIZONA CITIES AND TOWNS 1850-1990

COMMUNITY	1850	1860	1864	1870	1880	1884	1890	1900	1910	1920	1930	1940	1950	1960	1970	1980	1990
Chino Valley								465	275	450	350	300	300	300	550	2858	4837
Chloride									200		262	484	350	150	225	300	350
Christmas											129	122	129	190	190		
Chuichu																300	330
Cibecue											50			500	500	950	1254
Clarkdale										2435	4647	2280	1609	1095	892	1512	2144
Clay Springs											154	154	150	199	200	275	500
Claypool										75	1243	1500	1000	2505	2245	2362	1942
Clemenceau										603	603	500	300	300			
Clifton					750	500	600	864	4874	4163	2305	2668	3466	4191	5087	4245	2840
Cochise								48	175	212	65	75	85	120	115	100	200
Colorado City/Short Creek											90	100	90	350	500	1439	2426
Concho					84			238	401	275	363	250	175	175	100	150	400
Congress							242	727	471	220	123	75					
Congress Junction									75		50	101	200	250	300	450	750
Constellation									200								
Contention					150	200											
Coolidge											1200	2700	4306	4990	4651	6851	6927
Cordes Lakes																800	850
Cornville														200	250	200	2089
Cortaro								110	110						200	200	250
Cottonwood									914	1621	1950	1710	1626	1879	2815	4550	5918
Courtland										414	114	115					
Crane																	2650
Crittenden								162									
Crown King								177	250	128	77	100		200	40	50	80
Davis Dam													600		200	120	150
Davis-Monthan AFB																6279	6279
Dennehotso														200		500	616
Desert Hills																950	1700
Dewey								50	75	157		164			200	400	675
Dilkon																90	285
Dolan Springs																870	1090
Don Luis							24	46	200	321	175	455	200				
Dos Cabezos					126	300			100	264	152	159	80	51	40	70	90
Douglas									6437	9916	9828	8623	9442	11925	12462	13058	12822
Dragoon						200		29	30	275	60	50	150	100	150	150	150
Dudleyville							86	137	100							1205	1356
Duncan						100	114	106	738	897	1090	887	941	862	773	603	662
Duquesne									150	164	164	164					

POPULATION HISTORY OF ARIZONA CITIES AND TOWNS 1850-1990

COMMUNITY	1990	1980	1970	1960	1950	1940	1930	1920	1910	1900	1890	1884	1880	1870	1864	1860	1850
Eagar	4025	2791	1279	873	637	880	562	635	397	262							
East Fork	752	750															
Eden	110	110	200	200	215	300	231	405	500	34							
Ehrenburg	1226	900	400	250	50				50	34	34	75	248	223			
El Mirage	5001	4307	3258	1723	1111												
Elfrida	400	300	300	200	300	1000	400										
Eloy	7211	6240	5381	4899	3580												
Fairbanks				75	50	192	197	269	225	171	478	100					
Flagstaff	45857	34743	26117	18214	7663	5080	3891	3186	1633	1271	963	500					
Flecha Caida	3200	1600															
Florence	7510	3391	2173	2143	1776	1383	1318	1161	807	1500	1486	1000	902	218			
Fort Apache	350	350	400	500	400	300	300	264	360	360	413		275				
Fort Bowie												300	184			142	
Fort Buchanan									150							256	
Fort Defiance	4489	3431	950	800	645	600	600										
Fort Huachuca			6659			1850	1500	1214	400	370	296	150	250				
Fort Lowell											545		227	47			
Fort McDowell	230	200	150	150	226						132		250	192			
Fort Mohave													78	118	120	130	
Fort San Carlos											344						
Fort Thomas	250	200	200	275	250	250	250	216	300	163	143	100	112				
Fortuna										155							
Fountain Hills	10030	2771															
Franklin	120	120	120	200		300	256	263	200								
Fredonia	1207	1040	798	643	350	401	254	243	166	50							
Gadsden	500	500	300	250	350	150	150										
Ganado	3400	1200	900	500	493	150		58	100								
Gibson					819												
Gila Bend	1747	1585	1795	1813	873	750	585	250	199	250	135						
Gila City													45			150	
Gilbert	29188	5717	1971	1833	1114	837	791	865									
Gleeson					100	140	139	381	600	30							
Glendale	148134	97172	36228	15893	8179	4855	3665	2737	1000	300							
Globe	6062	6886	7333	6217	6419	6141	7157	7044	7083	1495	803	1500	704				
Golconda								102	198								
Goldroad							52	250	100								
Goodyear	6258	2747	2140	1654	1254	140	140										
Grand Canyon	1499	1348	1101	950	1001	701	193	69	150								
Greasewood	450		300	200													
Green Valley	13231	7999	2000														

POPULATION HISTORY OF ARIZONA CITIES AND TOWNS 1850-1990

COMMUNITY	1990	1980	1970	1960	1950	1940	1930	1920	1910	1900	1890	1884	1880	1870	1864	1860	1850
Gu Achi	450	339	339	250	300												
Guadalupe	5458	4506	3500	1200	646												
Hamburg									300								
Harshaw					100	150	259				260	150	640				
Hayden	909	1205	1283	1760	1494	2504	2364	2550	150								
Heber	950	600	500	400	300	109	80		300	50							
Helvetia										172							
Holbrook	4686	5785	4759	3438	2336	1184	1115	1206	609	233	206	300					
Hotevilla	869	700	900	577													
Houck	400	600	500	680			69	69	150								
Huachuca City	1782	1661	1233	1330													
Hualapai	450																
Humboldt	650	400	424	400	1108	1208	675	1060	525								
Inspiration		300	400	500	711	450	600										
Jerome	403	420	290	243	1233	2295	4932	4030	2393	2861	250						
Jerome Junction																	
Johnson							258	139	314	87							
Joseph City/St. Joseph	950	900	500	500	350	350	350	258	75	30			105				
Kaibito	641	275	275					82	64	64							
Kayenta	4372	3343	800	500	110												
Kearns Canyon	393	600	600	500	150	150	150	36	29		32	100	42				
Kearny	2262	2646	2829	902													
Kelvin									500	377							
Kingman	12722	9257	7312	4525	3342	2568	2275	1276	900	726	322	100					
Kykotsmovi/Oraibi	773																
La Paz														254	352		
Lake Havasu City	24363	15909	2500														
Lake Montezuma	500	900															
Lakeside	950	1333	900	750	500	425	160	38	114								
Laveen	950	600	500	500	300	300	100	68									
Lehi	3303	3657	1664	950	450	250	202		300	270	269		123				
Litchfield Park	600	600															
Little Acres			200	300													
Lowell					1136	2636	3479	3520	4356								
Lukachukai	1113	1049		500													
Luke AFB	4371	3515	5047														
McCabe									139	250							
McMillanville													350				
McNary	355	1320	950	1608	1902	2000	155	114									
Mammoth	1845	1906	1953	1913	800	800	200	300	500	210	46						

POPULATION HISTORY OF ARIZONA CITIES AND TOWNS 1850-1990

COMMUNITY	1990	1980	1970	1960	1950	1940	1930	1920	1910	1900	1890	1884	1880	1870	1864	1860	1850
Many Farms	1294	1364	300														
Marana	2187	1674	1000	950	900	250	275										
Maricopa	1600	900	500	200	127	100	125	129	200	75	75	75	96				
Maxey													145				
Mayer	1800	950	810	700	965	505	729	280	334	37	37						
Mesa	288091	152453	62853	33772	16790	7224	3711	3036	1692	722	319	400	151				
Mesa del Oro	1000																
Metcalf						235	533	1740	2868	525			53				
Miami	2018	2716	3394	3350	4329	4722	7693	6689	1390								
Midland City	1200	1200	1000	300	500												
Mineral Park								83	71	68	68	700	318				
Moenkopi	924	900	600	500	655												
Mohave City									175	30	30	50		159			
Mohave Valley	950	750	500														
Morenci	800	1200	950	2431	6541	5115	5108	7501	5010	1100	758						
Morristown	200	200	200	200	250	250	100	68	75	61							
Mount Lemmon	300	400															
Mountainaire	750	700															
Mowry									250						252		
Munds Park	950	150															
Naco	870	800	750	500	400	300	250	450	250	181							
Nazlini	400	400		121	85	70											
Nelson							69	69	300								
New River	300	300															
Nogales	19489	15683	8946	7286	6153	5135	6006	8460	3514	1761	1194						
Nutrioso	300	250	200	200	200	250	100			55	55	150	45				
Oak Creek	950																
Oatman	300	200	175	74	100	500	647	975	168	410							
Octave					100		100	100	500	43							
Oracle	3043	2478	900	700	400	300	200	89	150								
Oraibi	773	600	600	500	400	400	340	340	340	108			675				
Oro Blanco											31	225	400				
Oro Valley	6670	1489	200	150	150												
Overgaard	900	300	200	150	150												
Owens						100			384	384							
Page	6598	4907	1439	2960													
Palo Verde	100	100	100	250	150	150	250										
Palominas	400	400						267									
Paradise Valley	11671	11085	7155	2368													
Parker	2897	2542	1948	1642	1201	456	617	475	420	55							

POPULATION HISTORY OF ARIZONA CITIES AND TOWNS 1850-1990

COMMUNITY	1990	1980	1970	1960	1950	1940	1930	1920	1910	1900	1890	1884	1880	1870	1864	1860	1850
Patagonia	888	980	630	540	723	756	710	757	500	41							
Payson	8377	5068	1490	800	350	235	174	158	86	138							
Peach Springs	787	600	600	500	300	129	129	60	75	42	116						
Pearce	30	20	100	125	150	199	198	604	517	324							
Peeples Valley	300	150	110		100	150											
Peoria	50618	12251	4792	2593	701	700	700	320	75	68							
Peridot	957	300	200	300													
Phoenix	900013	789704	581562	439170	106818	65414	48118	29053	11134	5544	3152	2000	1708	240			
Picacho	600	550	400	400	100	100	100										
Pima	1725	1599	1184	806	824	867	980	515	500	521	282	100					
Pinal City												500	166				
Pine	950	500	200	175	175	150	220	213	100	77							
Pinedale	250	200			192	192	125	125	200								
Pinetop	2422	1527	750	400	300	65	50	37	95								
Pinon	468	100	250														
Pioneer	1364	1425	850	850	898	500						300					
Pirtleville	341	200	140	200	242												
Pisinemo	1000	1500	1077	1552													
Plantsite	1108	600	500	500													
Polacca					600	700	600	1000	1500								
Poland									117								
Polaris									339								
Pomerene	300	200	200	200	300	300	300										
Portal	150	100	100	100	100	300			50								
Poston	480	200			200		600										
Prescott	26455	20055	13030	12861	6764	6018	5517	5010	5092	3559	1759	3000	1836	668	300		
Prescott Valley	8858	2284															
Providence										217							
Quartsite	1876	1193	600	350	200	125	60	84	300								
Queen Creek	2667	1378	600	550	550												
Ramsey													156				
Randolph	350	300	400	400	245												
Ray				1468	1595	2454	4102	4272	250	175							
Red Rock	300	250	100						75								
Reymert											254						
Rillito	400	400	300	250	250												
Riviera		4500	900														
Rock Point	500	400	150	300	300												
Roll	200	200		100		300	300										
Roosevelt	500	175	125			126	220	221	287								

POPULATION HISTORY OF ARIZONA CITIES AND TOWNS 1850-1990

COMMUNITY	1850	1860	1864	1870	1880	1884	1890	1900	1910	1920	1930	1940	1950	1960	1970	1980	1990
Rough Rock															100	450	650
Round Rock																300	400
Rowood										100	200	200	842				
Sacaton						150	42	166	250	315	315	315	584	700	800	1951	1452
Safford					173	150	213	950	929	1336	1706	2266	3756	4648	5333	7010	7359
Sahuarita										64	200	200	200	230	250	600	600
St. David					84	100	132	170	500	300	350	467	600	650	750	950	1468
St. Johns					546	400	482	1100	835	1294	1386	1503	1469	1310	1320	3368	3294
St. Michaels										43	200		400	215	250	250	500
Salome										60	100	150	400	400	450	600	950
San Carlos					186		54	365	500			650		950	2542	2668	2918
San Jose														100	150	300	300
San Luis															200	1946	4212
San Manuel													2500	4524	4332	5443	4009
San Simon								81	81	319	300	350	350	300	300	400	450
San Xavier			112														900
Sanders										29	56	90	250	300	250	400	300
Santa Maria																	
Santa Rosa																	493
Santan																150	330
Sasco									300								
Sawmill															250	400	507
Scottsdale								94	100	194	515	1187	2032	10026	67823	88622	130069
Second Mesa												300	300	300	500	500	929
Sedona										112	116	196	350	850	2022	5368	7720
Seligman								50	338	566	417	685	764	850	950	950	950
Sells											250	500	789	750	750	1864	2750
Seymour					258												
Shongopovi					216						300	300	350	420	250	300	730
Shonto															700	700	710
Show Low					120		126	126	201	258	189	295	500	1625	2285	4298	5019
Sierra Vista														3121	6689	24937	32983
Signal					157	300											
Silver Bell									700	50	246				800	600	
Silver King					180	300	212	113									
Skull Valley											115	100	100	150	250	300	300
Smithville					148												
Snowflake					300	300	324	475	494	758	659	903	929	982	1833	3510	3679
Solomonsville					175	150	287	629	595	870	684	884	753	600	500	350	550
Somerton								50		938	891	1247	1825	1613	2225	5761	5282

POPULATION HISTORY OF ARIZONA CITIES AND TOWNS 1850-1990

COMMUNITY	1990	1980	1970	1960	1950	1940	1930	1920	1910	1900	1890	1884	1880	1870	1864	1860	1850
Sonora				1244	1821	2000	3075	3075									
South Tucson	5093	6554	6220	7004	2364	1066											
Springerville	1802	1452	1038	719	689	852	565	479	296	510	443	300	364				
Starfield	1700	900	400	300	250												
Stanton												200					
Stargo	1038	1038	1194	1075													
Steamboat Canyon	400	200	250	200													
Strawberry	300	130	100														
Sun City	38126	40505	13670	2000													
Sun City West	15997	3772															
Sun Lakes	6578																
Sunnyslope		1925			4420												
Sunset												100	161				
Sunsites	1100	200															
Supai	423	200	165	140	230	200	200			236							
Superior	3468	4600	4975	4875	4291	4000	4295	2464	200								
Surprise	7122	3723	2427	1574													
Swansea								337	400								
Tacna	500	500	400	195													
Tanque Verde		400	400	153													
Taylor	2418	1915	888	500	500	466	432	420	332	205	117	350					
Teec Nos Pos	317	250	175														
Tempe	141865	106743	62907	24897	7684	2906	2495	1963	1473	885	897	600	135				
Thatcher	3763	3374	2320	1581	1284	1106	895	899	904	644	118						
Thomas								283			195		112				
Tiptop												75	150				
Tiger					783	500	910	540									
Tolleson	4434	4433	3881	3886	3042	1731											
Tombstone	1220	1632	1241	1283	910	822	849	1178	1582	646	1875	6000	3423				
Tonalea	150	150	140														
Tonopah	300	150															
Tonto Basin	300	200		91													
Top Rock	900	300					55										
Topawa	250	250	220	200	300	304	425										
Total Wreck												200					
Truxton	150	150				150	170										
Tuba City	4000	3000	800	600	150	150	150	150	200	150		200	47				
Tubac	250	160	140	125	125	140	120						71	178		353	200
Tucson	405390	330537	262933	212892	45454	35752	32506	20292	13193	7531	5150	11000	7007	3224	1568	915	
Tumacacori	250	250	150	100													400

POPULATION HISTORY OF ARIZONA CITIES AND TOWNS 1850-1990

COMMUNITY	1990	1980	1970	1960	1950	1940	1930	1920	1910	1900	1890	1884	1880	1870	1864	1860	1850
Twin Buttes					74												
Vail	200	150		150				318	300								
Valencia	1200	1300		750													
Valentine	60	60	500	127		125	168	164									
Valley Farms	380	320	270	220													
Vulture										62	62	300	89	268			
Waddell	400	400			300	350											
Walker							39		162	162		50	165				
Warren					2610	3036	3034	2042	175								
Washington								374	250	139			120				
Welton	1066	911	970	700	150	200	250	110	200								
Wenden	450	300	300	245	250	100	80	163									
West Yuma			5552	2781	474												
Whipple Barracks					400	400					338		330	116	200		
White Hills										311							
White River	1600	1400	600	450	200	250	300	52									
Wickenburg	4515	3535	2698	2445	1736	955	734	527	570	217	149	150	104	174			
Wikiup	350	150	130		100	200	200										
Wilhoit	500	250															
Willcox	3122	3243	2568	2441	1266	884	806	905	600	466	396	250					
Williams	2532	2266	2386	3559	2152	2622	2166	1350	1267	1382	199	50					
Williams AFB	3435	3435	3443														
Window Rock	3306	2230	900	600	400	250											
Winkelman	676	1060	974	1123	540	524	729	573	484								
Winslow	8190	7921	8066	8862	6518	4577	3917	3730	2381	1305	363						
Wittman	950	700	350	200	50	248											
Woodruff	300	250	200	116	225	204	180		171	135	98	500	99				
Yarnell	1500	950	700	500	300	200	66										
Young	700	300	250	250	200		240	79									
Youngtown	2542	2254	1886	1599													
Yucca	200	175	150	100	60		75	89									
Yuma/Arizona City	54923	42433	29007	23974	9145	5325	4892	4237	2914	1519	1773	1000	1200	1144	151	130	
Yuma Proving Ground		1098	1349														
Yuma Station			3460														

1864: The 1864 Census of the Territory of Arizona. Phoenix: The Historical Record Survey, 1938.
1884: Colorado, New Mexico, Utah, Nevada, Wyoming, and Arizona Gazetteer and Business Directory. Chicago: R.L. Polk, 1884.

POPULATION HISTORY OF CALIFORNIA CITIES AND TOWNS 1850-1990

COMMUNITY	1990	1980	1970	1960	1950	1940	1930	1920	1910	1900	1890	1880	1870	1860	1850
Acampo	350	350	350	200	275	250	210	175	175	132	132	75			
Acton	1471	900	500	500	700		95	325	100	100					
Adelaida		2164	2115	950	623	303	47		79	79	79	203			
Adelanto	8517	575	500	200	300	300	210	219	376	246	376				
Adin	575											217			
Agnew	20390			900	300	300	300	316	125	68	68				
Agoura	1000	600	350	360	400	500									
Agua Caliente	900	1000	150		418		100	415	115	130	200				
Agua Dulce	900	900	900				415								
Ahwahnee	900	900	600	450	500		50		100	100					
Alameda	76459	63852	70968	63855	64430	36256	35033	28806	23383	16464	11165	5708	1560		
Alamo	6700	6700	4560	1791	750		69		69	69	69				
Albany	16327	15130	15561	14804	17590	11493	8569	2462	808						
Alberhill			45	200	300	450	210								
Albion	400	400	350	300	250	250	300	250	250	103	103	119	115		
Alcatraz	460	450	300	130	250	150	150	116	171	171	171	220			
Alderpoint															
Alhambra	82106	64615	62125	54807	51359	38935	29472	9096	5021	847	808	80			
Alleghany	175	175	135	200	300	614	871	519	200	145	200	277	240		
Alma					350	310	310	310	281	96	84	151		999	
Almonte			800	800	200										
Alondra	12215	12096	12193												
Alpaugh	9695	900	800	600	638	574	500	575	125						
Alpine	450	5368	1570	1044	460	200	239	116	67	159	135				
Alta	450	450	225	125	125	113	113	200	50	50		120			
Alta Hill/Altaville	1229	1229	1185	1078	320	321	320	320	250			71			
Alta Loma			4000	1821	550	500	500	50							
Alta Sierra	5709	2168	375												
Altadena	42658	40510	42380	40568	37560			400	400	400					
Alton	170	170	170	300	250	226	255	217	117	117					
Alturas	3231	3025	2799	2819	2819	2090	2338	979	916	1013	1013	148			
Alum Rock	16890	17471	18355	18942											
Alvarado					2000	1248	1032	1032	800	642	642	364	315		
Alviso				1174	652	677	381	517	402	207	207	141	100		
Amador City	196	136	156	202	151	249	171	377	984	988	984	824	200	500	
American Canyon	7706	5712	550	800											
Anaheim	266406	221847	166408	104184	14556	11031	10995	5526	2628	1456	1273	833	881		
Anderson	8299	7381	5492	4492	1501	1543	1399	837	700	600	508	201	623		
Angel Island									285	285	285	305			
Angels Camp	2409	2302	1710	1121	1147	1163	915	941	1390	2828	917	330	500	500	

POPULATION HISTORY OF CALIFORNIA CITIES AND TOWNS 1850-1990

COMMUNITY	1990	1980	1970	1960	1950	1940	1930	1920	1910	1900	1890	1880	1870	1860	1850
Angwin	3503	3526	2690	995	895	363	300		75	67	75				
Antioch	62195	43559	28060	17305	11051	5106	3563	1936	1124	674	635	626	-700		
Anza	400	400	200	220	220										
Apple Valley	46079	14305	6702	5836	550										
Applegate	600	600	800	300	300	261	250	262	65						
Aptos	9061	7039	8704	3000	1000	337	300	278	278	278	278	100	100		
Arbuckle	1912	1306	1037	950	1150	1855	1533	1533	800	480	375	187			
Arcade	47900	37600	37500												
Arcadia	48290	45994	45138	41005	23066	9122	5216	2239	696	500	300				
Arcata	15197	12338	8985	5235	3729	1855	1709	1486	1121	952	962	702	600		
Arden	62900	52000	46000	25000	6000										
Argus	800	800	1130	800	500										
Arlington				7000	4326	2505	1550	1550	500						
Armona	3122	2644	1392	1502	1274	1693	536	316		203	103				
Arnold	3788	2385	500	575	200	250									
Aromas	950	950	750	768	325	317	316	316	100						
Arroyo Grande	14378	11290	7454	3291	1723	1090	892	760	900	711	466	428	100		
Artesia	15464	14301	14757	9993	5920	4708	3891	2039	450	301					
Artois	200	200	200	260	125		120	240							
Arvin	9286	6863	5199	5007	5007	854	707	116							
Ashland	16590	13893	14810												
Ashview															
Atascadero	23138	16232	10290	5983	3443	2577	2000	1643							
Atherton	7163	7797	8085	7717	3630	1908	1242								
Atolia						102	150	213							
Atwater	22282	17530	11640	7318	2856	1235	917	319	150						
Atwood	1866	1100	900	800	250	165	235	62							
Auberry			350	400	400	185	100	183	75						
Auburn	10592	7540	6570	5586	4653	4013	2661	2289	2376	2050	1595	1229	800	814	1302
August	6376	5445	6735												
Avalon	2918	2022	1520	1536	1506	1637	1897	586	500	178					
Avenal	9770	4137	3035	3147	3982	582	750	162							
Avery	900	900	400	180	180		64	64	42	42					
Avila															
Avila Beach	600	600	450	300	300	315	315	315							
Avocado Heights	14232	11721	9810												
Azusa	41333	29380	25217	20497	11042	5209	4808	2460	1477	863	514	503	320	363	
Baker	650	650	500	200	150	102	109								
Bakersfield	174820	105611	69515	56348	34784	29252	26015	18638	12727	4836	2626	801	800		
Balboa		810			2500	1062	810	810							

POPULATION HISTORY OF CALIFORNIA CITIES AND TOWNS 1850-1990

COMMUNITY	1850	1860	1870	1880	1890	1900	1910	1920	1930	1940	1950	1960	1970	1980	1990
Baldwin Park							420	618	1015	5226	28000	33951	47285	50554	69330
Ballena				321	132	132									
Ballico												200	300	200	
Bangor			300	325	284	284	95	261	250	262	300	250	350	500	500
Banning					182	324	659	1810	2752	3874	7034	10250	12034	14020	20570
Banta				413	143	143	143								
Barstow					300	197	480	819	2455	3075	6135	11644	17442	17690	21472
Bass Lake											150	150	300	500	500
Batavia				205	114	114	114								
Bay Point							250	1225	1225	1229					
Bayshore										749	950	1500			
Bayside					300	207	207	319	300	320	450	450	250	450	450
Bayview											350	1800	1300	1400	1400
Baywood Park												800	1500	2900	2900
Beale AFB													9354	6329	6912
Bear Valley		250	200	150	166	166	166			100					
Beaumont					407	407	750	857	1332	2208	3152	4288	5484	6818	9685
Beckwith/Beckwourth				51	74	112	300	263	100	100	150		120	175	175
Bell						74	170	700	7884	11264	15430	19450	21836	25450	34365
Bell Gardens											9500	26467	29308	34117	42355
Bellflower					260	363	450	1245	6710	9900	30000	45909	52334	53441	61815
Belmont				202		434	481	619	984	1229	5567	15996	23538	24505	24127
Belvedere			150					616	500	457	800	2148	2599	2401	2147
Ben Lomond						300	360	458	458	553	1500	1814	2793	7238	7884
Benicia	480	470	600	1794	2361	2751	2360	2693	2913	2419	7284	6070	7349	15376	24437
Benton						100	100								
Berkeley				1400	5101	13214	40434	56036	82109	85547	113805	111268	114091	103328	102724
Berros						103	103	249	249	200	200				
Bethel Island												800	1398	1774	2115
Betteravia							80	310	310	250	450	335			
Beverly Hills								674	17429	26823	29032	30817	33416	32367	31971
Bicknell							100	259	100						
Bidwell Bar	600			30	22										
Bieber				43	513	513	513	150	150	565	500	300	300	600	600
Big Bar				75	100	67	67	73	73	140	200	225	165	400	400
Big Bear City										302	476	588	950	3500	3500
Big Bear Lake									250	1000	1434	1562	3274	4896	5351
Big Creek								158	350	350	368	400	450	700	700
Big Oak Flat			200	73	263	417	263	713	300	161	150	125	110	500	500
Big Pine	210	250	100	138	147	159	400	721	700	402	556	800	950	1510	1158

POPULATION HISTORY OF CALIFORNIA CITIES AND TOWNS 1850-1990

COMMUNITY	1990	1980	1970	1960	1950	1940	1930	1920	1910	1900	1890	1880	1870	1860	1850
Big River	1200	1200		125	250	200	75								
Big Sur	520	520	150												
Biggs	1581	1413	1115	831	784	547	463	683	403	700	571	95	250		
Bijou				500	350		121	121	90	90					
Biola	800	800	700	651	225	300	124								
Birds Landing									100	100	205	350			
Bishop	3475	3333	3498	2875	2891	1490	1159	1304	1190	307	340	159			
Black Point	300	300	900	644	431	125			292	292	292	85	200		
Blacks Station/Zamora															
Blairsden	150	150	100		350	261	262	262							
Blocksburg	40	40		170	125	124	121	266	266	266	266	200			
Bloomfield	180	180	150			200	75	200	206	206	206	192	300		
Bloomington	15116	6674	11957	9995	3500	1073	1287	775	95						
Blue Jay	500	500	300	500	300	200									
Blue Lake	1235	1201	1112	1234	824	503	555	441	507	398	398	60			
Blue Tent											100	350			
Blythe	8428	6805	7047	6023	4089	2355	1020	1622	200						
Boca							139	214	266	226	266	123	100		
Bodega Bay	500	500	300	350	463	300	200	200	220			388	350		
Bodfish	1283	1379	500	250	247	182	50	50	40						
Bodie						90	228	110	698	965	1595	2712	150		
Bolinas	1098	1225	600	400	250	125	190	559	190	110	110	163			
Bolsa Knolls	950	950													
Bombay Beach	450	450	800	600											
Bonadelle Ranchos	1750	1750													
Bonita	12542	6257	4000	3000	1000	200	100								
Bonny Doon	600	950	950				50	159			120				
Bonnyview			4882	4686											
Bonsall	1881	900	350		200		213	213	31						
Boonville	1000	1000	950	950	950		534	534	200	200	285	125	100		
Borden	2101	2040	1999							40	72	283	300		
Boron	2244	1405	900	650	236	250									
Borrego Springs				400		400									
Bostonia					985		306	219	300	300					
Boulder Creek	6725	5662	1806	1306	1497	862	713	713	544	498	489	150			
Boulevard	245	250	100		200	200	128	128							
Bowman	950	950	290		300	200	100	53	100						
Boyes Hot Springs	5973	4117	3558	2462	2391	302	400	62							
Bradbury	829	846	838	618					207	207	207				
Bradley	100	100			100	100									

POPULATION HISTORY OF CALIFORNIA CITIES AND TOWNS 1850-1990

COMMUNITY	1990	1980	1970	1960	1950	1940	1930	1920	1910	1900	1890	1880	1870	1860	1850
Brawley	18923	14946	13746	12703	11922	11718	10439	5389	881						
Brea	32873	27913	18447	8489	3208	2567	2435	1037							
Brentwood	7563	4434	2649	2186	1729	1000	696	325	369	369	369	52			
Bridgeport	900	900	500	300	250	247	200	250	224	214	224	150	80		
Bridgeville	200	200	100	100	300	200	300	50	90	41	41				
Brighton												303			
Brisbane	2952	2969	3003	4000	4200	1815	1200								
Broadmoor	3739	4600	4000												
Broderick/Washington		12700	10000	7500	3000	1500	1500	600	800	616					
Brookdale			450		150										
Brooklyn												5300	1603	1341	
Brown's Valley	75	75	300	225	250	150	212	212	150	217	100	168	200		
Brownsville	950	950	500		200	113	113	113	274	274	274	75	200		
Bryn Mawr			600	350	500	502	315	315	196	196					
Bryte		2800	2780	3000	3000	500	404								
Buck Meadows	200	200	100				362	362							
Buckingham Park	700	700	400												
Buellton	3506	2364	1402			107	107	55							
Buena Park	68784	64165	63646	46401	5483	2420	867	520	200	115	150				
Bulwinkle								519							
Burbank (Los Angeles)	93643	84625	88871	90155	78577	34337	16662	2913	450	306	183				
Burbank (Santa Clara)	4902	3400	5000	5000											
Burkett Gardens	4700	4100	4000												
Burlingame	26801	26173	27320	24036	19886	15940	13270	4107	1565	147					
Burnet												187			
Burney	3423	3187	2190	1294	1513	800	150	123	210	210	216	175			
Burrell	40	40	75		350										
Burson	400	400	250		70										
Burton				4635	2381										
Butte City	350	350	200		350	369	250	369	279	266	279	150		200	
Buttonwillow	1301	1350	1193	985	978	349	50	100	100	125					
Byron	900	900	800	600	600	449	400	260	320	289	289	61			
Cabezon	1588	900	598	498	300	153	150				100				
Cacheville												213			
Cahto										189	182	49			
Cajon			150		50	211									
Calabasas	900	900	200		300	150	150	218	35						
Calabasas Park	1700	1700	100												
Calavo Gardens	6100	6100	3500	1800											
Calexico	18633	14412	10625	7992	6433	5415	6299	6223	797						

POPULATION HISTORY OF CALIFORNIA CITIES AND TOWNS 1850-1990

COMMUNITY	1850	1860	1870	1880	1890	1900	1910	1920	1930	1940	1950	1960	1970	1980	1990
Calico				500											
Caliente				160	431	38									
California City												500	1309	2743	5955
Calimesa									100	200	500	2000	3000	2600	4647
Calipatria								785	1554	1799	1428	2548	1824	2636	2690
Calistoga			450	467	600	690	751	850	1000	1124	1418	1574	1882	3879	4468
Calla										150	300	225	650	650	950
Callahan				145	115	126	125	139	80		200		100	200	200
Calpela					82	82	140	217	217	219	300	500	700	300	300
Calpine									300	251	75		100	200	200
Calwa								700	210	168	880	5500	5191	6640	6640
Camarillo							101	166	871	1630	2500	2359	19219	37732	52303
Camarillo Heights								524				1704	3800	3800	3800
Cambria			400	1350	288	282	500	318	538	448	975	1600	1716	3061	5328
Cambrian Park												4000	5316	4000	2998
Cameron Park							500	700			700			5607	11897
Camino							100	516	516	518		750	900	900	1500
Campbell						377	550	940	1800	1138	7662	11863	23797	27067	36048
Camp Meeker						35	150	319	125	125	300	100	175	500	500
Camp Pendleton													25495	10017	21672
Campo			200	51	122	122	122	210	210	152	847	500	300	100	100
Campo Seco				105	110	168	168			100	200	100		300	300
Camptonville		600	500	351	387	387	387	168	168	200	300	400	200	450	450
Canby						45	45	427		300	600	500	450	450	450
Canoga Park/Owensmouth												64200	109127		
Cantil													80	260	260
Cantu/Andrade								218	65		100				
Cantua Creek											500		350	450	450
Canyon										150	400	200	200	250	250
Canyon Country														15728	
Canyon Lake														2309	7938
Capay									115	250	250		200	90	90
Capistrano Beach				260	304	448	304				950	2026	4149	6168	
Capistrano Highlands													1680	2400	2400
Capitola						203	240	275	255	308	1848	2021	5080	9095	10171
Carbon Canyon													680	680	680
Cardiff								85	450	504	1200	3149	5724	10054	
Carlotta								113	113	100		200	350	500	500
Carlsbad					100	76		121	1660	1998	4383	9253	14944	35490	63126
Carmel-by-the-Sea						50	400	638	2260	2837	4351	4580	4525	4707	4239

POPULATION HISTORY OF CALIFORNIA CITIES AND TOWNS 1850-1990

COMMUNITY	1990	1980	1970	1960	1950	1940	1930	1920	1910	1900	1890	1880	1870	1860	1850
Carmel Highlands	900	900	900	600											
Carmel Valley	4407	4013	3026	1143	1250										
Carmel Woods	1400	1400	1200	1043	600										
Carmichael	48702	43108	37625	20455	4499	550	550								
Carnelian Bay	1000	1000													
Carpinteria	13747	10835	6982	4998	2864	2208	1840	1260	300	206	206	113	100		
Carriage Hills	600	600													
Carson	83995	81221	71150	38059											
Carson Hill							113	113							1000
Cartago	100	100		106	126		80	158							
Caruthers	1603	1514	900	500	400	136	121	134							
Casa de Oro	9500	9500		2000	2000										
Casitas Springs	1038	1038	1113	800	300										
Casmalia	300	300	275	200	180	181									
Caspar	550	550	578	276	264	358	290	285	290	211	206	502	196		
Castaic	900	900	900	750	600	250	161								
Castella	525	525	300	300	600	500	500	150	90	65					
Castle Park	6300	6300	2500	2000	1000										
Castro Valley	48619	44011	44760	37120	22000										
Castroville	5272	4396	3235	2838	1865	779	1124	800	641	641	641	533	436		
Cathay	550	550	400	200	200										
Cathedral City	30085	4130	3640	1855	2058	800	300								
Cayucos	2960	2301	1772	1000	750	202	260	400	330	313	316				
Cazadero	500	500	300	230	200	186	150	184		80		51			
Cedar Glen	2000	2000	400	100	100	100									
Cedar Grove	700	700	350												
Cedar Ridge	400	400	600	375	310		60								
Cedarpines Park	325	325	250	180	200										
Cedarville	950	950	800	850	925	622	400	500	520	380	400	219	250		
Centerville (Alameda)					1401	2000	1025	1025	750	564	516	203	350		
Centerville (Fresno)	140	140	120	200	300										
Central											510	257			
Central Valley	4340	3424	2361	2854	2202	1210						140			
Ceres	26314	13281	6029	4406	2351	1332	981	637	206	206	205	166			
Cerritos	53240	53020	15856	3508		1000									
Cerro Gordo	650	650	300	150	300		61	61	61	61	42	55	474		
Challenge	1600	1600	2000	2000											
Chapman Woods	1600	1600	2000	2000											
Chapmantown/Mulberry	1946	1946	1795	2643	2545		150								
Charter Oak	8858	6840	5000	4000	1000	402	300	362							

POPULATION HISTORY OF CALIFORNIA CITIES AND TOWNS 1850-1990

COMMUNITY	1990	1980	1970	1960	1950	1940	1930	1920	1910	1900	1890	1880	1870	1860	1850
Chatsworth	700	700	24000	13250			864	517	250						
Chemeketa Park	50	50	350	350											
Cherokee					80	225	379	225	260	310	500	699	150	400	
Cherry Valley	5945	5012	3165	900											
Cherryland	11008	9425	9969		675										
Chester	2082	1756	1531	1553	1197					41					
Chicago Park	700	700	200	350	600				41	30					
Chico	40079	26601	19580	14757	12272	9287	7961	9339	3750	2640	2894	3300	2500	1482	
Chilcoot	230	230	100	100			113	113							
China Lake	4275	4275	11105	4000	2000										
Chinese Camp	175	175	150	100	150	239	237	237	180	146	314	184	400	500	
Chino	59682	40165	20411	10305	5784	4204	3118	2132	1444	1320	800	113	75		
Cholame	80	80			300	849	571								
Chowchilla	5930	5122	4349	4525	3893	1957	847	350		78		40			
Chrisman				3923	4211										
Chualar	500	500	600	500	450	220	200	107	107	107	107	46	150		
Chula Vista	135163	83927	67901	42034	15927	5138	3869	1718	100	60					
Citrus	9481	12450													
Citrus Heights	107439	85911	21760	17000	6000										
City of Industry/Industry	631	664	712	778											
Claremont	32503	30950	24776	12653	6327	3057	2719	1728	1114	242	100				
Clarksburg	250	250	400	350	300	100	100	290	84	84	84				
Clarksville								216	99	99	99	75			
Clayton	7317	4325	1385	400	300	198	285	268	320	268	268	175	150		
Clearlake Highlands	11804	8343	4148	850	660	225	225								
Clearlake Oaks	2419	1610	950	425	225	200									
Clearlake Park		800	900	450	150										
Clearwater					8586	1402	1000	615	150	150					
Clements	180	180	125	150	419	508	419	419	320	329	333				
Cleone									111	111	196				
Clifton	1500	1500	1800	1750		900		162	300						
Clio	185	185	125		130		62	143							
Clipper Mills	200	170	170	100	100	143	143	143	131	131	131				
Cloverdale	4924	3989	3251	2848	1292	809	759	718	823	750	763	501	150		
Clovis	50323	33021	13856	5546	2766	1626	1316	1157	900	273		430	700		
Clyde	100	100	400	450	250	250									
Coachella	16896	9129	8353	4854	2755	1331	1372	610							
Coalinga	8212	6593	6161	5965	5539	5026	2851	2934	4199						
Coarsegold	2000	2000	550		200			164	100	30	85				
Cobb	1477	950	300		60		50								

POPULATION HISTORY OF CALIFORNIA CITIES AND TOWNS 1850-1990

COMMUNITY	1990	1980	1970	1960	1950	1940	1930	1920	1910	1900	1890	1880	1870	1860	1850
Coeur							40	50	40						
Cohasset	300	300	200		200							194			
Coleville	40	40	60	275	300	150	85	100	58	58	93	102	75		
Colfax	1306	981	798	915	820	794	912	573	621	588	670	591	650		
College	150	150	350	350	200	325	250	300	300	310	387	237	250		
Collinsville	50	50	100	200	200	200		264	250	250	293				
Colma	1103	395	537	500	297	354	342	293	500	293	293	188			
Coloma	500	500	280	280	350	410	161	200	200	203	212	231	200	888	500
Colton	40213	27419	20016	18666	14465	9686	8014	4282	3980	1285	1315	300			
Columbia	1799	950	600	550	650	748	500	550	550	550	812	650	1125	2062	3000
Colusa	4934	4075	3842	3518	3031	2285	2116	1846	1582	1441	1336	1779	1C51		
Commerce	12135	10509	10635	9555											
Comptche	555	555	170	175	175	175	135	319	82	82	82				
Compton	90454	81286	78547	71812	47991	16198	12516	1478	922	663	636	448	160		
Concord	111348	103251	85164	36208	6953	1373	1125	912	703	586	373	399	400		
Cool	700	700	150	150	200	389	319	412	420	232	232	148			
Copperopolis	700	700	125					32	666				500		
Coram									500						
Corcoran	13364	6454	5249	4976	3150	2092	1768	1101							
Cordelia	300	300	300	300	365	318	300	316	287	287	287	149	200		
Corning	5870	4745	3573	3006	2537	1472	1377	1449	972	475	210	200			
Corona del Mar					850	450									
Corona	76095	37791	27519	13336	10223	8764	7018	4129	3540	1434	800				
Coronado	26540	16859	20020	18039	12700	6932	5425	3289	1477	935					
Coronita	2400	2400													
Corralitos	950	950	950	900	300	300	300	316	143	143	143	107			
Corte Madera	8272	8074	8464	5962	1933	1098	1027	607	360						
Costa Mesa	96357	82291	72660	37550	11844	3674	3037	213							
Cotati	5714	3475	1368	1852	990	1000	1200	100	100	40					
Cottonwood	1747	1553	1288	950	950	750	618	618	460	300	269				
Coulterville	500	500	180	180	350	455	400	450	525	525	525	224	400	250	
Country Club	9325	9585	300	120											
Courtland	500	500	400	550	950	750	500	672	135	135	135				
Covelo	1057	1488	950	600	500	400	400	419	350	350	498	183	250		
Covina	43207	33751	30395	20124	3956	3049	2774	1999	1652	255	93				
Cowan Heights	2600	2600	1400	750											
Coyote			400		150	321	300	319	200	200	200				
Crannell				450	428	300	300								
Crescent City	4380	3099	2586	2958	1706	1363	1720	955	1114	699	907	570	458	638	
Crescent Mills	375	375	250	250	205	230	160	113	150	200	202	100			

POPULATION HISTORY OF CALIFORNIA CITIES AND TOWNS 1850-1990

COMMUNITY	1850	1860	1870	1880	1890	1900	1910	1920	1930	1940	1950	1960	1970	1980	1990
Crescent North												3086	3053	2846	3853
Cressy												200	200	250	250
Crest Park											100	100	250	550	550
Crestline									55	1000	800	1250	3509	6715	8594
Creston									66		85		60	300	300
Crockett				75	301	850	1409	1845	2063	2233	3400	4000	3300	2900	3228
Cromberg							40	50	50		150		200	525	525
Crowley Lake														950	950
Crows Landing					59	59	250	319	300	350	500	650	500	525	525
Cucamonga				70	94	200	330	2012	3340	5744	5255	5796	19484	55250	101409
Cudahy										300	7500	9954	16998	17984	22817
Culver City								503	5669	8976	19720	32163	34451	38139	38793
Cupertino				80	65	50	140	1019	1019	1900	2438	3664	17895	25770	40263
Cutler								510	500	726	1768	2191	2503	3149	4450
Cutten									325	242	1340	1572	2228	2315	1516
Cuyama									50		100	100	150	170	170
Cypress								62	610	570	1318	1753	31569	40391	42655
Daggett			75		382	382	382	112	112	201	400	490	900	650	650
Dairyland										200	500	622			
Daly City								3779	7838	9625	15191	44791	66922	78519	92311
Dana Point									125	319	500	1186	4745	10602	31896
Danville			75	50	85	200	400	718	700	968	3130	3585	14059	26000	31306
Darwin				203	116	116	116		80		100	450	150	55	55
Daunt/Springville					207	207	207								
Davenport					50		300	317	300	318	500	500	300	300	300
Davis			500	441	547	579	750	939	1243	1672	3554	8910	23488	36640	46209
Deadwood		150			286	161	100	221	200					100	500
Death Valley										150	125				
Decoto					212	212	250	519	519	1500	2830				
Deer Park/Sanitarium									500	500	750	750	900	1454	1825
Del Aire												5000	5500	8487	8040
Del Dios												560	560	560	560
Del Mar					100	100	150	250	368	783	1800	3124	3956	5017	4860
Del Monte								200	100	750	650	1174	1500		
Del Paso										800	21000				
Del Rey						100	100	110	370	500	700	937	900	1126	1150
Del Rey Oaks											1509	1831	1823	1557	1661
Del Rosa								50	400	550	1154	6000			
Delano				75	401	421	600	805	2632	4573	8717	11913	14559	16491	22762
Delhi									95	250	1000	1175	2063	2832	3280

POPULATION HISTORY OF CALIFORNIA CITIES AND TOWNS 1850-1990

COMMUNITY	1850	1860	1870	1880	1890	1900	1910	1920	1930	1940	1950	1960	1970	1980	1990
Delkern												800	800	1300	1300
Delleker														350	350
Delsur						711									
Delways														400	400
Denair							110	219	437	377	860	900	1128	2892	3693
Descanso						55	70	116	230	230	250	350	350	680	680
Desert Hot Springs											770	1472	2738	5941	11668
Desert View Highlands													2172	2175	2154
Devore										125	180		670	2000	2000
Di Giorgio											450	450	250	175	175
Diablo														1500	1500
Diamond Bar												100	10576	28045	53672
Diamond Springs		200	200	102	267	267	267	265	550	600	640	617	900	2287	2872
Dillon Beach											310	100	200	500	600
Dinkey Creek									800	800	375	300			
Dinuba						110	970	3400	2968	3790	4971	6103	7917	9907	12743
Discovery Bay														1326	5351
Dixon			317	912	1082	783	827	926	1000	1108	1714	2970	4432	7541	10401
Dobbins					47	47	47	69	42						
Doheny Park									549	549					
Dominguez										1500	2700	6000	3680		
Donner Lake								58						650	650
Dorris							214	424	762	863	892	973	840	836	892
Dos Palos						100	520	550	945	978	1394	2028	2496	3123	4169
Dos Rios								217						180	180
Douglas City				221	175	145	75	142	142	100	95	200	250	950	950
Douglas Flat				165	83	107	83		85		63		100	500	500
Downey		500	411	237	489	700	1000	2550	4233	6621	35000	82505	88573	82602	91444
Downieville	1343	938	704	650	1022	500	500	600	835	665	450	350	375	950	750
Doyle								68	68	100	75	150	300	900	900
Drytown				200	216	216	216	216	200	150	155		150	50	50
Duarte	250		150		600	650	600	620	1033	1363	10000	13962	14981	16766	20688
Dublin			100		250	106		162	200	196	200	200	13641	15036	23229
Ducor							100	113	200	100	125			350	350
Duncan Mills			100	300	175	137	200	164	164				200	100	100
Dunlap					200	61	61	61	61	200	300	200	300	600	600
Dunnigan				121	214	214	214	161	141	141	150	125	100	400	400
Dunsmuir					300	783	1719	2528	2610	2359	2256	2873	2214	2253	2129
Durham				53	89	89	180	362	500	350	603	700	950	950	1500
Dutch Flat		500	850	939	682	750	750	700	701	502	220	250	200	250	250

POPULATION HISTORY OF CALIFORNIA CITIES AND TOWNS 1850-1990

29

COMMUNITY	1990	1980	1970	1960	1950	1940	1930	1920	1910	1900	1890	1880	1870	1860	1850
Eagle Mountain	1890	1890	2453	850	350										
Eagle Rock								2256							
Eagleville	185	185	70		95	210	210	210	200	123	116	500	100		
Earlimart	5881	4578	3080	2897	2162	1000	223	64	75						
Earp	950	950	200												
East Bakersfield				1199E							622	242			
East Blythe	1511	1660	1252		300										
East Compton	7967	6435	5853												
East Hemet	17611	14712													
East Highlands	500	500	400	270	350	300	300	516	150	150					
East La Mirada	9367	9688	12339												
East Los Angeles	126379	110017	105033	104270			8000								
East Palo Alto	23451	18191	17837	12000	9000	2000	1200								
East Pasadena/Lamanda Park					8044	8044	1500	1500							
East Porterville	5790	4042	5218	2000											
East Quincy	1750	1750	1500	1020											
East Richmond	5100	5100	5000	4500			6885								
East San Diego								4148	1661						
East San Jose															
East San Pedro							5000	817							
East Tustin	10000	10000	11000												
Easton	1877	1710	1065	1000	300	300	300	515	61	83	250				
Edgemont	5215	5215	3500	1628											
Edgewood	200	200	150	250	250	175	250	117	227	227	227	53	100		
Edison	500	500	350		500	100	50								
Edna							100	319	75	67					
Edwards AFB	7423	8554	7148	1000	425										
El Cajon	88693	73892	52273	37618	5600	1471	1050	469	420		293				
El Centro	31384	23996	19272	16811	12590	10017	8434	5464	1610						
El Cerrito (Contra Costa)	22869	22731	25190	25437	18011	6317	3870	1505							
El Cerrito (Riverside)	4490	2500													
El Dorado	950	550	550	525	600	504	400	417	360	311	311	200	200	558	
El Dorado Hills	6395	3453	2000	2000											
El Encanto Heights	7700	7700	6225												
El Granada	4426	3582	1473	850	206	122	122	151							
El Modina				1434	770	600	600	518	100	100	200				
El Monte	106209	79494	69892	13163	8101	4746	3479	1283	450	266	200	300	350		
El Nido	350	350	140	240	550	250	250			60					
El Portal	850	850	600						55						
El Pueblo	800	800	800	200	279	300	200	424							

POPULATION HISTORY OF CALIFORNIA CITIES AND TOWNS 1850-1990

COMMUNITY	1990	1980	1970	1960	1950	1940	1930	1920	1910	1900	1890	1880	1870	1860	1850
El Rio	6419	5674	6173	6966	1376	1516	500	219	200	178					
El Segundo	15223	13752	15620	14219	8011	3738	3503	1563				114			
El Sereno								516							
El Sobrante	9852	10535	12500	12000	4000										
El Sueno	475														
El Toro	62685	38153	8654	300	200	108	108	75	75	75					
El Toro Station	6869	7632	6970												
El Verano	3498	2384	1753	1236	796	605	518	518	300	103					
Eldridge	100	100	100												
Electric									325	325	400				
Elk	300	300	200	200	200	748	600	618	430	261	216				
Elk Creek	350	350	300	200	225		117	117	213	213	213	45			
Elk Grove	17483	10059	3721	2205	1200	610	784	467	470	375	202	301	150		
Elkham	570	570													
Elmhurst										1000					
Elmira	325	325	160	200	200	200	200	317	380	361	317	240			
Elverta	950	950	900	450	225	200	196								
Emerald Bay	2000	2000	1000	500	500										
Emerald Lake	3000	3000													
Emeryville	5740	3714	2681	2686	2889	2521	2336	2390	2613	1016	228				
Emigrant Gap	50	50	100	200	150										
Empire	2016	2016	2016	1636	1448	100	164	164	150	150	107	137			
Encanto						369	159	159							
Encinitas		10796	5375	2786	475	417	417	417	270	213	213				
Encino	55386		40000	29500	2100	1769	1463								
Engel							716	716							
Enterprise			11486	4946	150		56	56	84	84	84	149			
Escalon	4437	3127	2366	1763	1569	938	785	825	100	53					
Escondido	108635	62480	36792	16377	6544	4560	3421	1789	1334	755	541				
Esparto	1487	1303	1088	300	500	300	300	217	100	100					
Etiwanda			900	787	975	1000	500	419	150	150					
Etna	835	754	667	596	649	456	379	425	518	500	271	361			
Eucalyptus Hills				900											
Eureka	27025	24153	24337	28137	23058	17055	15752	12923	11845	7327	4858	2639	2049	617	55
Eureka Mills											350	370			
Evergreen	7276			950	500	250	314	314	169	169	169	100			
Exeter	7273	5606	4475	4264	4078	3883	2685	1852	820	236					
Fair Oaks (Sacramento)	26867	20253	11256	10000	2000	1000	500	519	300	75					
Fair Oaks (San Luis Obispo)				1622	1500	634	871	500	500	261					
Fairfax (Kern)	500	500													

POPULATION HISTORY OF CALIFORNIA CITIES AND TOWNS 1850-1990

COMMUNITY	1850	1860	1870	1880	1890	1900	1910	1920	1930	1940	1950	1960	1970	1980	1990
Fairfax (Marin)							120	120	2000	2198	4078	5813	7661	7391	6931
Fairfield			329	424	505	600	834	1008	1131	1312	3118	14968	44146	58099	77211
Fairmead								75	75		250	100	200	450	450
Falk								316							
Fall River Mills			100	122	311	208	310	369	350	400	400	500	600	900	900
Fallbrook					200	310	310	510	862	887	1735	4814	6945	14041	22095
Farmersville			100	108	117	117	140	319	300	386	952	3101	3456	5544	6235
Farmington			250	303	236	263	263	263	263	200	300	250	250	250	250
Fawnskin											250	640	500	700	700
Feather Falls								106	106	700	735	650	560	150	150
Fellows							150	516	516	750	825	900	950	750	750
Felton				271	259	360	360	439	445	535	964	1380	2062	4564	4000
Ferndale			300	178	763	846	905	919	889	901	1032	1371	1352	1367	1331
Fetters Hot Springs								335	200	300	600	450	300	675	675
Fiddletown/Oleta		250	300	295	268	367	225	250	250	363	250	250	150	250	250
Fieldbrook							80	1231	100	100	150		350	1200	1200
Fields Landing					100	80	120	345	345	200	350	600	320	250	250
Fig Garden													9000	9000	9000
Fillmore						150	520	1597	2893	3252	3884	4808	6285	9602	11992
Finley					75						300	300	300	450	450
Firebaugh				60	58	221	221	550	506	704	821	2070	2517	3740	4429
Flintridge									1474	1474	3300	5000	2650		
Florence	300	400		200	750	750	750	765	1287			38164	34100	38000	43900
Florin					385	385	385	392	400	466	500	1500	9646	16523	24330
Floriston							75	364	364	150	130	133	100	100	100
Folsom			1000	2000	699	950	1200	1525	1557	1745	1690	3925	5810	11003	29802
Fontana								261	426	3866	13695	14659	20673	37109	87535
Foothill Farms													14000	13700	17135
Forbestown			150	250	222	222	222	231	231	200	250	250	250	450	450
Ford City											4347	3926	3503	3392	3781
Forest City		765	152	620	238	317	350	342	243	100					
Forest Falls												175		110	600
Forest Hill		500	350	688	650	650	660	658	714	497	1000	900	900	1304	1409
Forest Knolls									500	400	950	800	900	2000	2000
Forestville			150	184	184	184	210	225	500	350	600	500	700	950	950
Fort Bidwell			100	260	362	362	410	462	462	482	275	330	200	230	230
Fort Bragg					945	1590	2408	2612	3022	3235	3826	4433	4455	5019	6078
Fort Dick								42	75	300	500	325	260	250	250
Fort Jones			500	302	266	356	316	331	302	360	525	483	515	544	639
Fortuna						776	883	986	1239	1413	1762	3523	4203	7591	8788

POPULATION HISTORY OF CALIFORNIA CITIES AND TOWNS 1850-1990

COMMUNITY	1990	1980	1970	1960	1950	1940	1930	1920	1910	1900	1890	1880	1870	1860	1850
Foster City	28176	23287	9327												
Fountain Valley	53691	55080	31886	2068											
Fowler	3208	2496	2239	1892	1857	1531	1171	1528	675	306	306				
Franklin				100	130	100	100	210	199	199	199				
Frazier Park	2201	1444	1167	250	250	150	150					115			
Freedom	8361	6416	5563	4206	2765	308	350		100		120	45			
Freeport							195		160	138	138	251			
Freestone						200	113		120	110	182	135			
Fremont	173339	131945	100869	43790											
French Camp	600	600	2500	1000	285	600	248	248	233	308	233	94			
French Corral	600	600	200	300	250		133	133	250	171	150	522	300	300	
French Gulch	500	500	200	300		618	618	618	218	208	218	199	100	100	
Freshwater				200	186	121	121	121	111	162	111				
Fresno	354202	218202	165655	133929	91669	60685	52513	45086	24892	12470	10818	1112			
Fresno Flats									149	149	149	1000	500		
Friant	500	500	350	300	375	400	110	110							
Fruitridge				5480											
Fruitvale	300	300	800							3500					
Fullerton	114144	102034	85987	56180	13958	10442	10860	4415	1725	698	212				
Fulton	950	500	400	250	250	150	200	175	194	194	194	76	300		
Gabilan Acres	950	950	400												
Gallinas				600									100		
Galt	8889	5514	3200	1868	1333	1290	1670	985	985	985	985	650			
Garberville	1200	1200	900	900	773	500	350	200	284	284	284	48			
Garden Acres	2600	2600	2400												
Garden Gate	1700	1700	1300												
Garden Grove	143050	123307	121155	84238	3762	2206	1824	522	350	126	126	175			
Garden Valley	900	900	300	225	200				120	120					
Gardena	49847	45165	41021	35943	14405	5909	4200	1250	425	100					
Garvanza										411	411				
Gasoline Alley	900	900													
Gasquet	400	400	340												
Gaviota				300	250	157	157	175	50	50					
Gazelle	200	200	150	275	175	150	116	116	100	100					
George AFB	5085	7061	7404		300				130	80					
Georgetown	2000	2000	900	900	600	607	705	724	730	400	320	415	600	700	462
Gerber	950	950	775	850	950	1000	1000	50							
Germantown	950	950	750	813	650	375	619	619	221	361	235	87			
Geyserville	950	950	750	175	125	120	120	520	550	398	246	100			
Giant									65						

POPULATION HISTORY OF CALIFORNIA CITIES AND TOWNS 1850-1990

COMMUNITY	1990	1980	1970	1960	1950	1940	1930	1920	1910	1900	1890	1880	1870	1860	1850
Gibsonville	200	200	250	150	150				200	170	238	373	350	350	
Gilman Hot Springs															
Gilroy	31487	21641	12684	7348	4951	3615	3502	2862	2437	1820	1694	1621	1625		
Glen Avon	12663	8444	5759	3416	950										
Glen Ellen	1191	1014	900	700	375	300	220	224	1000	1000	3500				
Glenbrook				600					139	139	139	60			
Glenbrook Heights	500	500	150		175										
Glenburn	300	300	100		100										
Glencoe	300	300	130					50		79	100	101			
Glendale	180038	139060	132664	119442	95702	82582	62736	13536	2746	200					
Glendora	47828	38654	32143	20752	3988	2822	2761	2028	900	492	164				
Glenhaven	300	300	300	150	100										
Glenview	250	250	500	250	400										
Glenville	350	350	200	150	120		50	95	94	78	85				
Glenwood									164	164					
Gloryetta															
Golden Gate											788				
Gold Run	125	125	200	225	125	130	114	114	100	150	211	377			
Goleta	28600	28100	8000	2000	1548	1000	866	519	500	475	300	400			
Gonzales	4660	2891	2575	2138	1821	1239	1670	1024	600	500	359	233			
Goodyear's Bar															
Goshen	1809	1809	1324	1061	525	254	364	210	69	69	200	251			
Graeagle	300	300	200	200	300	150	150	227	68	68	75				
Grafton								200			350				
Graham	10600	10600	8500												
Grainland															
Granada Hills			50000	31162											
Grand Terrace	10946	8498	5901	1450	755										
Grandview	400					400				89	89	302			
Grangeville						125	162		153	153	153	103			
Granite Bay Vista	950	950													
Graniteville					150	150	206	60	250	234	234	225	100		
Grass Valley	9048	6697	5149	4876	5283	5701	3817	4006	4520	4719	4032	4451	3500	3840	454
Graton	1409	1286	900	1055	800	500	500		200						
Grayson	500	500	350	300	600			163	200	220	331	133	250		
Greeley Hill	1500	1500													
Green Valley	800	800	600	165	150					96	96				
Green Valley Lake	350	350			65										
Greenacres	7379	5381	2116	1000											
Greenbrae	3400	3400	3500	2000	1500		100								

POPULATION HISTORY OF CALIFORNIA CITIES AND TOWNS 1850-1990

COMMUNITY	1990	1980	1970	1960	1950	1940	1930	1920	1910	1900	1890	1880	1870	1860	1850
Greenfield	7464	4181	2608	1680	1309	290	125	113	100						
Greenview	300	300	250	165	160	160	94		150						
Greenville	1396	1537	1073	1140	1153	703	877	520	531	531	531	403	240		
Greenwich						1000	1000				618				
Greenwood	250	250	175		375	385	300	318	307	307	307	181	100		200
Grenada	450	450	300	300	350	300	250	216							
Gridley	4631	3982	3534	3343	3054	2338	1941	1636	987	750	686	352			
Grimes	540	540	500	300	250	350	164	164	350	82	75	100			
Grossmont	2600	2600	2000	2000	500	175	175	62							
Groveland	350	350	300	350	350	300	300	143	250	184	184	59			
Grover City	11656	8827	5939	5210	2788										
Guadalupe	5479	3629	3145	2614	2429	1769	1540	919	480	295	295	431	450		
Gualala	700	700	600	300	100		94	150	173	173	173	207	236		
Guasti	150	150	100	500	640	600	600	164							
Guerneville	1966	1525	900	1000	1065	954	1042	633	780	633	633	363	150		
Guinda	400	400	200	150	250	235	235	315	125	125					
Gustine	3931	3142	2793	2300	1984	1355	1016	716	350						
Hacienda Heights	52354	49422	35969												
Half Moon Bay	8886	7282	4023	1957	1168	1360	1999	1500	1100	784	784	550			
Hamilton City	1811	800	800	800	703	500	200	125	200				150		
Hammondton	35	35			250	300	863	863							
Hanford	30897	20958	15179	10133	10028	8234	7028	5888	4829	2929	942	269			
Happy Camp	1110	1110	800	600	530	500	566	172	163	168	163	142			
Harbison Canyon	2122	2300	800	825	500										
Harbor City			17500	10000	7500	2500	1514	164							
Harbor Side	3700	3700	2000												
Hardwick		70	100												
Harrison Park	300	300		125	600	139	139								
Hathaway Pines	700	700	200	110	145										
Hatton Fields	300	300	400	362	350										
Havasu Lake	300	300	200												
Havilah					72				70	128	143	196	250		
Hawaiian Gardens	13639	10548	9052	10000	3500										
Hawkinsville	70	70	60		50					60	300	313			500
Hawkins Bar	235														
Hawthorne	71349	56447	53304	33035	16316	8263	6596	1062	200						
Hayfork	2605	1788	950	800	600	500	350	362	114	114	200	178	172		
Hayward	111498	94167	93058	72700	14272	6736	5530	3487	2746	1965	1419	1231	504		
Hazel Creek							134			189	189	200			
Healdsburg	9469	7217	5438	4816	3258	2507	2296	2412	2011	1869	1485	1133	959	334	

POPULATION HISTORY OF CALIFORNIA CITIES AND TOWNS 1850-1990

COMMUNITY	1990	1980	1970	1960	1950	1940	1930	1920	1910	1900	1890	1880	1870	1860	1850
Heber	2566	2221	800	400	510	335	240	219	80						
Hedges/Tumco									250	698					
Helendale	300	300													
Helm	250	250	150	125	300	175	175		250	250					
Hemet	36094	22454	12252	5416	3386	2595	2235	1480	992						
Henley									192	192	192	90			
Herald	300	300				100									
Hercules	16829	5693	252	310	343	343	392	373	279						
Herdlyn									679						
Herlong	1188	1188	900	1000	900										
Hermosa Beach	18219	18070	17412	16115	11826	7197	4796	2327	679						
Herndon	200	200	400	500	700		60	50	75						
Hesperia	50418	13540	4592	3226	750	710	210	127	95	121	250				
Hi Vista	600	600	350		100										
Hickman	550	550	400	400	500		158	158	80	58					
Hidden Hills	1729	1760	1529	1000	795	600	500	364	100	119					
Highgrove	3175	4200	2800	2400											
Highland	34439	10908	13290	8000	3500	1825	1155	715	1995	1600					
Highway City	1200	1200	1100	1331	350	359									
Hildreth											300				
Hills Flat	700	700	400	500											
Hillsborough	10667	10451	8753	7554	3552	2747	1891	931							
Hilltop	650	650													
Hilmar	3392	1706	900	539	500	200	100	94							
Hilt			420	530	528	500	500	216	60						
Hinkley	700	700	700	700	175	200	200	63	50						
Hite's Cove												251			
Hobart Mills							400	516							
Hollister	19212	11488	7663	6071	4903	3881	3757	2781	2308	1315	1234	1034	1000		
Hollydale	300	300	300	700		400									
Hollywood			185047		179749										
Hollywood-by-the-Sea					700										
Holt		50			125	125	210	415							
Holtville	4820	4399	3496	3080	2472	1772	1758	1347	729						
Home Garden	1549	1495													
Home Gardens	7780	5783	5116	1541	1400		1530								
Homeland	3312	2616	1187	700	900										
Homestead											637	367			
Homestead Valley	3500	3500	1500	2000	600	350									
Homewood	500	500	500												

POPULATION HISTORY OF CALIFORNIA CITIES AND TOWNS 1850-1990

COMMUNITY	1850	1860	1870	1880	1890	1900	1910	1920	1930	1940	1950	1960	1970	1980	1990
Honcut			150	190	85	461	500	419	220	150	271		270	100	100
Hondo									100	3150	5000				
Hood						78				100	125	225	350	435	435
Hoopa										140	125	425	600	800	800
Hope Ranch										500		1000	2500	4200	4200
Hopeton				201	32										
Hopland				403	417	417	417	515	515	860	600	600	900	900	900
Hornbrook		500	600	350	276	188	250	516	300	300	350	250	480	350	350
Hornitos						250	160	100	62	159	126	73	100	200	200
Horse Creek											125	125		200	200
Howland Flat		500	500	218	100		100	110							
Hueneme			250	166	789	583	789	750	600	600	1816	1898	2144	2943	3259
Hughson							300	640	600	590					
Huntington Beach							815	1687	3690	3738	5237	11492	115960	170505	181519
Huntington Park							1299	4513	24591	28648	29450	29920	33744	46223	56065
Huron					150	67	70	67	119		1373	1269	1525	2768	4766
Hyde Park						100	100	517	517	517	517				
Hydesville/Burnell			150	164	317	317	317	317	200	200	450	400	700	900	1131
Hynes								516	2000	5000					
Idria						64	200					250	300		
Idyllwild									376	300	604	850	900	2400	2400
Ignacio							50	110	198	134	180	1176	3200	2800	2800
Igo			50	225	200	48	180		40		60		75	300	300
Imperial						148	1257	1885	1943	1493	1759	2658	3094	3451	4113
Imperial Beach							80	113	113	363	285	17773	20244	22689	26512
Imusdale				130	321	321									
Independence			250	282	407	407	407	407	678	600	850	1000	950	1000	1000
Indian Wells											50		760	1394	2647
Indio						50	250	516	2000	2296	5300	9745	14459	21611	36793
Ingle											350	565			
Inglewood						361	1536	3286	19480	30114	46185	63390	89985	94245	109602
Ingot							50	415	200	100	100				
Inverness							45	113	132	300	450	450	600	1400	1422
Inyokern											600	660	800	900	900
Ione		500	600	636	806	806	880	876	1361	1200	1071	1118	2369	2207	6516
Iowa Hill		500	350	456	500	508	460	456	120	150	125			60	60
Irvine									150	125	150	316	7000	62134	110330
Irvington					467	467	800	819	1000	1000	1400				
Irwindale						141	150	218	367	250	700	1518	784	1030	1050
Isabella						84	84	50	200	200	215				

POPULATION HISTORY OF CALIFORNIA CITIES AND TOWNS 1850-1990

COMMUNITY	1990	1980	1970	1960	1950	1940	1930	1920	1910	1900	1890	1880	1870	1860	1850
Isla Vista	20395	16700	13441												
Isleton	833	914	909	1039	1597	1837	2090	917	100	100	100	200			
Ivanhoe	3293	2684	1575	1616	1172	230	200				332				
Jackson	3545	2331	1924	1852	1879	2024	2005	1601	2035	2300	1531	1040	800	1000	500
Jacumba	600	600	600	700	500	400	400	160							
Jamestown	2178	2206	950	875	743	982	814	814	650	382	385	212	400	250	400
Jamul	2258	1826	700	350	325	300	150	79	46	46	46	40			
Janesville	1200	1200	600	600	200	200	200	100	93	108	93	81			
Jenner	175	175	175	150	175	160	160	62							
Jenny Lind							100	216	78	78	78	54			
Johannesburg	300	300	300	312	200	135	530	300	300	272					
Johnson Park	1008	1008	500												
Johnsondale	150	150	600	300	285	400									
Johnsville							100	200	311	308	311	250			
Jolon							216		199	199	199	151			
Joshua Tree	3898	2083	1211	950	500										
Judsonville												301			
Julian	1284	1320	500	400	300	250	373	350	327	327	327	200	500		
Junction City	700	700	175	105	120	189	365	150	180	150	268	175	440	250	
June Lake	900	900	425	100	100										
Juniper Hills	350	350													
Keddie	285	285	250	300	350	150	250	261							
Keeler	135	135	100	203	302	300	164	52	85	53	50				
Keene	250	250	300	120	250	164	150	43	42	42	42				
Kelsey	400	400	200	100	150					87	87		150	100	
Kelseyville	2861	1567	950	800	550	423	877	520	900	994	282	156	500		
Kennett						150	124	464	1200	50	50				
Kensington	4974	5342	5823	6161											
Kent Woodlands	1600	2400	1500			1200									
Kentfield	6030	4800	5500	5000	4000	1000	100		130						
Kenwood	1400	1400	500	250	200	200	150	115	110	110					
Kerman	5448	4002	2667	1970	1563	400	250	213	400						
Kern									1500	1291					
Kern City			900												
Kernville	1656	1660	900	600	476	244	224	210	210	210	210	490	350		
Keswick	150	150	500	400	100	350	152	1800	2000	2980					
Kettleman	1411	1051	500	400	375		350								
Keyes	2878	1800	1875	1546	800	100	150	40							
King City	7634	5495	3717	2937	2347	1768	1483	1048	1000	330	253				
Kings Beach	2796	1942	2000	629	500	300									

POPULATION HISTORY OF CALIFORNIA CITIES AND TOWNS 1850-1990

COMMUNITY	1850	1860	1870	1880	1890	1900	1910	1920	1930	1940	1950	1960	1970	1980	1990
Kingsburg				101	291	328	634	1316	1322	1504	2310	3093	3843	5115	7205
Klamath						85		116	100	500	500	506	500	850	827
Klamath Glen											100	700	600	600	600
Klamathon						300	50								
Knight Landing/Grafton			600	367	287	369		376	600	462	700	725	846	1000	1000
Knights Ferry		200	500	191	573	573	573	573	337	184	100	125	100	100	100
Knightsen											500	150	100	135	135
Knoxville				300	27	27									
Konacti														230	230
Korbell				42		40	100	816	350	350	500	300	125	75	75
Kyburz								65	65		100	100	100	100	200
La Canada-Flintridge				250	325	175	250	420	2650	3800	8200	18338	20652	20153	19378
La Crescenta						150	150	320	2506	3561	12700	16000	19594	16531	12500
La Grange				145	285	237	237	261	102	102	250	150	150	175	175
La Habra						200	230	1255	2273	2499	4961	25136	41350	45232	51266
La Habra Heights												1500	4500	4874	6226
La Honda				50	68	68	100	100	150	250	500	900	600	750	750
La Jolla							250	1525	1525	3630	13000	12800	30000		
La Loma												5700			
La Mesa						290	290	1004	2513	3925	10946	30441	39178	50342	52931
La Mirada						161	161	213	362	300	350	22444	30808	40986	40452
La Palma												622	9687	15663	15392
La Porte/Rabbit Creek		500	400	274	214	214	214	225	250	200	75		75	40	40
La Presa												1500			
La Puente									250			24723	31092	30882	36955
La Quinta												500	800	4027	11215
La Riviera/Larchmont												2400	2500	10906	10986
La Selva Beach											250	500	1171	1603	1603
La Sierra										700	3802	19239			
La Verne/Lordsburg					100	500	954	1698	2860	3092	4198	6516	12965	23508	30897
Ladera												900	2000	1900	1900
Ladera Heights													6535	6647	6316
Lafayette				58	100	79	90	132	215	750	5500	7114	20484	20879	23501
Laguna Beach							100	316	1981	4460	6661	9288	14550	17860	23170
Laguna Hills													13676	16400	16400
Laguna Niguel													4644	12237	44400
Lagunitas								512	512	400	500	750	800	1200	1200
Lake Alpine									350						
Lake Arrowhead									510	605	667	950	2682	6272	2500
Lake Elsinore/Elsinore					800	279	488	633	1350	1552	2068	2432	3530	5982	18285

POPULATION HISTORY OF CALIFORNIA CITIES AND TOWNS 1850-1990

COMMUNITY	1850	1860	1870	1880	1890	1900	1910	1920	1930	1940	1950	1960	1970	1980	1990
Lake Forest											150	100		700	700
Lake Hughes											280	375	600	800	800
Lake Isabella									98	180		850	600	3428	3323
Lake Los Angeles														900	900
Lake San Marcos													1400	2000	3802
Lakehead											100		100	300	300
Lakeland Village												3539	3559	2796	5159
Lakeport			248	562	991	726	870	1024	1318	1490	1983	2303	3005	3675	4390
Lakeside						110	110	452	305	350	3500	6000	11991	23921	39412
Lakeview									200	200	300	300	500	950	1448
Lakewood										1200	31000	67126	83025	74654	73557
Lamanda Park					114	200	300	1520	8044	8044					
Lamont										700	3571	6177	7007	9616	11517
Lanare														400	400
Lancaster					305	300	400	1017	1694	2400	3594	26012	30948	48027	97291
Landers													900	1500	1500
Larkfield													1000	1500	1500
Larkspur							594	612	1241	1558	2905	5710	10487	11064	11070
Las Lomas						200							900	1740	2127
Las Posas													2100	2500	2500
Lassen								158				200		1500	1500
Lathrop				165	577	577	577	275	462	332	600	1123	2137	3717	6841
Laton						60	375	413	699	774	881	1052	1071	1100	1415
Latrobe			150	108	213	213	213	220	220		225				
Lawndale (Los Angeles)							100	261	369	2365	19500	21740	24825	23460	27331
Lawndale (San Mateo)										354	354				
Lawrence					300	152	152	415	415		425			1096	1133
Laytonville					200	100	100	125	116	116	500	500	900	1500	1205
Le Grand						103	300	362	350	500	769	900	900	900	900
Lebec						50	50	50	300	300	400	400	600		900
Lee Vining											325	350	400	900	900
Leggett									80		500	350	500	700	700
Lemon Grove						150	180	319	468	1200	7200	19348	19690	20780	23984
Lemon Heights													1500	2500	2500
Lemoncove							100	281	200	400	950	700	400	500	500
Lemoore				463	651	639	1000	1355	1399	1711	2153	2561	4219	8832	13622
Lennox								418	6720	8132	25000	31224	16121	18445	22757
Lenwood									200	181	250	2407	3834	2974	3190
Lerdo							75				990				
Leucadia										1400	1880	5665	5900	9478	9478

POPULATION HISTORY OF CALIFORNIA CITIES AND TOWNS 1850-1990

COMMUNITY	1850	1860	1870	1880	1890	1900	1910	1920	1930	1940	1950	1960	1970	1980	1990
Lewiston		200	338	301	182	182	240	200	327	254	300	500	750	950	1187
Liberty Acres												4000	4500	4600	4700
Likely						50	100	100	75	200	125	100	150	265	265
Limco													100	500	500
Lincoln			250	275	961	1061	1402	1325	2094	2044	2410	3197	3176	4132	7248
Lincoln Acres									1050	1050	1700	3500	2000	1800	1800
Lincoln Village												6000	6112	6476	4236
Linda												6129	7731	10225	13033
Linden			200	101	147	147	147	167	167	167	875	875	900	900	1339
Lindsay						100	1814	2576	3878	4397	5060	5397	5206	6924	8338
Linnell														150	150
Litchfield										109	900	900		350	350
Little Lake													3500	3500	
Little River			158	170	243	243	242	152	256	201	300	375	500	800	800
Little Rock						243	152		300	300	325	500	1500	800	1320
Little Stony				301	117										
Live Oak (Santa Cruz)												3518	6443	11482	15212
Live Oak (Sutter)				201	278	278	278	289	500	800	1770	2276	2645	3103	4320
Livermore			500	855	1391	1493	2030	1916	3119	2885	4364	16058	37703	48349	56741
Livingston					130	82	110	358	803	895	1502	2188	2588	5326	7317
Llancha Plana		1000	100		100	29	29								
Llano								50	100	100				350	350
Loch Lomond													100	300	300
Locke													300	175	175
Lockeford			300	472	472	369	472	612	619	750	750	900	890	1852	2722
Lockwood														250	250
Lodi				606	1013	1491	2697	4850	6788	11079	13798	22229	28691	35221	51874
Loleta						261	390	317	400	270	500	600	800	800	800
Loma Linda								50	1000	2500	2800	6000	9797	10694	17400
Loma Mar											125	100		190	190
Loma Prieta					500										
Lomita								725	7052	7122	8700	14983	19784	18807	19382
Lomita Park									800	1000	1400			875	
Lompico															875
Lompoc				226	1015	972	1482	1876	2845	3379	5520	14415	25284	26267	37649
London											200		600	1257	1638
Lone Pine			400	300	487	261	250	262	267	1022	1415	1310	1241	1684	1818
Long Barn													200	250	250
Long Beach				250	564	2252	17809	55593	142032	164271	250767	344168	358879	361334	429433
Long Valley				85	205	205	205								

POPULATION HISTORY OF CALIFORNIA CITIES AND TOWNS 1850-1990

COMMUNITY	1990	1980	1970	1960	1950	1940	1930	1920	1910	1900	1890	1880	1870	1860	1850
Lookout	350	350	200	125	230		80		40	73					
Loomis	5705	1284	1108	500	525	398	319	307	450	300					
Lordsburg									954	698	97				
Lorenzo					7500	1000			320						
Lorin											743				
Los Alamitos	11676	11529	11346	4312	1800	1206	696	619	300	280					
Los Alamos	950	950	600	630	600	500	291	410	607	462	607	75			
Los Altos	26303	25769	25062	19696	18198	2150	1000	520	200						
Los Altos Hills	7514	7421	6871	3412											
Los Angeles	3485398	2966763	2811801	2479015	1970358	1504277	1238048	576673	319198	102479	50395	11183	5728	4385	1610
Los Banos	14519	10341	9188	5272	3868	2214	1875	1276	745	240					
Los Gatos	27357	26593	22613	9036	4907	3597	3168	2317	2232	1915	1652	555	200		
Los Molinos	1709	1241	900	1060	600	500	200	264							
Los Nietos	7100	7100	7845	9000	9000	1152	500	125	114	114			350		
Los Olivos	350	350	300	300	300	193	193	250	220	180					
Los Osos	8000	8000	2000	900	550										
Los Ranchitos	1800	1700	2300												
Los Seranos	7099	4500	1700	900	220	200	200	300							
Lost Hills	1212	800	200	200	100	100	200	219	130						
Lotus	300	300	150							136					
Lower Lake	1217	1043	850	550	475	484	698	395	395	395	395	459	692		
Loyalton	931	1030	945	936	911	925	837	442	983	143	143	84	200		
Lucas Valley	2000	2000	1650												
Lucerne	2011	1767	1300	850	350										
Lucerne Valley	1300	1300	1000	1402	933	500	300	68							
Lundy									127	362	250	100			
Lynwood	61945	48548	43354	31614	25823	10982	7323	113							
Lytle Creek	700	700	500	300											
Lytton				160	250	220	220	112							
McArthur	600	600	400	400	300	150	112								
McCloud	1555	1656	1643	2140	1394	1000	296	250	200	100					
Macdoel	200	200	170	250	200	150	200	120	200						
McFarland	7005	5151	4177	3686	2183	605	500	517	100						
McKinleyville	10749	7772	2000	950	200										
McKittrick	300	300	300	127	124	295	300	207	300						
Mad River	500														
Madeline	85	500						320							
Madera	29281	21732	16044	14430	10497	6457	4665	3444	2404	1890	950	217			
Madera Acres	5245	2173	80												
Madera Ranchos	1500	1500													

POPULATION HISTORY OF CALIFORNIA CITIES AND TOWNS 1850-1990

COMMUNITY	1990	1980	1970	1960	1950	1940	1930	1920	1910	1900	1890	1880	1870	1860	1850
Madison	470	470	200	400	150	150	250	264	300	300	577	105			
Madron				360	300	100		100	65						
Magalia	950	950	350	125	100	100	200	257	243	243	243	103	250	100	
Magunden					340										
Malaga	750	750	900	700	800	125	125	90	81	81					
Malibu	10000	10000	7000	2300	950										
Malibu Canyon	2900	2300	1000												
Mammoth												473			
Mammoth Lakes	4785	3000	900	150	50										
Manchester	490	490	150	112	400	150	113	113	96	96	96	250			
Manhattan Beach	32063	31542	35352	33934	17330	6398	1891	859							
Manila	700	700	300						100						
Manteca	40773	24925	13845	8242	3804	1981	1614	1286	100	50					
Manton	300	300	150	150	100		47	47	140						
Manzanita					200	1000									
Mar Vista							1500								
March AFB	5523	3607	2002												
Maricopa	1193	946	740	648	800	670	1071	1121	750						
Marin City	2500	2500	1650	2500	2400										
Marina	26436	20647	8343	3310	600	400	113	113							
Marina del Rey	7431	8065	3300												
Marinwood	4500	4500	4500												
Mariposa	1152	1150	900	850	700	574	711	431	450	400	366	342	700	600	200
Mark West												183			
Markleeville	100	100	150	128	100	199	162	150	150	149	149	80	75		
Marshall	170	170	100	175	200	150	56	65	65	162	200				
Martell	100	100	235		200	150	150	50							
Martinez	31808	22582	16506	9604	8268	7381	6569	3858	2115	1380	1600	1150	560		
Marysville	12324	9898	9353	9553	7826	6646	5763	5461	5430	3497	3991	4321	4738	4500	2000
Mather AFB	4885	5245	7027												
Matheson/Copley					359	359	359								
Maxwell	800	800	850	820	750	900	613	480	480	420	500	202			
Mayfield						1800	2158	1127	1041	1009	821	425	600		
Mayflower Village	4978	5017													
Maywood	27850	21810	16996	14588	13292	10731	6794								
Meadow Lakes	400	400													
Meadow Vista	3067	2683	900	900	250										
Meadowbrook	500	500	500	200											
Mecca	1966	1698	400	300	560	500	500								
Meeks Bay	800	800													

POPULATION HISTORY OF CALIFORNIA CITIES AND TOWNS 1850-1990

COMMUNITY	1990	1980	1970	1960	1950	1940	1930	1920	1910	1900	1890	1880	1870	1860	1850
Meiners Oaks	3329	5600	7025	3513	2446										
Melones					150										1000
Melrose										260	100				
Mendocino	1008	1008	975	930	1250	1507	1500	1239	1100	1009	806	603	473		
Mendota	6821	5083	2705	2098	1516	435	364	210	100	50					
Menlo Park	28040	25673	26826	26951	13587	3258	2254	1100	820	885	385	225	150		
Mentone	5675	3800	3800	3216	2000	800	416	416	300	225					
Merced	56216	36499	22670	20068	15278	10135	7066	3976	3102	1969	2009	1446	1200		
Merced Falls					500	500	200	63	50	58	385	150			
Meridian	600	600	330	410	450	350	300	225	199	199	199	196			
Mesa Verde	300	300	250												
Metropolitan				260											
Michigan Bluff	30	30	50		50	123	72	479	480	400	377	468	300	500	
Michillinda	1100	1100	1500	2000	2000										
Middletown	2000	2000	900	500	450	726	736	434	327	327	327	271	200		
Midland				500	750	100									
Midpines	390	390	200	150	100	125									
Midway City	3500	3500	5200	4500	1421	585	485								
Mill Creek					400	100									
Mill Valley/Eastland	13038	12967	12942	10411	7331	4847	4164	2554	2551	919					
Millbrae	20412	20058	20920	15873	8972	1250	415	243	240	210	243	195			
Millville	300	300	150		150		200	217	361	361	361	253	300		
Milpitas	50686	37820	26561	6572	700	416	532	312	312	312	312	550	200		
Milton	90	90	125	150	125	100	200	118	408	408	408	87	250		
Mineral	320	320			100		50								
Mint Canyon			1500												
Mira Monte/Tico	3500	3500			750	293									
Mirabel Heights	300	300	150												
Mirabel Park	400	400	150	150											
Mirada Hills				22444											
Miraleste		3500	3500												
Mira Loma	15786	8707	8482	3932	1555	726	400								
Miramar	500	500	700	150	400	100									
Miramonte	350	350	350	830	250	293	47	59							
Miranda	350			150	150		44								
Mission Hills	3112	2729	2699												
Mission San Jose					850	531	531	531	759	750	759	216			
Mission Viejo	72820	50666	11933												
Miwuk Village	1175	250	200	125											
Moccasin	185	185	250	140	125										

POPULATION HISTORY OF CALIFORNIA CITIES AND TOWNS 1850-1990

COMMUNITY	1990	1980	1970	1960	1950	1940	1930	1920	1910	1900	1890	1880	1870	1860	1850
Modesto	164730	106602	61712	36586	17389	16379	13842	9241	4034	2024	2402	1693	1500		
Mohawk							45	45	70						
Mojave	3763	2886	2573	1845	2055	761	638	316	405	231	231	200			
Mokelumne Hill	950	950	560	570	600	1170	1622	968	700	782	573	515	700	1000	
Moneta								715	300						
Monitor												201			
Mono Vista	2599	1154	300												
Monolith/Cement			150	450	450	150	261	263	40						
Monoville														987	
Monrovia	35761	30531	30562	27079	20186	12807	10890	5480	3576	1205	907				
Monta Vista	3000	3000	3000	3000											
Montague	1415	1285	890	782	579	463	507	453	274	250	250				
Montalvin Manor	1800	1800	2300												
Montalvo			2400	2028	600	300	215	215	141	148					
Montara	2552	1972	1459	500	500	177	177	286							
Montclair	28434	22628	22546	13546											
Monte Nido	700	700	250	200											
Monte Rio	1058	1137	900	900	750	500	500	320							
Monte Sereno	3287	3434	2847	1506											
Montebello	59564	52929	42807	32097	21735	8016	5498	450							
Montecito	9300	9300	7000	5000	4052	3773	1573	916	500	350					
Monterey	31954	27558	26302	22618	16205	10084	9141	5479	4923	1748	1662	1396	1112	1653	1092
Monterey Park	60738	54338	49166	37821	20395	8531	6406	4108							
Montgomery Creek	800	800	200	150	200	200	200		135	135					
Monticello					250	100	274	274	250	250	233	102			
Montrose	4000	4000	6000	10000	8500	3840	1040	50							
Monument												246			
Moonridge	2700	2700	1000												
Moores Flat									120	103	175	459	200	250	
Moore's Station											437	103			
Moorpark	25494	4030	3380	2902	1146	726	367	216	50						
Morada	3570	3600	2936	2156	100		100	61							
Moraga	15852	15014	14205	1000	400	400	111	59							
Moreno Valley	118779	1175	500	250	225		105	59		59					
Morgan Hill	23928	17060	5579	3151	1627	1014	908	646	607	482					
Mormon Island											270	257			
Morongo Valley	1544	1137													
Morro Bay	9664	9064	7109	3692	1659	863	198	110	100	49	50				
Moss Beach	3002	1868	800	600	500	416	416	416				183	150		
Moss Landing	630	630	600	400	400	150	150	106	106	106					

POPULATION HISTORY OF CALIFORNIA CITIES AND TOWNS 1850-1990

COMMUNITY	1990	1980	1970	1960	1950	1940	1930	1920	1910	1900	1890	1880	1870	1860	1850
Mott										174	174				
Mount Baldy	500	500	300	225	100										
Mount Eden				150	475	500	500	145	210	155	300	400	100		
Mount Helix	1500	1500	1500												
Mount Herman	560	560	500	150	150	145									
Mount Laguna	500	500	350	450	75	210									
Mount Shasta	3460	2837	2256	1936	1909	1618	1009	542							
Mount View	3600	3600	3000												
Mountain Gate	400	400	400	150											
Mountain Mesa	1153	900	400												
Mountain Pass	700	450	225												
Mountain View	67460	58655	54132	30889	6563	3946	3308	1888	1161	921	921	250	400		
Mountain View Acres	2469	1684	1000	900											
Muir Beach	300	300	250												
Mulford			1000		950										
Murphys	1517	950	950	775	650	792	948	700	700	698	570	384	300	250	500
Murrietta	350	350	600	600	475	1080	283	162	200	200	537				
Murrietta Hot Springs	1938	1091	50												
Muscoy	7541	6188	7091	8000	400										
Myrtletown/Ryans Slough	4413	3959	3922	3624	1727										
Nanceville			400	400											
Napa	61842	50879	36103	22170	13579	7740	6437	6757	5791	4036	4395	3731	1879	1378	159
Napa Junction	535	535	500		224		210	210	100	100	150	100			
Naples						1500	250	310	50						
Narod			1000												
National City	54249	48772	43184	32771	21199	10344	7301	3116	1733	1086	1353	248			
Natividad										106	300	500			
Navarro	255	255	175	135	200	140	140	259	202	202	202	150	315		
Nebo Center	1459	1749													
Needles	5191	4120	4051	4530	4051	3624	3144	2807	1500	1100	285	75			
Nelson							113	200	80	217	217				
Nestor					725	150	56		65						
Nevada City	2855	2431	2314	2353	2505	2445	1701	1782	2689	3250	2524	4002	3000	3679	2683
New Almaden/Almaden	300	300	250	300	300	200	200	273	700	1261	1050	993			
New Cuyama	600	600	600	800	500										
New Jerusalem											300	400			
Newark	37861	32126	27153	9864	1532	628	519	519	400	318	318	179			
Newberry Springs	900	900	650	200	200	175	175	315							
Newberry Park			9000	450	150	135					85				
Newcastle	1500	1500	900	975	800	750	750	800	755	450	335	162	551		

POPULATION HISTORY OF CALIFORNIA CITIES AND TOWNS 1850-1990

COMMUNITY	1990	1980	1970	1960	1950	1940	1930	1920	1910	1900	1890	1880	1870	1860	1850
Newhall		12029	9651	4705	2527	1573	1104	1022	250	202	202	61			
Newman	4151	2785	2505	2148	1815	1214	1269	1027	892	621	621				
Newport Beach	66643	62556	49582	26564	12120	4438	2203	894	445	130	83	50			
Nicasio	100	100			200	200	200	159	96	95	96	183	100		
Nice	2126	1400	700	350	450	160	160								
Nichols	100	100	200	100	675	250									
Nicolaus				200	400	144	213	132	130	309	309		350		300
Niland	1183	1042	950	800	700	500	500	323							
Niles					1519	1500	1517	1517	1000	235	235	136			
Nipomo	7109	5247	3642	950	1000	750	870	513	260	215	215	136			
Norco	23302	21126	14511	4964	1584	1215	1005								
Norden	110	110	250	264	220	130									
Nordhoff									400	261	244	60			
Norman									250	200					
North Bloomfield	50	50	40			605	872	500	497	561	497	724	500	400	
North Columbia									156	156	156	290			
North Edwards	1259	1107	700												
North Fair Oaks	13912	10294	9740												
North Fork	950	950	800	850	453	134	218	130	130	100		50			
North Highlands	42105	37825	31854	21271	3000										
North Hollywood/Lankershim			190000	173341			5000	2026	200						
North Modesto		5800	4500		4300										
North Oaks															
North Ontario										280	96				
North Palm Springs	950	950	500		750										
North Richmond	3200	3200	4000	2000											
North Sacramento				12922	6029	3053	2097	1027							
North San Juan	300	300	135	130	250	225	135	320	400	400	303	656	500	700	
North Shafter		800	800	500											
North Temescal											2032				
North Turlock				1945	1586										
Northcrest			900												
Nortonville									76	76	76	900	350		
Norwalk	94279	85232	90164	88739	6300	6184	5111	1517	596	596	596	150			
Novato	47585	43916	31006	17881	3496	617	700	510	400	300	130	100	75		
Noyo	650	650	500	600	250	250	93	93	84	84	84				
Nubieber	250	250	250	150	150	250									
Nuevo	3010	1628	500	300	500	350	350				163				
Nyland	1800	1800	1500	1619											
Oak Knolls	3000	2700													

POPULATION HISTORY OF CALIFORNIA CITIES AND TOWNS 1850-1990

COMMUNITY	1850	1860	1870	1880	1890	1900	1910	1920	1930	1940	1950	1960	1970	1980	1990
Oak Knoll Hills														425	425
Oak Park														5000	5000
Oak Run													100	300	300
Oak View											150	2448	4872	4671	3606
Oakdale			150	376	1012	1012	1035	1745	2112	2592	4064	4980	6594	8474	11961
Oakhurst								153	150		500	500	500	1959	2602
Oakland		1442	10500	34555	48682	66960	150174	216261	284063	302163	384575	367548	361561	339337	372242
Oakley							200	261	761	400	2892	3000	1306	2816	18374
Oakridge												600			
Oakville				101	264	264	264	219	219	219	200	150	300	550	550
Occidental/Howards				97	516	516	516	220	350	500	500	200	300	200	200
Ocean Beach							100	713	713	713	16600				
Ocean View					216					200	500				
Oceano						108	250	425	669	574	1446	1317	2564	4478	6169
Oceanside					270	330	673	1161	3508	4651	12881	24971	40494	76698	128398
Ocotillo												200	250	500	500
Oil Center/Oil City							50	1046	1000	500	790				
Oil Fields								358	350	350	400				
Oildale								517	2000	2238	16615	19000	20879	23382	26553
Ojai								1400	1468	1622	2519	4495	5591	6816	7613
Olancha					147	147	147	100	100	100	275		260	450	450
Old Station													90	300	300
Olema				103	205	205	250	110	150	150	150	150		75	75
Oleum								217	217	217	250				
Olinda (Orange)							100	519	449	250	411				
Olinda (Shasta)								180	180	180	170			150	130
Olive					250			526	600	600	900	1000	600		
Olivehurst											3588	4855	8100	8929	9738
Olivewood					500										
Olympic Valley												250	600	900	900
Omo					85						125	300	250	200	
Ontario					683	722	4274	7280	13585	14197	22872	46667	64118	88820	133179
Onyx								75	500	125	95		80	550	550
Opal Cliffs												3825	5425	5041	5940
Ophir		100	150	595	400	262	170	210	250	181	100			500	500
Orange				679	866	1216	2920	4884	8066	7901	10027	26444	77365	91788	110658
Orange Cove									500	488	2395	2835	3392	4026	5604
Orange Park													800	900	900
Orangevale							80	50	150	250		8000	16493	20585	26266
Orcutt							350	719	719	470	1001	1414	1700	1500	1500

POPULATION HISTORY OF CALIFORNIA CITIES AND TOWNS 1850-1990

COMMUNITY	1990	1980	1970	1960	1950	1940	1930	1920	1910	1900	1890	1880	1870	1860	1850
Oregon House	200	150	150	300	350	200	197	197	182	182	182	130			
Orick	600	600	900	900	600	250	115	63	70	40	40				
Orinda	16642	16825	6790	5568	3300	225	225								
Orland	5052	4031	2884	2534	2067	1366	1195	1582	836	440	440	292			
Orleans	900	900	600	300	263	140	75	357	50	74	200				
Oro Grande/Halleck	900	900	700	859	685	350	350	350	108	108					
Orosi	5486	4076	2757	1048	855	1000	1200	510	330						
Oroville	11960	8683	7536	6115	5387	4421	3698	3340	3859	2981	1787	1743	1425	2429	
Otay	6400	6400	3500	1500	1774	308	219	219	140	112	175				
Oxnard	142216	108195	71225	40265	21567	8519	6285	4417	2555	1601					
Pacheco	3325	2000	2000	1518	375	425	200	169	322	232	232	400	500		
Pacific Beach			59000	43000	23600		1042	619		60	200				
Pacific Gardens	3600	4000	3500												
Pacific Grove	16117	15755	13505	12121	9623	6249	5558	2974	2384	1411	1336				
Pacific House	300	300	150												
Pacific Manor	500	500													
Pacific Palisades							1000								
Pacific Villas			430												
Pacifica	37670	36866	36020	20995											
Pacoima							1012	210							
Paicines	350	350	100		150	200		84	54	54	54				
Pajaro	3332	1426	1407	1273	1487	260	260	460	100	84	100	150	100		
Pala	350	350	250	250	250	260	250	219	84	50	75				
Palermo	5260	2572	1966	900	720	300	200	119	200						
Palm City			1200		500	200	200								
Palm Desert	23252	11801	6171	1295	600										
Palm Springs	40181	32271	20936	13468	7660	3434	1500	175	150						
Palmdale	68842	12277	8571	11522	3300	665	392	392	75	50	60				
Palmdale East	3052	2920	3560												
Palms						1218	1218	1218	250						
Palo Alto	55900	55225	56040	52287	25475	16774	13652	5900	4486	1658					
Palo Cedro	1800	950													
Palo Verde	600	600	600	250	300	108	108		100						
Palomar Park	900	900	700												
Palos Verdes Estates	13512	14376	13631	9564	1963	987	750								
Panoche	2400	2400	200						32	82	82	400			
Panorama Heights															
Paradise	25408	22571	14539	8268	4426	1123	250	150	150	93	93	299		100	
Paramount	47669	36407	34734	27249	16800										
Parker Dam	250	250	220	500	550	150									

POPULATION HISTORY OF CALIFORNIA CITIES AND TOWNS 1850-1990

COMMUNITY	1990	1980	1970	1960	1950	1940	1930	1920	1910	1900	1890	1880	1870	1860	1850
Parkfield					100	100	217	217	207	207	207				
Parksdale	1911	1267													
Parkway	12000	12000	13000	10000											
Parkwood	1659	1146	900												
Parlier	7938	2902	1993	1366	1419	776	564	819	400	50					
Pasadena	131591	118550	112951	116407	104577	81864	76086	45354	30291	9117	4882	391			
Pasatiempo	900	900	1115												
Paskenta	300	300	200		240		122	122	122	122	122	200			
Paso Robles/ El Paso de Robles	18583	9163	7168	6677	4835	3045	2573	1919	1441	1224	827	150			
Patterson (Stanislaus)	8626	3908	3147	2246	1343	1109	905	694	75	58	200	150			
Patterson (Tulare)	400	400													
Patton	700	700	500	600	850	800	400	215							
Pauma Valley	550	550	400	350	700										
Pearblossom	1800	1800	900	680	484	160	80								
Peardale	550	550	500												
Pearland	650	650	250												
Pebble Beach	4700	4700	2500	1250	300	300	295								
Pedley	4800	4800	4500	1554	2226										
Pedro Valley					350		57	97							
Penn Valley	1242	1032	700	530	500	200	160	89	100	40					
Penngrove	600	600	500	350	500	440	365	365	250	219	219	238			
Penryn	600	600	320						85	85	85	45			
Pentz				200	200	265	265	265	100						
Pepperwood	60	60													
Peralta	900	900									744				
Perkins				300	950	200	200	250	250	215	215				
Perris	21460	6827	4228	2950	1807	1011	763	499	480	318	318	238	500		
Pescadero	500	500	625	800	1000	864	1000	984	539	381	238	238			
Petaluma	43184	33834	24870	14035	10315	8034	8245	6226	5880	3871	3692	3326	3000	1505	
Peters	30	30				125	125	219	140	132	132				
Petrolia	190	190					50	319	199	199	199				
Phillipsville	250	250	250		150				90		50	200	150		
Philo	960	960	700	600	250	110	110	110	200						
Picacho									200	200					
Pico Rivera	59177	53459	54170	49150	9000	3630	2000								
Piedmont	10602	10498	10917	11117	10132	9866	9333	4282	1719		634				
Piedra	500	500													
Piercy	350	350	200		250	200									
Pike									210	278	210				

POPULATION HISTORY OF CALIFORNIA CITIES AND TOWNS 1850-1990

COMMUNITY	1990	1980	1970	1960	1950	1940	1930	1920	1910	1900	1890	1880	1870	1860	1850
Pilot Hill	500	500	250				50	75	113	113	123	85			
Pine Cove	350	500	200												
Pine Grove (Amador)	1500	1500	850	600	600	126	126	179	164	164	164	104			
Pine Grove (Shasta)	1049	1049	900	500	250										
Pine Hills	1200	1200	1000	200											
Pine Knot	950						500	67							
Pine Mountain Lake	200														
Pine Ridge					115		50	150	150						
Pine Valley		950	300	150	175	150	150								
Pinedale	1297		2900	2300	2220	518	518								
Pino											307	194			
Pinole	17460	14253	13266	6064	1147	934	781	967	798	508	340	502			
Pinon Hills	875	875	250												
Pioneer	800	800	480	270	300										
Pioneer Point	1300	1300	1200	900	400										
Piru	1157	1284	975	1000	1500	1452	868	521	200	122					
Pismo Beach	7669	5364	4043	1762	1425	1104	915	528	175	108					
Pitt River								760							
Pittsburg/Black Diamond	47564	33034	21423	19062	12763	9520	9610	4715	2372	603	300				
Pixley	2457	2488	1584	1327	700	350	342	107	75	58	50				
Placentia	41259	35041	21948	5861	1682	1472	1606	810	40						
Placerville	8355	6739	5416	4439	3749	3064	2322	1650	1914	1748	1690	1951	1562	2466	5623
Plainview	525	525	400	450	500										
Planada	3531	2406	2056	1704	950	350	350	69	106	106	106	181			
Plano				1500	1000	100									
Plaster City	50	50	150	230	400										
Playmor	800	800	600												
Pleasant Hill	31585	25124	24610	23844	5686										
Pleasant Valley	900						64	64	231	231	231	257	250		
Pleasanton	50533	35160	18328	4203	2244	1278	1237	991	1254	1100	984	600	350		
Plymouth	811	699	501	489	382	460	343	657	768	768	768	740	100		
Point Arena	407	425	424	596	372	374	385	394	497	709	709	198	956		
Point Dume	2809	2438													
Point Reyes	900	900	600	600	500	400	143	225	100	53	99				
Poland													350		
Pollack Pines	4291	1941	950	850	650	300	135								
Pomona	131723	92742	87384	67157	35405	23539	20804	13505	10207	5526	3634	250			
Pondosa	300	300	100	310	105	300									
Pope Valley	300	300	300	300	300	180	250	279	266	266	266	50			
Poplar	1901	1295	1239	1478		200	199	115	90	90					

POPULATION HISTORY OF CALIFORNIA CITIES AND TOWNS 1850-1990

COMMUNITY	1850	1860	1870	1880	1890	1900	1910	1920	1930	1940	1950	1960	1970	1980	1990
Port Chicago									1032	1700	3000	1746			
Port Costa				175	627	850	850	519	593	628	587	350	300	250	250
Port Hueneme			500	166	1100	789	800	800	501	862	3024	11067	14295	17803	20319
Porterville				202	606	1692	2692	4097	5303	6270	6904	7991	12602	19707	29563
Portola							200	617	1012	764	2261	1874	1625	1885	2193
Portola Valley												1800	4996	3939	4193
Potrero						77	77	91	91		125		120	400	400
Potter Valley				500	219	563	576	512	600	617	800	975	975	1500	1500
Poway				140	159	159	180	218	218	242	360	1921	9422	33439	43516
Pozo				300	115	128	115	264	264		200				
Prado												100	100	100	100
Prattville				50	239	239	239	251	251						
Press							100				350				
Princeton			132	142	309	300	310	309	319	386	400	400	500	540	540
Proberta								50			275	200	250	300	300
Project City										1500	1250	1200	1431	1657	1657
Prunedale												600	800	1500	1500
Pudding Creek										300	600	250	480	600	600
Puente					250	200	220	1034	2200	2200	3800				
Pulga											500			30	30
Pumpkin Center												225	700	700	700
Quail Valley													600	2000	1937
Quartz Hill						212	212	212			1200	3325	4935	7421	9626
Quincy		192	208	432	546	546	520	528	901	1331	1330	1700	2500	2700	2700
Rackerby									250	150	200	170	150	300	300
Railroad Flat			100	175	77	77	77	219	219	219	400		200	600	600
Rainbow							50		56	100			530	1092	2006
Raisin							50	125	100		250	250	450	300	300
Ramona					100	188	210	575	400	540	1158	2449	3554	8173	13040
Ramos															600
Rancho California														2500	2500
Rancho Cordova												7429	30451	42881	48713
Rancho Cucamonga														55250	101409
Rancho Del Mar													2200	1400	
Rancho La Costa													300	400	400
Rancho Mirage											550	700	1298	6281	9778
Rancho Palos Verdes														36577	41659
Rancho Rinconado													5149	5100	4206
Rancho San Diego														2400	2400
Rancho Santa Clarita													4860		

COMMUNITY	1990	1980	1970	1960	1950	1940	1930	1920	1910	1900	1890	1880	1870	1860	1850
Rancho Santa Fe	4014	4014	3000	950	750	400	400								
Rancho Santa Margarita	15000														
Rand				350											
Randsburg	280	280	300	315	500	535	1040	1000	1000	1099					
Ravenswood				650	775										
Raymond	425	425	300	300	300	150	175	175	520	323	114				
Raynor Park															
Red Bluff	12363	9490	7676	7202	4905	3824	3517	3104	3530	2750	2608	2106	992	391	
Red Dog														400	
Red Hill	2500	2500	1600												
Red Mountain	200	200	250	350	320	800									
Redcrest	300	300	200	250											
Redding	66462	41995	16659	12773	10256	8109	4188	2962	3572	2946	1821				
Redlands	60394	43619	36355	26829	18429	14324	14177	9571	10449	4797	1904	600	500		
Redondo Beach	60167	57102	57451	46986	25226	13092	9347	4913	2935	855	603				
Redway	1212	1094	900	900	500										
Redwood City	66072	54951	55686	46290	25544	12453	8962	4020	2442	1653	1572	1383	727		
Redwood Estates	1100	1100	1100	1284	400										
Redwood Valley	1300	1300	500	400	727										
Reedley	15791	11071	8131	5850	4135	3170	2589	2447	1600	267					
Represa	150	500		360	360	250									
Requa	500	150	100	150	250	150	150	417	50	53	200				
Rescue		500	100		125		100								
Reseda			60862	52000		2184	2600	306							
Reward							518	518							
Rialto	72388	37474	28370	18567	3156	1770	1642	961	400	178					
Ribier					500						600				
Rich Gulch							300								
Richfield	200	200		225	225										
Richgrove	1899	1398	1023	500	300	150	150								
Richmond	87425	74676	79043	71854	99545	23642	20093	16843	6802						
Richvale	400	400	550	300	425	150	100	65							
Ridgecrest	27725	15929	7629	5099	2028										
Rimforest	600	600	300	300											
Rio Del Mar	8919	7067			100										
Rio Dell (Humboldt)	3012	2687	2817	3222	1862	465	352	213	213	213	213				
Rio Dell (Sonoma)	500	500	350												
Rio Linda	9481	7359	7524	2189	1200	363	100								
Rio Nido	300	300	150	150	300		300								
Rio Oso	150	150	100		500	197									

POPULATION HISTORY OF CALIFORNIA CITIES AND TOWNS 1850-1990

COMMUNITY	1990	1980	1970	1960	1950	1940	1930	1920	1910	1900	1890	1880	1870	1860	1850
Rio Vista	3316	3142	3135	2616	1831	1666	1309	1104	884	682	648	666	319		
Ripley	500	500	500		300	200	200								
Ripon	7455	3509	2679	1894	1550	700	571	212	250	138	150	151			
Ripperdan	200	200	600												
River Pines	450	450	240	180	300										
River Road					650										
Rivera					2700	400	300	275	210	161	268				
Riverbank	8547	5695	3949	2785	2662	1130	803	1027							
Riverdale	1980	1866	1722	1012	713	316	312	281	200	200	130	100			
Riverside	226505	170876	140089	84332	46764	34696	29696	19341	15212	7973	4683	1366	75		
Robbins	500	500	450	200	150	100	100								
Rockaway Beach					300	150	250	82	50						
Rocking Horse	800	800													
Rocklin	19033	7344	3039	1495	1155	795	724	643	1026	1050	1056	624	542		
Rockport					550	250			50	261					
Rockville			120	125											
Rodeo	7589	8286	5356	5800	5500	2500	1288	564	400	208					
Rohnert Park	36326	22965	6133												
Rohnerville	400	400	1300	1000	1500	694	500	615	600	516	621	500	100		
Rolling Hills	1871	2049	2050	1664	300	250									
Rolling Hills Estates	7789	7701	6735	3941											
Rolling Hills Riviera	3600	3700	3000												
Rollingwood	1000	1500	2000												
Romoland/Ethanac	2319	1349	700	450	450	300	353								
Roosevelt Terrace	2500	2300	2200												
Rosamond	7430	2869	2281	950	469	200	135	83	100	64	97				
Rosedale	900	900	900		275			63	75	150					
Roseland	8779	7915	5105	4510	1552										
Rosemead	51638	42604	40972	15476	15230	5500	2717								
Rosemont	22861	18888	4000												
Roseville	44685	24347	18221	13421	8723	6653	6425	4477	2608	461	345	258	115		
Rosewood	900	900	900	1100	1200										
Ross	2123	2801	2742	2551	2179	1751	1355	727	556		100	252	100		
Rossmoor	9893	10457	12922	12000											
Rough and Ready	950	950	400		125	188	120	145	140	121	175	131	300	719	672
Round Mountain	700	700	150	200	300	117	117	117	107	107	107				
Rovana	400	400	400												
Rowland											100	200			
Rowland Heights	42674	28252	16881												
Rubidoux	13200	13200	13969	9500	3798										

POPULATION HISTORY OF CALIFORNIA CITIES AND TOWNS 1850-1990

COMMUNITY	1990	1980	1970	1960	1950	1940	1930	1920	1910	1900	1890	1880	1870	1860	1850
Running Springs	1200	1200	600	450	75										
Runnymeade								786							
Rupert									375						
Russell					4490										
Rust				1100											
Rutherford	700	700	450	200	300	319	319	319	225	261	308	45			
Ryde	300	300	200	200	191		300	312	150	30					
Sacramento	369365	275741	257105	191667	137572	105958	93750	65908	44696	29282	26386	21420	16283	13785	6820
St. Helena	4990	4898	3173	2722	2297	1758	1582	1346	1603	1582	1705	1339	1000		
St. John									108	108	108	54	300		
St. Marys		2600	900	850	995	750	500								
Salada Beach						700									
Salida	2000	2000	1456	1109	1300	300	200	125							
Salinas	108777	80479	58896	28957	13917	11586	10263	4308	3736	3304	2339	1854	599		
Salton City	900	900	900	350											
Salvador			700												
Salyer	950	950	600	300	200			318							
Samoa	450	850	600	600	546		600	517							
San Andreas	2115	1912	1564	1416	1263	1210	2615	1638	1500	750	462	597	600		
San Anselmo	11743	12053	13031	11584	9188	5790	4650	2475	1531	161					
San Antonio	2935	2900	2000	1100	950	220	346							281	
San Ardo	450	450	350	400	270	150	150	150	100	79	100				
San Bernardino	164164	118057	106869	91922	63058	43646	37481	18721	12779	6150	4012	1673	2000	940	
San Bruno	38961	35417	36254	29063	12478	6519	3610	1562	710	200	175	50			
San Carlos	26167	24710	26053	21370	14371	3520	1132	113	100						
San Clemente	41100	27325	17063	8527	2008	479	667								
San Diego	1110554	875538	697471	573224	334287	203341	147995	74361	39578	17700	16159	2637	2300	731	500
San Dieguito												302			
San Dimas	32397	24014	15692	7743	1840	2524	2000	2541	800	263	100				
San Fernando	22580	17731	16571	16093	12992	9094	7567	3204	1100	608	296	174	150		
San Francisco	723959	678974	715674	740316	775357	634536	634394	506676	416912	342782	298997	233959	149473	56802	34870
San Gabriel	37120	30072	29336	22561	20343	11867	7224	2640	737	737	737	237	200	586	300
San Geronimo	500	500	350												
San Gregorio	240	240	200	200	205	110	250	264	100	89	85	45			
San Jacinto	16210	7098	4385	2553	1778	1356	1346	945	898	583	661	100			
San Joaquin	2311	1930	1506	879	632	240	163	320							
San Jose	782248	629442	459913	204196	95280	68457	57651	39642	28946	21500	18060	12567	9089	4579	3500
San Juan Bautista	1570	1276	1164	1046	1031	678	722	501	326	449	463	484	500	250	250
San Juan Capistrano	26183	18959	3781	1120	1250	946	861	519	326	400	500	376	175	150	250
San Leandro	68223	63952	68698	65962	27542	14601	11455	5703	3471	2258	1879	1369	426		200

POPULATION HISTORY OF CALIFORNIA CITIES AND TOWNS 1850-1990

COMMUNITY	1990	1980	1970	1960	1950	1940	1930	1920	1910	1900	1890	1880	1870	1860	1850
San Lorenzo	19987	20545	24633	23373	10750	1000	589	358	350	198	198	158	150		
San Lucas	150	150	100	100	200		360	360	349	349	349				
San Luis Obispo	41958	34252	28036	20437	14180	8881	8276	5895	5157	3021	2995	2243	1500	800	500
San Luis Rey				1000	950		320	320	150	150	200	299	100		300
San Marcos	38974	17479	3896	900	300	200	300	319	62	62	62	55			
San Marino	12959	13307	14177	13568	11230	8175	3730	584	200						
San Martin	1713	1731	1392	1162	800	400	375	314							
San Mateo	85486	77561	78991	69870	41782	19403	13444	5979	4384	1832	1170	932	400		
San Miguel	1123	800	800	800	800	788	706	520	500	458	458	65			
San Pablo	25158	19750	21461	19637	14476	590	489	487	367	367	367	251	1075		
San Pedro			91000	60000	74000			6500	6000	1787	1240	200		359	
San Quentin	140	140	450	215	500	328	328	328	200	165	140	298			
San Rafael	48404	44700	38977	20460	13848	8573	8022	5512	5934	3879	3290	2276	841	636	300
San Ramon	35303	22356	4084	300	250	121	70	115	110	110	110	100	100		
San Simeon	260	260			100	100	100	123	132	58	132	100	100		
San Tomas				1500	900										
San Ysidro					2381	1368	1368	324							
Sand City	192	182	212	520											
Sand Hill	2606	2606													
Sanders											33	199			
Sanger	16839	12558	10088	8072	6400	4017	2967	2578	1500	551	428				
Santa Ana	293742	203713	155710	100350	45533	31921	30322	15485	8429	4933	3628	711	500	756	
Santa Ana Heights	3300	3300	900		350		2069	100	88	88	100				
Santa Anita															
Santa Barbara	85571	74414	70215	58768	44854	34958	33613	19441	11659	6587	5864	3460	4500	2351	1500
Santa Clara	93613	87746	86118	58380	11702	6650	6302	5220	4348	3650	2891	2416	2000	1559	600
Santa Clarita	110642														
Santa Cruz	49040	41483	32076	25396	21970	16896	14395	10917	11146	5659	5596	3898	2561	950	
Santa Fe Springs	15520	14520	14750	16342	8000	2020	2020	112	100	63	65				
Santa Margarita	1200	1200	950	375	600	700	700	512	300	207					
Santa Maria	61284	39685	32749	20027	10440	8522	7057	3943	2260	1413	1433	200	75		
Santa Monica	86905	88314	88289	83249	71595	53500	37146	15252	7847	3057	1580	417			
Santa Paula	25062	20552	18001	13279	11049	8986	7452	3967	2216	1500	1047	188	150		
Santa Rita Park	350	350	300	500	400	150					75	125			
Santa Rosa	113313	83320	50006	31027	17902	12605	10636	8758	7817	6673	5220	3616	2000	425	
Santa Susana	6000	6000	2900	2310	985	907	134	124							
Santa Venetia			4000	3000											
Santa Ynez	4200	3335	500	500	500	542	451	300	300	211	211	150			
Santee	52902	40313	21107	2000	1000	400	400	259	67	67					
Saranap				6450	2362										

POPULATION HISTORY OF CALIFORNIA CITIES AND TOWNS 1850-1990

COMMUNITY	1990	1980	1970	1960	1950	1940	1930	1920	1910	1900	1890	1880	1870	1860	1850
Saratoga	28061	29261	26810	14861	1329	1500	1091	519	439	361	439	297	250		
Saticoy			2400	2283	2216	1028	877	520	400	218	218	105	250		
Saugus		16283	5100	800	550	200	151	113	100						
Sausalito	7152	7338	6158	5331	4828	3540	3667	2790	2383	1628	1334	476	100		
Sawtelle								5031	2143						
Sawyers Bar	100	100			125	150	100	250	250	303	225	88	160	200	
Scales									200	200	217				
Scotia	1200	1200	950	1122	1017	1448	860	1024	500	454	454				
Scotts Bar	120	120				150	220	215	210	328	210	165	250		
Scotts Valley	8615	6891	3621												
Seal Beach	25098	25975	25551	6994	3553	1553	1156	669	250						
Searles Valley	2740	3439	3828	2450											
Seaside	38901	36567	36883	19353	10226	2500	1800		80	78					
Sebastopol	7004	5595	3993	2694	2601	1856	1762	1493	1233	567	263	197	200		
Sedco Hills	3008	2678	800	800			200								
Seeley	1228	1058	900	700	600	300	375	375							
Seiad Valley	460	460	275	200	115			110	106	106	106	152			
Selby					403	141	141	141	123	123	123				
Selma	14757	10942	7459	6934	5964	3667	3047	3158	1750	1083	1150	650			
Sepulveda			40000	28339	4500	1890	200								
Serena Park	400	400	300												
Serra															
Sespe	350	350	350		650	549	113	113							
Seville	250	250	200		575	500	50	113							
Shafter	8409	7010	5327	4576	2207	1258	500	421							
Shandon	800	800	400	500	500	300	112	54	80						
Sharp Park					865	700									
Shasta	700	700	750	800	900	568	645	645	640	500	500	448	800	1000	
Shasta Dam					660	750									
Shaver Lake	400	400	300												
Sheep Ranch	60	60	100		75	368	372	249	300	300	358	200			
Shell Beach			1900	1820	849	200									
Shell Point					4674										
Sheridan	800	800	400	250	500	198	198	198	213	213	213	125	100		
Sherman								1047	375						
Sherwood Forest	2600	2600	800	325	200	200	119	119							
Shingle Springs	2049	1268	300	300	350	300	320	320	175	175	197	126	200		
Shingletown	450	450	150	100	185	216	216	216	103	103	103				
Shively	200	200	130						100						
Shore Acres	3800	3800	3000	3093											

POPULATION HISTORY OF CALIFORNIA CITIES AND TOWNS 1850-1990

COMMUNITY	1990	1980	1970	1960	1950	1940	1930	1920	1910	1900	1890	1880	1870	1860	1850
Short Acres	1266	1266	1476												
Shoshone	250	250	200	115	100										
Sierra Buttes												247			
Sierra City	800	800	100	150	180	268	250	525	650	650	632	401	500		
Sierra Madre	10762	10837	12140	9732	7273	4581	3550	2026	1303	481	149	75			
Sierra Valley	390	390	300	200	250	133	360	370	370	309	510	350			
Sierraville												126			
Signal Hill	8371	5734	5588	4627	4040	3184	2932								
Silverado	950	950	900	865	865	200	200								
Silveyville													279		
Simi Valley	100217	77500	59832	2167	1550	1860	362	213	120	109					
Simons					700	500									
Sisson							905	542	636	556	556				
Sisquoc	80	80			500										
Sky Valley	800	800	100												
Skyforest	650	650													
Sleepy Hollow (Marin)	2400	2400	1200	1200											
Sleepy Hollow (San Bernardino)	2000	500	500								250				
Slide				375											
Sloat	100	100	150	200	250	217	500	217	500	389	389	372		400	
Smartville	200	200	300	275	350	432	150	516	60	108	48	162	250		
Smith Flat	450	450	400	500	300	150		126				280	150		
Smith River	1000	1000	900	800	700	300	300	645	683	683	683	187	400		
Snelling	260	260	225	265	350	426	324	324	400	318	318				
Soda Bay	700	700	300												
Soda Springs	300	300	200	300	250										
Solana Beach	12962	13047	5023	4439	1350	662	259								
Soledad	7142	5928	4222	2837	2441	861	594	503	510	300	217	136	100		
Solemint			500												
Solvang	4741	3091	2004	1325	1025	487	300	312							
Somerset	500	100	100				50	117							
Somersville									50	308	371	501	200	400	
Somis	950	950	900	630	325	308	308	150	80	57					
Sonoma	8121	6054	4259	3023	2015	1158	980	801	957	652	757	910	700	597	500
Sonora	4153	3239	3100	2725	2448	2257	2278	1684	2029	1922	1441	1492	1322	1960	4000
Soquel	9188	6212	5795	1950	1400	1089	1000	900	430	400	426	328	450	651	
Soscol												332			
Soulsbyville	700	700	300	200	325	250	321	321	250	143	143	125	50		
South Dos Palos	1214	850	700	600	503	170									

POPULATION HISTORY OF CALIFORNIA CITIES AND TOWNS 1850-1990

COMMUNITY	1990	1980	1970	1960	1950	1940	1930	1920	1910	1900	1890	1880	1870	1860	1850
South El Monte	20850	16623	13443	4850											
South Gate	86284	66784	56909	53831	51116	26945	19632	57							
South Laguna	6013	6013	2566	2000	982	309									
South Lake Tahoe	21586	20681	12921												
South Modesto	12492	12492	7889	5465	3800										
South Oroville	7463	7246	4111	3704											
South Pasadena	23936	22681	22979	19706	16935	14356	13730	7652	4649	1001	623				
South Riverside											573				
South Sacramento			28574	16443											
South San Francisco	54312	49393	46646	39418	19351	6629	6193	4411	1989	680					
South San Gabriel	7700	5421	5051	2850											
South San Jose Hills	17814	16049	12386												
South Shafter	600	600	600	700											
South Taft	2170	2073	2214	1910	2918										
South Turlock		1700	1762	1577	1492										
South Whittier	49524	43815	46641	9500											
South Yuba City	8816	7530	5352	3200											
Spadra					2162	1210	275	113	125	150	200	225	250		
Spanishtown												461	500		
Spreckles	500	500	750	800	545	200	100	150	140	100					
Spring Valley	55331	40191	29742	10000	4000	1000									
Springdale						600									
Springfield															
Springville	1500	950	950	900	832	665	300	142	50	58	58	163	100	500	
Squaw Valley	1500	1500						75	31	31		75			
Standard	600	600	300	300	525	600	800	813							
Stanford	18097	11045	8691	6800	5000	950	720	720	750	720					
Stanton	30491	23723	18186	11163	1762	920	1157	695							
Stateline				900	527										
Stege							520	475	520	100					
Stent								250	250	250					
Sterling Park	1700	1700	700												
Stinson Beach	900	900	600	500		159	159	118							
Stirling City	300	300	375	350	632	450	450	250	350						
Stockton	210943	149779	109963	86321	70853	54714	47963	40296	23253	17506	14424	10282	10066	3679	2000
Stony Ford	250	250	175	125	250	150	300	320	221	221					
Stratford	850	850	800	800	750	550	400	240							
Strathmore	2353	1955	1221	1095	770	500	419	262	80						
Strawberry Point	4000	4000	3300	1500											
Sugarloaf	1500	1500	500					161							

POPULATION HISTORY OF CALIFORNIA CITIES AND TOWNS 1850-1990

COMMUNITY	1990	1980	1970	1960	1950	1940	1930	1920	1910	1900	1890	1880	1870	1860	1850
Suisin City	22686	11087	2917	2470	946	706	905	769	641	625	499	554	462	394	
Sultana	700	700	500	450	500	200	200	213	250						
Summerland	1000	1000	1000	600	600	300	466	263	350	312					
Summersville/Carters										400			100		
Summit City	1136	1136	1000	800	720	500	250	789				100			
Sumner											622	242			
Sun City	6500	6500	5519												
Suncrest/Crest	1300	1300	2000	1166	550										
Sunland		22200	17614	5000	1356	862	1000	515	165	60	100				
Sunnybrae			950	700											
Sunnymead	11554	11554	6708	3404	885	100	100								
Sunnyside (Fresno)	5000	5000	2000												
Sunnyside (Placer)	500	550	300												
Sunnyside (San Diego)	700	700	300	175	175	153									
Sunnyslope	2000	2000	2000			700	700								
Sunnyvale	117229	106618	95976	52898	9829	4373	3094	1675	850						
Sunol	750	750	750	750	650	400	600	340	340	340	328	135	100		
Sunset	700	700	200	2000	1500	181	150		100						
Sunset Beach	2500	2500	1900	200	600										
Surfside															
Susanville	7279	6520	6608	5598	5338	1575	1358	918	688	950	882	943	500		
Sutter	2606	2225	1488	1219	930	750	500	942	400	237	237	145			
Sutter Creek	1835	1705	1508	1161	1151	1134	1013	920	1500	1500	1351	1324	700	1000	
Swasey											300				
Sweetland									100	84	247	202			
Sycamore							50		207	207	207				
Sylvia Park	400	400	200	190											
Table Rock										125	497	501			
Taft	5902	5316	4285	3822	3707	3205	3442	3317	2000						
Taft Heights	2050	2111	2108	2661	2176										
Tahoe City	1300	1300	1394	731	250	268	165	97	130	87	87		150		
Tahoe Vista	1144	500	250												
Tahoma	300	300	100		200										
Talbert					400	200	200	264	100						
Talmage	1514	1000	900	400	408	350	350	50							
Tamalpais Valley	5000	5000	5000	2000	500	475									
Tanglewood				300	200										
Tara Hills	6000	6000	4000												
Tarpey	4000	4000													
Tarzana			24165	15000	10000										

POPULATION HISTORY OF CALIFORNIA CITIES AND TOWNS 1850-1990

COMMUNITY	1850	1860	1870	1880	1890	1900	1910	1920	1930	1940	1950	1960	1970	1980	1990
Taylor						2000					900			500	500
Taylorsville			250	176	205	209	205	219	275	150	200	225	150	200	200
Tecate							50				50		90	250	250
Tecopa										200	100	100	200		
Tehachapi			100	275	255	600	385	458	736	1264	1685	3161	4211	4126	5791
Tehama				328	546	546	221	196	190	175	314	261	317	365	401
Temecula			500		163	207	290	325	325	250	500	500	500	1783	27099
Temelec															750
Temescal			100	122	648	285									
Temple City									3400	3400	25000	31838	31034	28972	31100
Templeton					308	313	350	308	538	450	586	750	900	1000	1000
Tennant										100	500	250			
Terminal Island						100	220	1046	1046						
Terra Bella								165	200		900	900	1037	1807	2740
Terra Linda													5000		
Tesla						55	500	100							
The Oaks												700	550	350	350
Thermal							700	518	895	795	942	950	900	800	800
Thermalito						78	73			250	485	950	4217	4961	5646
Thorn											700				
Thornton								135	200	750	896	850	800	850	850
Thousand Oaks									250	750	1243	2934	35873	77072	104352
Thousand Palms										100	100	150	600	1718	4122
Three Rivers				300	276	100	100	100			192	250	900	900	900
Thurin									500						
Tiburon					207	207	260	327	350	395	594	4704	6209	6685	7532
Tierra Buena										250	250		900	2374	2878
Timbuctoo		250	150	86										20	20
Tionesta										300					
Tipton				86	366	366	450	314	414	500	980	950	969	1185	1383
Tobin														30	30
Todd Valley				226		187		187			250			800	800
Tolenas										600					
Tollhouse			100		213	213	213	89	70		70		65	300	300
Tomales		250	200	251	225	300	420	425	696	500	500	500	200	280	280
Topanga							160	116	199	968	3728	4000	4800	2000	2000
Topanga Beach													4500	700	700
Topanga Park													400		
Topaz								64	80		80			235	235
Torrance								1027	7271	9950	22241	100991	134968	129881	133107

POPULATION HISTORY OF CALIFORNIA CITIES AND TOWNS 1850-1990

COMMUNITY	1990	1980	1970	1960	1950	1940	1930	1920	1910	1900	1890	1880	1870	1860	1850
Towles	140	140	200	300	300	1000	50	159	172	172	317	225			
Toyon	600	600	300		350	165									
Trabuco Canyon															
Tracy	33558	18428	14724	11289	8410	4056	3829	2450	1000	362	362	75			
Tranquillity	950	950	600	750	539	165	165	165							
Traver	600	600	400	350	200	218	216	128	438	438	438				
Tres Pinos	400	400	200	200	330	330	175	187	300	194	194				
Trinidad	362	379	300	289	188	94	107	100	100	100	100	104	160		
Trinity Center	650	650	180	100	125	125		113	95	106	95	51	160		
Trona	1400	1400	975	1138	2450	876	775	114							
Tropico	60	60						300	350	78					
Truckee	3484	2389	1392	1800	1025	1936	1525	1239	1250	1378	1350	1147	1000		
Tudor											65				
Tujunga			22000	21030	14000	2600	2311	621				447	250	120	
Tulare	33249	22475	16235	13824	12445	8259	6207	3539	2758	2216	2697				
Tulare East		2168	2361	1342	1028	785	75								
Tulelake	1010	783	857	950											
Tuolumne	1686	1708	1365	1433	1284	1597	2107	1200	1200	722		175	200		
Tupman	280	280		530			98								
Turlock	42198	26287	13992	9116	6235	4839	4276	3394	1573	203	203	227			
Tustin	50689	32073	22313	2006	1143	953	926	920	800	671	288		200		
Tustin Foothills	24358	26174	26598												
Tuxedo Country Club	3100	3400	3300												
Twain-Harte	2170	1369	1484	900	285	150	78								
Twentynine Palms	11821	7465	5667	1450	1022	550	250								
Twentynine Palms Base	10606	7079	5647	6818	6733										
Twin Lakes	5379	4502	3012	1849											
Twin Oaks	900	900				145	306	155							
Twin Peaks	1500	1500	400	500	450	480									
Ukiah	14599	12035	10095	9900	6120	3731	3124	2305	2136	1850	1627	933	900	624	
Union City	53762	39406	14724	6618											
Union Hill	400	400	300	500											
Union Park						500									
University Heights	4400	4400	5000												
University Park			3100	450											
Upland	63374	47647	32551	15918	9203	6316	4713	2912	2384						
Upper Lake	950	950	900	600	600	358	540	320	320	296	296	147	200		
Upper Placerville													343	515	
Vacaville	71479	43367	21690	10898	3169	1614	1556	1254	1177	1220	725	361		331	
Val Verde Park	500	500	700												

POPULATION HISTORY OF CALIFORNIA CITIES AND TOWNS 1850-1990

COMMUNITY	1850	1860	1870	1880	1890	1900	1910	1920	1930	1940	1950	1960	1970	1980	1990
Valencia													4243	12163	
Valinda													18837	18700	18700
Valle Vista												3000	1500	5474	8751
Vallecito		500	100	214	200	200	250	200	160	242	200	200	400	800	800
Vallejo	1600	1564	3500	5987	6343	7965	11340	16845	16072	20072	26038	60877	71710	80303	109199
Valley Center										250	600	750	800	1242	1711
Valley Dale				130	67	67	67	358	360		400	1000	1500	4800	
Valley Ford			150	102	312	200	310	162	200	200	160		130	270	270
Valley Springs					298	298	298	312	312	500	500	550	800	600	600
Valona					374										
Valyermo													50	80	80
Van Nuys								3037			90000	168475	231600		
Vandenburg AFB													13193	8136	9846
Vandenburg Village													4874	5839	5971
Venice/Ocean Park						3119	3119	10385	23124		58000	40000	80500		
Ventura/San Buenaventura	400	628	1600	1370	2320	2470	2945	4156	11603	13264	16534	29114	57964	74393	92575
Verdugo City					50	137	137		1500	1500	500				
Vernalis							50	50	210	150	300			25	25
Vernon							775	1005	1269	850	432	229	261	90	152
Victor						103		50	160	225	400	250	275	250	250
Victorville					112	112	200	617	1030	2617	3241	8931	10845	14220	40674
Vidal									200		100			50	50
View Park								789				2500	5000	5900	5700
Villa Park									150	150	100	1000	2723	7137	6299
Villa Verona													1000	1000	1000
Vina										363	325	350	300	400	400
Vine Hill				93	232	232	300	218	367		552	3958	3000	4100	3214
Vineburg								164	100	100		100		150	150
Vinton						92			75		75		70		
Virgilia										350	200			250	250
Virginia				514											
Visalia		548	913	1412	2885	3085	4550	5753	7263	8904	11749	15791	27130	49729	75636
Vista						38	60	50	268	658	1705	14795	24688	35834	71872
Vista Park												1500	1500	950	950
Volcano	500	500	400	499	358	421	450	433	541	432	150	120			
Waddington						311	300	319							500
Walker									50	230			250	500	500
Walnut							100	213	362		700	934	5992	12478	29105
Walnut Creek			250	94	447	447	550	538	1014	1578	2420	9903	39844	53643	60569
Walnut Creek West													8330	5893	5893

POPULATION HISTORY OF CALIFORNIA CITIES AND TOWNS 1850-1990

COMMUNITY	1990	1980	1970	1960	1950	1940	1930	1920	1910	1900	1890	1880	1870	1860	1850
Walnut Grove	1500	950	800	950	925	962	631	631	200	218	212	160			
Walnut Heights	1600	1600	700	580											
Walnut Park	14722	11811	8925	7500	8500										
Walteria	1600				595	536	536								
Warm Springs					950	150	59	200	170	100					
Warner Ranch	1400	1400													
Warner Springs	30	30		150	300	180									
Wasco	12412	9613	8269	6841	5592	2848	1581	720							
Washington (Nevada)								69	400	359	359	195	100		
Washington (Fresno)	200	200	130	115	150	121	100	359	430		929	118	200		
Waterford	4771	2683	2243	1780	1777	514	198	200	175	137	137	63	75		
Waterman				1500					156	156					
Watsonville	31099	23543	14719	13293	11572	8937	8344	5013	4446	3528	2149	1799	1151	398	
Watts								4529	1922						
Waukena	300	300	150	200			50	78	50						
Waverly Park				900	300										
Wawona	200	200	150	200			50	50		62	50				
Weaverville	3370	2787	1489	1736	1800	1354	1374	824	1100	913	913	863	816	777	210
Weed	3062	2879	2983	3223	2739	1845	4227	1525	400	733					
Weed Patch	1892	1553	250	400	700	500									
Weimar/New England Mills	900	900	900	500		125	50	50		150					
Weitchpec				100			64	64	41						
Weldon	430	430	200		196		189	189	99	99	99	75			
Weott	450	450	450	350	350	250	150								
West Alhambra								314							
West Athens	8859	8531	8000							1278	370				
West Berkeley	20143	17997	15918												
West Carson	5451	5907	5605												
West Compton															
West Covina	96086	80291	68034	50645	4499	1072	769								
West Duarte										591					
West Hollywood	36118	35703	29448	28870	25600										
West Los Angeles			38805												
West Modesto	6135	6135	6135	1697	2038										
West Parlier	2811	2811													
West Pittsburg	6000	6000	5969	5188	4647	320	326	200	266	266	266	173	100		
West Point	1500	1500	950	950	950										
West Puente Valley	20254	20445	20733												
West Sacramento	28898	10875	12002	13300	8200										
West Whittier	13800	13800	13000			610	100								

POPULATION HISTORY OF COLORADO CITIES AND TOWNS 1860-1990

COMMUNITY	1990	1980	1970	1960	1950	1940	1930	1920	1910	1900	1890	1885	1880	1870	1860
Acres Green	3000	900													
Adams	2200	2200	2000	1500	800	400	50	110							
Agate	90	100	120	120	150	135	135								
Aguilar	520	624	699	777	1039	1397	1383	1236	858	698		60			
Akron	1599	1716	1775	1890	1650	1417	1135	1401	647	351	559	100			
Alamo							162								
Alamosa	7579	6630	6985	6205	5354	5613	5107	3171	3013	1141	973	1000	802		
Alcott										707					
Alden					350	350									
Allenspark	300	50			100		60		70	70					
Alma	148	132	73	107	149	469	110	127	301	297	367	500	446	250	
Alpine										32	75	200	508		
Altman								45	145	659					
Ames															
Anaconda									164	1059		200			
Andersonville	200	200													
Animas City					712	712	457	250	200	154	180	200	286		
Animas Fork												170	158		
Antonito	875	1103	1113	1045	1255	1220	858	946	681	347	315	350	87		
Applewood	8130	7200	6200												
Arbourville															
Argo									443	443	300	150	159		
Arlington									80	80	162	200			
Arriba	220	236	254	296	367	286	337	334	200	40					
Artesia				318	281										
Arvada	89235	84576	49844	19242	2359	1482	1276	915	840	300		200			
Ashcroft												300			
Aspen	5049	3678	2437	1101	916	777	705	1265	1834	3303	5108	3500	125		
Aspen Park	900	500	500												
Atwood	200	150	100	200	200	250	250	261	100						
Ault	1107	1056	841	799	866	761	737	769	569						
Aurora	222103	158588	74974	48548	11421	3437	2295	983	679	202					
Austin	1798	640	1163	1021	125	100			150						
Avon	950	800	300	500	100	134									
Avondale			700		300	350	350	358	160						
Barela															
Basalt	1128	529	419	213	173	212	148	183	235	382		220	203		
Bayfield	1090	724	320	322	335	372	277	267	227	125					
Bear River		500					265	265							
Belle Plain	500	500													

POPULATION HISTORY OF COLORADO CITIES AND TOWNS 1860-1990

COMMUNITY	1990	1980	1970	1960	1950	1940	1930	1920	1910	1900	1890	1885	1880	1870	1860
Bellevue	250	200	200	250	150	150	319	319	104	99					
Bennett	1757	942	613	287	272	199	211	100	105	52	80		51		
Berkeley										707					
Berthoud	2990	2362	1446	1014	867	811	811	852	738	305	228		50		
Berwind							150	550	700	700					
Bessemer											3317	200			
Bethune	173	149	99	70	71	79	97	261	300	205	205	300			
Beulah	600	500	400	300	275	275	275								
Black Forest	8143	3372	2700	800											
Black Hawk	227	232	217	171	166	289	253	253	668	1200	1067	1500	1540	1068	
Blanca	272	252	212	233	376	407	252	380	550						
Blende	1330	1500	1500	600	400	400	350								
Blue River	440	230		19	51	140	445	91	96	141	96		72		
Bonanza							115	115							
Boone	341	431	448	548	250	250									
Boulder	83312	76685	66870	37718	19999	12958	11223	11006	9539	6150	3330	3500	3069	343	
Bow Mar	854	930	945	748											
Bowie				125	250	350	300	319	80						
Brandon								219							
Branson	58	73	70	124	157	250	237	200							
Breckenridge	1285	818	548	393	296	381	436	796	834	976	714	2000	1657	165	
Briggsdale	95	85	100	120	200	250	200	210							
Brighton	14203	12773	8309	7055	4336	4029	3394	2715	850	366	306	100	50		
Bristol	250	250	250	300	250	200	200	315	200			100	79		
Broadmoor		1900	2000	2000	1585	643	643								
Broadway Estates	3260	4300	4300												
Brodhead							400								
Brookridge	760	1200	1200												
Brookside	183	178	173	163	175	196	198	202							
Broomfield	24638	20730	7261	4353	200	125	125								
Brownsville	900	800										200	450	350	
Brush	4165	4082	3377	3621	2431	2481	2312	2103	997	381	112				
Buckskin													227		
Buena Vista	1752	2075	1962	1806	783	779	751	903	1041	1006	1317	2000	2141		
Buffalo	225	150	75	75			156	168	150	150					
Burlington	2941	3107	2828	2090	2247	1280	1280	991	368	183	146				
Byers	1065	1100	900	500	400	400	400	260	75	75		100	45	50	
Calhan	562	541	465	347	375	352	399	420	400	65					
Campion	300	200	200	200	200	200	200								
Campo	121	185	206	235	266	200	200	45							

POPULATION HISTORY OF COLORADO CITIES AND TOWNS 1860-1990

COMMUNITY	1860	1870	1880	1885	1890	1900	1910	1920	1930	1940	1950	1960	1970	1980	1990
Canfield				200		200	110								
Canon City		229	1501	2500	2825	3775	5162	4551	5938	6690	6345	8973	9206	13037	12687
Capitol City			140	100											
Capps										800					
Capulin				136		100	300	825	106	106	200	500	400	400	400
Carbonateville			157	200											
Carbondale			158		166	173	284	310	283	437	441	612	726	2084	3004
Cardiff						225	225						120		
Caribou		275	549	300											
Cascade						52	52				100	200	600	600	1000
Castle Rock			88	200	315	304	365	461	478	580	741	1152	1531	3921	8708
Castleton				200											
Castlewood														16413	24392
Cedaredge							295	455	463	556	574	549	581	1184	1380
Center						71	385	547	1011	1515	2024	1600	1470	1630	1963
Central City	598	2360	2626	3250	2480	3114	1782	552	572	706	371	250	228	329	335
Centreville			151	166	153	153									
Chama						50	45		350	350	733	500	350	250	250
Chandler							50		425	450	450				
Cheraw							200	186	293	184	174	173	129	233	265
Cherry Hills											750	1931	4605	5127	5245
Cherry Knolls													2500	2500	2670
Cherry Park															770
Cherrywood													800	800	2800
Cheyenne Wells					179	179	270	508	595	695	1154	1020	982	950	1128
Chihuahua			141	100											
Chipita Park										200	200		350	350	800
Chromo										203	150				
Cimarron Hills														6597	11160
Clark															500
Cleora			184												
Clifton							500	319	300	300	300	500	800	5223	12671
Climax									250	500	860	1609	300	190	
Coal Creek			701	1200	600	698	676	618	435	261	195	206	225	90	157
Cokedale								515	500	500	214	219	101		116
Collbran						50	156	286	341	301	237	310	225	344	228
Colorado City (El Paso)												100	950	950	1149
Colorado City (Pueblo)		81	347	500	1788	2914	4333								
Colorado Springs		1480	4226	5000	11140	21085	29078	30105	33237	36789	45472	70194	135517	215150	281140
Columbine													4700	13300	13300

POPULATION HISTORY OF COLORADO CITIES AND TOWNS 1860-1990

COMMUNITY	1860	1870	1880	1885	1890	1900	1910	1920	1930	1940	1950	1960	1970	1980	1990
Columbine Valley												385			1071
Commerce City												8970	17407	16234	16466
Como			134	300	374	407	411	121	80	95	39	108	150	100	100
Concrete							75	261	35						
Conejos		100	339	500	342	348	158	319	300	206	175	150	150	100	100
Conifer													500	500	550
Cordova							50								
Coronado				400									4800	6300	6890
Cortez					332	125	565	541	921	1778	2680	6764	6032	7095	7284
Cotopaxi				200		125	125	125	238	238	120	100	100	100	100
Cottonwood			250												
Craig						133	392	1297	1418	2123	3080	3984	4205	8133	8091
Crawford							210	149	157	221	170	147	171	268	221
Creede					857	938	741	500	384	670	503	350	653	610	362
Crested Butte			300	1500		988	904	1213	1251	1145	730	289	372	959	878
Crestone					36	150	231	74	86	172	72	51	34	54	39
Creswell			158	100	157										
Cripple Creek						10147	6206	2325	1427	2358	853	614	425	655	584
Crook							125	232	251	236	259	209	199	177	148
Crowley								224	323	318	379	263	216	192	225
Cucharas			350		348	250	100							85	400
Dacono							180	172	275	296	258	302	360	2321	2228
Dallas					541	50									
De Beque						83	149	292	347	280	253	172	155	279	257
Decatur			250	100											
Deer Trail			275	250	54	54	400	200	390	387	421	764	374	463	476
Del Norte		560	729	1000	736	705	840	1007	1410	1923	2048	1856	1569	1709	1674
Delagua							958	1035	1021	422	239				
Delcarbon									300	300	300				
Delta				250	470	819	2388	2623	2938	3717	4097	3832	3694	3931	3789
Denver	4749	4759	35629	65000	106713	133859	213381	256491	287861	322412	415786	493887	514678	491396	467610
Derby									83		2840	10124	10206	8578	6043
Dillon			55	250	133	143	134	126	92	161	191	814	182	337	553
Dinosaur												318	247	313	324
Divide			125	100		72	120		50					50	600
Dolores						108	320	465	557	804	729	805	820	802	866
Dora			300	50											
Dove Creek									120	418	702	986	619	826	643
Drake														70	300
Dream House Acres													3600	3600	2010

POPULATION HISTORY OF COLORADO CITIES AND TOWNS 1860-1990

COMMUNITY	1990	1980	1970	1960	1950	1940	1930	1920	1910	1900	1890	1885	1880	1870	1860
Dumont												200			
Dupont	5200	2000	1500	800	350	200	200								
Durango	12430	11426	10333	10530	7459	5887	5400	4116	4686	3317	2726	3000	450		
Eads	780	878	795	929	1015	700	518	406	210	85	100				
Eagle	1580	801	790	546	445	518	341	358	186	124			130		
East Canon			1805	1101	761	699	595	445							
East Idaho Springs											323				
Eastlake	500	165	165	200	100	150									
Eastridge		700	700												
Eaton	1959	1932	1389	1267	1276	1322	1221	1289	1157	384	300	100			
Eckley	211	262	193	207	295	358	359	332							
Edgewater	4613	5714	4910	4314	2580	1648	1473	664	712	50					
Edith									293	282					
El Jebel	900	900	900												
Elbert	200	200	250	176	250	325	325	360	350	200	118	150			
Eldora								35	81	395					
Eldorado Springs				130											
Elgin												200			
Elizabeth	818	789	493	326	253	275	266	230	194	215	156	100			
Elkhorn												200			
Elkton							50	150	390	1900					
Ellicott									50	250					
Elmoro							206	219	125	335	355	300			
Elyria										1384					
Empire	401	423	249	110	228	174	93	105	179	276	134	200	203	600	
Engle							75		710						
Englewood	29387	30021	33695	33398	16869	9680	7980	4356	2983	710	701	250			
Enterprise	1258	1254	1090	875	937	1019	930	697	596	697	662	800			
Erie															
Espinoza						410	410	410							
Estes Park	3184	2703	1616	1175	1617	994	417	475	425	155		150	160		
Eureka							197	160	87	39	49	200	123		
Evans	5877	5063	2570	1453	862	792	540	505	600	400	306	400	349	189	
Evanston	300	300	300												
Evergreen	7582	6376	2321	2000	596	596	275	265	125	67	67	100	45		
Fairplay	387	421	419	404	476	739	221	183	265	319	301	500	450	316	
Farisita					150	300									
Farr							800								
Federal Heights	9342	7846	1502	391	173										
Firestone	1358	1204	570	276	297	262	240	214	110						

POPULATION HISTORY OF COLORADO CITIES AND TOWNS 1860-1990

COMMUNITY	1990	1980	1970	1960	1950	1940	1930	1920	1910	1900	1890	1885	1880	1870	1860
Flagler	564	550	615	693	793	506	540	544	300	99	99				
Fleming	344	388	349	384	377	400	365	518							
Fletcher									202						
Florence	2990	2987	2846	2821	2773	2632	2475	2629	2712	3728	239	150	70		
Florissant	250	110	100	53	53	62	26	48	268	131	439		42		
Forbes							50	315	200						
Forest City													163		
Fort Carson	11309	13219	19399												
Fort Collins	87758	64632	43337	25027	14937	12251	11489	8755	8210	3053	2011	2500	1356	200	
Fort Garland	300	300	300	500	621	250	250	210	160	147	147	150	131	157	52
Fort Lewis												500			
Fort Logan					300	800	800								
Fort Lupton	5159	4251	2489	2194	1907	1692	1578	1000	400	442	113	300			
Fort Lyon			650	500	500	1180	1180	1014	614	214	65	70	64	520	
Fort Morgan	9068	8768	7594	7379	5315	4884	4423	3818	2800	634	488	500			
Fort Sedgewick														210	
Fountain	9984	8324	3515	1602	713	571	577	595	431	108	108	150	99		
Fowler	1154	1227	1241	1240	1025	922	968	1062	925	200					
Franktown	300	75	221	253	250	260	260	260	260	97	97	60	63	200	
Fraser	575	470													
Frederick	988	855	696	595	599	652	596	361	266	100	200	500	447		
Freeland											77	200	48		
Frisco	1601	1221	471	316	87	60		81	81	91					
Fruita	4045	2810	1822	1830	1463	1466	1053	1193	881	126					
Fruitvale	5222	400	400	332		100									
Galena	170	170	170	200	200	200	200	125				125	300		
Galeton	75	75	100	250	200	325	325		75						
Garcia	199	85	142	129	104	87									
Garden City	75	50	150	175	200	125	125								
Gardner				150				215	130	100	129	250	130		
Garfield	300	200	200										140		
Gateway															
Genoa	167	165	161	185	257	214	218	210	350			250			
Georgetown	891	830	542	307	329	391	303	703	950	1418	1927	3000	3294	802	
Gilcrest	1084	1025	382	357	429	352	324	222	265						
Gill	200	200		230	150	350	300	150	150						
Gillett								60	33	524					
Gilman	100	350	350	375	356	225	225	232	222	222	442				
Glen Haven	150	150	150												
Glendale	2453	2496	765	468											

POPULATION HISTORY OF COLORADO CITIES AND TOWNS 1860-1990

COMMUNITY	1860	1870	1880	1885	1890	1900	1910	1920	1930	1940	1950	1960	1970	1980	1990
Glenwood Springs				250	920	1350	2019	2073	1825	2253	2412	3637	4106	4637	6561
Globeville						2192									
Gold Hill			250	400	238	300	150		50				150	150	150
Golden	1014	587	2730	3000	2383	2152	2477	2484	2426	3175	5238	7118	9817	12237	13116
Goldfield						2191	1122	633	159	195	81				
Goodnight														1400	1050
Gorham						340	340		91		91				
Gothic			949	250	48										
Granada			121	200	163	204	359	308	352	342	551	593	551	557	513
Granby							40		90	251	463	503	554	963	966
Grand Junction				2500	2030	3503	7754	8665	10247	12479	14504	18694	20170	28144	29034
Grand Lake			156	250	100	100	115	160	209	600	309	170	189	382	259
Grand Valley							268								
Granite		176	800	200	142	250	300	315	50		40	55	75	30	30
Gray Creek						200	576	160							
Greeley		480	1297	2500	2395	3023	8179	10958	12203	15995	20354	26314	38902	53006	60536
Green Mountain Falls			300	300				100	41	87	106	179	359	607	663
Greenwood						50	50								
Greenwood Village												572	3095	5729	7589
Grover							300	195	165	137	146	133	121	158	135
Guadalupe						348	158						150	150	150
Guffey			196			200	200								
Gunbarrel													800	5172	9388
Gunnison			838	3000	1105	1200	1026	1329	1415	2177	2770	3477	4613	5785	4636
Gwillimville			172		172										
Gypsum					129	76	100	164	165	245	345	358	420	743	1750
Hahns Peak				500											
Hamilton															
Hancock		240	100	250											
Harman					743	743									
Hartman							450	175	269	148	181	164	129	122	108
Hastings/Victor						1174	693	587	307						
Hasty											180	200	150	150	150
Haswell								265	156	163	163	169	150	126	62
Haxtun							341	1118	1027	985	1006	990	899	1014	952
Hayden			175	100		66	314	453	554	640	767	764	763	1720	1444
Heatherwood													900	900	1470
Henderson							110	260	150	150	280	250	200	200	500
Henson			78	100		200	50								
Heritage Place															1820

POPULATION HISTORY OF COLORADO CITIES AND TOWNS 1860-1990

COMMUNITY	1860	1870	1880	1885	1890	1900	1910	1920	1930	1940	1950	1960	1970	1980	1990
Hesperus							150	219	125		240				100
Hideaway Park												125	200	450	50
Higbee				100			50	185	185						
Highland Hills															740
Highlands			132	2500	5161										
Highlands Ranch															3000
Hillerton															
Hillrose				100			225	275	210	177	190	157	121	213	169
Hiwan Hills														900	1420
Hoehne						50	75	110	320	550	550	500	200	200	200
Holly				150		364	724	940	971	864	1236	1108	993	969	877
Holy Cross				200											
Holyoke					649	451	659	1205	1226	1150	1558	1555	1640	2092	1931
Homelake									225	225	225		250	250	150
Hooper						177	131	156	155	170	103	58	80	71	112
Horseshoe				300											
Hortense			125		114										
Hot Sulphur Springs			100	60	80	60	182	123	142	235	263	237	220	405	347
Hotchkiss						261	600	572	541	653	715	626	507	849	741
Howard				250	109	109	170	210	200		43		43	40	160
Howland			212	100											
Hudson						120	275	322	346	295	365	430	518	698	918
Hugo			140	250	120	100	343	838	712	852	943	811	759	776	660
Hygiene						200	130	148	250	250	250	200	300	350	450
Ibex															
Idaho Springs		229	733	2000	1338	2502	2154	1192	1207	2112	1769	1480	2003	2077	1834
Idalia					98	100	100	100	198		75	87	100	110	110
Ideal								520							
Idledale												475	500	500	400
Ignacio						50	200	290	464	555	526	609	613	667	720
Iliff				50	50		250	238	266	322	235	204	193	218	174
Independence			75			1200	485	160	80	100	50				
Indian Hills					200	200					162	700	900	900	2000
Irondale								73	139	71	71	700	700	700	420
Ironton				125	100	71	48								
Irwin			526	450	500	26									
Ivywild									1472	1472	2849	4000	4000	4000	4000
Jamestown			250	400	212	164	157	150	150	190	118	107	185	223	251
Jansen							80				260	230	270	270	300
Jaroso								415	150	150	150	100	75	40	40

POPULATION HISTORY OF COLORADO CITIES AND TOWNS 1860-1990

COMMUNITY	1990	1980	1970	1960	1950	1940	1930	1920	1910	1900	1890	1885	1880	1870	1860
Johnson	300	250	250												
Johnstown	1579	1535	1191	976	897	961	767	274	198						
Julesburg	1295	1528	1578	1840	1951	1619	1467	1320	962	371	202	100			
Kassler					300	300									
Keenesburg	570	541	427	409	432	284	297	164	55						
Ken Caryl	24391	10661													
Keota					21	34	108	129	130						
Kersey	980	913	474	378	304	268	307	319	304	50					
Keystone	300														
Kim	76	100	200	275	260	200	200	120							
Kiowa	275	206	235	195	173	195	185	148	260	116	116	150	113		
Kit Carson	305	278	220	356	379	333	325	158	75	50	151		473		
Kittredge	750	500	500	400	400	350	350	525							
Kline					115		56								
Knob Hill				3400	3612										
Kremmling	1166	1296	764	576	623	567	261	254	141	35					
Lafayette	14548	8985	3498	2612	2090	2052	1842	1815	1892	970	410				
Laird	110	110	150	245	156	165	165	210	240						
La Jara	725	858	768	724	912	897	602	521	448	208	380	1000			
La Junta	7637	8338	8205	8026	7712	7040	7193	4964	4154	2513	1439	1000	56		
La Plata	1783	1929	1227	1070	797	755	564	460	400			200			
La Salle	726	611	589	632	701	897	782	737	691	254	361	400	600		
La Veta	223	206	91	106	141	185	259	317	405	700	607	1000	1950		
Lake City	300	150	150												
Lake George															
Lakeborough			750												
Lakeside	750	750													
Lakewood	126481	112848	92743	19338	8000	5000									
Lamar	8343	7713	7797	7369	6829	4445	4233	2512	2977	987	566				
Langford											233	600			
Laporte	1300	900	900	700	300	300	100	115	100	100	100	100	62		
Lariat				900											
Larkspur	232	141	175	200	175	150	150	115	90	75	178	60	175		
Las Animas	2481	2818	3148	3402	3223	3232	2517	2252	2008	1192	611	600	52	400	
Lavalley	130	130	150	200	340	340	198								
Lawrence									62	299					
Lawson	175	100	100	125	150	100	100	113	162	162	162				
Leadville	2629	3879	4314	4008	4081	4774	3771	4959	7508	12455	10384	16000	14820		
Leawood		600	600												
Left Hand													425	213	

POPULATION HISTORY OF COLORADO CITIES AND TOWNS 1860-1990

COMMUNITY	1990	1980	1970	1960	1950	1940	1930	1920	1910	1900	1890	1885	1880	1870	1860
Limon	1831	1805	1814	1811	1471	1053	1100	1047	534	70					
Lincoln															
Lincoln Park	3728	3426	2984	2085	1345										
Littleton	33685	28631	26466	13670	3378	2244	2019	1636	1373	738	289	400	160	180	
Livermore	60	60			285	285			161	161		100	200	150	
Lochbuie	1168	895	934												
Log Lane Village	667	709	329	310											
Loma	200	100	100	150	110	110	460	213							
Lombard	620	350	350												
Longmont	51555	42942	23209	11489	8099	7406	6029	5848	4256	2201	1543	1600	773	800	
Loretto							240		72	72					
Louisville	12361	5593	2409	2073	1978	2023	1681	1799	1706	966	596	500	450		
Louviers	600	350	350	305	350	350	350	318							
Loveland	37352	30244	16220	9734	6773	6145	5506	5065	3651	1091	698	750	256		
Ludlow					210	210	210	210	210						
Lula													150		
Lyman											322				
Lyons	1227	1137	958	706	689	654	567	570	632	547	574	400			
McClave	150	120	120	175	120	250	250	75	100						
Mack	180	150	150	150	150	250	250	73	50						
McPhee					716	774	350								
Magnolia									100	88	109	100	157		
Malta							50			109		350	220		
Manassa	988	945	814	831	832	1008	953	906	788	739	642	500	250		
Mancos	842	870	709	832	785	748	646	682	567	383	120	50	112		
Manitou Springs	4535	4475	4278	3626	2580	1462	1205	1129	1357	1303	1439	1000	422	150	
Manzanola	437	459	451	562	543	531	578	562	428	250					
Marble	64	30	50			240	217	81	782	101					
Marshall									50				270		
Masonville	500	300	300	200	200	105									
Matheson	100	100	100	100	150	200	200	215							
Maxwell	120	50								217	217				
Maysville										78	78	100	561		
Mead	456	356	195	192	186	191	152	145	114						
Meadowbrook	450	450	450												
Mears										148	148		150		
Meeker	2098	2356	1597	1655	1658	1399	1069	935	807	507	260	200			
Merino	238	255	260	268	209	259	230	263	350						
Mesa	150	150	150	317	60		92	69	210	210					
Mesa Verde	150	150	150												

POPULATION HISTORY OF COLORADO CITIES AND TOWNS 1860-1990

COMMUNITY	1990	1980	1970	1960	1950	1940	1930	1920	1910	1900	1890	1885	1880	1870	1860
Mesita					150	250									
Milliken	1605	1506	702	630	510	531	483	372	230						
Milner	150	150	150	112	150		75	46							
Mineral Point												200			
Minturn	1066	1060	706	662	509	596	400	298	241	189	189				
Model	120				225	150	150								
Moffat	40	105	98	104	109	149	150	210	210	87					
Mogote	100	100	100		150		50	360							
Monarch															
Montclair									410	415	380	450			
Monte Vista	4324	3902	3909	3385	3272	3208	2610	2484	2544	555	780	600	53	93	
Montezuma	60	25			48	59	38	69	134	40		125	280		
Montgomery												1200			
Montrose	8854	8722	6496	5044	4964	4764	3566	3581	3254	1217	1330				
Monument	1020	690	393	204	126	175	192	192	149	156	177	250	125	100	
Morley				300	450	600	600	115							
Morrison	465	478	439	426	306	216	177	195	251	254	254	400	186	150	
Mosca	90	110	110	130	150		75	162	200	200					
Mount Crested Butte	264	272													
Mount Harris				730	891	800	1500	820							
Mount Morrison						216	177	195	380						
Mountain View	550	584	706	826	600	600	664	372	390						
Nathrop	434						145	47	30	144	144	100	139		
Naturita		819	820	979	600	600			47	47		50			
Nederland	1099	1212	492	272	266	384	285	291	446	50		350	279		
Nevadaville/Bald Mountain	679	563	499	447	483	484	470	51	367	823	933	2000	1084	973	897
New Castle								447	493	431	311				
New Windsor										305	173				
Ninaview						300									
Niwot	2666	500	400	185	175	175	175	113	150	114	114	50	140		
Nob Hill	2720	800	800												
North Cherry Creek Valley	4800	1300	1000												
North Creede/Amethyst									122	235					
North Glenn	27195	29847	27785												
North La Junta	1076	1076	1249	950	1502										
North Veta						300									
North Washington	1460	2000	1500												
Norwood	429	478	408	443	294	412	299	365	212	61					
Nucla	656	1027	949	906	457	361	221	217	110						
Nunn	324	295	269	228	182	190	196	149	143						

POPULATION HISTORY OF COLORADO CITIES AND TOWNS 1860-1990

COMMUNITY	1990	1980	1970	1960	1950	1940	1930	1920	1910	1900	1890	1885	1880	1870	1860
Oak Creek	673	929	492	666	1483	1769	1211	967	222						
Oakview/Tropic								265	50						
Ohio City						78	72	50	153	96	96	200	100		
Olathe	1263	1262	756	773	810	705	593	491	458	100					
Olney Springs	340	253	264	263	279	260	228	240	130	50					
Ophir	69	38					100	29	124	127	113		130		
Orchard	100	75	75		150		350	225	140	50					
Orchard City/Eckert	2218	1914	1163	1021	956	865	350	531	125						
Orchard Mesa	5977	4876	5824	4956											
Ordway	1025	1135	1017	1254	1290	1150	1139	1186	705	138					
Oro	100	100	100	108	250	252	252	253	150	125	222	150	400	250	438
Ortiz									80	40	129				
Otis	451	534	521	568	532	498	529	467							
Ouray	644	684	741	785	1089	951	707	1165	1644	2196	2534	1800	864		
Ovid	349	439	463	571	664	687	649	250	250						
Padroni	100	120	150	153	110	180	180	100	100						
Pagosa Springs	1207	1331	1360	1374	1379	1591	804	1032	669	367	227				
Palisade	1871	1551	874	860	361	855	851	855	900						
Palmer Lake	1480	1130	947	542	263	269	244	160	163	166					
Palos Verdes	1640	250	250												
Paoli	29	81	52	81	91	85	143	175	65						
Paonia	1403	1425	1161	1083	1257	1117	958	925	1007						
Papeton				2300											
Parachute/Grand Valley	658	338	270	245	296	230	209	228	268	75					
Paradox												200			
Park															
Parker	5450	290	150	132	100	200	200	155	200	85		200	267		
Parrott											308	250	303		
Peetz	179	220	186	218	232	207	244	322	80						
Penrose	800	125	175	250	500	500	90	89	55						
Peyton									140						
Phippsburg	175	150	150	125	400	400	150								
Pictou					100	150		42		107					
Pierce	823	878	452	424	372	343	281	327	107						
Pikeview				200	200	150	150	315	410						
Pine	500	250	250												
Pine Grove							60	75			109		225		
Pitkin	53	59	44	94	152	156	228	165	250	203	371	2000	1891	400	
Placerville								160	80	50	36	100	70		
Platteville	1515	1662	683	582	570	561	533	479	430	263	213	100			

POPULATION HISTORY OF COLORADO CITIES AND TOWNS 1860-1990

COMMUNITY	1990	1980	1970	1960	1950	1940	1930	1920	1910	1900	1890	1885	1880	1870	1860
Pleasant View	3460	4500	3800	2500	200	250	80	37	43	97	101	300	170		
Poncha Springs	244	321	198	201	114	94									
Ponderosa Hills	900	300	300												
Portland		75	73	73	205	377	435	473	300	69	116	50	100		
Poughkeepsie												250			
Powderhorn												70	200		
Primero								1650							
Pritchett	153	183	170	247	286	495	451								
Prospect Heights		34	38	39	50	51	138	109	157						
Pryor	25	25	25		200	200	500		100						
Pueblo	98640	101686	97774	91181	63685	52162	50096	43050	41747	28157	24558	20000	3217	666	
Pueblo West	4386	900	900												
Quartz												500			
Querida											756				
Ramah	94	119	101	109	142	186	171	213	200						
Ramona					159	159	105								
Rangely	2278	2113	1591	1464	808										
Ravenwood						125	125	219							
Raymer/New Raymer	98	80	68	91	130	169	254	267	75	75	74				
Recen/Kokomo				74	53	101	44	93	183	344	147	1000	818		
Red Cliff	297	409	621	586	556	715	544	347	383	256	383	600	500		
Red Elephant												300			
Red Mountain											172	1000			
Red Wing							223								
Redlands	9355	800	800												
Redmesa	125	100	85	163	135	270	270								
Redstone	150	150	150	100											
Richards						300	300	50							
Rico	92	76	275	363	212	388	447	326	368	811	1134	1500	894		
Ridge				350	100	207	362								
Ridgeview Hills	2200	350	350												
Ridgeway	423	369	262	254	209	354	239	400	378	245					
Rifle	4636	3215	2150	2135	1525	1373	1287	805	698	273					
River Bend					75	110			53	50	53		50		
Riverside					50					50	107	50			
Robinson									78	61	228	300	168		
Rockvale	321	338	359	413	380	575	710	1249	1413	870		300			
Rocky Ford	4162	4804	4859	4929	4087	3494	3426	3746	3230	2018	468	180	47		
Roggen	150	150	150	146	75	110	110	164	120	44					
Rollinsville	300	100	100		50		53	49	160	50		170	198		

POPULATION HISTORY OF COLORADO CITIES AND TOWNS 1860-1990

COMMUNITY	1860	1870	1880	1885	1890	1900	1910	1920	1930	1940	1950	1960	1970	1980	1990
Romeo							200	213	188	392	404	339	352	308	341
Rosita			1008	1000	304	110	42	45	27						
Roswell						66		362	500	500	1029	1000			
Rouse						200	200	562	250	250	250				
Ruby City	483		1123												
Rugby						43	200	315	135	135					
Russell Gulch		973	543	700	673	500	700	215	93						
Rye		250	325	100			105	275	275	163	166	179	207	232	168
Saguache				400	660	389	620	948	1010	1219	1024	722	642	656	584
St. Elmo				500	267	64	46	37							
St. Thomas										450	450				
Salida			432	3000	2586	3722	4425	4689	5065	4969	4553	4560	4355	4870	4737
Salina			220	175	172	176	100	210	38						
San Acacio								140	150	150	150	160		60	60
San Luis		350	341	200		350	550	945	750	1000	1239	1000	781	842	800
San Miguel				200											
San Pablo						77	145	145	476	476	75		100	100	100
San Rafael/Paisaje			90		43	700	261	293	221	221					
Sanford					67	210	564	555	597	736	666	697	638	687	750
Sarcillo										200	125				
Sargents				100	99	99	105	105	110	110	110	80	60	30	50
Security												9017	8700	11000	6660
Sedalia					169	169	169	115	202	202	202	240	250	250	350
Sedgewick			103	100			375	380	444	373	332	299	208	258	183
Segundo			210	300		200	550	613	800	1500	827	300	250	200	125
Seibert					64	100	350	311	273	249	346	210	192	180	181
Severence							155	219	200	138	108	70	59	102	106
Shamballa Ashrama													200	200	300
Shaw Heights													2300	2300	3070
Sheridan						442	498	455	587	712	1715	3559	4787	5377	4976
Sheridan Lake												90	86	87	95
Sherman			184	100	207	100	110	100	100		100				
Sherrelwood													8600	11450	10200
Silt					546	576	275	165	264	359	361	384	434	923	1095
Silver Cliff			5040	1300			250	241	201	309	217	153	126	280	322
Silver Plume			260	700	908	775	460	272	126	139	136	86	164	140	134
Silverthorne													400	989	1768
Silverton				1500	1154	1360	2153	1150	1301	1127	1375	822	797	794	716
Simla			574				100	387	351	421	424	450	460	494	481
Skyline													3500	3500	2500

POPULATION HISTORY OF COLORADO CITIES AND TOWNS 1860-1990

COMMUNITY	1860	1870	1880	1885	1890	1900	1910	1920	1930	1940	1950	1960	1970	1980	1990
Skyway													1500	3600	3600
Smuggler						110	110	710	30						
Sneffels														999	1449
Snowmass			60			300	300	110	300		95	160	150	150	150
Snyder							100								
Somerset						600	600	465	600	600	500	150	180	180	140
Sopris								1032	300	500	653	1330			
South Boulder											3807				
South Canon						958	1321	1281	1471	1729	1588				
South Fork						55	55	164	250	250	175	200	250	250	250
South Glenn													2800	3800	43087
South Pueblo			1443	5000											
Southwind													900	900	1190
Southwood													2600	2600	2050
Spavik									350	350	273				
Springfield					90	45	100	295	1393	1082	2041	1791	1660	1657	1475
Sprucedale													300	300	400
Starkville			500	300	928	600	1000	2050	1650	945	795	261	166	127	104
Steamboat Springs			125	500	91	450	1227	1249	1198	1613	1913	1843	2340	5098	6695
Sterling				150	540	998	3044	6415	7195	7411	7534	10751	10636	11358	10362
Stoneham							75	260	100	100	100				
Stonewall				250											
Strasburg							100	216	216	216	300	490	900	1005	1005
Stratmoor													1150	5519	5854
Stratton							500	421	507	623	720	680	790	705	649
Stratton Meadows												3500	6223		150
Stratton Park									375	375	375			75	150
Stringtown												500			
Strong							50	225	340						
Sugar City						689	808	836	598	565	527	409	307	306	252
Sulpher Springs				500		106	182		123	235					
Summitville						70	70			300				30	
Sunnyside										300	250				
Sunnyslopes											827		400	400	500
Sunshine			200	100	179	179	179								
Superior							349	233	160	205	134	173	171	208	255
Swink							310	465	418	374	336	348	381	668	584
Tabernash							50	615	150	150	275	250	200	150	300
Teller			109	175		175	175	315							
Telluride				1400	786	2446	1756	1618	512	1337	1101	677	553	1047	1309

POPULATION HISTORY OF COLORADO CITIES AND TOWNS 1860-1990

COMMUNITY	1990	1980	1970	1960	1950	1940	1930	1920	1910	1900	1890	1885	1880	1870	1860
Ten Mile												1000			
Thornton	55031	40343	13326	11353											
Tiffany	190	185			150		100	265	150	38	38				
Timnath			177	150	177	147	169	160							
Tin Cup								210	95	64	170	800	325		
Tioga				250	400	300	300	260							
Tomichi															
Tourtellotte											614	600	134		
Towaoc	700	300	300	500			60	168	150						
Towner									150						
Trinchera	70	30		150	200	200									
Trinidad	8580	9663	9901	10691	12204	13223	11732	10906	10204	5345	5523	5000	2226	562	
Trondale				700									353		
Trout Creek															
Troy					150	300	300	420							
Twin Lakes	63	84	138	111	121	158	158	93	65			250			
Two Buttes												200			
Ula															
Uravan	350	800	800	1005	400	400									
USAF Academy	9062	8655	8000	5000											
Vail	3659	2261	484												
Valdez	200	150	150	700	682	250	250	262							
Vallecito					800	800									
Valverde								675		665					
Vancoram	60	60		200											
Vicksburg												200			
Victor	258	265	258	434	684	1784	1291	1777	3162	4986					
Vilas	105	94	83	107	132	129	175	40		49	43				
Villa Grove	50	50	75	100	200	125	125	210	130	103	294	300			
Vineland				500											
Virginia City													344		
Vista Verde	1100	500	500												
Vona	104	94	114	130	209	226	183	268	150						
Wah Keeney Park	692	500	500	300											
Walden	890	947	907	809	696	668	284	260	162	141	64	300			
Walnut Hills	4260	1700	1700												
Walsenburg	3300	3945	4329	5071	5596	5855	5503	3565	2423	1033	928	850	377		
Walsh	692	884	989	856	897	406	454							60	
Ward	159	129	32			118	34	74	129	300	424	150	275		
Watkins	890	100	100	100					50	50		100			

POPULATION HISTORY OF COLORADO CITIES AND TOWNS 1860-1990

COMMUNITY	1990	1980	1970	1960	1950	1940	1930	1920	1910	1900	1890	1885	1880	1870	1860
Wattenburg															
Webster	250	200	200	150						70	188	50			
Welby	10218	9668	900												
Weldona	300	175	175	150	250	300	300	114	150						
Wellington	1340	1215	691	532	541	485	533	439	459						
West Las Animas												400	454		
West Village		400	400												
Westcliffe	312	324	243	306	390	429	355	338	232	256	192				
Westcreek									34	161					
Western Hills	744	6000	4500	1500											
Westminster	74625	50211	19512	13850	1686	534	436	235	127						
Westminster East/Perl-Mack	5197	6002	7576	3000											
Weston	175	150	200	300	350	510	510	618	400						
Westridge	320														
Wheat Ridge	29419	30293	29778	21619	10000	3500	500								
Wheeler												250			
White Pine	350	175	175	170	125	125		115	69	69	143	500			
Whitewater									80	61					
Widefield	12112	7500	6600												
Wiggins	499	531	475	400	275	275	275	89	220	53					
Wild Horse									200						
Wiley	406	425	357	383	417	413	589	565	197						
Williamsburg	253	72	75	57	65	97	155	402	556	337	324	450			
Willowbrook	830	280	280												
Willow Creek	3140	700	700												
Windsor	5062	4277	1564	1509	1548	1811	1852	1290	935	305	173				
Winfield												250			
Winona					1004										
Winter Park	528	480	100		78	100									
Woodglen			900												
Woodland Park	4610	2634	1022	666	391	372	194	125	163	269					
Woodmar	2150														
Woodmen					250	400									
Woodmoor	3858	1490													
Woody Creek	450	450	450												
Wray	1998	2131	1953	2082	2198	2061	1785	1538	1000	271	125				
Yampa	317	472	286	312	421	426	310	200	332						
Yuma	2719	2824	2259	1919	1908	1606	1360	1177	333	139	241	50			
Zapato										50	579	50			

POPULATION HISTORY OF COLORADO CITIES AND TOWNS 1860-1990

1885: Croffut, George A. Croffut's Grip-sack Guide of Colorado. 1885

POPULATION HISTORY OF HAWAII CITIES AND TOWNS 1832-1990

COMMUNITY	1990	1980	1970	1960	1950	1940	1930	1920	1910	1900	1880	1853	1836	1832
Ahuimanu	8387													
Aiea	38500	32879	12560	11826	3714	3553	3021	2020	600			500	51	404
Amauulu											250	300	232	
Anahola	1181	915	638	326	326	367	105		100					
Barbers Point	2218	1373	1947											
Captain Cook	2595	2008	1263	1687	316		150	100						
Eleele	1489	580	758	617	993	1184	312	312	200		150			
Ewa	3780	2637	2906	3257	3429	3570	4739	1475	1000	100				
Ewa Beach	14315	14369	7765	2459	1500									
Foster Village	3700	3700	3755	2500										
Haiku	2000	619	464	422	729	431	2186	300	50	50	500	100		
Haina			300	450	670									
Hakalau	250	250	742	650	688	1138	525	250	200	160	500	150		
Halaula - Kohala	496	300	600	400	900						350	200		
Halawa (Hawaii)	55			80				132	150			200		
Halawa (Molokai)								100			200	150		
Halawa Heights	7000	7000	5809	2000	800		400	267	200					
Haleiwa	2442	2412	2626	2504	2142	1849								
Haliimaile	841	741	638	600	575									
Hamakuapoko			250	250				400	100	100	150			
Hana	683	643	459	435	547	1185	400	293	258	258	250	200	2858	3816
Hanalei	461	483	153	370	364	313	325	325	200		300	500	522	
Hanamaulu	3611	3227	2461	977	1031	1337	750	500	300	200		400		
Hanapepe	1395	1417	1388	1383	1259	1166	1088	368	125					
Hauula	3479	2997	2048	806	631	411	200	150	100		200	150	135	111
Hawaii National Park	400													
Hawaiian Ocean View	969													
Hawi	924	795	797	985	951	1194	1703	1539	600	550	100	200	233	505
Heeia	5010	5432		500	1500				427	427	300	400	483	
Hickam AFB	6553	4425	7352											
Hilea								100	91	100	220			
Hilo	37808	35269	26656	25966	27198	23353	19468	10431	6745	4550	2000	1500	1077	
Holualoa	3834	1243	700	704	475	541	250	200	73	100				
Honaunau	600	600	200	150	250			50			100	200		
Honoipu					75						400			
Honokaa	2186	1936	1555	1247	1021	1132	1069	168	128	128	300	200		
Honokahua	309	309	431	354	475	729	250	250				200		
Honokohau	190	200	300					50			100	500		
Honokowai	1000	500		100										
Honolulu	365272	365114	324871	294194	248034	179326	137582	83327	52183	39306	17000	11455	6000	5522

POPULATION HISTORY OF HAWAII CITIES AND TOWNS 1832-1990

COMMUNITY	1990	1980	1970	1960	1950	1940	1930	1920	1910	1900	1880	1853	1836	1832
Honomu	532	559	737	663	600	868	2110	2110	500	500	100	150		
Honouliuli	600	600	350	300				100	150	100		400		
Honuapo	60			22				100	64	100	200	150		
Hookena		60				54		175	200	200		150		
Hoolehua	250	250	100	990	973	1050								
Hoopuloa							50			100		150		
Iroquois Point	4188	3915	4572											
Kaaawa	1138	959	848	581	650							100	198	234
Kaanapali	579	541					172	172				200		
Kaawaloa								30			150	250		
Kahakuloa	100			70								300	465	728
Kahaluu (Hawaii)	380	380		50								200		
Kahaluu (Oahu)	3068	2925	1657	1125	400		200	150			100	300	242	267
Kahana (Maui)		900		375	375									
Kahana (Oahu)	100	100	100	100	150	150	150			150	200	150	203	233
Kahuku	2063	935	917	1238	1602	2251	1505	1836	400	400	150	100	413	334
Kahului	16889	12978	8280	4223	6306	2193	2353	910	210	210				
Kailua	36818	35812	33783	25622	7740	1540	200	350	350	350	50	400	762	760
Kailua - Kona	9126	4751	1365	466	325	381	350				200	500	1616	
Kainaliu	512	512	500	549	510	490	100				50			
Kalaheo	3592	2500	1514	1185	972	770	220							
Kalalau													131	
Kalapana	130	60		60	60	211	150	150			70	300		
Kalaupapa		144	250	270	446			600	385	385	100	120		
Kalawao					340			150			400			
Kalihiwai	435													
Kaluaihakoko				270	270									
Kamaee				302	302									
Kamalo								100	100	100	50	200		
Kamooloa	350		350	150										
Kaneohe	35448	29919	29903	14414	3208	1762	400	300	200		300	500	1168	1159
Kapaa	8149	4467	3794	3439	3177	2828	2818	330	300		300			
Kapaau/Halaula	1083	612	237	937	1309	1255	1239	300	200		75	200	145	
Kapalua	408													
Kapehu	100	100	150		181									
Kapoho	400			250	335	483	261	261				250		
Kapulena	100		100	235	235									
Kaumakani/Makaweli	803	888	1014	921	1283	1010	974		400	97	150			
Kaunakakai	2658	2231	1070	740	709	722		200		175		50		
Kaupakuea	200										320			

POPULATION HISTORY OF HAWAII CITIES AND TOWNS 1832-1990

COMMUNITY	1990	1980	1970	1960	1950	1940	1930	1920	1910	1900	1880	1853	1836	1832
Kaupo	200	200												
Kawaihae	100	100		100	152	123	125	50	50	100	100	100	437	
Kawailoa	400	400	250	300	391		400	125	100			200		
Kawanui				80	250									
Kawela	366													
Keaau - Olaa	1584	775	951	1334	1620	2509	1301			150			550	
Keahua				250	250									
Kealakekua	1453	1033	740	579	325	373	350	350	50	50			462	
Kealia	700	700	600	655	655	758	400	300	250	100	100			
Kealia/Kai Malino	100	100	100	100	184	195					200			
Keanae	250	250		54	54	106	67	67			50	300		
Keauhou	185	185	150	250	200			50	53	100				
Keei	210	210	150	100				54			50			
Kekaha	3506	3260	2404	2082	1989	2536	1500	1000	400	112				
Kemoo				250	250									
Keokea	900	900	500	436	698	454	100	57	97	97				
Kihei	11107	5644	900	938	95			75	300	150	350	100	117	
Kilauea	1685	895	671	665	757	548	1232	1232	46	46	100	150		
Kipahulu	110	110						150						
Kohala				550	400	960	720	720	550	550	400			
Kokomo	250	250	150	250	181	208								
Koloa	1791	1457	1368	1426	1470	1903	1844	1000	1000	1000		500		
Kualapuu	1661	502	441	566	607	641		100						
Kukuihaele	316	332	310	424	590	408	300	250	200	107	160			
Kukuiula	280	280	110	146										
Kula	1300	1300	500	570	570									
Kunia	550	550	1025	1500										
Kurtistown	910	1200				542		542						
Lahaina	9073	6095	3718	3423	4025	5217	2730	1560	1000	1000	2000	2750	3195	4028
Laie	5577	4643	3009	1767	841	761	521	400	350	350	200	200	375	452
Lanai City	2400	2092	2122	2056	2746	3597	1000							
Lanikai					7740	570	100							
Laupahoehoe	508	500	452	407	401	534	430	430	400					
Lawai	1787	950	600	145	145		110		100	400	150	200		
Lihue - Nawiliwili	5536	4000	3124	3908	3870	4254	2399	640	625	425	400	500	164	
Lower Paia	1500	1500	1105	925	1137	1235	1081	519						
Maalaea	443	200		200	200									
Mahukona				100	100	147	116	150	275	275			147	
Maili/Lualualei	6059	5026	4397	5045	1528	371								
Makaha	7990	6582	4644	2720	800							100		

POPULATION HISTORY OF HAWAII CITIES AND TOWNS 1832-1990

COMMUNITY	1990	1980	1970	1960	1950	1940	1930	1920	1910	1900	1880	1853	1836	1832
Makakilo	9828	7691	3499											
Makapala	190	190	201	353	381	527	450	250	150					
Makawao	5405	2900	1066	977	1098	903	525	525	200	200	500		295	346
Makaweli/Pakala	565	700	500	600	514		200	250	200	100				
Makena				30	150				150	150		250		
Mana	50	50		225	225									
Maunaloa	405	633	872	789	926	979		60	100	100				
Maunawai				570	570		218	218						
Maunawili	4847	5239	5303											
Mililani	29359	20351	2035											
Milolii	50	50		95	95	66	100	100				250		
Mokapu	11662	11615	7860											
Mokuleia				200	200			115					115	
Moloaa				176	176		150	75			150			
Mountain View	3075	540	419	566	747	955								
Naalehu	1027	1168	1014	952	1004	1038	700	400	250	250	400	150		
Nahiku							100	325				150		
Nanakuli	9575	8185	6506	2745	2002	777								
Napili	3000	1900	200	50										
Napoopoo				90	103	103	220	220	200	200		300		
Ninole	150	150	200	112	112	77	352	352	200		200	150	200	
Niulii				250	250			250			200	200		
Numila	150	150	250	260	568						250			
Okala											250	250		
Olaa				1334		1416	597	597	150	150				
Olomana	1000	1000	100											
Olowalu	180	180	200	75										
Omao	1142	500			250			100						
Onomea				485					250			150		
Ookala	401	401	486	562	662	735	526	200	100	87		150		
Opihikao	40	40		116	116			50			50	250		
Paauhau	380	380	450	400	617	584	536	536	178	178		100		
Paauilo	620	755	710	1059	975		1233	1233	200	100		150		
Pacific Palisades	10000	9500	7846											
Pahala	1520	1619	1507	1329	1602	1651	1000	750	250	250				
Pahoa	1027	923	924	1046	990	1114	400	240						
Paia	2091	1000	541	2149	3195	4272	4171	1000	300	300				
Panaewa	480	400	300											
Papaaloa	350	350	319	449	597	662	500	400	300					
Papaikou	1634	1567	1888	1591	1427	1566	518	500	400	150	400	150		

POPULATION HISTORY OF HAWAII CITIES AND TOWNS 1832-1990

COMMUNITY	1990	1980	1970	1960	1950	1940	1930	1920	1910	1900	1880	1853	1836	1832
Paukaa	495	544		365	530				150					
Pauwai					200									
Pauwela/Kuiaha	468	468	355	558	618	465	572	572				150		
Peahi							312	312				250	250	250
Pearl City	45900	42575	19552	7072	2663	1938	1071	639	200	200				
Pelekunu												200		
Pepeekeo	1813	1800	600	400	623	691	520	520	250		400	150		
Piihonua					350	500								
Pohakupu	2000	2000		1100										
Poipu	975	685	466											
Pomoho	340	340	340	330	368									
Port Allen				609	609									
Princeville	1244	500												
Puako	397										100			
Puhi	1210	991	772	704	765	886	165	165						
Pukalani	5879	3950	1629	600	600									
Pukoo				75	42	52	50		50	50	100	200		
Punaluu	672	400	300	300	320							300		
Pupukea	1500	900		100	100									
Puuiki	150			100	100									
Puukolii	150	150	250	418	689	1042	500	400						
Puuloa							215							318
Puunene		572	1132	3054	4418	4456	4080	4080						
Schofield Barracks	19597	18851	13516	14873	7179	16331	11694	2960	965	965				
Spreckelsville	280	280	120	1200	2634	2634	2655	1000			500			
Sunset Beach	1500	800	500	400										
Ulupalakua	400	400	150	150		372	30	30						
Union Mill	400	900	300						300	300	100			
Volcano	1516			90	90		30	36						
Wahiawa	17386	16911	17598	15512	8369	5420	3370	1027						
Wahiawa New Mill					568	771								
Waiahole	350	350	200		80									
Waiakea							1536	1536			200	200	210	419
Waiakoa - Kula				416	517	695	52	52						
Waialua	3943	4051	4047	2689	2602	2512	4511	3200	1000		300	1000	2414	2640
Waianae	8758	7941	3302	6844	1000	1078	1202	1320	750		300	300		
Waiau	100		140	47										
Waiehu	2000				700							400		
Waihee	717	413	346	436	500		90	150	150	250	350	500		
Waikane														

POPULATION HISTORY OF HAWAII CITIES AND TOWNS 1832-1990

COMMUNITY	1990	1980	1970	1960	1950	1940	1930	1920	1910	1900	1880	1853	1836	1832
Waikapu	729	698	598	513	549	643	120	200			300	700		733
Waikiki												1200	3000	2571
Waikoloa	2248											200		
Waikolu												200		
Wailau														
Wailea	3799	1125	150	250	341	414	42				100	250		
Wailua	2018	1587	1379	1129	500							700		
Wailuku	10688	10260	7979	6969	7424	7319	6998	7200	1400	1400	1000		1364	2256
Waimalu	29967	3600	2982											
Waimanalo	3508	3562	2081	3011	868	971	1008	700	200	400	300	500	903	1208
Waimanalo Beach	4185	4161	3045											
Waimea (Kauai)	1840	1569	1596	1312	1648	1921	2091	2075	1000	450	300	700		
Waimea/Kamuela	5972	1179	756	657	560	445	816	450	450	400	200	300		
Waimea (Oahu)	750	600	400										189	217
Wainaku	1243	1045				214	200							
Waiohinu	200	200	200	163	163			200	100	100	400	500	222	
Waipahu	31435	29139	22798	7802	7169	6906	5874	2085	1000	85	200	640		1200
Waipio (Hawaii)	60	60	50	80	95	216	170	250	300	250	300			
Waipio (Oahu)	11812													
Waipio Acres	5304	4091	2146	1158										
Wheeler AFB	2600													
Whitmore	3373	2318	2015	1820	1700									

1880: Bower, George. The Hawaiian Kingdom: Statistical and Commerical Directory and Tourists Guide 1880-1881. Honolulu: George Bower and Co., 1880.
1853: Coulter, John Wesley. Population and Utilization of Land and Sea in Hawaii, 1853. Honolulu: Bernice P. Bishop Museum, 1931. (Bulletin 88)
1836 and 1832: Schmitt, Robert C. The Missionary Census of Hawaii. Honolulu: Bernice P. Bishop Museum, 1973. (Pacific Anthropological Records No.20)

POPULATION HISTORY OF IDAHO CITIES AND TOWNS 1863-1990

COMMUNITY	1863	1864	1870	1880	1890	1900	1910	1920	1930	1940	1950	1960	1970	1980	1990
Aberdeen							280	471	646	1016	1486	1484	1542	1528	1406
Acequia							75	83	55	110	125	107	107	100	106
Ahsahka						100	200								
Alameda									1885	2691	4694	10660			
Albion				257	179	306	392	388	262	357	610	415	229	286	305
Almo						80	180	200	310	310	310	100		100	100
American Falls					47	150	953	1547	1280	1439	1874	2123	2769	3626	3757
Ammon					100	100	214	378	270	363	447	1882	2545	4669	5002
Antelope								300							
Arbon							65	100	55		55				
Archer							251	325	400	400	250				
Arco					65	50	322	737	572	548	961	1562	1224	1241	1016
Arimo					97		80	215	290	291	337	303	252	338	311
Ashton							502	1022	1003	1203	1256	1242	1187	1219	1114
Athol						48	281	180	116	120	226	214	190	312	346
Atlanta		147	72	300	108	108	108		35	50	50	50	50	50	45
Atomic City/Midway											250	141	24	34	25
Avery								250	200	200	280	450	430	430	125
Bancroft						100	300	374	403	406	495	416	366	505	393
Basalt/Monroe						140	201	245	259	252	227	275	349	414	407
Bay Horse					237	92						25			
Bayview							50					250	200	320	320
Beaver					156			82	136	136	136				
Bellevue				613	892	356	702	526	375	502	528	384	537	1016	1275
Bennington				152	196	250	200	233	250	250	200	100	160	200	175
Bem											75	50		60	60
Black Pine							151	252	67						
Blackfoot				285	538	1000	2202	3937	3199	3681	5780	7378	8716	10065	9646
Blanchard								45	82	150	150	100	120	130	130
Bliss						45	200	200	188	188	126	91	114	208	185
Bloomington			316	505	400	417	539	475	393	418	302	254	186	212	197
Blowout												174			
Boise City	725	1658	995	1899	2311	5957	17358	21393	21544	26130	34393	34481	74990	102451	125738
Bonanza				352	154	208									
Bonners Ferry						349	1071	1236	1418	1345	1776	1921	1909	1906	2193
Booneville			160												
Bovill							400	589	572	447	437	357	343	289	256
Bruneau				75	63	105	150	490	300	300	300	200	100	190	190
Bryan						300	300								
Buena Vista			880	100											

POPULATION HISTORY OF IDAHO CITIES AND TOWNS 1863-1990

COMMUNITY	1990	1980	1970	1960	1950	1940	1930	1920	1910	1900	1890	1880	1870	1864	1863
Buhl	3516	3629	2975	3059	2870	2414	1883	2245	639						
Bullion City															
Burke	15	80	150	300	800	963	1027	1135	1400	1081	200				
Burley	8702	8761	8279	7508	5924	5329	3927	5408	900		482				
Burton					300	500									
Butte City	59	93	42	104						68					
Cabinet															
Calder	200	200	130				45	263	251						
Caldwell	18400	17699	14219	12230	10487	7272	4974	5106	3543	997	779				
Camas							30	100	75		182	300			
Cambridge	374	428	383	473	354	405	336	404	349	525					
Carey	600	600	300	200	100	100	600	740	701						
Cascade	977	945	833	923	943	1029	726	299							
Castleford	179	191	174	274	300	330	265	370	40	50					
Cataldo	300	300	100	100	70		100	113	100						
Centerville					133		208	206	130	257	142	217	474	2000	2638
Central						225	225	380							
Challis	1073	758	784	732	728	620	418	484	338	387	356	614			
Chatcolet	72	181	95	10	92		45	40	50						
Chester	420	420	420	300	275	342	185	200	200	200					
Chesterfield				190	196	196	196	290	325	300					
Chubbock	7791	7052	2924	1590	120										
Clarkia	150	150	190	200	150				100						
Clarks Fork	448	449	367	452	387	430	432	325	280	259					
Clawson				120	120	120									
Clayton	26	43	36	75	100	114	311	215	170	186	252				
Clearwater							58		250	90					
Cleveland				50	243	243	243	163	151	200					
Clifton	228	208	137	150	201	268	217	234	350	440	375	200			
Cobalt/Blackbird	225	200	200	120	250	100	180	160	100						
Coeur d'Alene	24563	20054	16228	14291	12198	10049	8297	6447	7291	508	491	150			
Collister		2700	2700	5456		780									
Conda	200	200	200	200	321	300	300								
Coolin	300	300	100	100	122	100	100		100						
Corral															
Cottonwood	882	941	867	1081	689	673	519	610	555	400	72	50			
Council	831	917	899	827	748	692	355	388	312	177	77	60			
Craigmont/Vollmer	542	617	554	703	594	528	496	549	332		200				
Crawford									100	61					
Culdesac	280	261	211	239	175	219	287	397	436						

POPULATION HISTORY OF IDAHO CITIES AND TOWNS 1863-1990

COMMUNITY	1863	1864	1870	1880	1890	1900	1910	1920	1930	1940	1950	1960	1970	1980	1990
Cuprum						137	45								
Custer				210	213	266	201								
Dalton Gardens											100	1083	1559	1795	1951
Dayton							75	225	271	364	287	212	198	368	357
De Lamar/Wagontown			160		438	876	560	423	126			35			
Deary								316	295	320	320	349	411	539	529
Declo								240	196	238	219	237	251	276	279
Delta					390	67	60								
Dempsey						246	50								
Denver						300	30								
Desmet						150	501	525	250	100	100	100		100	100
Dietrich								400	300	112	160	118	84	101	127
Dingle						50	50	250	300	300	300	200	200	230	230
Dixie						280								20	20
Donnelly								56	325	325	295	161	114	139	135
Dover								50	412	226	240	250	400	190	294
Downey						250	300	522	553	673	748	726	586	645	626
Driggs							250	683	719	1040	941	824	727	727	846
Drummond								115	61	66	59	31	25	25	37
Dubois						180	200	290	312	332	430	447	400	413	420
Eagle							151	412	412	250	250	200	359	2620	3327
East Hope								123	115	115	149	154	175	258	215
Eastport								39	40		125	100	125	70	70
Eden								359	409	413	456	426	343	335	314
Egin					33	58	125	185							
Elba						212	301	311	250	250	200	70		90	90
Elk City	372	219		276	42	252	250	210	150	150	180	300	450	670	670
Elk River								847	862	337	312	382	383	265	149
Elva							220								
Emida							150		200	200	150	225	100	150	150
Emmett					197	508	1351	2204	2763	3203	3067	3769	3945	4605	4601
Enaville							150								
Era					121										
Fairfield								280	306	511	502	474	336	404	371
Fairview				35		500	400	336	348	414	398	350		300	
Farnum							201	112				25			
Felt							51	390	50			25		45	
Ferdinand						40	300	255	196	223	206	176	157	144	135
Fernan Lake												134	179	178	170
Fernwood							200	87	150	150	210	250	315	680	680

POPULATION HISTORY OF IDAHO CITIES AND TOWNS 1863-1990

COMMUNITY	1863	1864	1870	1880	1890	1900	1910	1920	1930	1940	1950	1960	1970	1980	1990
Filer							214	1012	1011	1239	1425	1249	1173	1645	1511
Firth						100	102	270	236	242	293	322	362	460	429
Fish Haven				133		135	52	205	125	125	125	130	100	150	150
Florence	575	254	154	175	390										
Fort Boise			86	120											
Fort Hall			67	57					100	100	200	700	600	900	900
Fort Lapwai				149											
Fort Sherman				250											
Franklin (Ada)											2300	7222			
Franklin (Franklin)			300	700	537	435	534	589	531	523	467	446	402	423	478
Fruitland							250	400	499	500	573	804	1576	2456	2400
Garden City											764	1681	2368	4571	6369
Garden Valley					54	54	125	100	50				150	320	320
Gem				195	339	1077	375	348	417	386	300	280	100	50	50
Genesee				150	282	731	742	676	555	678	552	535	619	791	725
Georgetown				134	212	333	410	456	391	463	404	551	421	544	558
Gibbonsville				150	188	641	176	144	136	200	162	100	125	125	150
Gibbs							90	112	130	277	277	130			
Gifford							153	154	70	85	51	52			
Gilmore							153	437	455	113	50			30	
Glenns Ferry					333	372	800	1243	1414	1290	1515	1374	1386	1374	1304
Gold Hill			179			50									
Gooding							1444	1843	1592	2568	3099	2750	2599	2949	2820
Goshen						40	40			200	250	200	150		
Grace						53	75	515	626	701	761	725	826	1261	973
Grand View							80	140		200	160	200	150	366	330
Grangemont															
Grangeville				129	540	1132	1534	1439	1360	1929	2544	3642	3636	3666	3226
Granite						234	252	261	102	102	151				
Grant											350				
Gray					100	204	201		110	110	157	200			
Greenleaf							175	190	111	111	111		323	663	648
Greer						42						70		70	70
Groveland												220	150	150	150
Haden						150	130								
Hagarman						40	308	327	328	435	520	430	436	602	600
Hailey					1073	1240	1231	1201	973	1443	1464	1185	1425	2109	3687
Hamer							75	285	250	220		144	81	93	79
Hammett								115	234	234	234	200	200	200	250
Hansen							130	278	379	527	463	427	415	1078	848

· POPULATION HISTORY OF IDAHO CITIES AND TOWNS 1863-1990

COMMUNITY	1990	1980	1970	1960	1950	1940	1930	1920	1910	1900	1890	1880	1870	1864	1863
Harrison	226	260	240	249	322	362	493	674	932	702					
Hatwai	200	200	200												
Hauser	380	305	349	270	350		200	62	51	38					
Hayden	3744	2586	1285	901											
Hayden Lake	338	273	260	247	39		50		101						
Hazelton	394	496	396	433	429	417	388	295							
Headquarters	250	300	300	300	100		75								
Heyburn	2714	2889	1637	829	539	413	201	292	440						
Hibbard				350	445	300									
Holbrook	100	100			200	240	240	300							
Hollister	144	167	57	60	80	100	113	159	130						
Homedale	1963	2078	1411	1381	1411	857	225	282	100						
Hope	99	106	63	96	111	116	111	160	215	316					
Horseshoe Bend	643	700	511	480	401	415	396	385	202						
Howe	50	50		25	20		150	260	51	47					
Huetter	82	65	49	114	84			35							
Huston	140	140	100				51	80	110	110	110				
Idaho City	322	300	164	188	246	273	187	104	262	390	459	672	889	7000	6275
Idaho Falls/Eagle Rock	43929	39590	35776	33161	19218	15024	9429	8064	4827	1262	938	300			
Ilo							270	263	209						
Independence										415					
Indian Valley		60		40	30	465	150	240	50						
Inkom	769	830	522	528	434	518	515	112	80						
Iona	1049	1072	890	702	502		386	430	353	100					
Irwin	108	113	228	330	147	275	270	285	252						
Island Park	159	154	136	53			50								
Jerome	6529	6891	4183	4761	4523	3537	1976	1759	970	287					
Julietta	428	522	423	368	365	337	274	427	414		213				
Junction								57	101	83	83	105			
Kamiah	1157	1478	1307	1245	812	568	487	653	324	495					
Kellogg	2591	3417	3811	5061	4913	4235	4124	3017	1273	823	324				
Kendrick	325	395	426	443	409	407	363	522	543	490					
Ketchum	2523	2200	1454	746	757	330	224	213	250	300	450				
Keuterville									150	100	50				
Kilgore					116	116	116	120		75					
Kimberly	2367	2307	1558	1298	1347	963	648	501	350						
King Hill	125	125	100	200	100	150	150	190	125						
Kingston	1000	750	500	500	200	200	200	112	105	80	263				
Kooskia	692	784	809	801	629	490	411	405	301	297					
Kootenai	327	280	168	180	199	214	199	245	250	100					

POPULATION HISTORY OF IDAHO CITIES AND TOWNS 1863-1990

COMMUNITY	1863	1864	1870	1880	1890	1900	1910	1920	1930	1940	1950	1960	1970	1980	1990
Kuna							150	366	398	443	534	516	593	1767	1955
Laclede							402	435	150		150	150	200	400	400
Lago						300	200	153	160	160	160	160			
Landore						500									
Lane						63	201	210	100		100	100			
Lapwai			91	166		61	350	359	416	426	480	503	400	1043	932
Lardo						300									
Lava Hot Springs								662	544	647	591	593	516	467	420
Leadore							25	307	307	330	159	141	111	114	74
Leesburg			180		128	50	75	33	34						
Leigh						250									
Leland						150	250	158	207						
Lenox								219	150						
Lewiston	414	359	1560	739	849	2425	6043	6574	9403	10548	12985	12691	26068	27986	28082
Lewiston Orchards											4494	9680			
Lewisville				193		175	346	383	285	371	402	385	468	502	471
Liberty				191		300	281	310	310	225	225	160	120	140	140
Lincoln							401	300	250	250	250	300	300	700	700
Loon Creek			480												
Lorenzo							252	311	250	250	250	200	100	40	40
Lost River/Grouse											37	58	40		
Lund						100	301	261	60	120	120				
Lyman						178	182		120	300	250	150			
McCall						293	403	467	651	875	1173	1423	1758	2188	2005
McCammon						98	321	307	497	489	578	557	623	770	722
Mace							150					75			
Mackay							638	869	777	776	760	652	539	541	574
Malad City			591	759	713	1050	1303	2598	2535	2731	2715	2274	1848	1915	1946
Malta					54	147	275	400	412	550	518	250	196	196	171
Manard							152								
Marion									200	200	200	20			
Market Lake			100	150	89	100	100		113						
Marsing						112			188	194	643	555	610	786	798
Marysville						104	298	334	307	218	190	201	200	200	250
May							75	65		100	100	50		110	110
Meadows						212	251		150	150	200	250	100	120	120
Melba								157	420	213	203	197	197	276	252
Menan						212	294	393	384	432	430	496	545	605	601
Meridian						200	619	1013	1004	1465	1810	2091	2616	6658	9596
Mesa								270	270	150	150			65	65

POPULATION HISTORY OF IDAHO CITIES AND TOWNS 1863-1990

COMMUNITY	1990	1980	1970	1960	1950	1940	1930	1920	1910	1900	1890	1880	1870	1864	1863
Middleton	1851	1901	739	541	496	477	372	585	450	147	190				
Midvale	110	205	176	211	231	262	203	278	380				125		
Milown	350	350													
Miner				50				85	300	201					
Minidoka	67	101	131	154	113	174	193	253	150						
Mink Creek		50		109	124	170	221	209	200	313	360				
Montour			150	100	150	100	100	150							
Montpelier	2656	3107	2604	3146	2682	2824	2435	2984	1924	1444	1174	546	299	74	
Moore	190	210	156	358	256	114	150	150	101						
Moreland	400	300	300	250	400	400	400	400	301						
Moscow	18519	16513	14146	11183	10593	6014	4476	3956	3670	2484	1139	76			
Mount Idaho	70	75		90	50		70	105	100	539	190	159	125		
Mountain Home	7913	7540	6451	5984	1887	1193	1243	1644	1411	529	233	100			
Mountain Home Base	5936	6403	6038	4898	3084										
Mountain View															
Moyie Springs	415	386	203	196	109	100	100								
Mud Lake	179	243	194	187											
Mullan	821	1269	1279	1477	2036	2291	1891	1320	1668	1217	818				
Murphy	150	150	100	50	50		75	150	102	80					
Murray	100	100	100	107	158	332	268	511	400	302	1172	500			
Murtaugh	134	114	124	214	239	272	400	300	102						
Nampa	28365	25112	20768	18897	16185	12149	8206	7621	4205	799	347				
Naples	120	120	130	100	175	200	327	255	251	156					
New Meadows	534	576	605	647	621	264	220	141							
New Plymouth	1313	1186	986	940	942	804	510	400	274	61					
Newdale	377	329	267	272	312	356	368	381							
Nezperce	453	517	555	667	543	590	444	677	599	300					
Niter				150			150		402						
North Fork	250	170	170					55							
North Pocatello/Alameda					575			436							
Notus	380	437	304	324	313	277	144	150	101						
Oakley	635	663	656	613	684	813	882	1273	911	678	644	100			
Oldtown	151	257	161	211	358										
Onaway	203	254	166	191	400	400	250								
Oneida									80	118	118	90			
Oreana							75	150	302	118					
Orofino	2868	3711	3883	2471	1656	1602	1078	537	384	300			113	145	
Osburn	1579	2220	2248	1788	954	800	300	115	100	78	59				
Osgood				200	500										
Ovid	155	145	145	200	207	135	135	154	200	200	123	146			

POPULATION HISTORY OF IDAHO CITIES AND TOWNS 1863-1990

COMMUNITY	1990	1980	1970	1960	1950	1940	1930	1920	1910	1900	1890	1880	1870	1864	1863
Oxford	44	66	75	85	110	275	309	300	320	260	246	300			
Page			250	200	200										
Palisades	75	150	150	75											
Paris	581	707	615	746	774	932	825	1333	1038	906	893	611	502		
Parker	288	262	266	284	306	384	286	400	432	40					
Parma	1597	1820	1228	1295	1396	1085	750	583	338	62					
Patterson				24	112	300									
Paul	901	940	911	701	560	606	363	527							
Payette	5592	5448	4521	4451	4032	3322	2618	2433	1948	614	396				
Pearl			8	24	38	21	12	39	123	217					
Peck	160	209	238	186	170	165	164	191	236	200					
Picabo	100	100		75	100	100	100	132	60						
Pierce	746	1060	1218	522	544	381	400	120	220	281	238	45	850	131	275
Pinehurst	1722	2183	1934	1432	125	125									
Pioneerville							58	157	102	143	137	192	477	2000	2743
Placerville				100	200	146	116	187	187	230	173	427	318	2500	3254
Plano				160	108	300	300	375							
Pleasant View		250				180			180						
Plummer	804	634	443	344	395	399	346	450							
Pocatello	46080	46340	40036	28534	26131	18133	16471	15001	9110	4046	1639				
Ponderay	449	399	275	231	248	160	119	110	102						
Post Falls	7349	5736	2371	1933	1069	843	509	576	658	287	400	49			
Pollatch	790	819	871	830	1105	1409	1500	1505	750						
Preston	3710	3759	3310	3640	4045	4236	3381	3235	2110	1074	313				
Priest River	1560	1639	1493	1749	1592	1056	949	545	248	280					
Princeton	130	130	100	90	87	175	175	210	201						
Quartzburg							75	130	60	214	84	57			
Rathdrum	2000	1369	741	710	610	511	496	509	725	407	218				
Raymond				35	35		160	207	152	100					
Reubens	46	87	81	113	116	119	191	176	400						
Rexburg	14302	11559	8272	4767	4253	3437	3048	3569	1893	1081	293				
Reynolds				75			75		201	150					
Richfield	383	357	290	329	429	390	193	333	158						
Rigby	2681	2624	2293	2281	1826	1978	1531	1629	555	107					
Riggins	443	527	533	588	287	150	66	60	60						
Ririe	596	555	575	560	527	493	422	396	192						
Roberts	557	466	393	422	341	319	297	313	130						
Robin							50	250		200					
Rockland	264	283	209	258	277	277	374	344	190	113	37				
Rocky Bar							40	50	100	296	505	350	440	540	560

POPULATION HISTORY OF IDAHO CITIES AND TOWNS 1863-1990

COMMUNITY	1990	1980	1970	1960	1950	1940	1930	1920	1910	1900	1890	1880	1870	1864	1863
Rogerson	70	70				100	100								
Rose Lake	200	200	100		100										
Roseberry							32	280	400						
Ross Fork				32				113	1400						
Roy					50		70	200							
Ruby City															640
Rupert	5455	5476	4563	4153	3098	3167	2250	2372	297						
St. Anthony	2010	3212	2877	2700	2695	2719	2778	2957	1237	411					
St. Charles	189	211	200	300	363	429	360	508	400	321	322	474	294		
St. Joe									450						
St. John	125	125	220				300	300				118			
St. Maries	2442	2794	2511	2435	2220	2234	1996	1962	869	209					
Salem				200	400	400	400	110	60	41					
Salmon	2941	3308	2910	2944	2648	2439	1371	1311	1434	398	613	292	186		
Salmon Falls												200	270		
Salubria	135	135	137	172				302	309	309	309				
Samaria					322	322	134	379	366	326	198				
Samuels	650	650			200										
Sandpoint	5203	4460	4144	4355	4265	4356	3290	2876	2993	507					
Sawtooth											50	1000			
Shelley	3536	3300	2614	2612	1856	1751	1447	1223	537	459					
Shelton					300	300									
Shoshone	1249	1242	1233	1416	1420	1366	1211	1165	1155	685	958				
Silver City					110	165	183	630	650	976	583	593	960	117	216
Silverton	750	800	800	700	200										
Slate Creek					300	400	200								
Smelterville	464	776	967	1127											
Soda Springs	3111	4051	2977	2424	1329	1087	831	935	501	428	446	250	144		
Soldier							215		266	113	108				
South Boise				1452	1281				885						
South Mountain															
Spalding	100	150	150	200	200	155	155	150	100	200		180	200		
Spencer		29	45	100	170	116	154		90	81					
Spirit Lake	790	834	622	693	823	1006	1241	940	907						
Springfield	100	100	100	80	350	350	350	295	200						
Stanley	71	99	47	35	33	158	159	155	75						
Star	600	600	450	275	353	443	414	402	300	88					
Sterling				70		120	250	255							
Stibnite					717		120								
Stites	204	253	263	299	227	258	278	317	300						

POPULATION HISTORY OF IDAHO CITIES AND TOWNS 1863-1990

COMMUNITY	1990	1980	1970	1960	1950	1940	1930	1920	1910	1900	1890	1880	1870	1864	1863
Stuart										297					
Sugar City	1275	1022	617	584	684	697	621	680	391						
Sun Valley	938	545	180	317	428	300									
Swan Valley	141	135	235	217	203	171									
Swanlake	125	125	135	150	170			80	50	49	49				
Sweet	90	90		100	100	125	200	250							
Tendoy	150	150													
Tensed	90	113	151	184	189	150	150	80							
Terreton	400	400		40	50		30								
Teton	570	559	390	399	463	514	481	537	494	250					
Tetonia	132	191	176	194	232	387	325	311							
Thatcher	145	145		100	50	150	50	150	201	150					
Thornton	100	100	150	200	200	300	300	300	252						
Treasureton				250		210	210	261	151						
Triumph		30			100	150									
Troy	699	820	541	555	531	580	619	591	543	283					
Twin Falls	27591	26209	21914	20126	17600	11851	8787	8324	5258						
Twin Lakes	400	400	250												
Ucon	895	833	664	523	356	449	349	364							
Ulysses								110	102						
Ustick	200						200	211	80						
Van Wyck							292		279	67	67				
Victor	292	323	241	240	431	294	250	277	300	300		300			
Vienna								56							
Virginia					250	250	250								
Volcano														180	
Wallace	1010	1736	2206	2412	3140	3839	3634	2816	3000	2265	878				
Wardner	246	423	492	577	772	861	903	704	1369	2278	858				
Warren/Washington		35	30	12	30	209	180	131	100	159	113	470	543	521	660
Wayan		25			10		96	125	122	70					
Weippe	532	828	713	600	800	396	110		60	180					
Weiser	4571	4771	4108	4208	3961	3663	2724	3154	2600	1364	901				
Wendell	1963	1974	1122	1232	1483	1001	725	664	482						
West Boise					3024										
Weston	390	310	230	284	382	439	429	452	398	500	84	297			
White Bird	108	154	185	253	175	275	209		400	176			71		
Whitney (Ada)				13303	3900										
Whitney (Franklin)	85	85	100	80			278	310	202						
Wilder	1232	1260	564	503	555	507	381	349							
Wilford										250					

POPULATION HISTORY OF KANSAS CITIES AND TOWNS 1860-1990

COMMUNITY	1990	1980	1970	1960	1950	1940	1930	1925	1920	1915	1910	1905	1900	1895	1890	1885	1880	1875	1870	1860
Asherville											125		150							
Ashland	1032	1096	1244	1312	1493	1186	1232	1067	1147		910		493		459		300			
Ashmead		35															200			
Ashton	35						66		84		125		75	320						
Assaria	387	414	303	322	221	232	201	209	234		246		214		180		56			
Atchison	10656	11407	12565	12529	12792	12648	13024	15028	12630	15263	16429	18159	15722	15482	13963	15599	15105	10927	7054	2616
Athol	86	90	108	140	203	248	280	317	294		305		100							
Atlanta	232	256	216	267	309	286	348	375	379		330		192		275		250			
Attica	716	730	639	845	622	708	756	629	744		737		311	271	553					
Atwood	1388	1665	1658	1906	1613	1408	1166	1125	919		680		486		450		150			
Aubry	100	150	150	150	110	110	128		115		100		72		72		100			
Auburn	908	890	261	160													100			
Augusta	7876	6968	5977	6434	4483	3821	4033	3297	4219	1378	1235	1212	1197	1025	1343	1476	922		400	
Aulne	35	25					185				150		53							
Aurora	101	130	120	150	221	274	256	272	275		269		193				60			
Avoca													50		152					
Axtell	432	470	456	493	510	545	607	559	617		748		651	501	643	674	255			
Baileysville											250		120		170					
Baker											122		166		272					
Bala							87				100		100		183					
Baldwin City	2961	2829	2520	1877	1741	1096	1127	1243	1137	1231	1386	1265	1017	1135	935	933	325		200	
Barnard	129	163	190	205	242	306	416	406	359		425		146		76					
Barnes	167	257	209	247	308	391	361	348	395		454		383	379	311	156	156			
Bartlett	107	163	138	137	143	161	167	204	222		249		136		52					
Basehor	1591	1483	724	500	275	211	200	177	225		225		105							
Bassett	20	31	62	67	117	124	194	282	319		415				40					
Bavaria	100	75			200	200	110				110		110		110		100			
Baxter Springs	4351	4773	4489	4498	4647	4921	4541	3591	3608	1343	1598	1791	1641	1566	1248	1240	1177	1059	1284	
Bazine	373	385	386	429	456	465	423	301	164		120		89		200					
Beagle	65	80	150	150	100		293				183		183							
Beattie	221	316	288	314	321	389	434	406	452		497		633	628	648	476	270			
Beaumont	100	140	175	150	150	291	388		360		200		157		157		100		100	
Beaver						100	100		146		200		105				200			
Bel Aire	3695	2395	1535																	
Belle Plaine	1649	1706	1553	1579	971	878	825	685	839		849		551	516	659		348		100	
Belleville	2517	2805	3063	2940	2858	2580	2383	2271	2254	2216	2224	2029	1833	1445	1868	719	238		250	
Belmont	30	40		32	48	194	155		141				36		36		150		79	176
Beloit	4066	4367	4121	3837	4085	3765	3502	3032	3315	3240	3082	2124	2359	2039	2455	2003	1835	300	400	
Belpre	116	154	191	211	231	300	382	351	488		485		75							
Belvue	207	212	161	179	193	226	186	210	199		218		146				100			

POPULATION HISTORY OF KANSAS CITIES AND TOWNS 1860-1990

COMMUNITY	1990	1980	1970	1960	1950	1940	1930	1925	1920	1915	1910	1905	1900	1895	1890	1885	1880	1875	1870	1860
Benedict	16	111	91	128	176	213	223	203	275		215		205		127					
Bennington	568	579	561	535	325	369	374	378	371		386		389	351	390		200			
Bentley	360	311	260	204	200	205	191	235	175		130		107							
Benton	669	609	517	452	269	235	253	235	224		240		225		241					
Bern	190	220	191	206	216	236	306	279	472		256		433		175					
Beulah													100		244		100			
Beverly	131	171	193	199	255	292	328	369	344				116		108					
Bigelow					225	250							200		275					
Bird City	467	546	671	678	784	694	740	570	489		190		88	98	145		100			
Bison	252	279	285	291	326	366	397	357	357		285		82							
Blaine	45	45			120	175	118				250		156		279					107
Blair	40	70	100		100	150	50				50									
Blakeman				100							100		100		280					
Blue Mound	251	319	308	319	424	446	545	573	570		596		738	703	689	851	100			
Blue Rapids	1131	1280	1148	1426	1430	1433	1465	1570	1534	1326	1756	1400	1100	1134	936		829	685	685	
Bluff City	69	95	109	152	172	252	233	223	272		307		200	148	194					
Bogue	150	197	257	234	211	157	149		135		100		52							
Bonner Springs	6413	6266	3884	3171	2277	1837	1837	1776	1626	1541	1462	890	609							
Brainerd	60	55									150		70	103	180					
Brazilton			100		100	117	73													
Breezy Hill					125	100	716													
Brewster	296	327	320	317	467	408	487	403	213		200		70		227					
Bridgeport							90				120		120							
Bronson	343	414	397	354	415	421	450	555	590		595		361	324	352		240			
Brookville	226	259	238	246	213	221	237	235	212		280		292		345	474	511		201	
Broughton											160		160							
Brownell	44	92	98	118	211	162	207	202	234		175		137							
Bruce													164							
Bucklin	710	786	771	752	824	832	917	787	835		696		167		158					
Bucyrus						115	134				200									
Buffalo	293	386	321	422	437	555	799	694	739		807		299		269					
Buffalo Park					223	200	163								300		147			
Buffville							316													
Buhler	1277	1188	1019	888	750	634	520	496	486		406		166							
Bull City																	173			
Bunker Hill	111	124	181	200	271	253	298	268	268		242		146	139	157	649	135			
Burden	518	518	503	580	541	522	507	492	441		424		519	480	508	157	157			
Burdett	248	275	285	375	355	291	345		320		200		157		157					
Burdick											225									
Burlingame	1074	1239	999	1151	1065	1019	1127	1477	1330	1474	1422	1581	1436	1513	1472	1574	1370	500	655	

POPULATION HISTORY OF KANSAS CITIES AND TOWNS 1860-1990

COMMUNITY	1860	1870	1875	1880	1885	1890	1895	1900	1905	1910	1915	1920	1925	1930	1940	1950	1960	1970	1980	1990
Burlington	118	960	975	2011	2819	2239	2322	2418	2257	2180	2251	2236	2533	2273	2379	2304	2113	2099	2901	2735
Burns				75		250		250		489		622	451	455	409	294	314	268	224	226
Burr Oak				425	546	597	595	671		746		638	574	595	560	505	473	426	366	278
Burrton				386	579	695	681	627		689		679	622	649	842	749	774	808	976	866
Bushong								97		150		218	115	193	135	93	51	39	62	57
Bushton						86		133		222		326	343	325	473	532	499	397	388	341
Byers												510	212	185	153	83	52	46	47	46
Cactus				200																
Cain						83														
Caldwell				1005	1970	1642	1448	1575	1917	2205	2215	2191	1954	2046	1962	2000	1788	1540	1401	1351
Callahan																				
Camargo																		900	900	
Cambridge				150		198		198		230		233	291	277	246	221	140	110	113	74
Camp Forsyth																		2334	2054	1967
Camp Funston																		4147		
Camp Sturgis		320																		
Caney		100		200		542	1004	887	2651	3597	3104	3427	2801	2794	2629	2876	2682	2192	2284	2062
Canton				396	453	420	357	493		684		700	700	728	796	771	784	893	926	794
Capaldo												412	395	395	261	150	150	150	150	150
Carbondale		250		710	1230	847	683	625		461		383	427	399	415	453	664	1041	1518	1526
Carlton						121		125		210		225		138	101	76	78	40	49	39
Carlyle										200										
Carona										350					300	300	125	125	130	130
Cassoday										300		162		200	134	150	112	123	122	95
Catharine								38		50					712	525	145	145	145	120
Cato				200		208		112												
Cawker City		300		1039	960	898	747	816		870		788	738	739	657	691	686	726	640	588
Cedar				150		160		161		350		149	158	148	144	86	73	46	53	25
Cedar Junction										161										
Cedar Point				113		230		163		167		190	134	141	140	107	87	73	66	39
Cedar Vale		200		218		640	544	932		948		1044	976	1000	952	1010	859	665	848	760
Cedarville				265		285		150									150	150	125	125
Centerville								100		175					200	200	150	150	125	125
Centralia				289	540	534	604	655		665		619	589	682	607	574	527	511	486	452
Centre				400		38														
Centreville				300		58		31												
Chalk Mound				200		78														
Chanute				887	1911	2826	3551	4208	9074	9272	9033	10286	9829	10277	10142	10109	10849	10341	10506	9488
Chapman		448	448	114		435	509	627		781		853	813	819	782	990	1095	1132	1255	1264
Chase				150		358		316		263		286	262	278	825	961	922	800	753	577

POPULATION HISTORY OF KANSAS CITIES AND TOWNS 1860-1990

COMMUNITY	1860	1870	1875	1880	1885	1890	1895	1900	1905	1910	1915	1920	1925	1930	1940	1950	1960	1970	1980	1990
Chatauqua				100		286		263		348		401	332	282	254	215	205	137	156	132
Chelsea				200				66												
Cheney		300		75		304	312	429		734		636	597	669	714	777	1101	1160	1404	1560
Cherokee		200		556	1003	1087	1314	1326	1647	1452	1149	1091	1570	1158	1101	849	797	790	775	651
Cherryvale		960	1068	690	2601	2104	2386	3472	5089	4304	4235	4698	4216	4251	3185	2952	2783	2609	2769	2464
Chetopa				1305	1629	2265	2640	2019	1913	1548	1899	1519	1629	1344	1606	1671	1538	1596	1751	1357
Chicopee						409	496	256		273		520	390	400	578	250	125	300	250	250
Childs Acres																			390	440
Cimarron				300		895	224	237		587		599	740	1035	1004	1189	1115	1373	1491	1626
Circleville				122		215	229	223		265		226	208	211	216	169	151	178	164	153
Claflin						300	234	300		554		648	617	607	747	921	891	887	764	678
Clarence																				
Clay Center		255		1753	3830	2802	2723	3069	3240	3438	3742	3715	4315	4386	4518	4528	4613	4963	4948	4613
Clayton				50		52		105		191		258	199	226	153	157	161	127	102	91
Clearwater				50		408	276	368		569		647	615	669	591	647	1073	1435	1648	1875
Cleburne								150		225				210	150	150	150			
Clements						320		200		200				184	104		100	100	100	
Clifton		100		142	309	622	552	609		614		631	674	713	670	743	746	718	695	561
Climax						87		93		100		113	138	129	157	91	81	64	81	57
Cloverdale								123		123						850	550	580	120	
Clyde		165		956	1770	1137	1129	1157	1187	1057	1211	1063	1207	1174	1060	1067	1025	946	909	793
Coalvale				195		78		53											30	
Coats								49		269		383	303	345	304	255	152	152	153	127
Cockerill															250	100				
Codell								62		175				184	120	200	125	125	120	70
Coffeyville		554		753	1813	2282	3424	4953	13196	12687	15228	13452	16220	16198	17355	17113	17382	15116	15185	12917
Colby						516	514	641	353	1130	1088	1114	1665	2153	2458	3859	4210	4658	5544	5396
Coldwater						480		263		684		1207	1042	1296	1214	1208	1164	1016	989	939
Collyer				100		100		100		200		190	205	243	268	282	233	182	151	144
Colony				114		474		483		530	473	997	633	596	420	386	419	382	474	447
Columbia	143																			
Columbus		402		1164	2354	2160	2204	2310	2927	3064	3500	3155	3327	3235	3402	3490	3395	3356	3426	3268
Colwich						212	223	225		258		262	261	260	284	339	703	879	935	1091
Concordia		250		1853	3002	3184	3011	3401	4427	4415	5229	4705	5488	5792	6255	7175	7022	7221	6847	6167
Conway Springs						681	549	714		1292		1120	988	981	849	816	1057	1153	1313	1384
Cookville				300		35		35												
Coolidge				350		472	198	288		145		144	102	135	132	168	117	102	82	90
Coonsville				250																
Cope				300																
Copeland												163		423	262	242	247	267	323	290

POPULATION HISTORY OF KANSAS CITIES AND TOWNS 1860-1990

COMMUNITY	1860	1870	1875	1880	1885	1890	1895	1900	1905	1910	1915	1920	1925	1930	1940	1950	1960	1970	1980	1990
Cora						180														60
Corbin						174		175		180		123		136	170	100	100	100	60	60
Corning				63	192	291	347	425		411		419	323	340	352	254	240	162	158	142
Coronado						310														
Cottonwood				324																
Cottonwood Falls		520	377	518	693	770	730	842		899		1044	920	963	1078	957	971	987	954	889
Council Grove		712	600	1042	1742	2211	2145	2265	2418	2545	2405	2857	2406	2898	2875	2722	2664	2403	2381	2228
Countryside																358	428	411	346	312
Courtland						267	207	286		454		411	414	430	383	367	384	403	377	343
Coyville		100		168		268		286		227		232	203	196	175	106	133	93	98	78
Cresson				200																
Crestline						162		162		162										
Crisfield			500	500		320		100		50		42		46	250	250	150	100		
Croweburg										125		1025	603	603						65
Cuba				75		415	424	445		466		432	432	403	363	345	336	290	286	242
Cullison						288		136		256		249	235	256	239	174	129	117	154	120
Culver						89		160		326		234	243	206	195	153	200	148	167	162
Cunningham								257		395		462	371	412	451	510	618	483	540	535
Curranville							578			773										
Damar								46		200		138		194	263	305	361	245	204	112
Danville						471		213		150		167		130	134	122	118	80	71	56
De Soto		100		219	257	257		333		337		345	375	384	383	518	1271	1839	2061	2291
De Witt				150																
Dearing								33		250		295	280	324	273	261	249	338	475	428
Deerfield				61				61		152		284	385	325	356	440	442	474	538	677
Delavan										175					150	300			50	100
Delaware City				126		58														
Delia										110		244	237	269	222	164	163	168	181	172
Delphos				256	511	561	466	648		767		870	767	678	714	676	619	599	570	494
Denison		100						146		295		240	183	202	176	166	184	248	231	225
Dennis						96		175		175					212	212	150	150	150	100
Densmore						174		100		225										
Denton						256		247		337		193		193	156	157	161	162	156	166
Derby/El Paso				200		200	257	250		235		247	284	294	256	432	6458	7947	9786	14699
Detroit										142				219	204	101	100	100	120	120
Devon								115		200				167	159	125	100	100	75	100
Dexter				146		371	299	380		512		497	449	484	424	354	291	286	366	320
Dighton						304	164	194		370		503	554	803	974	1246	1526	1540	1390	1361
Dillon								161		161										
Dodge City		200	500	996	2446	1763	1857	1942	2627	3214	4101	5061	6099	10059	8487	11262	13520	14127	18001	21129

POPULATION HISTORY OF KANSAS CITIES AND TOWNS 1860-1990

COMMUNITY	1990	1980	1970	1960	1950	1940	1930	1925	1920	1915	1910	1905	1900	1895	1890	1885	1880	1875	1870	1860
Doniphan					50	135	140		171		134		196		347		518		528	343
Dorrance	195	220	234	331	365	414	325	286	299		281		156	190	175		140			
Doster																	200		150	
Douglass	1722	1450	1126	1058	729	763	804	850	1010		657		755	723	737	1152	369			
Dover	135	135	135		100	200					175		100		100		100			
Downs	1119	1324	1268	1206	1221	1219	1383	1618	1508	1552	1427	1287	938	801	938	800	465			
Dresden	73	84	103	134	162	180	231	166	315		325		162				200			
Drycreek													85							
Dunavant							184				85									
Dunkirk		20			100	100		232	513		125									
Dunlap	65	82	102	134	134	219	273	254	300		333		400	385	408		247			
Durham	119	130	143	183	229	245	254	268	288		268		190	134			150			
Dwight	365	320	322	281	281	295	334	265	246		298		136		207					
Eads																	200			
Earlton	69	79	102	104	141	174	166	138	381		250		158		320		43			
East Genda Springs															169					
Eastborough	896	854	1141	1001	708	312														
Easton	405	460	435	320	255	255	277	237	228		310		170		126		125			
Eden Prairie																	200			
Edgarton	1244	1214	513	414	266	264	278	305	323		443		310	332	321	1316	229		100	
Edison	37	56	90	91	110	200	197	175	213		250		215		276		75			
Edmond						180														
Edna	438	537	418	442	422	507	502	514	500		489		374		321					
Edwardsville	3979	3364	619	513	274	243	228	188	203		250		206		206		106		100	
Effingham	540	634	605	564	525	676	646	634	616		674		634		361		187		75	
El Dorado	11504	10510	12308	12523	11037	10045	10311	9500	10995	2710	3129	3462	3466	3518	3339	4573	1411	500	680	
El Paso						256					235									
Elbing	184	175	128	105	98	101	110	128	230		175		100				55			
Elgin	118	139	115	148	212	356	446	446	600		400		298		156		357			
Elk											45		45							
Elk City	334	404	432	498	524	680	607	635	725		659		709	770	796	671	383	250	225	
Elk Falls	122	151	124	179	276	294	288	255	293		271		383	306	350	565	513		315	
Elkhart	2318	2243	2089	1780	1132	902	1435	1138	1160											
Ellinwood	2329	2508	2416	2729	2569	2059	1115	1155	1103	1032	976	875	760	692	684	553	352			
Ellis	1814	2062	2137	2218	2649	2042	1957	1932	1876	1457	1404	1291	932	1017	1107		689			
Ellsworth	2294	2465	2080	2361	2193	2227	2072	1954	2065	1982	2041	1800	1549	1415	1620	1584	929		360	
Elmdale	83	109	102	114	180	239	246	229	248		253		297		350		95			
Elmo	35	30				250	146				225		100							
Elsmore	91	104	116	128	152	180	203	208	237		216		330	326	377		323		180	
Elwood	1079	1275	1283	1191	1020	1014	849	780	750		636		623	395						

POPULATION HISTORY OF KANSAS CITIES AND TOWNS 1860-1990

COMMUNITY	1990	1980	1970	1960	1950	1940	1930	1925	1920	1915	1910	1905	1900	1895	1890	1885	1880	1875	1870	1860
Emmett	165	223	156	128	143	191	268	221	217		141									
Empire											982		2258	838	923	641	1367			
Emporia	25512	25287	23327	18190	15669	13188	14067	12243	11273	10664	9058	8974	8223	8258	7551	7759	4631	2194	2168	
Englevale	30				150	165	150	262	416		140		140							
Englewood	96	111	158	243	341	377	477	437	466		518		181		175					
Ensign	192	209	237	255	227	202	244		320		41									
Enterprise	865	839	868	1015	795	671	764	748	975		706		798	935	804	802	411		180	
Erie	1276	1415	1414	1309	1296	1286	1184	1361	1167	1202	1300	1483	1111	1225	1176	1337	270		418	
Esbon	167	234	206	237	278	292	319	344	375		347		555							
Eskridge	518	603	589	519	601	648	726	634	759		797		612	554	548		114		100	
Eudora	3006	2934	2071	1526	929	603	599	591	627		640		640	640	618	650	572		375	
Eureka	2974	3425	3576	4055	3958	3803	3698	3575	2606	2261	2333	2412	2091	2188	2259	2207	1127	400	740	
Everest	310	331	304	348	363	375	386	370	403		436		502	490	478	357	357			
Everett																165				
Excelsior																175				
Fairlawn																150				
Fairmount	75	60	135	135			150	86	113		99		107		168		138		100	
Fairview	306	258	283	272	336	333	367	360	386		386		395		68					
Fairway	4173	4619	5227	5398	1816															
Fall River	113	173	191	226	261	336	339	348	376		383		371	366	454		102			
Falun											200									
Fame																				
Farlington	100	90		100	96	134	140	114	211		211		211		320		150			
Farmington	25	45		250	700								46		46		75			
Farms																	300			
Florence	636	729	777	853	1009	1329	1493	1777	1517	1258	1168	1076	1178	1474	1229	1297	954		330	
Fontana	131	173	160	138	168	174	187	197	206		246		237	248	256		174		50	
Ford	247	272	246	252	244	296	382	259	272		205		82	86	148					
Formoso	128	166	180	192	271	293	381	344	374		453		318		102					
Fort Dodge	450	450	450	550	500	550	547		515		450		450						427	
Fort Harker																136			293	
Fort Hays																	200		320	
Fort Larned																			179	
Fort Leavenworth		2147	8060	7000	4000	4814	5327	2550	5025		2500		2000			628	1122		1975	166
Fort Riley	112		2310		2531	2208	2767		2650		2500		1000			396	168		560	320
Fort Riley North	12848	16086	12469																	
Fort Scott	8362	8839	8967	9410	10335	10557	10763	11763	10693	11422	10463	12248	10322	11108	11946	7867	5372	4572	4174	262
Fort Wallace											125						85			127
Fostoria													60		220		200			
Fourth Creek																				

POPULATION HISTORY OF KANSAS CITIES AND TOWNS 1860-1990

COMMUNITY	1860	1870	1875	1880	1885	1890	1895	1900	1905	1910	1915	1920	1925	1930	1940	1950	1960	1970	1980	1990
Fowler						148		90		473		490	470	724	563	778	717	588	592	571
Frankfort		150		652	1013	1053	1084	1167	1300	1426	1256	1314	1330	1346	1243	1237	1106	960	1038	927
Franklin										150	1649	1819	1440	1683	650	600	600	620	400	500
Frederick						123		126		151		145	130	135	84	53	48	39	29	18
Fredonia		555	555	923	1427	1515	1638	1650	2255	3040	3473	3954	3463	3446	3524	3257	3233	3080	3047	2599
Freedom				300																
Freeport				200		138	54	83		161		56	111	105	67	30	31	21		
Frontenac						600	951	1805	2790	3396	3338	3225	3002	2085	1766	1569	1713	2223	2586	2588
Fruitland																		500	400	
Fulda				200																
Fuller										351										
Fulton				263		506	438	424		416		411	408	393	309	243	207	213	194	191
Galatia								65		65		59	162	194	150	89	73	78	69	47
Galena					1378	2496	2882	10155	6449	6096	5926	4712	4786	4736	4375	4029	3827	3712	3587	3308
Galesburg				63		241		236		183		205	171	199	165	189	128	146	181	160
Galva				87		255	228	300		322		350	273	358	465	426	442	522	651	651
Garden City				250	378	1490		1590	1267	3171	3016	3848	4099	6121	6285	10905	11811	14790	18256	24097
Garden Plain						300		225		296		361	297	336	323	323	560	678	775	731
Gardner		180				515	391	475		514		514	511	493	510	676	1619	1839	2392	3191
Garfield				100		175		175		333		368	355	451	335	297	278	261	277	236
Garland						276		276		276				380	250	250			60	100
Garnett	237	1219	1048	1389	2107	2191	2145	2078	2121	2334	1999	2329	2464	2768	2607	2693	3034	3169	3310	3210
Garrison				145		245		160		150		135		149	116	80	80			
Gas								90		1281		367	328	326	357	294	342	438	543	505
Gaylord		50		231	333	314	271	302		308		356	310	291	245	231	239	211	203	173
Geary City	91	102				52		35		52										
Gem				200						250		259		200	125	118	116	80	101	104
Geneseo						399	283	466		566		561	538	536	632	660	558	453	496	382
Gettysburg				150																
Geuda Springs						355	186	218		254		266	344	340	275	245	223	223	217	219
Girard		695	695	1289	2410	2541	2703	2473	2513	2446	2917	3161	3102	2442	2554	2426	2350	2591	2888	2794
Glade										200		218		218	200	107	133	180	131	101
Glasco		75		207		461	415	509		720		724	693	707	741	803	812	767	710	556
Glen Elder		100		165		407	354	481		565		615	616	617	555	582	444	422	491	448
Glenwood				200				50												
Goddard				50		210		225		225		255	235	255	248	274	533	955	1427	1804
Goessal								27		150		116		129	200	270	327	386	421	506
Goff						182	339	365		422		398	407	437	339	315	259	207	196	156
Goode				200																
Goodland						1027	988	1059	1410	1993	1742	2664	2887	3626	3306	4690	4459	5510	5708	4983

POPULATION HISTORY OF KANSAS CITIES AND TOWNS 1860-1990

COMMUNITY	1990	1980	1970	1960	1950	1940	1930	1925	1920	1915	1910	1905	1900	1895	1890	1885	1880	1875	1870	1860
Goodman	284																			
Gorham		355	379	429	385	385	238		219		155		76		76					
Gould					375	295											306			
Gove City	103	148	172	228	206	284	241	169	132		196		162	128	118					
Grainfield	357	417	374	389	371	341	343	352	290		309		115		99		77			
Grand Prairie																	200			
Grandview			250																	
Grandview Plaza	1233	1189	734	450																
Grantville	225	215	190	168	100	100	100				103		103		103					
Grasshopper Falls																			603	202
Great Bend	15427	16608	16133	16670	12665	9044	5548	5389	4460	4751	4622	3365	2470	2134	2450	1498	1071			
Greeley	339	405	368	415	436	387	504	465	496		492		394	450	514	491	285	400	330	
Green	150	155	163	190	219	246	293	295	297		289		198	219	138		100		145	
Greenleaf	353	462	448	562	614	739	660	767	778		781		854	827	916	877	316			
Greensburg	1792	1885	1907	1988	1723	1417	1338	1168	1215	1298	1199	486	343	387	515		300			
Greenvale															35		200			
Greenwich Heights	900	600	120	350							72									
Grenola	256	335	290	349	380	517	552	571	547		532		666	582	608	787				
Gridley	356	404	328	321	360	418	434	586	321		283		243	106	146					
Grinnell	348	410	449	396	364	289	303	284	162		250		100		152					
Grinter			500																	
Gross	30	60	100	100	142	142	275	480	316											
Grove City																	200			
Gypsum	365	423	391	593	523	615	638	611	732		623		552	620	530					
Haddam	195	239	289	311	375	384	381	404	392		408		355	357	419		93			
Hallowell	120	150	160	160	225	205					210		210		300					
Halstead	2015	1994	1716	1598	1328	1397	1373	1238	1163	1040	1004	754	914	694	1071	802	200		100	
Halton																	205			
Hamilton	301	363	349	400	456	519	549	437	398		325		296		206					
Hamlin	50	80	95	99	118	174	183	208	211		208		258		216		135		100	
Hanover	696	802	793	773	854	896	880	951	947	1030	1039	1064	987	938	903	979	578		210	
Hanston/Olney	326	257	282	279	286	251	254		219		177		41							
Hardtner	198	336	300	372	373	313	341	385	385		297									
Harlan	45	45		91	125	120	200				175		60		109		100			
Harper	1735	1823	1665	1899	1672	1695	1485	1527	1770	1458	1638	1432	1151	1068	1579	2769	1760			
Harris	39	80	41	36	84	127	134	97	241		250		233		230		350			
Harrison															52					
Hartford	541	551	478	337	395	491	516	549	575		589		553	558	441		500			
Hartland							50		46		80		139		193		100			
Harts Mill																	150			

POPULATION HISTORY OF KANSAS CITIES AND TOWNS 1860-1990

COMMUNITY	1860	1870	1875	1880	1885	1890	1895	1900	1905	1910	1915	1920	1925	1930	1940	1950	1960	1970	1980	1990
Harveyville						112		213		331		333	282	321	302	236	204	279	280	267
Havana				100		102		179		227		318	279	289	253	215	162	144	169	121
Haven						273		221		528		1301	530	553	653	720	982	1146	1125	1198
Havensville				180		374	260	437		412		333	293	263	232	208	166	163	183	135
Haviland						126	73	88		568		607	617	641	499	606	725	705	770	624
Hayne										1136										
Haynesville					265															
Hays		320		850		1242	979	1136	1711	1961	2339	3165	4444	4618	6385	8625	11947	15396	16301	17767
Haysville				50				50		50		50		50		105	5836	6531	8006	8364
Hazelton						319	174	143		315		281	281	299	260	250	246	176	143	128
Healy								60		175		219		219	250	200	251	251	250	250
Hepler						269	261	215		276		241	241	210	259	224	178	152	165	150
Herington						1353	1446	1607	3052	3273	4255	4065	4010	4519	3804	3775	3702	3165	2930	2685
Herkimer						128		186		225					170	160			90	100
Herndon								118		273		411	461	430	448	321	339	268	220	170
Hesston							75	72		340		189	425	526	403	686	1103	1926	3013	3012
Hewins								77		225				225	200	100			35	50
Hiattville						288	146	170		225		200		200	125	150	150		60	100
Hiawatha		713	713	1375	2248	2486	3062	2829	3017	2974	2878	3222	3202	3302	3238	3294	3391	3365	3702	3603
Highland	120	282		441		493	576	780		763		809	601	788	764	717	755	899	954	942
Highland Station						178		130												
Hill City				100		545	348	468		983		732	919	1027	1115	1432	2421	2071	2028	1835
Hillsboro		105		133	575	555	649	754	738	1134	1223	1451	1462	1458	1580	2150	2441	2730	2717	2704
Hillsdale				157		457		331		260		283		214	142	150	180	250	250	300
Hodgeman						52		52		52				124	225					
Hoisington						446	611	789	1414	1975	2089	2395	2926	3001	3719	4012	4248	3710	3678	3182
Holcomb										75		64		64	130	206	258	272	816	1400
Hollenberg				167		166		109		169		210		229	128	97	55	47	57	28
Holliday						79		150		150				163						
Hollis						142		50		50				94						
Holmdel Gardens																1248	1436	1960		
Holton		650	650	1500	1899	2727	3020	3082	3555	2842	2666	2703	2668	2705	2885	2705	3028	3063	3132	3196
Holyrood				75		200		266		361		421	470	432	559	748	737	593	567	492
Home				50		134		163		200		218		237	275	200	143	120	125	150
Hope				60		632	503	557		567		589	554	556	500	480	463	438	468	404
Horace						150		90		189		212	208	230	234	258	195	137	137	168
Horton						3316	3157	3398	3936	3600	3839	4009	4212	4049	2872	2354	2361	2177	2130	1885
Howard		125		683	1302	1015	1063	1207	1079	1163	1080	1060	1166	1069	1170	1149	1017	918	965	815
Hoxie				300		245	203	250		532		616	747	800	957	1157	1289	1419	1462	1342
Hoyt						300		250		293		282	279	228	238	246	283	420	536	489

POPULATION HISTORY OF KANSAS CITIES AND TOWNS 1860-1990

COMMUNITY	1860	1870	1875	1880	1885	1890	1895	1900	1905	1910	1915	1920	1925	1930	1940	1950	1960	1970	1980	1990
Hudson								54		253		235	216	197	221	194	201	181	157	159
Hugoton						136		54		105		644	817	1368	1349	2781	2912	2739	3165	3179
Humboldt		1202	1141	1542	2045	1361	1474	1402	2329	2548	2131	2525	2812	2558	2290	2308	2285	2249	2230	2178
Hunnewell				300		168	132	233		208		209	216	205	166	103	83	77	86	87
Hunter										50		205	211	219	199	236	229	150	135	116
Huron				259		325		200		200		188	155	149	163	128	119	106	107	75
Hutchison		1040	1040	1540	4251	8682	8515	9397	11215	16364	19200	23298	25970	27085	30013	33575	37574	36885	40284	39308
Idana							123	175		225		225		225	170	115	103	100	40	100
Independence		435		2915	4115	3127	3663	4851	11206	10480	12144	11920	10900	12782	11565	11335	11222	10347	10598	9942
Industry						225		154		250										
Indianola				200																
Ingalls						87	67	176		250		213		273	187	173	174	235	274	301
Inman							264	352		484		482	412	533	507	615	729	836	947	1035
Iola		960	600	1096	1614	1706	1565	5791	10287	9032	7866	8513	7990	7160	7244	7094	6885	6493	6938	6351
Ionia				135		152		187		250						179	120	100	80	50
Iowa Point	310	242		187		250		150		150		228		108		110	46		30	30
Irving		125		257	357	375	342	366		409		341	362	356	310	279	47			
Isabel				114		257				222		277	293	279	252	205	181	147	137	104
Iuka				101	257		312	69		228		198	147	185	183	129	225	210	235	197
Jamestown						372		400		462		495	502	507	490	494	422	470	440	325
Jefferson								55												
Jennings				150		200		139		259		253	235	344	311	330	292	224	194	188
Jetmore				130		324	258	230		317		559	569	914	881	988	1028	936	862	850
Jewell		210		372	710	702	619	736	1022	839		805	769	707	669	593	582	569	589	529
Jimtown				200																
Johnson City						143		150		100		62	212	514	524	994	860	1038	1244	1348
Junction City		1782	1782	2684		4502	4769	4695	5264	5598	5798	7533	6699	7407	8507	13462	18700	19018	19305	20604
Jurrett				400																
Kackley										250				135						
Kanapolis				125		272	205	240		577		762	805	860	868	743	732	626	729	605
Kanorado										175		210	324	359	322	285	245	278	217	276
Kansas City				3200	3802	38316	40676	51418	67614	82331	91658	101177	116053	121857	121458	129553	121901	168213	161087	149767
Kechi				150				50		125		75		82	200	160	245	229	288	517
Kedron										250										
Kelly																				
Kendall						67	67	67		75		60		65	150	125	160	160	110	250
Kenneth										24										
Kensington							247	350		497		595	520	546	597	635	619	653	681	553
Key				200																
Keysville				200																

POPULATION HISTORY OF KANSAS CITIES AND TOWNS 1860-1990

COMMUNITY	1990	1980	1970	1960	1950	1940	1930	1925	1920	1915	1910	1905	1900	1895	1890	1885	1880	1875	1870	1860
Kickapoo											200									
Kimbal											165		165				219			
Kimeo											50		50				140			
Kincaid	170	192	189	220	309	431	380	441	443		426		364	299	284		300			
Kingman	3196	3563	3622	3582	3200	3213	2752	2403	2407	2255	2570	2116	1785	1700	2390					
Kings Gardens		400	500	400	400															
Kingsdown											150									
Kinsley	1875	2074	2212	2263	2479	2178	2270	1917	1986	1794	1547	1132	780	703	771	623	457			
Kiowa	1160	1409	1414	1674	1561	1579	1501	1441	1539		1520		765	373	893		42			
Kipp	100	70			100	100	162				150		60							
Kirkwood	100	115	250	250		592	500	559	553		626		586	502	689	824	807			
Kirwin	269	249	293	356	374	227	169	168	69		100		260		261		260		135	
Kismet	421	368	294	150	180	140	141		207		300									
Labette	74	123	105	114	145															
La Crosse	1427	1618	1583	1767	1769	1407	1355	899	808		806		536	428	513		178			
La Cygne	1066	1025	989	810	794	932	1019	950	1028		957		1037	943	1135	1081	835	600	820	
La Fontaine	125	150	150	150	168	190					250		212		212					
La Harpe	650	687	509	529	511	624	756	997	1001	1182	2080	2757	610							
Lake City	70	70			165	200					250		162		162					
Lake Quivira	983	1087	959	450																
Lakeshore	1370	700																		
Lakin	2060	1823	1570	1432	1618	709	739	579	556		337		259	352	258				75	
Lancaster	299	274	279	196	200	163	188	192	184		220		292		238		166			
Lane	247	249	254	282	200	234	291	278	351		272		483		310		61			
Langdon	62	84	93	97	128	208	181	181	204		216		200							
Lansing	7120	5307	3797	1264	1100	812	860		682		824		650	629	1468		933			
Larned	4490	4811	4567	5001	4447	3533	3532	3141	3139	2900	2911	1998	1583	1566	1861	1507	1066		240	
Latham	160	148	156	203	218	307	291	242	334		364		268		268					
Latimer	20	31	29	40	34	84	124		113											
Lawrence	65608	52738	45698	32858	23351	14390	13726	12341	12456	12884	12374	11708	10862	10084	9997	10685	8510	7268	8320	1645
Le Roy	568	701	551	601	695	751	788	797	815		861		772	830	893	685	545		410	222
Leavenworth	38495	33656	25147	22052	20579	19220	17466	20889	16912	22090	19363	20934	20735	20822	19768	19286	16546	15136	17873	7429
Leawood	19693	13360	10645	7466	1167															
Lebanon	364	440	517	583	610	652	723	731	822		731		590	342	301		100			
Lebo	835	966	589	498	575	522	590	612	572		560		605	532	538					
Lecompton	619	576	434	304	263	250	288	307	310		386		408	413	450	653	284		105	
Lehigh	180	189	168	178	240	296	315	371	370		385		254		425	516	416		75	
Lenexa	34034	18699	5549	2487	803	502	452	401	472		382		231		173		102			
Lenora	329	444	439	512	511	537	519	556	268		454		247	216	231		34			
Leon	707	667	510	541	518	573	587	476	427		494		527	487	456		113			

POPULATION HISTORY OF KANSAS CITIES AND TOWNS 1860-1990

COMMUNITY	1990	1980	1970	1960	1950	1940	1930	1925	1920	1915	1910	1905	1900	1895	1890	1885	1880	1875	1870	1860
Leona	39	73	72	110	130	164	285		268		275		250		171		135			
Leonardville	374	437	412	378	320	342	392	326	325		376		335	355	410		300			
Leoti	1738	1869	1916	1401	1250	816	618	471	392		288		151		341					
Levant	85	150	115	115		160	113													
Lewis	451	551	525	486	475	481	512	391	439		557				100					
Liberal	16573	14911	13862	13813	7134	4410	5294	3372	3613	2314	1716	530	426							
Liberty	140	174	185	233	185	254	246	266	247		385		314	311	344		93		75	
Liebenthal	112	163	169	191	211	265	268		362		125									
Limestone																			360	
Lincoln Center	1381	1599	1582	1717	1636	1761	1732	1630	1613	1142	1508	1322	1262	652	1100	470	422		150	
Lincolnville	197	235	218	244	228	255	270	235	260		258		143		97					
Lindsborg	3076	3155	2764	2609	2383	1913	2016	2077	1897	1953	1939	1927	1279	1305	968	885	466		150	
Linn	472	483	388	466	395	395	340	264	282		277		225	190	323		125			
Linwood	409	343	323	375	261	299	295	442	364		323		349	308	306					
Litchfield													100	416	835		100			
Little River	496	529	493	552	635	603	618	641	749		661		457		340		100			
Logan	633	720	760	846	859	703	743	750	585		714		449	329	390	300	275			
Lone Elm	32	55	66	69	82	97	131	133	160		150		118		122					135
Longford	68	109	99	146	178	160	200	188	155		159		150							
Long Island	170	187	195	229	247	257	242	246	286		291		337		374		100			
Longton	389	396	304	401	478	629	744	699	583		611		564	548	624	590	255		165	
Lorette																	250			
Loring											31		31		31					
Lorraine	147	157	153	157	195	236	177	205	218		204		176				300			
Lost Springs	106	94	103	139	184	255	265	203	261		276		200		137					
Louisburg	1964	1744	1033	862	677	590	616	589	556		603		665	615	760	933	499		285	
Louisville	215	207	204	204	190	188	227	213	207		246		336	343	382	417	432		344	
Lovewell											200									
Lowell	300	300	300	300	200	200	200		164		156		237		156					
Lucas	452	524	524	559	631	648	630	606	651		573		277	117	183		157		150	
Luddell	90	90	100	100	100	200							103							
Luray	261	295	303	328	351	392	464	469	475		341		150		103					
Lyman					250															
Lyndon	964	1132	958	953	729	751	742	852	732		763		1004	941	935	807	500		165	
Lyons	3688	4152	4355	4592	4545	4497	2939		2516		2071		1736		1754		509			
McCraken	231	292	333	406	553	534	594	566	491		371		312	202	281					
McCune	462	528	487	433	532	556	584	579	591		736		657	706	700	846	170			
McDonald	184	239	269	323	426	425	442	410	341		350		92							
McFarland	224	242	209	256	279	336	399	386	579		388		83							
Mackie						200														

POPULATION HISTORY OF KANSAS CITIES AND TOWNS 1860-1990

COMMUNITY	1990	1980	1970	1960	1950	1940	1930	1925	1920	1915	1910	1905	1900	1895	1890	1885	1880	1875	1870	1860
Macksville	488	546	484	546	624	723	868	800	753		626		248	195	156					
McLouth	719	700	623	494	477	515	517	435	575		571		529	495	311	301				
McPherson	12422	11753	10851	9996	8689	7194	6147	4209	4595	4057	3546	3348	2996	2666	3172	2530	1590		135	
Madison	845	1099	1061	1105	1212	1198	1488	1439	795		721		683	595	623		123		135	
Mahaska	98	119	122	160	179	195	218	208	210		246		105	115						
Maize	1520	1294	785	623	266	198	229	161	189		200		126							
Makenny					300															
Manchester	80	98	92	153	151	215	241	256	263		250		127							
Manhattan	37712	32644	27575	22993	19056	11659	10136	10112	7989	6816	5722	4205	3438	2980	3004	2735	2105			
Mankato	1037	1205	1287	1231	1462	1425	1404	1508	1326	1054	1155	962	890	767	800	652	506	1381	1173	
Marsfield							224													
Manter	186	205	219	183	200	133	224	146												
Maple Hill	406	381	327	244	176	247	256	248	255		277		130		83		100			
Mapleton	96	121	112	127	213	226	251	239	230		230		166		175		53			
Marienthal	100	100	100	100			162													
Marion	1906	1951	2052	2169	2050	2066	1959	1884	1928	1951	1841	1802	1824	2077	2047	1691	857			
Marquette	593	639	578	607	666	609	714	701	780		715		489	433	367		175		60	
Marvin													173		188		156			
Marysville	3359	3670	3588	4143	3866	4055	4013	3946	3048	2166	2260	2094	2006	2297	1913	1932	1249	1000	300	171
Matfield Green	33	71	77	95	119	146	182	166	213		220		200	197	417		324		195	
Mathewson													25				230			
Mayetta	267	287	246	218	247	275	294	267	309		337		200		103					
Mayfield	110	128	110	119	134	150	187		225		200		130		67					
Mayview											35		35				250			
Meade	1526	1777	1899	2019	1763	1400	1552	902	838		664		326	266	457		150			
Media													150							
Medicine Lodge	2453	2384	2545	3072	2288	1670	1655	1139	1305	1304	1229	1037	917	659	1095	700	373		197	
Medina	100	100				200	210						40		76					
Melrose											175		100							
Melvern	423	481	455	376	389	368	445	606	422		505		469	413	461	525	103			
Menlo	50	42	48	99	113	144	204		113		225		78							
Meriden	622	707	472	402	378	421	390	371	422		467		433	546	441	574	277		100	
Merriam	11821	19794	10955	5084	1649	336			350		127		106		127					
Michigan Valley					270	200	113													
Midian																				
Midland				300									164							
Midland Park	1200	1350	400																	
Midway							557		525		400		356	352	246					
Milan	109	135	162	144	165	224	198	221	222		240		229		229		50			
Milburn					200	350														

POPULATION HISTORY OF KANSAS CITIES AND TOWNS 1860-1990

COMMUNITY	1990	1980	1970	1960	1950	1940	1930	1925	1920	1915	1910	1905	1900	1895	1890	1885	1880	1875	1870	1860
Mildred	46	64	42	60	79	155	341	487	336		236									
Milford	384	465	296	318	284	271	300		262		250		200		250		118		135	
Milton	85	95			110	163	163				150		54		108		250			
Miltonvale	484	588	718	814	911	800	814	784	821		829		396	412	591		500			
Minneapolis	1983	2075	1971	2024	1801	2087	1741	1795	1842	1922	1895	1772	1727	1559	1756	1779	1084		225	
Minneola	705	712	630	679	660	490	617	487	493		348		30							
Mission	9504	8643	8125	4626	6500	1152														
Mission Hills	3446	3904	4198	3621	1275		600													
Mission Woods	182	213	237	243	205															
Missouri Flat																	521			
Moline	473	553	555	698	871	870	897	861	950		808		695	618	527		79			
Monmouth											179		179		179	608				
Mont Ida							119				200		139		73				100	
Montana											180		212		153		123			
Montezuma	838	730	606	543	509	340	424	200	163											
Monticello	70	115	150	150	141	141					63		63		63		150			
Monument											150		50		74		150			
Moran	551	643	550	549	616	592	651	681	676		559		464	515	463					
Morganville	181	261	257	226	278	264	281	276	262		285		350		233		206			
Morland	234	223	300	317	287	356	385	409	296		237		100							
Morrill	399	336	308	299	362	387	519	567	552		398		400	344	308		186			
Morrowville	173	180	201	195	229	308	246		213		210		100							
Moscow	252	228	228	211	222	177	249	190	163											
Mound City	789	755	714	661	707	703	655	675	720		698		809	780	888	940	443	1323	635	
Mound Valley	405	381	467	481	566	648	666	722	803		956		533	646	545		138		75	
Moundridge	1531	1453	1271	1214	942	864	870	724	733		626		557	404	443					
Mount Hope	805	791	665	539	473	442	466	497	513		519	519	327	251	241		105			
Mount Muncie																	182			
Mulberry	555	647	622	642	779	1175	1596	2298	2697	1662	997	448	341		343				60	
Mullinville	289	339	376	385	410	428	436	400	361		289		75	72	79					
Mulvane	4674	4254	3185	2981	1387	940	1042	1143	1239	1024	1084	696	667	614	724		215			
Munjor	250	260	230	230	150		113				100		100				215			
Murdock	75	85	100	100	100	140	162													
Munden	143	152	123	177	169	193	205	214	339		275		115							
Muscotah	194	248	206	228	248	331	365	376	427		491		462		524	538	412		225	
Narka	113	120	130	166	220	193	252	228	207		278		258							
Nashville	118	127	107	137	159	212	234	204	219		200		50							
Natoma	392	515	603	775	775	651	583	607	518		407		221							
Navarre	55	85				125	213				75		35		35					
Neal	70	90		99	150	150	178		162		150		136		144					

POPULATION HISTORY OF KANSAS CITIES AND TOWNS 1860-1990

COMMUNITY	1990	1980	1970	1960	1950	1940	1930	1925	1920	1915	1910	1905	1900	1895	1890	1885	1880	1875	1870	1860
Nelson											419									
Neodesha	2837	3414	3295	3594	3723	3376	3381	3626	3943	3011	2872	3470	1772	1783	1528	1095	924	655	665	
Neosho Falls	157	157	184	222	355	452	462	621	628		571		763	952	606	689	552	400	532	
Neosho Rapids	235	289	234	178	204	255	306	241	267		256		264	420	308		80		180	
Ness City	1724	1769	1756	1653	1612	1355	1509	1003	905		712		505		869		100			
Netawaka	167	218	192	225	213	226	229	235	267		250		330	266	267	353	253			
New Albany	60	78	59	104	152	165	150	158	223		213		261		227		232		120	
New Cambria	152	175	160	187	160	144	130	153	127		185		212		212		47			
New Gottland																	350			
New London																	180			
New Murdock													100							
New Pittsburg															156		624			
New Strawn /Strawn	428	457	81	64	150	187	169		169											
Newton	16700	16332	15439	14877	11590	11048	11034	9831	9781	7620	7862	6601	6208	5148	5605	5128	2601	769	769	
Nickerson	1137	1292	1187	1091	1013	1052	1052	1081	1049	1167	1195	1024	1038	1560	1162	1503	597			
Niles	65	75				200	215				200		103		51					
Niotaze	99	104	83	124	162	241	235	230	186		317		150							
Noble																				
Norcatur	198	226	284	302	368	440	524	526	476		482		194	176	165					
North Branch																				
North Newton	1262	1222	963	890	566	130	134				125		100							
North Wichita											220									
Norton	3017	3400	3627	3345	3060	2762	2767	2276	2186	1513	1787	1441	1202	914	1074	609	634		105	
Nortonville	643	692	727	595	568	562	606	659	696		638		700	686	669		350			
Norway	50	100	100	98	100		112	91	113		150		58		58					
Norwich	455	476	414	430	378	411	477	415	430		392		311	306	301		200			
Oak Hill	13	35	41	69	92	147	147		216		250		103		103					
Oak Valley	25			50	60	94	238		219		149		202		202					
Oakland							2473	2333	1721	1651	1465		50			287	100			
Oaklawn	4200	4200	5000	5000																
Oakley	2045	2343	2327	2190	1915	1138	1159	931	768		681		269	160	176					
Oberlin	2197	2387	2291	2337	2019	1378	1629	1404	1247	1019	1157	1132	937	718	976					
Odell	120	120	150	150																
Odin					105						30									
Offerle	228	244	212	208	269	273	298	239	225		200		88				39			
Ogden	1494	1804	1491	1780	845	494	418	352	596		230		232	167	173					
Oil Hill					501	400														
Oketo	116	130	133	128	169	218	225	220	225		253		347	338	334		50			
Olathe	63352	37258	17917	10987	5593	3979	3656	3372	3268	3335	3272	3183	3451	3456	3294	3021	2285	2146	1817	

POPULATION HISTORY OF KANSAS CITIES AND TOWNS 1860-1990

COMMUNITY	1990	1980	1970	1960	1950	1940	1930	1925	1920	1915	1910	1905	1900	1895	1890	1885	1880	1875	1870	1860
Olivet	59	65	64	116	127	172	145		280		200		46							
Olmitz	130	140	161	141	125	130	166	158	189		165		76		76					
Olpe	431	477	453	722	293	331	317	246	235		215		131		123					
Olsburg	192	166	151	137	140	177	175	175	213		182		188	181	185					
Onaga	761	752	761	850	882	741	930	779	838		759		598	519	423	475	242			
Oneida	79	120	112	119	138	187	224	233	276		211		279	353	311	349	163			
Opolis	130	165	160	150	160	180	150	187	237		185		175	169	178		135			
Oronoque							95				200									
Osage City	2689	2667	2600	2213	1919	2079	2402	2957	2376	2823	2432	2937	2792	4273	3469	3633	2098	1062	1062	
Osawatomie	4590	4459	4294	4622	4347	4145	4440	3560	4772	2870	4046	3889	4191	2612	2662	543	681		135	
Osborne	1778	2120	1980	2049	2068	1876	1881	1810	1635	1601	1566	1352	1075	991	1174	1072	719		225	
Oskaloosa	1074	1092	955	807	721	800	733	719	700		851		978	869	773	759	725		640	
Oswego	1870	2218	2200	2027	1997	1953	1845	2039	2386	2258	2317	2228	2208	2145	2574	2511	2351	1212	1196	631
Otis	385	410	387	362	410	413	407	381	505		328		100							
Ottawa	10667	11016	11036	10673	10081	10193	9563	8498	9018	9127	7650	7727	6934	7059	6248	6626	4032	2595	2941	
Ottumwa											139		337	273	139		125		263	
Overbrook	920	930	748	509	387	428	588		472		580				172					113
Overland Park	111790	81784	77934	21110	5000	1500	1600				150									
Oxford	1143	1125	1113	989	798	1020	1129	828	748		624		567	549	665	663	403		195	
Ozawkie/Osawki	403	472	137	195	204	288	240		240		290		219		308	311	144		135	
Padonia											104		104		150					
Palco	295	329	398	575	405	276	290	278	281		279		110							
Palermo									279				279							
Palmer	121	149	166	169	150	182	187	150	179		209		305	222	203				138	151
Paola	4698	4557	4662	4784	3972	3511	3762	3425	3238	3392	3207	3636	3144	3000	2943	2932	2312	1523	1811	
Paradise	66	89	145	134	145	161	178	191	260		97		52							
Park City (Gove)	150	183	178	218	223	156					60		60							
Park City (Sedgewick)	5050	3778	2529	2687																
Parker	256	270	255	181	251	361	364	375	436		398		306						210	
Parkerville	28	42	25	59	78	105	127	123	144		157		146	152	202	191	250		105	
Parsons	11924	12898	13015	13929	14750	14294	14903	14839	16028	12118	12463	11720	7682	7573	6736	7245	4199	2120	2120	
Partridge	213	268	302	221	221	226	270	250	253		246		184		204					
Paw Paw																	150			
Pawnee Rock	367	409	442	380	359	388	399	429	428		458		210	164	204		84			
Paxico	174	168	216	276	196	237	261	279	784		234		209		174					
Peabody	1349	1474	1368	1309	1194	1367	1491	1786	2455	1401	1416	1276	1369	1361	1474	1588	1087		620	
Penalosa	21	31	32	84	71	118	128	150	162		200									
Perry	881	907	664	495	399	392	418	438	481		400		464	440	372	405	319		403	
Perth	60	80			240	300	219				150		115							

POPULATION HISTORY OF KANSAS CITIES AND TOWNS 1860-1990

COMMUNITY	1860	1870	1875	1880	1885	1890	1895	1900	1905	1910	1915	1920	1925	1930	1940	1950	1960	1970	1980	1990
Peru		135		135		322		218		575		570	620	628	487	368	340	289	286	206
Peterton				226		426	555	307		225									75	100
Petrolia										200				216	200	125	125	125	75	100
Pfeifer								150		150				60		200			100	100
Phillipsburg				309	316	992	916	1008	1285	1302	1237	1310	1582	1543	2139	2589	3233	3241	3229	2828
Piedmont						110		175		250		182		182	200	130	190	116	100	230
Pierceville				75		137		60		150							120	120	180	100
Piper								75		75					221	305	100	733	730	100
Piqua								145		225				258	258	258	150	150	75	100
Pittsburg				624	2605	6697	8982	10112	15012	14755	17685	18052	19182	18145	17571	19341	18678	20171	18770	17775
Plains /West Plains				100		62		50		330		361	424	883	619	718	780	857	1044	957
Plainville				39		347	308	378	1005	1090	1008	1004	1054	1058	1232	2082	3104	2627	2458	2173
Pleasant Grove				300		27		45		45										
Pleasant View				160		27														
Pleasanton				709	1479	1139	990	1097	1559	1373	1516	1291	1229	1214	1227	1178	1098	1216	1303	1231
Plevna			500	300		93		93		182		202	173	174	61	200	117	124	115	117
Plum Grove															150					
Pollard																				
Polk																	100	200	60	60
Pomeroy				250		74		100												
Pomona			195	259	512	466	561	547		523		485	436	501	485	453	489	541	868	835
Pontiac				300		29		29		65				34						
Portis				143				160		304		390	345	340	349	286	232	178	172	129
Potter								100		250				184	360	150	100	100	160	115
Potwin				100		143		143		249		415	460	427	487	465	635	497	563	448
Powhattan						100		237		216		247	282	221	184	150	128	111	95	111
Prairie View						46		78		191		183	192	198	205	192	188	201	145	111
Prairie Village																5359	25356	28378	24657	23186
Pratt					569	1418	1330	1213	1346	3302	3739	5183	5245	6322	6591	7523	8156	6736	6885	6687
Prescott				151		241		298		255		291	262	238	277	283	278	222	319	301
Preston/Haynesvil						147		210		278		401	383	383	328	307	278	239	227	177
Pretty Prairie				55		78		262		327		432	413	429	452	484	525	561	655	601
Princeton				103		126		303		270		252	191	210	187	177	174	159	244	275
Protection						110		72		390		1109	1011	1072	846	814	780	673	684	625
Quaker																150				
Quenemo				122	410	643	608	682		556		733	575	564	557	391	434	429	413	369
Quincy								95							225	150			60	50
Quindaro				700		220		500		500				530	500	500	500			
Quinter						260		100		450		383	494	570	481	741	776	930	951	945

POPULATION HISTORY OF KANSAS CITIES AND TOWNS 1860-1990

COMMUNITY	1860	1870	1875	1880	1885	1890	1895	1900	1905	1910	1915	1920	1925	1930	1940	1950	1960	1970	1980	1990
Radium												34		37	85	64	64	65	47	47
Radley										75	1183	2096	700	400	250	250	170	170	150	100
Rago								66		125				125	200	150			60	40
Ramona						239		43		265		303	270	240	236	190	132	170	116	106
Randall								268		325		304	305	262	281	240	201	195	154	96
Randolph		150		262		305	406	372		455		401	389	408	369	391	35	106	131	129
Ransom				100		87		100		204		285	326	431	403	405	387	416	448	386
Rantoul				50		78		178		176		317	208	224	164	197	157	163	212	200
Raymond				208		137		200		150		139		153	163	205	143	133	132	125
Reading		75		93		222	296	304		289		358	396	341	302	289	249	247	244	264
Reamsville						160		100		100										
Redfield						162		193		232		269	236	233	194	173	133	138	185	143
Reece						179		188		200		162		178	246	250	150		80	60
Reno				43		112		112		112					150					50
Republic				50		228	206	241		450		442	437	396	376	360	333	243	223	177
Reserve				146		132		270		153		319	167	197	172	169	138	117	105	108
Rexford								107		300		237	73	375	244	304	245	231	204	171
Richey																703				
Richardson															250	100				
Richfield						164		61		53		62		106	96	105	122	82	81	50
Richland						102		165		275				267	150		170			
Richmond				60		230		313		350		400	481	411	418	433	352	464	510	528
Ridgeway		225						43												
Riley				93		250		300		343		364	357	431	392	414	575	668	779	804
Ringo												50	743	350					35	35
Riverton												96		383	383	250	450	500	550	600
Riverview																		1700	2500	1970
Robinson		120		210	288	343		493		492		500	424	457	413	381	317	278	324	268
Rock						123		100		150					200	200	150	150	125	90
Roeland Park																1373	8949	9760	7962	7706
Rolla												139	212	437	284	433	464	400	417	387
Rolling Hills																	2000			
Rosalia										110		156		218	190	100	90	130	100	150
Rosedale				962	1114	2276	1963	3270	4741	5960	7498	7674							1557	2399
Rose Hill								71		200		139		153	198	200	273	387		
Roseland										396		482		190	181	118	100	113	119	98
Rossville		105		323	478	420	559	555		672		664	688	701	601	577	797	934	1045	1052
Roxbury				200		52		52		100					110	120	150	150	115	100
Roy																				
Rozel										160		210		220	203	233	207	236	219	187

POPULATION HISTORY OF KANSAS CITIES AND TOWNS 1860-1990

COMMUNITY	1860	1870	1875	1880	1885	1890	1895	1900	1905	1910	1915	1920	1925	1930	1940	1950	1960	1970	1980	1990
Rush Center				119	119	214	121	188		178		163		179	184	300	278	237	207	177
Russell		120		861	818	961	952	1143	1165	1692	1601	1700	2452	2352	4819	6483	6113	5371	5427	4781
Russell Springs						117	97	117		82		115	103	141	198	161	93	83	56	29
Rutland				150																
Sabetha		495		849	1352	1368	1488	1646	1857	1768	1856	2003	2210	2332	2241	2173	2318	2376	2286	2341
Saffordville						22		106		200				135	210	125				
St. Bridget				239				51												
St. Francis				206		375		336		492		733	795	944	1041	1892	1594	1725	1610	1495
St. George	78	118		56		149		179		254		211	222	216	203	251	259	241	309	397
St. John						865	732	869	1086	1785	1637	1671	1511	1552	1735	1735	1753	1477	1501	1357
St. Marys		300		884	1200	1174	1196	1390	1227	1397	1031	1321	1216	1304	1132	1201	1509	1434	1598	1791
St. Paul/Osage Mission		791	1230	1306	1508	1097	1057	1047	1017	927		974	714	800	869	783	675	804	746	687
St. Peter								50						263		100			100	50
Salina		918	980	3111	4009	6149	5703	6074	7829	9688	10488	15085	15624	20155	21073	26176	43202	37714	41843	42303
Santa Fe						166		128		200		22		22						
Satanta												263	229	508	345	667	686	1161	1117	1073
Savonburg						158	319	300		257		258	207	230	158	155	131	109	113	93
Sawyer								120		300		263	268	276	239	223	192	164	213	183
Scammon				200		748		1549	2373	2233	2364	1694	1370	1093	737	561	429	457	501	466
Scandia				573	768	653	592	598		579		547	628	608	614	611	643	567	480	421
Schoenchen										200		415		446	259	170	188	182	209	128
Scott City						229		212		918		1112	1273	1544	1848	3204	3555	4001	4154	3785
Scottsville				95		364		364		248		165	132	169	187	108	60	46	56	26
Scranton				835	1613	1572	1449	1099		770		622	627	538	500	487	576	575	664	674
Seabrook															300	450				
Sedan		150		665	1151	970	1085	1067	2211	1211	1454	1885	1556	1776	1948	1640	1677	1555	1579	1306
Sedgewick				415	878	652	611	622		626		731	694	832	738	732	1095	1083	1471	1438
Selden								144		297		280	391	399	431	438	347	271	266	248
Seneca		900		1203	2225	2032	1961	1846	1853	1806	1961	1855	1931	1864	2015	1911	2072	2182	2389	2027
Severence		375		375	424	377	391	424		383		350	329	312	256	197	146	128	134	98
Severy				306		389	379	489		608		551	521	525	570	477	492	384	447	357
Seward						100		108		225		113		127	125	130	92	66	88	71
Shannon								50						2500						
Sharon						304		116		350		325	290	316	296	278	272	265	283	256
Sharon Springs						178		180		440		815	764	792	760	994	966	1012	982	872
Shawnee		300		427		427		336		450		448	460	553	597	845	9072	20946	29653	37993
Sherwin						210		110		110				110						
Sherwood																			400	500
Shorey								400		400					200					

POPULATION HISTORY OF KANSAS CITIES AND TOWNS 1860-1990

COMMUNITY	1860	1870	1875	1880	1885	1890	1895	1900	1905	1910	1915	1920	1925	1930	1940	1950	1960	1970	1980	1990
Silver Creek																				
Silver Lake		159		200	367	256	360	259		260		260	344	336	362	331	392	811	1350	1390
Simpson				268		253		253		211		295	219	273	235	234	149	131	123	107
Sitka				100				90		90				115	250	250				
Skiddy						328														
Smith Center		100		254	342	767	704	1142	1293	1292	1405	1567	1513	1736	1686	2026	2379	2389	2240	2016
Smolan								80		130		119		132	144	180	200	175	169	195
Soldier				98		193		302		358		346	297	274	247	193	171	173	165	135
Solomon		780		618	1002	839	777	817	1003	949	1110	1071	987	1032	872	834	1008	973	1018	939
South Haven				124		465	340	411		483		423	410	442	405	358	408	413	439	420
South Hutchison						321		225		387		639	583	669	915	1045	1672	1879	2226	2444
South Park										50					620	753	1500			
Southridge															350					
Sparks										175										
Spearville				136		460		157		576		629	538	703	603	610	602	738	693	716
Speed								100						139	111	70	75	58	41	64
Spivey						205		134		200		263	178	219	181	109	98	78	83	88
Spring Creek				200		66				252		226								
Spring Hill		400		502	631	573	622	580		605		555	408	566	489	619	909	1186	2005	2191
Spring Valley				150		42		42												
Springdale																				230
Springfield																			160	
Stafford				50	206	640	702	1068	1312	1927	1728	1752	1543	1614	2011	2005	1862	1414	1425	1344
Stanford				200		400		42												
Stanley				44		63		125		200				219	200	200	350	350	200	200
Stanton						173		169		160										
Stark						246		246		191		189	184	197	160	157	96	124	143	79
Sterling				1014	1455	1641	1815	2002	2013	2133	2214	2060	1832	1868	2215	2243	2303	2312	2312	2115
Stemerton				200																
Stilwell								150		200				195	240	240	175	175	185	200
Stippville								200		200										
Stockton		60		411	534	880	789	1030	1037	1317	1291	1324	1440	1291	1418	1867	2073	1818	1825	1507
Strong City				324	961	976	923	1128		762		944	1009	805	848	680	659	545	675	617
Sublette												275	238	673	582	838	1077	1208	1293	1378
Sugar Valley				200																
Summerfield						102	375	505		554		539	431	398	396	305	237	254	225	169
Sun City				81		100		78		130		139		404	305	231	188	119	85	88
Sunflower																	877	1744	1050	
Sunset Park																	1000	750		
Superior				250																

POPULATION HISTORY OF KANSAS CITIES AND TOWNS 1860-1990

COMMUNITY	1860	1870	1875	1880	1885	1890	1895	1900	1905	1910	1915	1920	1925	1930	1940	1950	1960	1970	1980	1990
Susank												110		110	140	100	87	59	52	61
Sutphens Mill				214		46		72		27										
Sycamore						59		319		175					187	187	150	150	175	200
Sylvan Grove						205		220		464		450	571	530	540	506	400	403	376	321
Sylvia							197			634		542	460	540	477	496	402	390	353	308
Syracuse				52		324	413	460		1126		1059	969	1383	1226	2075	1888	1720	1654	1606
Talmage								80		200				181	212		100	100	125	120
Tampa								52		256		262	258	275	222	216	145	154	113	113
Tapley				200																
Tecumseh				169				35		150		210		350	150	107	270	270	350	600
Tescott						209	238	270		421		377	432	382	402	412	396	393	331	317
Thayer		146	146	311	509	544		542		542		528	406	495	461	423	396	430	517	435
Timken								52		50		116		129	170	138	147	123	99	87
Tipton						111		111		200		230	230	294	248	246	252	315	321	267
Tonganoxie		270		426	480	673	800	848		1018		971	1123	1109	1114	1138	1354	1717	1864	2347
Topeka	759	5790	7272	15452	23499	31007	30151	33608	37644	43684	46747	50022	55411	64120	67833	78791	119484	125011	115266	119883
Topsey				200																
Toronto		100		88		552	607	695		627		829	719	706	737	600	524	431	466	317
Torrance						142		30		30										
Towanda				53		156		165		275		718	489	424	374	417	1031	1190	1332	1289
Traer														165	125				35	30
Travel Air										200									680	540
Treece						90	87	62		158		991	1073	749	568	378	280	225	194	172
Tribune										35		243	262	436	607	1010	1036	1013	955	918
Trousdale														162	202	125			50	40
Troy		639		694	702	730	859	947	840	940	1109	1013	986	1042	1049	977	1051	1047	1240	1073
Turner						76		200		200					750	800	1500			
Turon						320		337		572		631	461	576	594	632	559	430	481	393
Tyro								106		603		454	185	272	322	279	289	206	289	243
Udall				85		338	263	282		330		381	410	436	419	410	600	668	891	824
Ulysses						198														
/New Ulysses								90		116		103	387	1140	824	2243	3157	3779	4653	5474
Uniontown		240		136		344	244	293		256		300	280	298	277	232	211	286	371	290
Utica						98		63		243		285	330	382	379	365	322	297	275	208
Valley Center				71		167	301	343		381		486	443	896	700	854	2570	2551	3300	3624
Valley Falls			1000	1016	1335	1180	1172	1078	1056	1129	1244	1218	1239	1238	1241	1139	1193	1169	1189	1253
Vasser								40		75									100	100
Vermillion		75		122		272	253	362		366		294	315	288	300	283	265	191	191	113
Vesper										100									35	25
Victoria				135				118		450		600	496	637	884	988	1170	1246	1328	1157

POPULATION HISTORY OF KANSAS CITIES AND TOWNS 1860-1990

1875: Kansas State Board of Agriculture. Census and Other Statistical Exhibits. Topeka, 1876.

1885: Kansas State Board of Agriculture. Compendium of the Census of the State for the Decennial Period Ending March 1st 1885. Topeka, 1886.

1895: Kansas State Board of Agriculture. State Decennial Census 1895. Topeka, 1896.

1905: Kansas State Board of Agriculture. Decennial Census, 1905. Topeka, 1907.

1915: Kansas State Board of Agriculture. Decennial Census, 1915. Topeka, 1916.

1915: Kansas State Board of Agriculture. Decennial Census, 1925. Topeka, 1926.

POPULATION HISTORY OF MONTANA CITIES AND TOWNS 1863-1990

COMMUNITY	1990	1980	1970	1960	1950	1940	1930	1920	1915	1910	1905	1900	1890	1880	1870	1863
Absarokee	1067	830	700	667	425	400	570	261	250	175						
Adobetown											200	27	100	100		
Alberton	354	368	363	356	326	283	276	310	300	100						
Alder	125	110	100		100	158	158	158	100	125						
Aldridge										400	700	400				
Anaconda	10278	12518	9771	12054	11254	11004	12494	11668	12000	10134	12000	9453	3975	700		
Antelope	130	100	100	150	142	157	142	285	100							
Argenta									75	48	75	48	216	50	47	
Arlee	135	100	100	200	300	450	150	215	200	100	100	100	49			
Armington	75	120		168	163					100		150				
Armstead				250	100		50		100	275						
Ashland	484	200	200	150	153		82	75	100	75		75				
Augusta	420	450	500	500	475	410	300	350	250	375	200	300	50			
Avon	175	150	200	175	120	162	162	162	150	175	100	116	116			
Bainville	165	245	217	285	356	403	471	396	300	425						
Baker	1818	2354	2584	2365	1772	1304	1212	1067	600	400						
Ballantine	160	200	350	350	298	250	275	275	150	125						
Bannack City							170	157	300	193	100	193	193	232	381	3780
Basin	200	175	230	280	300	315	355	420	400	650	1000	600	104	146	144	
Bearcreek	37	61	31	61	162	324	472	744	1000	302						
Beartown													38	361	355	
Belfry	270	250	250	250	250	250	250	169	300	325						
Belgrade	3411	2336	1307	1057	663	618	533	499	800	561	200	170	300			
Belle Creek	100	160	400													
Belmont							35	175	100	175				225		
Belt	571	825	656	757	702	744	810	967	1000	1158	2000	2000	112			
Big Fork	1080	1080	500	500	425	425	415	415	500	300	150					
Big Sandy	740	835	827	954	743	596	633	589	400	178	100	86				
Big Sky	500	450	250													
Big Timber	1557	1690	1592	1660	1679	1533	1224	1282	1500	1022	1000	850	265	100		
Billings	81151	66798	61581	52851	31824	23261	16380	15100	15000	10031	7500	3221	836	600		
Billings Heights	8480	8480														
Bivens Gulch																450
Black Eagle	850	1100	1200	1395	1449	1000	81	81								
Black Pine													244			
Blackfoot City									50	60			66	82	499	
Blossburg									200			200	175			
Bonita																
Bonner	200	250	300	400	500	500	350	718	600	261	600	261	62	214	182	
Boulder	1316	1441	1342	1394	1017	510	926	682	700	922	850	922	500			

POPULATION HISTORY OF MONTANA CITIES AND TOWNS 1863-1990

COMMUNITY	1990	1980	1970	1960	1950	1940	1930	1920	1915	1910	1905	1900	1890	1880	1870	1863
Bowdoin	250	250	275	275	284	275	70	515	50	75		31				
Box Elder							127	185	200							
Bozeman	22660	21645	18670	13361	11325	8665	6855	6183	8000	5107	6000	3419	2143	894	168	
Brady	200	225	230	235	240	240	185	264	200	150						
Bridger	692	724	717	824	854	783	567	679	300	514	500	178				
Broadus	572	712	799	628	517	500	240	165								
Broadview	133	120	123	160	164	140	260	191		375						
Broadwater			900	250												
Brockton	365	374	401	367	359	385	118	113	50	50						
Brockway	60	70		185	130	130	130									
Browning	1170	1226	1700	2011	1691	1825	1172	986	175	225	125	100				
Buffalo	30	30			200	125	125	150	150	225						
Burlington												344	344			
Busby	409	300	400	400	100		50	50			150					
Butte	33336	37205	23368	27877	33251	37081	39532	41611	75000	39165	40000	30470	10723	3363	241	
Bynam	40	40					94	210	50		50	62	62			
Cable									100	27		27	82	200	260	
Carroll												600	549			
Carter	75	100	120		129	209	105		100	75						
Cascade	729	773	714	604	447	419	520	465	450	600	300	300	187			
Castle										100	60	150	383			
Cat Creek	15	15		200	100	100	106	58								
Centerville			2284	3398	1825	1030	997			1000						
Charlo	358	250	150	200	260	310	81									
Chester	942	963	936	1158	733	548	387	402	600	850	85	65				
Chestnut				200						200	200	200		100		
Chico										43	55	43	43	150		
Chinook	1512	1660	1813	2326	2307	2051	1320	1217	1200	780	1000	310				
Choteau	1741	1798	1586	1966	1618	1181	926	1043	750	700	400	396	236			
Church Hill	300	200	250	200												
Circle	805	931	964	1117	856	685	519	345	100	75						
Clancy	1000	700	550	300	161	113	315	310	250	510	250	510	100	76	300	
Clinton	200	150	200	200	150		50	100		200	100	66				
Clyde Park	282	283	244	253	280	216	302	352	425	400	50					
Coalville										250						
Coburg	65			100			50	159	150	50						
Coffee Creek		50				158	158	318								
Cokedale											300		284			
Collins									75		50					
Colstrip	3035	1475	160	200	200	160	160									

POPULATION HISTORY OF MONTANA CITIES AND TOWNS 1863-1990

COMMUNITY	1990	1980	1970	1960	1950	1940	1930	1920	1915	1910	1905	1900	1890	1880	1870	1863
Columbia Falls	2942	3112	2652	2132	1232	637	637	611	925	601	1000	620	620			
Columbus	1573	1439	1173	1281	1097	962	834	987	900	521	500	175				
Comet														300		
Concord/Devon									115	375	150					
Conrad	2891	3074	2770	2665	1865	1471	1499	988	1250	888						
Cooke City	100	100					45	120	50	130	150	300	42			
Coram/Citadel	330	300	400	440	500	300	200	50								
Corbin	35	25					60	162	150	150	50	100	39			
Corvallis	500	400	467	450	500	500	275	315	300	250	200	250	194	60		
Craig	75	50							65	125	40	63	63			
Crow Agency	1446	750	750	700	900	900	113	113	100	100		56				
Culbertson	796	887	821	919	779	585	536	547	600	528	400	75				
Custer	280	250	193	236	257	150	150	96	100	175						
Cut Bank	3329	3688	4004	4539	3721	2509	845	1181	550	500	250	43				
Dagmar	50	50					50	210	100	150						
Darby	625	581	538	398	415	481	285	325	400	375	65	70				
Dayton	100	75					43	159	100	175	40					
Dearborn													75	160		
Deborgia									200							
Deer Lodge	3378	4023	4306	4681	3779	3278	3510	3780	4000	2570	1100	1324	1463	941	788	96
Denton	350	356	398	410	435	406	345	431	500							
Diamond City											35	48	51	64	460	
Dillon	3991	3976	4548	3690	3668	3014	2422	2701	2800	1835	2000	1530	1012	711		
Divide			145				113	113	100	97	50	31				
Dixon	145	125	170	132	132	132	132	162	200	50	50	100	97	196	200	
Dodson	137	158	196	313	330	397	249	365	275	100		45				
Dooley							220	220								
Drummond	264	414	494	577	531	360	380	375	300	425	300	150	213	50		
Dublin Gulch					875											
Dunkirk									100	300						
Dupuyer	100	100	125	115	150	447	350	316	150	300	250	300	100			
Dutton	392	359	415	504	431	300		262	105	275						
East Glacier	326	500	340	300	300	300										
East Helena	1538	1647	1651	1490	1216	1143	1039	840	1100	800	1200	750	380			
East Missoula	1707	1707	450	600												
Edgar			130	178	157	111					100	200				
Ekalaka	439	620	663	738	904	719	475	433	400	275						
Electric/Horr							26	100	50	210		210				
Elkhorn										150		300	430			
Elliston	180	150	200	200	225	225	225	225	450	225	350	250	114			

POPULATION HISTORY OF MONTANA CITIES AND TOWNS 1863-1990

COMMUNITY	1990	1980	1970	1960	1950	1940	1930	1920	1915	1910	1905	1900	1890	1880	1870	1863
Ennis	773	660	501	525	500	285	259	234	200	150	50	49	49			
Eureka	1043	1119	1195	1229	929	912	860	1082	900	603						
Evergreen	4109	3746	1000													
Fairfield	660	650	638	752	693	400	157	157	1000	200						
Fairview	869	1366	956	1006	942	901	576	513								
Fallon	235	265	280	251	251	300	200	110		175						
Flaxville	88	142	185	262	220	260	272	267								
Floral Park			5113	4079	2600											
Florence	250	200	300	350	350	150	68	68	100	200	75	100	67	100		
Forest Park	780	750														
Forsyth	2175	2553	1873	2032	1906	1696	1591	1838	2000	1398	1000	500	308	200		
Fort Assineboine							88			365		450	660	450		
Fort Belknap	530	500	185	200	106									50		
Fort Benton	1660	1693	1863	1887	1522	1227	1109	1065	1400	1004	1275	1024	624	1618	367	132
Fort Custer													582	739		
Fort Ellis														267	158	
Fort Harrison				350	300	300	550									
Fort Keogh				265	265	265	133			100	350	156	614	600		
Fort Logan												29	29	136	68	
Fort Maginnis							41			100		48	43	100		
Fort Missoula													271			
Fort Owen					400	400	400			475						107
Fort Peck	325	600	650	950	1214	3100	443	80								
Fort Shaw	200	200	250	120	180	269			250	380	330		275	125	473	
Fortine	130	150	100	150					50		100					
Frazier	335	300	400	400	378	300	300	164								
French Gulch																
Frenchtown	140	75			125	125	300	316	200	216	350	250	216	110	155	
Froid	195	323	330	418	555	441	434	410	250					50	100	
Fromburg	370	469	364	367	442	533	446	520	660	500	150					
Galata	25	40			100		75	210	250							
Gallatin																
Gallatin Gateway	260	200	200	200	200	160	160							40		
Gardiner	670	600	600	600	602	600	524	519	350	500	300	75	132	100		
Garneill	20	20			160	160	150	150	200	150	200	45				
Garnet	50	100				103	266	261	300	250	300					
Garrison	50	100	200		100	100	100		50	175	50	302	97			
Gebo											250	350				
Geraldine	299	305	370	364	374	262	279	354								
German Gulch									300						239	

POPULATION HISTORY OF MONTANA CITIES AND TOWNS 1863-1990

COMMUNITY	1990	1980	1970	1960	1950	1940	1930	1920	1915	1910	1905	1900	1890	1880	1870	1863
Geyser	130	150	300	175	175	175	175	230	300	200						
Gildford	250	300	340	350	340	250	250	180	175	350	100					
Gilman							35	216	200							
Giltedge							25			225	300	221	300			
Glasgow	3572	4455	4700	6398	3827	3799	2216	2059	2600	1158	900	458	338			
Glendale													371	678		
Glendive	4802	5978	6305	7058	5254	4524	4629	3816	5000	2428	2000	1200	720	500		
Glenwood Park					1889											
Gloster														250		
Granite								157		350	600	1079	1310			
Grantsdale	150	150	175	150	150	125	161	150	120	150	175	150	362			
Grass Range	159	139	181	222	234	206	212	435	200	100						
Great Falls	55097	56725	60091	55244	39214	29928	28822	24121	25000	13948	16000	14930	3979			
Grizzly					200											
Gunderson												1100	1075	400		
Hall	100	80		100			90	213	80	100						
Hamilton	2737	2661	2499	2475	2678	2332	1839	1700	2600	2240	2583	1257		50	200	
Hanover				125	175	235	150	214								
Hardin	2940	3300	2733	2789	2306	1886	1169	1312	1000	700						
Harlem	882	1023	1094	1267	1107	1166	708	721	600	383	500	150				
Harlowton	1049	1181	1375	1734	1733	1547	1473	1856	1200	770	150					
Harrison	130	115	275	151	151	151	151	164	50	125						
Hasmark												300				
Hassel/St. Louis											150					
Haugan	90	60	100	100	200	125										
Havre	10201	10891	10558	10740	8086	6427	6372	5429	5000	3624	3295	1033				
Havre North	1110	1230	1073	1168												
Hays	333	300	600	500	550	550	412	412		412	440	412				
Heart Butte	499	150	250	150	100											
Hecla									110				103	300		
Hedges								250		250						
Helena	24569	23938	22730	20227	17581	15056	11803	12037	18000	12515	14000	10770	13834	3624	3106	
Helmville	80	60				200	113	200	100	200	75	50	39			
Heron	75	45				215	215	161	150	150	120	63	46			
Highwood	150	200	200	200	225	225	225	264	50	75	50					
Hilger	60	60			100	100	225	167	225							
Hingham	181	186	262	254	214	205	251	154	250			48				
Hinsdale	225	200	400	400	400	359	359	420	350		100					
Hobson/Philbrook	226	261	192	207	205	239	240	389	400	600						
Hoffman											225					

POPULATION HISTORY OF MONTANA CITIES AND TOWNS 1863-1990

COMMUNITY	1990	1980	1970	1960	1950	1940	1930	1920	1915	1910	1905	1900	1890	1880	1870	1863
Opportunity			350		350	350										
Orchard Homes	4500	4000	3500	2019	1545											
Oswego							150	210								
Outlook	109	122	153	226	235	208	302	295	250	160						
Ovando	100	70	90	100	100	100	100		100		80	54				
Pablo	240	200	300	150	100	150	150	213								
Paradise	325	300	300	280	300	300	259	259	350	175						
Park City	375	300	400	400	450	350	350	313	400	300	60	100	43			
Park Grove				100		300										
Peerless	135	110	145	110	220	103										
Pendry	70	40					85	165								
Philipsburg	925	1138	1128	1107	1048	1304	1300	1724	1100	1109	1000	995	1058	299	150	
Pinesdale	670	300														
Piltzville	500	500	235													
Pioneer									50		80	87	199	271	560	
Plains	992	1116	1046	769	714	624	522	452	1100	481	300	100				
Pleasant Valley												275				
Plentywood	2136	2476	2381	2121	1862	1574	1226	888	900	300						
Plevna	140	191	189	263	247	291	258	241	100							
Polson	3283	2798	2464	2314	2280	2156	1455	1132	1250	700						
Polytechnic					250	250										
Pony	150	150	150	150	185	200	242	242	400	369	350	437	207	100		
Poplar	881	995	1389	1565	1169	1442	1046	1152	600	250	200	100				
Power	120	120	175						40							
Prickly Pear City															233	
Pryor	654	50	150	100	300	300										
Radarsburg	60	90	100	100	152	137	245	375	250	270	150					
Rapelje	100	75	100	115	100	175			100							
Rattlesnake	3474	3474	1492													
Red Bluff													150			
Red Lodge	1958	1896	1844	2278	2730	2950	3026	4515	5500	4860	4500	2152	624			
Redstone	70	70		150	200	200	150	217	250							
Reedpoint	130	100	100	130	158	158	260	260	100							
Reserve	75	100		250	200	120	65	100								
Rexford	132	130	243	300	200	260	200		70		75					
Richey	259	417	389	480	595	373	362	350	125	100	200	110				
Rimini	70	60					118	113	100							
Ringling	320	300			125	125	125	162	100	300			200			
Roberts	225	300	291	275	200	200	200	216	75	100		61				
Rollins		200	200	150	150	107	107		50							

POPULATION HISTORY OF MONTANA CITIES AND TOWNS 1863-1990

COMMUNITY	1990	1980	1970	1960	1950	1940	1930	1920	1915	1910	1905	1900	1890	1880	1870	1863
Ronan	1547	1530	1347	1334	1251	1032	537	600	500	175	50	175	100			
Rosebud	170	140	140	250	250	250	250	263	300	180	100	60	43			
Roundup	1808	2119	2116	2842	2856	2644	2577	2434	2000	1513			300			
Roy	175	150	175	175	175	175	280	280	125	125						
Ruby							30	210	100							
Rudyard	500	600	600	628	521	350	165	225	60							
Ryegate	260	273	261	314	339	348	292	405	300	120						
Saco	261	252	356	490	539	452	506	425	400	350	50	64	50			
St. Ignatius	778	877	925	940	781	768	380	375	200	80	50	50	100			
St. Labre	250	250														
St. Peter						300	361	361		300	300	300	300			
St. Regis	650	600	500	500	500		213		200	240	100	240				
Salesville									200		50					
Saltese	70	85		100	150	200	200		250	280	250					
Sand Coulee	275	250	400	500	590	1030	619	630	900	1000	700	1500	600			
Santa Rita	100	100	150	110	110	110	400	319	200							
Savage	300	300	300	350	300	250										
Savoy							175	158								
Scobey	1154	1382	1486	1726	1623	1311	1259	1170	300							
Seeley	870	800	500	450	250											
Shawmut	50	70			150	100			50							
Shelby	2763	3142	3111	4017	3058	2538	2004	537	550	400	200	100				
Sheridan	652	646	636	539	572	597	521	538	500	399	700	581	207	150	100	
Sidney	5217	5726	4543	4564	3987	2978	2010	1400	700	345	100	75	129	100	425	
Silver Bow Park			5524	4798	5128		92	129	100	129	75	129				
Simms	200	300	299	295	250	250	150	220	100							
Smelter												180				
Somers	800	800	800	831	750	800	375	761	500	300	750					
South Butte								158					801			
Southern Butte							85									
Southern Cross					130	100										
Square Butte																
Stanford	529	595	505	615	542	529	509	375	500	450						
Sterling								300			50	54		150	100	
Stevensville	1221	1207	829	784	772	703	692	744	1200	796	793	346	306	150	100	
Stockett	175	200	300	400	500	500	815	815	1700	700	1000	500				
Sun River	180	200	190	165	115		224	200	100	316	100	200	316	300	176	
Sunburst	437	476	604	882	845	709	486	63								
Superior	881	1054	993	1242	626	500	215	210	100	150	150	76	50			
Swan Lake	145	130	200	200												

POPULATION HISTORY OF MONTANA CITIES AND TOWNS 1863-1990

COMMUNITY	1863	1870	1880	1890	1900	1905	1910	1915	1920	1930	1940	1950	1960	1970	1980	1990
Sweet Grass				100	112	45	200	200	260	356	356	356	205	205	200	100
Terry				339	300	160	700	500	794	779	1012	1191	1140	870	929	659
Thompson Falls						300	400	550	508	468	736	851	1274	1356	1478	1319
Three Forks			200	142	50		674	1200	1071	884	876	1114	1161	1188	1247	1203
Toston					54	75	200	160	316	200	200	100	100	100	75	100
Townsend			200	245	446	800	759	1000	897	735	1309	1316	1528	1371	1587	1635
Trapper																
Trident			228							80		100	200	100	50	35
Troy				65	250	200	200	300	213	498	796	770	855	1046	1088	953
Turner								475	763		227	227	175	175	175	175
Twin Bridges		200	210	250	550	325	491	600	755	671	534	497	509	613	437	374
Twodot					86	150	250	240	213	125	125	125			60	40
Ulm					42	40	42		42	75		150	250	350	350	325
Utica				100	100	100		50								
Valier							750	1000	613	575	641	710	724	651	640	519
Vaughn								50	43	50	228	190	205	265	2270	2270
Victor				89	136	200	374	400	516	350	380	350	375	400	450	500
Virginia City	3450	867	624	675	568	800	467	500	342	242		323	194	149	192	142
Walkerville			444	1743	2621	2700	2491	3000	2391	2052	1880	1631	1453	1097	887	605
Warmsprings				62	62		62	50			1900	875				
Washoe								500	318	275	275	275	115		60	50
West Glacier												350	300	348	250	300
Waterloo											200	200	200			
West Riverside													150	400	500	530
West Yellowstone										200	300	400	500	756	735	913
Westby									253	287	369	396	309	287	291	253
Wheeler											200	850				
White Sulphur Springs			300	640	446	450	417	800	574	575	858	1025	1519	1200	1302	963
Whitefish						250	1479	1350	2867	2803	2602	3268	2965	3349	3703	4368
Whitehall				100	600	450	417	550	629	553	818	929	898	1035	1030	1067
Whitepine											175	175	275	200	95	25
Whitetail							100	250	210	200	200	200	100	200	30	100
Wibaux				200	300	525	487	800	611	619	625	739	766	644	782	628
Wickes			200	627	158	100	200	50	216	221		70	44	40	30	40
Willow Creek				150	175	200	175	75	219	350	350	350	250	150	150	180
Wilsall							100	250	517	300	200	300	275	200	180	225
Windham							200	140			125	125	100		30	40
Winifred								200	262	251	300	217	220	190	155	150
Winnett									316	408	399	407	360	271	207	188
Winston					150	150	75	150	162	100	100				30	50

POPULATION HISTORY OF MONTANA CITIES AND TOWNS 1863-1990

COMMUNITY	1990	1980	1970	1960	1950	1940	1930	1920	1915	1910	1905	1900	1890	1880	1870	1863
Winston	50	30				100	100	162	150	75	150	150				
Wisdom	135	150	155	175	250	387	387	264	250	250	250	86				
Wolf Creek	150	150	175	175	110	110			75	100		57				
Wolf Point	2880	3074	3095	3585	2557	1960	1539	2098	400	35	30	35				
Worden	380	300	350	310	375	250	250	219	130							
Yates									150							
Yellowtail	270	250	250													
Zortman	60	60	175	120	100		70	361	150	300	125					
Zurich	65	65					305	219								

1905: Minnesota, North and South Dakota and Montana Gazetteer and Business Directory. Chicago; R.L. Polk, 1906.
1915: Minnesota, North and South Dakota and Montana Gazetteer and Business Directory. Chicago; R.L. Polk, 1915.

POPULATION HISTORY OF NEBRASKA CITIES AND TOWNS 1860-1990

COMMUNITY	1860	1870	1880	1890	1900	1910	1920	1930	1940	1950	1960	1970	1980	1990
Abie				110	113	210	132	196	134	113	117	78	107	106
Adams			52	350	417	647	574	535	516	457	387	463	395	472
Ainsworth			266	733	605	1045	1508	1378	1833	2150	1982	2073	2256	1870
Albion		150	330	926	1369	1584	1978	2172	2268	2132	1982	2074	1997	1916
Alda			79	110	78	200	175	153	151	190	229	456	601	540
Alexandria			387	515	332	447	432	421	369	317	257	225	255	224
Allen					236	371	485	489	404	374	350	309	390	331
Alliance				829	2535	3105	4591	6669	6523	7891	7845	6862	9869	9765
Alma			298	905	923	1066	1058	1235	1272	1768	1342	1299	1369	1226
Alvo					161	230	208	163	215	190	159	151	144	164
Amherst					183	256	259	262	238	219	220	259	269	231
Angus						250								
Anoka						145	129	107	117	60	32	25	24	10
Anselmo				150	145	351	457	472	388	316	269	180	187	189
Ansley				400	468	700	775	817	753	711	714	631	644	555
Antioch								139	114	30	26			
Aoway Creek			300				764							
Arago	193	364	154	100	118	22								
Arapahoe			470	734	701	901	894	1017	1002	1226	1084	1147	1107	1001
Arborville		100	78		246	75	210	63						
Arcadia			93	429	374	618	745	711	663	574	446	418	412	385
Argo				43										
Arlington			278	412	579	645	695	622	569	593	740	910	1117	1178
Arnold			145	100	114	231	933	899	884	936	844	752	813	679
Arthur							104	142	110	176	165	175	124	128
Ashland		653	978	1601	1477	1379	1725	1786	1709	1713	1989	2176	2274	2136
Ashton				50	251	404	397	435	488	381	320	277	273	251
Aspinwall		350	175		26									
Atkinson				701	595	810	1300	1144	1350	1372	1324	1406	1521	1380
Atlanta			195		248	250	258	207	173	147	107	101	102	114
Auburn		250	450	1537	2664	2729	2863	3068	3639	3422	3229	3650	3482	3443
Aurora			678	1862	1921	2630	2962	2715	2419	2455	2576	3180	3717	3810
Avoca			92	166	255	249	231	222	197	196	218	229	242	254
Axtell			127	262	329	394	385	328	295	352	477	500	602	707
Ayr			128	173	141	142	164	177	152	121	111	140	112	101
Bancroft			135	344	733	742	673	660	599	596	496	545	552	494
Barada			70	102	147	118	118	108	132	83	58	58	36	24
Barneston			50	300	250	228	258	221	219	208	177	149	155	122
Bartlett				150	135	112	132	133	179	145	125	193	144	131
Bartley				220	307	511	251	465	380	399	309	283	342	339

POPULATION HISTORY OF NEBRASKA CITIES AND TOWNS 1860-1990

COMMUNITY	1990	1980	1970	1960	1950	1940	1930	1920	1910	1900	1890	1880	1870	1860
Bassett	739	1009	983	1023	1066	931	635	664	383	270	231	50		
Battle Creek	997	948	768	587	630	702	755	743	597	506	352	123	75	
Bayard	1196	1435	1338	1519	1869	2121	1559	2127	261	230				
Bazile Mills	34	54	44	45	46	76	76	91	77	175	276			
Beatrice	12354	12891	12389	12132	11813	10883	10297	9664	9356	7875	13836	2447	850	
Beaver City	707	775	802	818	913	1015	1024	1103	975	911	763	153	125	
Beaver Crossing	448	458	400	439	425	550	522	543	542	359	395	49		
Bee	209	192	156	149	160	205	205	228	207	180				
Beemer	672	853	699	667	613	585	571	548	494	455	350			
Belden	149	151	162	157	192	235	248	285	247	197				
Belgrade	157	195	210	224	284	406	386	493	400	240				
Belle Creek												200	200	
Bellevue	30982	21813	21953	8831	3858	1184	1017	695	596	527	387	211		929
Bellwood	395	407	361	361	389	434	391	369	397	410	413	42	150	
Belvidere	117	158	162	185	274	325	358	424	475	458	359	264	150	
Benedict	230	228	209	170	206	221	279	313	336	292	200			
Benkelman	1193	1235	1349	1400	1512	1448	1154	1009	538	296	357	75		
Bennett	544	523	489	381	396	412	428	473	457	495	474	214	100	
Bennington	866	631	683	341	315	326	375	314	276	229	75			
Benson					1892		1732		3170	510				
Bertrand	708	775	662	691	584	615	645	697	643	344	265			
Berwyn	122	104	110	104	138	170	196	205	200	115				
Bethany							1143	1078	948	330				
Big Springs	495	505	472	506	527	569	595	408	325	88	75			
Black Bird										26	26	175		
Bladen	280	298	293	322	282	272	448	445	494	300	100			
Blair	6860	6418	6106	4931	3815	3289	2791	2702	2584	2970	2069	1317	494	
Bloomfield	1181	1393	1287	1349	1455	1467	1435	1431	1264	678				
Bloomington	129	138	165	176	293	361	431	503	554	488	464	524	125	
Blue Hill	810	883	784	723	574	565	669	726	761	823	796	138		
Blue Springs	431	521	506	509	581	681	700	742	712	786	963	513	225	
Boelus/Bollus/Howard City	203	228	182	181	167	228	296	259	233	289	250			
Boone	50	75		35	100	119	138	157	125	180				
Bostwick				50	54	113	238	219	125	100				
Boys Town	794	622	989	997	975									
Bradshaw	330	373	347	306	352	339	340	391	359	365	434	200		
Brady	331	377	311	275	320	460	387	400	308	361	368			
Brainard	326	275	309	300	373	444	400	468	465	384	306	61		
Brewster	22	46	54	44	69	125	126	113	230	125				
Bridgeport	1581	1668	1490	1645	1631	1520	1421	1235	541	178				

POPULATION HISTORY OF NEBRASKA CITIES AND TOWNS 1860-1990

COMMUNITY	1990	1980	1970	1960	1950	1940	1930	1920	1910	1900	1890	1880	1870	1860
Bristow	107	123	127	153	146	188	183	255	175					
Broadwater	160	161	141	235	300	344	368	364	115					
Brock	143	189	192	213	283	373	328	274	434	543	348	153		
Broken Bow	3778	3979	3734	3482	3396	2968	2715	2567	2260	1375	1647			
Bromfield									282	282	195	112		
Brownville	148	203	174	243	357	581	426	463	457	718	980	1309	1305	425
Brule	411	438	423	370	330	374	329	492	230	255	150			
Bruning	332	330	315	289	246	232	316	326	353	191				
Bruno	141	154	142	155	155	189	202	245	245	142				
Brunswick	182	190	229	254	260	289	352	359	278	142				
Bryants Grove												200		
Burchard	105	122	131	132	201	263	275	265	315	297	201	75		
Burlingame												161		
Burnett											400	200		
Burr	75	101	108	81	91	126	122	133	113	238	100			
Burwell	1278	1383	1341	1425	1413	1412	1156	1214	915	460	378			
Bushnell	119	187	211	266	225	252	341	321						
Butler Center										30				
Butte	452	529	575	526	614	623	569	593	550	350		200		
Byron	140	154	171	147	159	171	206	137	184	200	150			
Cairo	733	737	686	503	422	411	425	427	364	224	150			
Callaway	539	579	523	603	744	768	833	833	765	406	234			
Cambridge	1107	1206	1145	1090	1352	1084	1203	1042	1029	840	510	106		
Campbell	432	441	447	424	412	478	565	561	573	368	200			
Carleton	144	160	163	207	291	350	363	350	393	309	458	274	100	
Carroll	237	246	235	220	309	351	401	448	382	252	68			
Cedar Bluffs	591	632	616	585	505	504	517	516	500	371	181	75		
Cedar Creek	334	311	119			189	217	131	180	188	311			
Cedar Rapids	396	447	449	512	541	695	743	766	576	559	484	229	100	
Center	112	123	111	147	148	146	130	198	119					
Central City/Lone Tree	2868	3083	2803	2406	2394	2460	2474	2410	2428	1571	1368	648	325	
Ceresco	825	836	474	429	374	342	391	398	296	226	211			
Chadron	5588	5933	5921	5079	4687	4262	4606	4412	2687	1665	1867	100		
Chambers	341	390	321	396	395	388	259	256	300	100	100			
Champion	150	105	100	100	170		100	110	100	75				
Chapman	292	349	371	303	274	204	283	224	266	209	429	110		
Chappell	979	1095	1204	1280	1297	1093	1061	1131	329	177				
Cheney									75	75	159			
Chester	351	435	459	480	539	634	579	529	560	439	407	194		
Clarks	379	445	480	439	464	454	540	540	605	554	512	210		

POPULATION HISTORY OF NEBRASKA CITIES AND TOWNS 1860-1990

COMMUNITY	1990	1980	1970	1960	1950	1940	1930	1920	1910	1900	1890	1880	1870	1860
Clarkson	699	817	805	797	764	829	918	884	647	344	147			
Clarksville												208	100	
Clatonia	296	273	224	203	192	194	242	239	233	130		50		
Clay Center	825	962	952	792	824	715	933	965	1065	590	390	68		
Clear Creek												145		
Clearwater	401	409	398	418	472	568	504	479	414	198	215	50		
Clinton	33	80	55	46	36	119	157	131						
Cody	177	177	246	230	296	375	408	428	185	205				
Coleridge	596	673	608	604	621	627	616	674	535	471	315	108		
College View							2384	2249	1508	865				
Colon	128	148	109	110	127	88	126	146	160	193		36		
Columbus	19480	17328	15471	12476	8884	7632	6898	5410	5014	3522	3134	2131	526	
Comstock	135	168	155	235	302	408	450	450	323	95	60			
Concord	156	145	180	150	194	242	257	261	198	175				
Cook	333	341	328	313	332	305	354	360	387	278	100			
Cordova	147	129	141	152	147	188	195	205	201	149				
Cornlea	39	40	54	44	69	67	105	95	90					
Cortland	393	403	326	285	288	307	318	322	364	390	509	200		
Cotesfield	60	82	76	81	106	134	153	214	300	40	65	50		
Cottonwood Springs											18	250		55
Covington	42	48	57	55	130	158	224	220	190	368	364	224	194	
Cowles											310	50	75	
Cozad	3823	4453	4225	3184	2910	2156	1813	1293	1096	739	542	150		
Crab Orchard	47	82	96	103	120	218	238	278	274	258	229	260		
Craig	228	237	295	378	384	437	452	418	339	462	290			
Crawford	1115	1315	1291	1508	1824	1845	1703	1646	1323	731	571			
Creighton	1223	1341	1461	1388	1401	1272	1388	1446	1373	909	822	310	125	
Creston	220	210	171	177	228	302	346	381	338	337	200			
Crete	4841	4872	4444	3546	3692	3038	2865	2445	2404	2199	2310	1870	850	
Crofton	820	948	677	604	630	600	733	811	610	46				
Crookston	99	86	86	139	168	262	373	157	100	50				
Cropsey												175		
Culbertson	795	767	801	803	770	815	820	686	580	422	460	108	175	
Cuming City														132
Curtis	791	1014	1166	868	964	952	960	1017	613	435	378			
Cushing	25	48	43	56	71	102	141	125	125	68				
Custer														
Dakota City	1470	1440	1057	928	622	477	417	399	474	521	310	500	300	
Dalton	282	345	354	503	417	358	453	295	207		510	364		
Danbury	109	143	137	185	218	236	321	293	268	219	198			

POPULATION HISTORY OF NEBRASKA CITIES AND TOWNS 1860-1990

COMMUNITY	1860	1870	1880	1890	1900	1910	1920	1930	1940	1950	1960	1970	1980	1990
Dannebrog			53	280	301	380	436	427	379	318	277	384	356	324
Davenport		125	150	513	446	484	495	477	450	459	416	427	445	383
Davey					140	150	123	154	125	112	121	163	190	160
David City			1000	2028	1845	2177	2216	2333	2272	2321	2304	2380	2514	2522
Dawson		150	93	153	322	340	351	389	394	309	263	251	215	157
Daykin				100	189	220	204	187	165	157	144	192	207	188
Decatur		350	533	593	800	782	657	683	905	808	786	679	723	641
Deer Creek	166			216										
Delcama	122													
Deloit			200	260	27									
Denton					65	200	145	114	126	101	94	151	164	161
Deshler				75	258	609	944	1177	1037	1063	956	937	997	892
Desoto			50	62	35	25	25	28					50	50
Deweese	336				125	200	144	156	134	115	100	86	69	74
DeWitt		525	305	751	662	675	623	534	490	528	504	651	642	598
Dickens						100	45	103	115	60	25	22	24	16
Diller			150	126	399	506	418	405	378	314	286	287	311	298
Dix							248	279	199	270	420	342	275	229
Dixon					157	217	241	222	226	159	139	128	127	87
Dodge				338	554	661	648	693	656	633	649	704	815	693
Doniphan			85	437	473	399	482	436	395	412	390	542	696	736
Dorchester			309	540	521	610	522	579	558	478	460	492	611	614
Douglas				100	253	305	242	233	234	213	197	175	207	199
Douglas Grove			175											
Dublin				388	35	25								
Dubois				316	307	339	332	350	315	236	218	185	178	119
Dunbar			250	412	208	216	312	292	336	228	232	252	216	171
Duncan			175	85	188	150	182	241	241	228	294	298	410	387
Dundee					400	1023		1417						
Dunning					53	400	289	212	272	254	210	162	182	131
Dwight					160	184	309	323	294	218	209	224	221	227
Eagle				125	297	360	368	309	289	255	302	441	832	1047
Eddyville					101	254	227	224	237	188	119	128	121	102
Edgar		275	577	1105	1040	1080	996	987	708	724	730	707	705	600
Edison					310	334	315	329	321	302	249	199	210	148
Edith				130										
Elba				318	257	302	276	286	270	216	184	211	218	196
Elgin				200	451	606	854	917	853	820	881	917	807	731
Elk Creek			139	216	347	240	218	260	199	176	170	151	144	116
Elkhorn			113	325	299	291	333	411	429	476	749	1184	1344	1391

POPULATION HISTORY OF NEBRASKA CITIES AND TOWNS 1860-1990

COMMUNITY	1860	1870	1880	1890	1900	1910	1920	1930	1940	1950	1960	1970	1980	1990
Ellis					180	100	90	100	110	69	80		50	75
Elm Creek			158	357	301	620	600	708	730	799	778	798	862	852
Elmwood			38	303	544	635	558	515	456	445	481	548	598	584
Elsie	63				230	200	201	262	223	219	198	125	133	153
Elwood			100	373	377	464	473	509	633	562	581	601	716	679
Elyria					35	100	100	111	77	87	89	55	62	61
Emerson			100	234	617	838	864	891	879	784	803	850	874	791
Emmett						150	130	88	89	62	66	70	73	70
Endicott			179	256	234	204	197	242	246	195	166	167	198	163
Ericson					53	150	192	272	279	186	157	122	132	111
Eustis			146	145	232	403	434	497	459	413	386	400	460	452
Ewing				348	275	440	543	588	681	705	503	552	520	449
Exeter			412	754	673	916	910	941	841	747	745	759	807	661
Fairbury	473	450	1251	2630	3140	5294	5454	6192	6304	6395	5572	5265	4885	4335
Fairfield		225	400	1233	1203	1054	784	757	640	503	495	487	543	458
Fairmont		525	600	1029	784	921	785	740	810	729	829	761	767	708
Falls City		607	1583	2102	3022	3255	4930	5787	6146	6203	5598	5444	5374	4769
Farnum					218	462	408	394	346	323	258	270	268	188
Farwell/Fardale/Posen					130	246	337	230	200	172	137	172	165	152
Febing			150	200										157
Filley			77	301	248	194	169	183	174	136	149	138	172	471
Firth		150	230	259	307	343	332	322	323	245	277	328	384	
Florence			176	198	688	1526								
Fontanelle	175		199			143	157	134	133	103	103			
Fordyce				113	89	250	150	192	202	165	143	146	148	190
Forest City	137													
Fort Calhoun	306	236	240	354	346	324	309	309	329	314	458	642	641	648
Fort Crook					646	203	402	719	375		416			
Fort Kearny	206	49												
Fort McPherson		500	250											
Fort Niobara			350	400	600	220	220							
Fort Omaha		620		118	700	122		175						
Fort Robinson				500	500		140	122	128	136	200			
Foster			200		100					114	60	79	60	60
Francis					180	36							81	57
Franklin		100	78	556	756	949	1055	1103	1272	1602	1194	1193	1167	1112
Fremont	237	1195	3013	6747	7241	8718	9592	11407	11862	14762	19698	22962	23979	23680
Friedensau				260	30	30								
Friend		275	555	1347	1200	1261	1263	1214	1169	1148	1069	1126	1079	1111
Fullerton			436	968	1464	1638	1595	1680	1707	1520	1475	1444	1506	1452

POPULATION HISTORY OF NEBRASKA CITIES AND TOWNS 1860-1990

COMMUNITY	1990	1980	1970	1960	1950	1940	1930	1920	1910	1900	1890	1880	1870	1860
Funk	198	189	143	141	123	120	117	147	300	112				
Gandy	51	53	50	41	88	169	194	191	300	268	300			
Garland/Germantown	247	257	244	198	184	205	228	279	275	194	142			
Garrison	71	68	60	82	88	124	126	138	177	250	217			
Geneva	2310	2400	2275	2352	2031	1888	1662	1768	1741	1534	1580	376		
Genoa	1082	1090	1174	1009	1026	1231	1089	1069	1376	913	793	187	75	
Gering	7946	7760	5639	4585	3842	3104	2531	2508	627	433	100			
Gibbon	1525	1531	1388	1083	1063	836	825	883	718	660	646	154	75	
Gilead	37	69	60	79	109	148	147	155	181	115	50			
Giltner/Huntington	367	400	408	293	284	325	355	387	410	282	195			
Glen Rock							30	105	83	120	82	50	175	
Glenville	304	363	332	323	281	285	376	400	304	246	203	54		
Goehner	192	165	113	106	67	125	126	150	300	55	50			
Gordon	1803	2167	2106	2223	2058	1967	1958	1581	920	542	500	116		
Gothenburg	3232	3479	3158	3050	2977	2330	2322	1754	1730	819	535			
Grafton	167	185	128	171	159	240	284	324	353	287	730	178		
Grainton	16	20	20	35	91	100	139	27						
Grand Island	39386	33180	32358	25742	22682	19130	18041	13947	10326	7554	7536	2963	975	
Grant	1239	1270	1099	1166	1091	897	798	585	358	162	315			
Greeley Center	562	597	580	656	787	891	857	919	845	552	492			
Green Meadows	885													
Greenwood	531	587	506	403	364	350	404	340	387	516	495	179	75	
Gresham	253	320	248	239	267	352	442	492	344	297	350			
Gretna	2249	1609	1557	745	438	482	477	491	484	466	255			
Gross				17	29	23	51	84	111	325				
Guide Rock	290	344	318	441	676	596	690	611	690	416	366	158	100	
Gurley	198	212	233	329	219	203	232	291	200	88				
Hadar	291	286	172	100	129	133	141	110	205	240				
Haigler	225	225	237	268	398	507	535	450						
Hallam	309	290	280	264	172	168	193	212	168	160	250			
Halsey	110	144	131	111	165	120	39	36	75					
Hamlet	60	74	64	113	154	220	199							
Hampton	432	419	387	331	289	310	369	457	383	367	430	134		
Hansen	50	30					90	210		100	72	45		
Harbine	66	50	44	58	85	63	106	107	150	242		90		
Hardy	206	232	250	285	348	341	399	445	496	345	343	170		
Harrisburg	60	85	80	144	94	140	212	200	140	114	137			
Harrison	291	361	377	448	492	500	480	401	186	168	111			
Hartington	1583	1730	1581	1648	1660	1688	1568	1467	1413	971	750	250		
Harvard	976	1217	1230	1261	774	704	865	991	1102	849	1076	768	375	

POPULATION HISTORY OF NEBRASKA CITIES AND TOWNS 1860-1990

COMMUNITY	1990	1980	1970	1960	1950	1940	1930	1920	1910	1900	1890	1880	1870	1860
Hastings	22837	23045	23580	21412	20211	15145	15490	11647	9338	7188	13584	2817	475	
Havelock							3659	3602	2680	1480				
Havens										850				
Hayes Center	259	231	237	283	361	314	229	210	330	250	150			
Hays Springs	693	794	682	823	1091	819	853	577	408	345	378			
Hazard	78	75	72	104	130	142	148	167		100				
Hazel Dell												180		
Heartwell	69	87	104	113	125	141	182	140	150	175				
Hebron	1765	1906	1667	1920	2000	1909	1804	1513	1778	1511	1502	466	275	
Hemingford	953	1023	734	904	946	792	1025	708	272	133	150			
Henderson	999	1072	901	730	536	495	480	485	391	208	100			
Hendley	42	39	58	79	130	147	211	200	238	139	100			
Hendricks												250		
Henry	145	155	147	138	171	176	167	129	75					
Herman	186	340	323	335	380	427	421	385	345	321	319	95		
Hershey	579	633	526	504	573	487	473	482	332	75				
Hickman	1081	687	415	288	279	320	302	380	388	382	341	83		
Hildreth	364	394	352	305	374	361	400	453	450	249	141			
Holbrook	233	297	307	354	398	441	488	455	414	214				
Holdredge	5671	5624	5635	5226	4381	3360	3263	3108	3030	3007	2601	400		
Holmesville	100	100	100	100	110	105	217	241	272	238				
Holstein	207	241	231	205	187	241	254	227	323	267	272	225		
Homer	553	564	457	370	345	477	452	491	397	341	251	118		
Hooper	850	932	895	832	859	802	985	1014	741	840	670	204	200	
Hordville	164	155	147	128	116	160	175	191	300					
Hoskins	307	306	271	179	171	212	255	274	262	175				
Howe	80	90		56	75	192	194	184	200	248				
Howells	615	677	682	694	784	861	952	904	800	515	197			
Hubbard	199	234	151	138	145	188	180	152	150	90	97			
Hubbell	55	71	83	126	199	250	233	231	295	375	330	357		
Humboldt	1003	1176	1194	1322	1404	1386	1435	1277	1176	1218	1114	917	575	
Humphrey	741	799	862	801	761	841	854	835	868	869	691	266		
Huntington									410	282				
Huntley	58	64	67	91	98	148	179	170	190	118				
Hyannis	210	336	345	373	432	449	384	384	262	299				
Imperial	2007	1941	1589	1423	1563	1195	946	723	402	258	159			
Inavale	150	180	180	185	188	243	145	132	200	100	153			
Indianola	672	856	672	754	738	800	815	742	681	626	579	233		
Inglewood	286	257	275	480										
Inman	156	181	160	192	237	206	285	315	300	135				

POPULATION HISTORY OF NEBRASKA CITIES AND TOWNS 1860-1990

COMMUNITY	1860	1870	1880	1890	1900	1910	1920	1930	1940	1950	1960	1970	1980	1990
Ionia			175											
Irvington		375	150	85	36	100	64	64	175				500	150
Isla			200											
Ithica			60	410	276	171	156	137	139	140	126	121	156	133
Jackson		125	550	308	339	290	274	242	226	200	224	232	287	230
Jamestown				32										
Jansen				100	271	308	258	264	255	244	204	191	204	140
Johnson			100	234	352	273	255	288	301	262	304	350	341	323
Johnstown				205	480	350	290	229	173	109	81	82	78	48
Julian				50	206	168	181	156	136	123	131	80	87	71
Juniata		325	494	528	543	471	329	367	338	365	422	480	703	811
Kearney		750	1782	8074	5634	6202	7702	8575	9643	12115	14210	19101	21158	24396
Kelso			50	195										
Kenesaw			214	500	504	657	646	614	551	584	546	728	854	818
Kennard			50	310	275	319	363	319	315	273	331	336	372	371
Keystone						150	162	176	115	55	127		75	75
Kilgore					50	200	274	232	173	189	157	110	76	79
Kimball				193	254	454	1620	1711	1725	2048	4384	3680	3120	2574
La Platte				200	71		123	79	68				300	250
La Vista												4858	9588	9840
Lake Forest													400	2700
Lakeside						40	213	232	144	175	59		25	30
Lamar				60	140	76	110	122	120	81	50	30	60	31
Lanham					200	250		133	154	75	49		40	50
Laurel					514	514	830	864	861	944	922	1009	1031	981
Lawrence				156	406	475	538	528	445	376	338	343	350	323
Lebanon			75	243	180	197	245	262	238	213	143	118	102	75
Leigh			54	249	439	567	516	692	575	551	502	501	509	447
Lemoyne								300					90	150
Leshara						86	102	110	84	61	103	102	133	118
Lewellen						300	361	419	532	510	411	376	368	307
Lewiston				70	108	127	167	187	158	94	77	88	102	64
Lexington				1392	1343	2059	2327	2962	3688	5068	5572	5654	7040	6601
Liberty		75	227	469	450	394	375	348	340	246	174	118	105	74
Lincoln		2441	13003	55154	40169	43973	54948	75933	81984	98884	128521	149518	171932	191972
Lindsay				125	316	465	490	456	332	247	218	291	383	321
Linwood		50	75	309	317	329	297	235	247	168	151	108	119	91
Lisco							68	238		150	150	150	150	125
Litchfield				150	240	403	428	404	412	337	264	248	256	314
Lodgepole			75	284	460	245	451	436	479	555	492	407	413	368

POPULATION HISTORY OF NEBRASKA CITIES AND TOWNS 1860-1990

COMMUNITY	1990	1980	1970	1960	1950	1940	1930	1920	1910	1900	1890	1880	1870	1860
Long Pine	396	521	363	487	567	824	937	1200	781	486	562	156		
Loomis	376	447	323	299	218	249	213	238	284	240				
Lorton	61	47	47	58	75	65	74	102	115	290				
Louisville	998	1022	1036	1194	1014	977	969	645	778	738	653	321	150	
Loup City	1104	1368	1456	1415	1508	1675	1446	1364	1128	826	671	225	75	
Lowell	28	33	34	45	60		51	46	46	28	46	100	275	
Lushton						126	148	186	205	238	125			
Lyman	452	551	561	626	666	672	656	589	583	231				
Lynch	296	357	375	409	440	487	498							
Lyons	1144	1214	1177	974	1011	1033	985	1025	865	847	532	90	75	
McCook	8112	8404	8285	8301	7678	6212	6688	4303	3765	2445	2346	554		
McCool Junction	372	404	289	246	297	272	356	338	369	276	204			
McGrew	99	110	79	90	105	139	128	128						
McLean	49	46	67	73	67	82	96	81	130	138		53		
Macey	836	500	550	545	356		203	35	35					
Madison	2135	1950	1595	1513	1663	1812	1842	1735	1708	1479	930	417	150	
Madrid	288	284	234	271	379	410	449	218	124	53	178			
Magnet	69	59	88	116	115	152	160	153	178	389				
Malcolm	181	355	132	116	93	121	121	125	200	88	111			
Malmo	114	100	131	135	151	167	179	189	214	259				
Manley	170	124	150	113	93	190	184	184	250	100	50			
Mapleville											195			
Marion	30	35			100	160	232	213	250					
Marquette	211	303	239	210	218	245	318	305	290	210	261	90		
Marsland	10	27	17	39	84	123	175	165	200	73	50			
Martell									250					
Martinsburg	90	100	73	68	79	105	93	303	291	180	154			
Maskell	54	76	43	54	84	138	131	165	150					
Mason City	160	196	196	277	305	396	447	487	480	241	250			
Max	100	100		150	135	140	65	62	100	40				
Maxwell	285	410	282	324	347	480	409	410	289	83				
Maywood	313	332	309	337	409	426	525	533	443	200				
Mead	513	506	488	428	388	260	310	329	330	330	324			
Meadow Grove	332	400	372	430	461	479	483	449	388	237	75	75		
Melbeta	116	151	124	118	138	145	138	129						
Memphis	117	89	71	77	92	103	149	186	162	250				
Merna	377	389	322	349	385	414	439	553	459	141	150			
Merrick												250		
Merriman	151	159	172	285	260	321	362	346	254	40				
Milford	1886	2108	1846	1462	951	759	832	792	716	542	555	402	75	

POPULATION HISTORY OF NEBRASKA CITIES AND TOWNS 1860-1990

COMMUNITY	1990	1980	1970	1960	1950	1940	1930	1920	1910	1900	1890	1880	1870	1860
Millard			7460	1014	391	315	321	300	260	323	328	131		
Miller	130	147	130	137	179	205	263	223	330	194	100			
Milligan	328	332	319	323	367	392	412	418	336	283	184			
Minatare	807	969	939	894	890	1125	1079	660	338					
Minden	2749	2939	2669	2383	2120	1848	1716	1527	1559	1238	1380	98		
Mitchell	1743	1956	1842	1920	2101	2181	2058	1298	640					
Monowi		18	16	40	67	99	123	100	109					
Monroe/Munroe	309	294	295	261	269	315	293	309	282	214	59			
Moorefield	52	36	56	55	58	97	156	151	300	125	60			
Morrill	974	1097	937	884	849	877	756	772	346					
Morse Bluff	128	132	162	119	142	170	179	216	196	177				
Mt. Claire					35		217	200	125	76				
Mullen	554	720	667	811	652	725	524	499	400	100				
Murdock	267	242	262	247	225	199	233	206	222	240				
Murray	418	465	286	279	244	209	169	210	300	138				
Naper	130	136	159	198	188	195	176	199	300	94	347	96		
Naponee	97	160	187	206	391	272	252	263	195	188				
Nebraska City	6547	7127	7441	7252	6872	7339	7230	6279	5488	7380	11941	4183	6050	1922
Nehauka	260	270	298	262	272	353	298	289	350	309	258			
Neligh	1742	1893	1764	1776	1822	1796	1649	1724	1566	1135	1209	326		
Nelson	627	733	746	695	806	963	903	955	978	978	913	196		
Nemaha	188	209	207	232	288	379	296	351	325	400	532	908	628	
Nenzel	25	28	27	43	24	125	76	42	42	25				
New Helena									25		67	150		
Newcastle	271	348	347	357	426	447	446	500	436	331	62	82		
Newman Grove	787	930	863	880	1004	1036	1146	1260	850	696	330			
Newport	136	141	141	162	207	275	273	430	268	208	100			
Nickerson	291	254	214	168	140	159	183	141	225	230	138	200		
Niobara	376	419	602	736	577	629	761	736	633	459	633	475		
Nora	24	24	43	60	88	119	157	130	200	88	50	93		
Norfolk	21479	19449	16607	13640	11335	10490	10717	8634	6025	3883	3038	547	350	
Normal	48	58	52	57	68	98	107	127		258				
Norman									200	68				
North Bend	1249	1368	1350	1174	906	1003	1108	1087	1105	1010	897	415	150	
North Loup	361	405	441	453	526	567	657	637	519	420	386	255		
North Platte	22605	24479	19447	17184	15433	12429	12061	10466	4793	3640	3055	363	540	
Northport	40	70	100	128	164	125	123	110						
Oak	68	79	100	125	131	177	218	201	237	198	50	75		
Oakdale	362	410	322	397	502	561	663	707	631	585	630	338		
Oakland	1279	1393	1355	1429	1456	1380	1433	1356	1073	1008	807	345		

POPULATION HISTORY OF NEBRASKA CITIES AND TOWNS 1860-1990

COMMUNITY	1990	1980	1970	1960	1950	1940	1930	1920	1910	1900	1890	1880	1870	1860
Obert	39	44	36	42	91	112	112	116	200	114				
Oconto	147	176	155	219	258	260	243	272	245	188				
Octavia	132	127	97	94	103	151	142	162	200	200	300	216		
Odell	291	322	349	358	420	404	472	403	427	359	896			
Offutt AFB	10833	8787	8445											
Ogallala	5095	5638	4976	4250	3456	3159	1631	1062	643	355	494	114		
Ohiowa	146	135	156	195	253	326	394	433	373	319	369	48		
Omaha	335795	314255	346929	301598	251117	223844	214006	191601	124096	102555	140452	30518	16083	1883
Omarel												150		
O'Neill	3852	4049	3753	3181	3027	2532	2019	2107	2089	1107	1226	57		
Ong	69	104	129	128	173	193	250	265	285	200	75			
Orchard	439	482	467	421	458	493	505	444	532	180				
Ord	2481	2658	2439	2413	2239	2240	2226	2143	1960	1372	1208	181		
Ordville					1332									
Orford												220		
Orleans	490	527	592	608	956	815	985	954	942	656	812	409	150	
Osceola	879	975	923	1013	1098	1039	1054	1209	1105	882	947	527	100	
Oshkosh	986	1057	1067	1025	1124	910	843	707	350	501				
Osmond	774	871	883	719	732	796	750	642	567	150				
Otoe/Berlin	196	197	204	225	230	298	263	261	196			279		
Overton	547	633	538	523	497	491	600	515	574	255	416	60		
Oxford	949	1109	1116	1090	1270	1141	1155	739	593	787	428	186		
Page	191	172	177	230	275	335	359	608	600	248				
Palisade	381	401	372	528	694	799	731	527	380	176	126			
Palmer	753	487	391	418	434	516	588	577	373	185				
Palmyra	545	572	386	377	372	401	344	317	334	301	487	239		
Panama	207	160	153	155	168	174	198	210	230	200	135	120		
Papillion	10372	6399	5606	2235	1034	763	718	666	624	594	600	444	250	
Parkview			1089											
Pauline	60	40		88	70	235	178	162	250	128				
Pawnee City	1008	1156	1267	1343	1606	1647	1573	1595	1610	1969	1550	763	575	
Paxton	536	568	503	566	606	551	507	430	179	58	50			
Pell				1709										
Pender	1208	1318	1229	1165	1167	1135	1006	992	804	943	429			
Peru	1110	998	1380	1151	1265	1024	835	783	950	848	624	567	425	
Petersburg	388	381	370	400	508	657	585	501	533	478	150			
Phillips	316	405	341	192	190	205	221	274	274	186	212	112		
Pickrell	201	184	118	130	161	170	183	160	200	118	197			
Pierce	1615	1535	1360	1216	1167	1249	1271	1105	1200	770	563	73	75	
Pilger	361	400	470	491	512	537	578	563	471	250	162			

POPULATION HISTORY OF NEBRASKA CITIES AND TOWNS 1860-1990

COMMUNITY	1990	1980	1970	1960	1950	1940	1930	1920	1910	1900	1890	1880	1870	1860
Plainview	1333	1483	1494	1467	1427	1411	1216	1199	941	603	375	75		
Platte Centre	387	367	384	402	422	509	525	464	388	392	302			
Plattford														135
Plattsmouth	6412	6295	6371	6244	4874	4268	3793	4190	4287	4964	8392	4175	1944	474
Pleasant Dale	253	259	258	190	163	140	138	221	257	238	183	200		
Pleasant Hill					29	110	145	210	140	246	199	115	200	
Pleasanton	372	349	261	199	188	235	282	262	252	103				
Plum Creek												344	325	
Plymouth	455	506	424	372	348	434	418	453	438	195		60		
Pode			19	19	33	72	104	105	100	50				
Polk	345	440	413	433	508	493	532	561	396					
Ponca	877	1057	984	924	893	1003	920	1014	1000	1043	1009	594	200	101
Poole									250					
Potter	388	369	356	554	421	387	515	486	100	121	75			
Powell	30	30		60	70	215	100	175	200	100	300			
Prague	282	285	291	372	396	385	421	353	394	324	185			
Preston	40	45	64	66	81	120	77	113	122	149	141	50		
Primrose	69	102	88	117	154	176	210	155	158					
Princeton	50	60		70		125	100	100	100	129				
Prosser	77	98	70	70	81	99	144	154	163	175				
Ragan	59	71	60	90	102	163	216	222	214	208	150			
Ralston	6236	5143	4731	2977	1300	834	809	455	400					
Randolph	983	1106	1130	1063	1029	1094	1145	1338	1137	850	374			
Ravenna	1317	1296	1356	1417	1451	1429	1559	1703	1359	808	628			
Raymond	167	179	187	223	196	199	205	249	236	200	482	96		
Red Cloud	1204	1300	1531	1525	1744	1610	1519	1856	1686	1554	1839	677	150	
Republican City	199	231	179	189	580	331	417	424	476	386	428	282	150	
Reynolds	104	125	115	131	166	211	213	208	246	260	271	207		
Richland/Benton	96	114	123	139	141	160	174	133	156	160	230	75		
Rising City	341	392	344	308	374	420	472	460	456	499	610	247		95
Riverdale	208	204	155	144	134	121	129	133	200					
Riverton	162	212	220	303	348	390	328	399	369	327	389	426	125	
Roca	84	130	118	123	105	127	107	133	129	177	191	115		
Rock Bluffs									45	45	45	172	150	
Rockville	87	116	114	153	164	233	241	208	201	158	181			
Rogers	89	89	95	162	113	121	138	128	155	124	100			
Rosalie	178	224	204	182	212	250	279	321	147					
Roseland	247	254	212	163	154	187	180	243	249	227				
Rosemont	20	20			42	150	105	100	200					
Royal	81	86	86	93	157	193	217	202	250	140				

POPULATION HISTORY OF NEBRASKA CITIES AND TOWNS 1860-1990

COMMUNITY	1990	1980	1970	1960	1950	1940	1930	1920	1910	1900	1890	1880	1870	1860
Rulo	191	261	299	412	639	808	719	744	661	877	786	673	611	440
Runelsburgh												200		
Rushville	1127	1217	1137	1228	1226	1125	1006	955	633	483	484			
Ruskin	187	224	229	203	214	223	239	360	339	178	75	125		
Sacramento								25	40	42	195			
St. Deroin										41	50	90	325	
St. Edward	822	891	853	777	917	893	1030	1002	814	625	293	158		
St. Helena	87	111	102	63	77	92	83	124	148	151	189	200	350	69
St. James								157		198		100	125	
St. John											177			44
St. Libory	300	250	200	175	142	140	142	125	125	37				
St. Paul	2009	2094	2026	1714	1676	1571	1621	1615	1336	1475	1263	482	100	
St. Stephens											155	75		404
Salem	160	221	214	261	341	380	387	373	391	533	504	473	304	694
Santee	365	388		150	175		150	36	36	121		126		
Sargent	710	828	789	876	818	847	834	1078	651	250	317	150		
Saronville	38	63	74	71	87	124	148	141	175	176	100	50		
Sartoria							56	51	51	58	300			
Schuyler	4052	4151	3597	3096	2883	2808	2588	2636	2152	2157	2160	1017	675	
Scotia	318	349	354	350	474	453	474	559	328	267	418	127		
Scottsbluff	13711	14156	14507	13377	12858	12057	8465	6912	1746	50				
Scribner	950	1011	1031	1021	913	904	1066	1021	891	827	664	193	125	
Seneca	78	90	111	160	219	255	272	476	250	75		70		
Seward	5634	5713	5294	4208	3154	2826	2737	2368	2106	1970	2108	1525	825	
Shelby	690	724	647	613	624	627	630	559	503	425	333	128		
Shelton	954	1046	1028	904	1032	983	927	1037	1005	861	706	258		
Sheridan													50	
Shickley	360	413	385	371	316	342	389	396	429	372	307	200		
Sholes	22	27	22	26	32	72	90	50	100					
Shubert	237	267	240	231	295	404	387	397	311	303	200			
Sidney	5959	6010	6403	8004	4912	3388	3306	2852	1185	1001	1237	1069	300	
Silver Creek	625	496	483	431	444	421	464	583	379	291	513	86		
Smithfield	53	68	58	85	102	158	165	229	190	100	100			
Snyder	280	387	383	325	369	395	458	359	314	229				
South Auburn									900	710	800	400		
South Bend	93	107	86	86	100	100	99	143	125	141	132	232		
South Creek												175		
South Omaha									26259	26001	8062			
South Sioux City	9677	9339	7920	7200	5557	4556	3927	2402	1196	889	603			
Spalding	592	645	676	683	713	830	839	878	637	148	100			

POPULATION HISTORY OF NEBRASKA CITIES AND TOWNS 1860-1990

COMMUNITY	1990	1980	1970	1960	1950	1940	1930	1920	1910	1900	1890	1880	1870	1860
Spencer	536	596	606	671	540	635	653	728	671	135				
Sprague	157	168	119	120	110	121	135	112	150	165				
Springfield	1426	782	795	506	377	370	419	413	463	400	607	265		
Springview	304	326	260	281	298	347	307	354	216	188	300			
Stamford	188	214	207	220	265	260	297	302	301	138				
Stanton	1549	1603	1363	1317	1403	1526	1479	1487	1342	1052	857	248		
Staplehurst	281	306	227	240	224	234	254	235	228	211	408	122		
Stapleton	299	340	311	359	363	399	431	401						
Steele City	101	137	176	173	214	291	295	300	300	313	380	375		
Steinauer	92	108	118	124	141	207	172	213	248	213	100			
Stella	248	289	282	262	324	396	385	449	430	498	399	188		
Sterling	451	526	476	471	547	640	702	804	714	782	913	560		
Stockham	64	68	65	69	82	197	211	239	189	169	211	50		
Stockville	32	45	61	91	181	238	186	196	232	269	227	75		
Strang	42	59	47	68	100	110	153	175	238	234	269			
Stratton	427	499	481	492	628	630	663	509	367	225	326			
Stromsburg	1241	1290	1215	1244	1231	1127	1320	1361	1355	1154	1362	63		
Stuart	650	641	561	794	785	760	763	739	467	382	245	160		
Sumner	210	254	222	254	267	296	297	345	321	210				
Sunrise										210				
Superior	2397	2502	2779	2935	3227	2650	3044	2719	2106	1577	1614	458		
Surprise	55	60	77	79	120	228	257	279	323	348	300			
Sutherland	1032	1238	840	867	856	862	753	651	447	361				
Sutton	1353	1416	1361	1252	1353	1403	1540	1603	1702	1365	1541	922	525	
Swanton	145	131	160	190	203	233	238	276	285	266	184			
Sweetwater				20		125	52	49	100	31	116	45		
Syracuse	1646	1638	1562	1261	1097	982	947	889	842	861	728	510	300	
Table Rock	308	393	429	422	513	562	673	750	814	852	673	455	375	
Talmage	246	246	285	361	398	423	474	525	461	489	429	193		
Tamora	51	50	93	88	91	131	139	205	205	139	184	75		
Tarnov	61	63	63	70	74	98	82	128	121	50				
Taylor	186	278	240	280	311	349	272	251	300	231	200			
Tecumseh	1702	1926	2058	1887	1930	2104	1829	1688	1748	2005	1654	1268	600	
Tekamah	1852	1886	1848	1788	1914	1925	1804	1811	1524	1597	1244	776	500	
Terrytown	656	727	747	164	228									
Thayer	64	70	78	78	90	135	192	168	200	189				
Thedford	243	313	303	303	275	288	270	260	230	162	50			
Thurston	98	139	117	140	156	221	236	204	112	35				
Tilden	895	1012	947	917	1033	984	1106	1101	901	553	539	258		
Tobias	127	138	124	202	240	316	402	357	445	672	539			

POPULATION HISTORY OF NEBRASKA CITIES AND TOWNS 1860-1990

COMMUNITY	1990	1980	1970	1960	1950	1940	1930	1920	1910	1900	1890	1880	1870	1860
Trenton	656	796	770	914	1239	920	865	592	497	329	267			
Trumball	225	216	220	173	150	126	181	236	300	135	50			
Tryon	150	175		91	150		198	36	100	88				
Uehling	273	273	249	231	250	253	297	267	228					
Ulysses	256	270	312	357	374	429	492	460	551	563	621	305		
Unadilla	294	291	271	254	216	223	194	227	209	243	195	178		
Union	299	307	275	303	277	364	316	292	302	282	200		100	
University Place							4358	4112	3200	1130	571			
Upland	169	192	205	237	251	317	367	433	390	281	75			
Utica	718	689	602	564	550	539	566	571	520	487	466	194		
Valentine	2826	2829	2662	2875	2700	2188	1672	1596	1098	811	896	315		
Valley	1775	1716	1595	1452	1113	985	1039	764	810	534	378	42		
Valparaiso	481	484	415	394	392	403	523	599	560	614	515	300		
Venango	192	230	218	227	233	214	286	285	175	83	75			
Verdel	59	72	74	123	142	108	155	162	162					
Verdigre	607	617	570	584	570	556	618	528	403	200	207			
Verdon	242	278	265	267	366	397	355	347	406	340	253	146		
Verona							85	105	150	115				
Vesta				75	75	225	175	210	250	114	126	67		
Virginia	94	90	83	88	113	144	157	116	154	243	50			
Wabash	50	60				175	75	105	200	190	150			
Waco	211	225	214	166	180	203	266	297	293	310	278	173	300	
Wahoo	3681	3555	3835	3610	3128	2648	2689	2338	2168	2100	2006	1064		
Wakefield	1082	1125	1160	1068	1027	961	1112	1114	861	755		296		
Wallace	308	349	241	293	361	335	406	327	175	130				
Walnut Hill											300			
Walthill	747	847	897	844	958	1204	1162	1145	810					
Washington	125	113	76	44	55	84	76	117	130	58				
Waterbury	95	92	81	81	141	164	204	190	199	130				
Waterloo	479	450	455	516	382	381	432	431	402	345	272	164		
Wauneta	675	746	738	794	926	770	793	572	327	181	75			
Wausa	598	647	720	724	708	732	754	688	604	441				
Waverly	1869	1726	1152	511	310	306	315	334	297	266	319	155		
Wayne	5142	5240	5379	4217	3595	2719	2381	2115	2140	2119	1178	450		
Weeping Water	1008	1109	1143	1048	1070	1139	1029	1084	1067	1156	1350	317	250	
Wellfleet	63	83	51	67	93	111	178	210	300	186	443			
West Lincoln				507	426	277	264	162	200	220				
West Point	3250	3609	3385	2921	2658	2510	2225	2002	1776	1890	1842	1009	520	
West Union									103	90	169	49		
Western	264	336	344	351	434	437	511	427	499	412	397	147	125	

POPULATION HISTORY OF NEBRASKA CITIES AND TOWNS 1860-1990

COMMUNITY	1990	1980	1970	1960	1950	1940	1930	1920	1910	1900	1890	1880	1870	1860
Westerville	30	45		45	50	160	91	84	175	140	186	53		
Weston	299	286	285	340	345	371	365	372	432	426	341	53		
Whitman	100	100		108	180	123	75	105	125	126				
Whitney	38	72	82	98	132	154	177	75	125	58	100			
Wilbur	1527	1624	1483	1358	1356	1355	1352	1255	1219	1054	1226	710	175	
Wilcox	349	379	280	260	296	310	343	358	382	266	250			
Wilsonville	136	189	266	289	327	382	489	470	385	296	309	100		
Winnebago	705	902	675	682	684	800	653	648	399			500		
Winneton	59	82	84	85	120	141	159	208	220					
Winside	434	439	453	416	454	451	483	488	450	400	130			
Winslow	140	143	145	136	138	130	156	154	99					
Wisner	1253	1335	1315	1192	1233	1256	1327	1210	1081	963	610	282	350	
Wolbach	280	301	366	382	442	523	501	589	563	256				
Wood Lake	59	89	117	197	238	323	293	323	198	123	210			
Wood River	1156	1334	1147	828	858	829	751	820	796	589	481	222		
Woodland Park	1100													
Wymore	1611	1841	1790	1975	2258	2457	2680	2592	2613	2626	2420	779		
Wynot	213	222	226	209	233	416	348	368	258					
York	7884	7723	6778	6173	6178	5383	5712	5388	6235	5132	3405	1259	250	
Yutan	626	631	507	335	287	268	313	300	353	263	168	115		

POPULATION HISTORY OF NEVADA CITIES AND TOWNS 1860-1990

COMMUNITY	1990	1980	1970	1960	1950	1940	1930	1920	1910	1907	1900	1890	1884	1880	1870	1861	1860
Alamo	400	260	250	250	25	250	150	200	93	75	75						
Aurora	370	350	300	400	221	580	681	666	755	300	702	225	200	341	160	1985	
Austin										600		1215	2200	1679	1324		
Babbitt		1800	1579	2159	264												
Battle Mountain	3542	2755	1856	800	735	462	661	602	878	350	365	360	250	522	244		
Beatty	1623	900	570	383	485	216	200	164	122	500							
Belleville												26	400	380			
Belmont							28	129	117	200	242	250	330	289	500		
Beowawe	250	250	100	150	75		200	75	75	100	75	75	75	62			
Berlin										250							
Blair									375	1000							
Blue Diamond	420	300	300	440	250												
Boulder City	12567	9590	5223	4059	3303	1342											
Bristol										500				167			
Buckskin										200							
Bullfrog																	
Bullionville													1000				
Bunkerville	300	180	180	150	200		200	200	200	300	63	63	117	159			
Caliente	1111	982	916	792	970	622	644	541	755	500	160	345	350				
Candelaria									32					756			
Carlin	2220	1232	1313	1023	203	832	825	673	423	600	344	413	400	392	295		
Carson City	40443	32022	15468	5163	3082	2478	1596	1685	2466	4000	2100	3950	4227	4229	3042	1466	714
Casazza Moana					812												
Cherry Creek	50	50	75	78	75	158	247	327	365	500	414	139	300	566			
Columbia									549	2000							
Crystal Bay	1200	1200	900	250	400												
Dayton	600	300	350	200	300	390	358	358	517	700	458	576	400	391	918	558	78
Deeth									200	150	82	82	60	355			
Delamar									78	500	904						
Diamondfield										400							
Dutch Creek										350							
East Ely			1992	1796	813		695	699	738	400							
East Las Vegas	11087	6449	6501	200						50							
Eldorado Canyon											103	54	150				
Elko	14736	8758	7621	6298	5393	4094	3217	2173	1677	1600	849	766	800	752	1160		
Ely	4756	4882	4176	4018	3558	4140	3045	2090	2055	2000	525	203	100	348	626		
Empire	300	300		500	375				50	150		327	500				
Eureka	650	500	300	491	470	705	711	708	661	800	785	1609	6000	4207	640		
Fairview										360							
Fallon	6438	4262	2959	2734	2400	1911	1758	1753	741	1000							

POPULATION HISTORY OF NEVADA CITIES AND TOWNS 1860-1990

COMMUNITY	1990	1980	1970	1960	1950	1940	1930	1920	1910	1907	1900	1890	1884	1880	1870	1861	1860
Ramsey																	
Rawhide							26	57	518	500							
Reipetown					250		125		967								
Reno	133850	100756	72863	51470	32497	21317	18529	12016	10867	12000	4500	3563	1500	1302	1035		
Reveille							20	14	26	125	26	263	100	100			
Rhyolite									675	2000							
Rio Tinto					517												
Rochester							300	1100	500								
Round Mountain	210	130	100	180	305	345	231	371	362	600							
Ruby Hill									182		263	142	1200	2165			
Ruby Valley									52	100	52	52	250				
Ruth	550	735	750	800	1244	1560	2281	1312	175	200							
St. Clair													250				
St. Joseph														54	198		
St. Thomas							128	150	93	125	43	105		214	252		
Schurz	617	325	300	300	100		75	475	50								
Searchlight	430	300	279	217	229	181	164	161	387	600	65						
Sheridan									238		238		110	107			
Shermantown														26	874	1022	637
Silver City	100	100	100	125	125		67	100	337	350	307	342	600	605	879		
Silver Peak	190	150	150	63	90		89	112	140	250	48	48					
Silver Springs	420	300	220		60												
Sparks	53367	40780	24187	16618	8203	5318	4508	3238	2500	2000							
Stateline	1379	1500	900	400	125												
Steamboat	450	150	100	250	100		200					87	50	34			
Stewart					500		412			340							
Stillwater									60	100	60	64	100	214			
Sun Valley	11391	8822	2414														
Sunrise Manor	95362	44155	9684														
Sutro									52	100	109	60	100	435			
Tonopah	3616	1952	1716	1679	1375	1904	2116	4144	3900	7500							
Treasure City														44			
Tuscarora	90	75	50	40	40	164	127	241	342	500	669	1156	1500	1364	1920		
Tybo							35	55		50	124	58	500	255	119		
Unionville	30	40	25	32	25		41		85	55	71	33	300	398	470		
Valmy	130	50	50														
Vegas Creek			8970	50	75		100										
Verdi	1140	800	500	250	350		275	419	156	500	156	236	300	300			
Vernon										600							
Victory Village					1776												

POPULATION HISTORY OF NEVADA CITIES AND TOWNS 1860-1990

COMMUNITY	1990	1980	1970	1960	1950	1940	1930	1920	1910	1907	1900	1890	1884	1880	1870	1861	1860
Virginia City	920	600	600	610	500	500	590	1200	2244	4000	2695	6433	13705	10917	7048	2704	2345
Wadsworth	640	350	375	250	275	531	400	403	212	200	1309	537	500	661	253		
Walker Lake	700																
Ward													350	318			
Washoe											29	29	100	91	552	270	
Washoe City	400	400	350	175													
Weed	230	650	650	1092	950												
Wellington	280	200	100	300			75	75	75	100	46	46	100	148			
Wells	1256	1218	1081	1071	947	830	655	521	598	500	440	254	200	243			
Winchester	23365	19728	13981	600													
Winnemucca	6134	4140	3587	3453	2847	2485	1989	1934	1786	1500	1110	1307	1200	763	290		
Wonder									275	1500		577					
Yerington/Mason	2367	2021	2010	1764	1157	964	1005	1169	682	709	709						
Zypher Cove	1434	1316	900	150	100												

1861: Census Report. Council and House Journal, 1st Terr. Ass'y., 1861. Appendix. pp.307-403.
1884: Colorado, New Mexico, Utah, Nevada, Wyoming, and Arizona Gazetteer and Business Directory. Chicago: R.L. Polk, 1884.
1907: Nevada State Gazetteer and Business Directory. Chicago: R.L. Polk, 1907.

POPULATION HISTORY OF NEW MEXICO CITIES AND TOWNS 1850-1990

COMMUNITY	1850	1860	1870	1880	1884	1890	1900	1910	1920	1930	1940	1950	1960	1970	1980	1990
Abiquiu							108	108	500	530	625		250	150	150	350
Acoma	384	522		300	300	566	492	823						150		200
Acomita													980	600		800
Adelino										400	1125					
Adobe Acres															3400	2400
Agua Fria															850	850
Alameda		649	648	570		554	500	554	778	1006	1440	1792	5000	5000	7800	5900
Alamogordo							1050	2315	2363	3096	3950	6783	21723	23035	24024	27596
Albuquerque		1203	1307	2315	5000	3785	6238	11020	15157	26570	35449	96815	201189	244501	331767	384736
Alcalde				168					314	377	375	325	650	800	800	308
Algodones			50	376			95		275	290	125	150	200	250	250	400
Alhambra							221									
Allison										500						
Alma					160											
Alto										123				104		800
Amalia										100	190	300	300	200	190	190
Amistad								250								
Ancho									113	140	101					
Anthony							91	150	265	1000	1162	916	1500	1728	3285	5160
Anton Chico			100	900	1000	305	790	790	500	435	380	435	500	450	200	200
Arenas Valley										100	250	150	150	200	500	500
Armijo										298	256	4516	7000	9000	18900	14600
Arrey										500	187	110	120	100	200	200
Arroyo Hondo							104	200	500			541	300	300	200	250
Arroyo Seco					500	100	100	220	810	620	525	727	500	400	500	300
Artesia								883	1115	2427	4071	8244	12000	10315	10385	10610
Atrisco				740								7367	5000	5000	5512	5479
Aztec					50	439	458	509	489	740	756	885	4137	3354	3036	2598
Barelas			309	350		642				1055		1846				
Bayard									202	243	764	2119	2327	2908		
Belen	540	634	720	690	1000	685	653	680	1306	2116	3038	4495	5031	4823	5617	6547
Bellview										400	196	100				
Bent									315	200						
Berino									119	300	438	300	150			
Bernalillo		619	745	1223	1500	924	900	907	988	2213	2100	1922	2574	2016	3012	5960
Black Rock								65			220	135			500	858
Blanco								128		80			300	150	160	160
Bland							615									
Bloomfield						65	65		255	305	500	619	1292	1574	4881	5214
Blossburg						829	75		218	263						

POPULATION HISTORY OF NEW MEXICO CITIES AND TOWNS 1850-1990

COMMUNITY	1990	1980	1970	1960	1950	1940	1930	1920	1910	1900	1890	1884	1880	1870	1860	1850
Bluewater	500	500	250	500	350	375	250									
Bonanza												200				
Bosque Farms	3791	3353	900	300	400	572	550	218								
Brilliant/Swastika					225	280										
Broadview	50	30		40	80											
Buckeye				160	225	325	210				555					
Buena Vista		150	100	171	265	125	82	69		70	46					
Cabezon								110	100							
Canjilon	150	300	200	800	900	1000	644									
Cannon AFB	3312	3798	5461													
Canoncito	978	600		100	60								147			
Capitan	842	762	439	552	575	932	551	635	567	165	247					
Capulin	50	50	100	120	200	388	283	303								
Carlisle									45		278					
Carlsbad/Eddy	24952	25496	21297	25541	17975	7116	3708	2205	1736	963						
Carrizozo	1075	1222	1123	1546	1389	1457	1171	1301	1082							
Carthage						212	24	163								
Casa Blanca	350	350	350	300	135											
Catskill										200	257					
Cebolla	100	100	150	200	250	360	480									
Cedar Crest	1200	900	450	215	200	200	200									
Cedar Hill	50	50	145	125	130	218	229									
Central	1835	1968	1864	1075	1511	1250	1223	1262	510	508	257	385	126	89		
Cerrillos	350	200	118	238	148	380	475	516	410	491	446	100	500			
Cerro	250	250	150	300	400	164	555	535	100	75						
Chacon	250	300	200		400	200	205	205	150	60						
Chama	1048	1090	899	950	791	625	743	600	533	300	295	100				
Chamberino	300	200	200	250	210	125	125	600		40						
Chamisal	272	600	400		195	125	95	175	75							
Chamita	600	300	300	300		300	275	405	300	52						
Chaparral	975	800										400				
Chaperito												250				
Cherryville																
Chilili	50	100	80	100	100	312	250	68	80	46	46					
Chimayo	2789	1993	900	700	800	1250	500	325	250	50			145			
Chloride	700	500	500	300	56		110	67	50	341	341	300				
Church Rock					300					363						
Cimarron	774	888	927	997	855	744	698	481	791	512	335	200	290	250		
Clarkville																
Clayton	2484	2986	2931	3314	3515	3188	2518	2157	970	750	140					

POPULATION HISTORY OF NEW MEXICO CITIES AND TOWNS 1850-1990

COMMUNITY	1990	1980	1970	1960	1950	1940	1930	1920	1910	1900	1890	1884	1880	1870	1860	1850
Cleveland	300	300	300	300	300	218	300	622	200	55						
Cliff	200	400	250	175	175	100	161	50	50							
Cloudcroft	636	521	525	464	251	215	118	200	225	52						
Clovis	30954	31194	28495	23713	17318	10065	8027	4904	3255							
Clyde									50	250						
Cochiti	434	400	400	250	400		391		345							
Columbus	641	414	241	307	251	265		2110	75							
Continental Divide	200	200		100												
Cooney										50	206					
Cordova	600	600	350	350	320	162	320	360								
Corona	215	236	262	420	530	468	215	215	180							
Corrales	5453	2791	1925	950							500		664			
Costilla	200	200	200	450	500	500	400	550	200	52	62	75				
Coyote										70			368			
Craig												350				
Crown Point	2108	1134	900	550	300	130	90									
Cuba	760	609	415	800	733	250	69	56	110	92						
Cubero	600	400	300	300	225	683	300	350	200	118	118	100	252			
Cuervo							150	319	250							
Cuyamungue	329	160														
Datil	300	100	150	115	80	255	203									
Dawson					1206	1613	2698	4045	3119							
Dayton									280							
Dedman								303								
Deming	10970	9946	8343	6764	5672	3608	3377	3212	1864	1341	1136	1000				
Des Moines	168	178	204	207	282	289	362	287	500							
Dexter	898	882	746	885	784	734	459	333	242							
Dilia	75	75	125	140	250	128	150	110								
Dixon	850	550	600	800	800	750	301		65							
Dona Ana	1202	800	800	800	800	838	842	1019	830	748	872		875	728	667	498
Dora	167	168	196	113	120	115	119									
Dulce	2438	1648	900	500	150	125										
Duran	100	115	130	195	210	437	300	163	200							
Eagle Nest				300	300	110										
East Vaughn	189	202	300		423	608	423	810								
Edgewood	600	600	100	200	125	132										
El Prado	700	700	650	200	100											
El Rito	150	100	100	600	707	1210	500	650	327	350	350	400	600			
Elida	201	202	233	534	430	330	325	300	229							
Elizabethtown						190	142	422		577	338	100	175			

POPULATION HISTORY OF NEW MEXICO CITIES AND TOWNS 1850-1990

COMMUNITY	1990	1980	1970	1960	1950	1940	1930	1920	1910	1900	1890	1884	1880	1870	1860	1850
Encinal	300	300	200	346	408	652	151	124	200							
Encino	131	155	250	346	375	500	375	113	60							
Ensenada	100	100	200	200												
Espanola	8389	6803	4528	1976	1446	643	314	560	400	172	176	50				
Estancia	792	880	721	737	916	668	634	578	517							
Eunice	2676	2970	2641	3531	2352	1227	313	228								
Fairacres	600	600	300	350	200		500									
Fairview				900	800		285	240	120	85	110	100				
Farmington	33997	31222	21979	23786	3637	2161	1350	728	785	548	336	50				
Fierro	50			300	498	586	940	753	361	650						
Five Points	4200	5500		2500	3200											
Flora Vista	1021	500	500	500	250	156	250	250	60							
Floyd	117	146	248	423	50											
Folsom	71	73	75	142	206	360	392	761	484	297	377					
Fort Bascom													127	133		
Fort Bayard			390	500	483	425	509	509	550	509	509	400	250	241		
Fort Craig												500		146		
Fort Cummings															346	
Fort Marcy														292		
Fort McRae																
Fort Seldon	300	300	389	350	250	188	218	218	200	150	253	100	118	126		
Fort Stanton	1269	1421	1615	1809	1982	1669	839	777	400	200	215	100		134		
Fort Sumner					250	185	261	284	276	288	229	300	164	244		
Fort Union											480	500	400	464		
Fort Wingate	950	900	400	200	250	312	513	432								
French	700	700	700	256	150	190	218	210	175	60						
Fruitland		700	700	200	200	250	200	481	250	258						
Galisteo	400		100	150	125	256	282	735	65							
Gallina	400	400	300	100	100	260	250	255	65							
Gallup	19154	18161	14596	14089	9133	7041	5992	3920	2204	2946	1208	350	506			
Gamerco	400	400	400	700	600	600	600	1000								
Gardiner									1120	965						
Garfield	300	300	150	300	200		200									
Georgetown										88	409	500	540			
Gibson									550	550						
Gila	375	350	100	150	300	205	250	381	60			50				
Glenwood	250	180	175	150	100		58	110								
Glorieta	240	200	100	200	100	190	280	268	43	43	45	250				
Golden	50			80		100	112	330	150	100	45	400				
Grady	110	122	104	100	130	237	155	125	125							

POPULATION HISTORY OF NEW MEXICO CITIES AND TOWNS 1850-1990

COMMUNITY	1990	1980	1970	1960	1950	1940	1930	1920	1910	1900	1890	1884	1880	1870	1860	1850
Grants	8626	11439	8768	10274	2251	1926	840	297	87	87	87	100				
Grenville	24	39	21	55	102	143	231	100								
Guadalupita	300	250	260	475	520	325	312	300	155	155		500	428			
Hachita	90	150		200	200	250	300	450				300				
Hacienda Acres	850	300														
Hagarman	961	936	953	1144	1024	854	609	476	449	45						
Hanover	500	500	350	950	1040	970	397	598	360	79						
Happy Valley	700	630	630													
Hatch	1136	1028	867	888	1064	822	364	110	40	40						
Heaton								318								
Highrolls/Mountain Park	400	650	650	235	100	130	85									
Hillsboro	200	150	125	200	250	285	403	429	400	557	621	500	500			
Hobbs	29115	29153	26025	25275	13875	10619	598	178								
Holloman AFB	5891	7245	8001													
Holman	260	400	300	510												
Hondo	250	180	250	250	200		200									
Hope	101	111	90	108	186	289	275	430	417							
House	85	117	119	139	125	138	115	46	75							
Hurley	1534	1616	1796	1851	2079	2500	2673	2959								
Isleta	1703	1246	1080	1870	1400	1688	1298	1100	1085	1050	1059	700			440	
Jal	2156	2675	2602	3051	2047	1157	404									
Jarales	350	250	525	1000	1190	815	890	849	756	848	676	450	196	897	473	
Jemez	1301	1503	1197	1050	878	875	465	525	525	455	428				790	
Jemez Springs	413	316	356	223	135	495	200	250	130							
Kelly					55	101	224	407	1015	616	351	75				
Kenna									440							
Kingston	50			43	50		28		109	284	816	300				
Kirtland	3552	2358	900	800		375	72	55	45							
Knowles									210							
Koehler				385	300		1090	1070	100							
La Cienega	1066	200	115													
La Cueva							375		200	66						
La Huerta			950		500	500	300									
La Jara				250	350	125										
La Joya	100	100	100	150			418	350		110	312	250	347			
La Land	1625	1194	600	400	250	188	150	245	230							
La Luz	200	100	200	350	150		200	250	85	85	85					
La Madera	900	900	600		601	500	600	315	175				289			
La Mesa		900		956												
La Plata	50	50		150	300	178	300	225	50	50	50					

POPULATION HISTORY OF NEW MEXICO CITIES AND TOWNS 1850-1990

COMMUNITY	1990	1980	1970	1960	1950	1940	1930	1920	1910	1900	1890	1884	1880	1870	1860	1850
La Union	500	200	200	350	350	218	300									
Laguna	434	800	900	462	502	800	766	1092	1342	1077	1140	1000			931	748
Lake Arthur	336	327	306	387	380	279	215	141	344							
Lake Valley	300	300							125	77		1000				
Lake Wood				58	46	100	75	275	200							
Lamy		65		103	235	191	306	164	80	91	91					
Las Cruces	62126	45086	37857	29367	12325	8385	5811	3969	3836	2906	2340	2000	1298	1304	768	414
Las Padillas					487	438										
Las Vegas	14753	14322	13835	13818	13763	12362	9097	8206	6934	6319	4697	6000	6000	2526	1094	1550
Ledoux	175	125	400	500	400				40							
Lemitar	400	400	300	500	600	300	400	436		52		500	169			
Lincoln	100	100	100	100	80	375	495	504	524	565	577	600	638	100		
Llano	150	200	150	350	504		87									
Loco Hills	175	300	350	450	300											
Logan	870	785	386	320	400	500	400	125	320							
Loma Beach											127		300			
Lordsburg	2951	3195	3429	3436	3525	3101	2069	1325	1323	796	228	500				
Lorenzo													244			
Los Alamos	11455	11039	11310	12584	9934											
Los Chaves	250	500	230		100											
Los Duranes					2873	794										
Los Griegos					325	310										
Los Lunas	6013	3525	973	1186	889	666	513	470	375	458	345	1000	876	598	484	226
Los Ojos/Park View	300	350					500	800	473	473						
Los Padillas	2400				789	750										
Los Ranches de Albuquerque	3955	2702	1900				905	559	479		538					
Los Ranchos	3200	4300														
Loving	1243	1355	1192	1646	1487	380	302	110	60							
Lovington	9322	9727	8915	9660	3134	1916	961	411	100							
Lumberton	120	200	190	300	350	625	600	450	386	465	504					
Luna	250	250	200	225	220		170		60							
McCartys	400	400	400													
Madrid	150				477	938	1116	555	427	422						
Magdalena	861	1022	652	1211	1297	1323	1371	1867	1226	300	273	300				
Malaga	200	200	250	500	701	564	701	650	100							
Maljamar	50	175	400	350	350											
Manzano		50	200	250	500	500	500	300		90	80					
Maxwell	247	316	393	392	404	483	439	384	270	104						
Mayhill	300	200	200	300												
Medanales	150	250	150		200	104	150									

POPULATION HISTORY OF NEW MEXICO CITIES AND TOWNS 1850-1990

COMMUNITY	1990	1980	1970	1960	1950	1940	1930	1920	1910	1900	1890	1884	1880	1870	1860	1850
Melrose	662	649	636	698	936	851	655	364	700							
Mentmore	200	100	315	230	300		350	175								
Mescalero	1159	1259	900	1480	1200	750	175	175	80	70	70					
Mesilla	1975	2029	1718	1264	1264	1625	1675	1011	1271	1274	1389	2000	1497	1578	2420	
Mesilla Park				2000	500	500	350	275	150	150						
Mesita	627	300	300													
Mesquite	600	400	400	500	210	375	100									
Mexican Springs	242	500	300	109												
Miami	100	100	150	120	150		200									
Milan	1911	3747	2222	2658												
Mills				22	136	136	171	300	50							
Mimbres			155	125	136	157	177									
Mogollon					26	454	299	482	779	599						
Monero			150	207	500	558	216	185	87	87						
Montezuma	175	250	110	137	300	300										
Monticello	60	125	125	150	150	220	175	200	150	60						
Montoya				81	70	125	300	310	250							
Mora	1200	900	1400	1250	1250	1250	1049	1011	817	741	688	700	915	1083		
Moriarty	1399	1276	758	720	500	380	396	300	250							
Mosquero	164	197	244	310	583	742	401	210								
Mountain Park	250					187	320	320	75							
Mountain View	2300	1900	1900		300											
Mountainair	926	1170	1022	1605	1418	1477	1027	577	350				350			
Nacimiento																
Nambe	1246	1017	400	486	879	625	534	118	108							
Naravista	200	200	350	350	250	384	300	275	450							
Navajo	1985	909	700													
New Laguna	600	600	300	150	150											
Newcomb	388	300	300	150	200											
Newkirk	60	60	75	250	250	115	77									
Nogal	120	100	80	75	50	100	211	180	93	93	93					
North Valley	12507	13006	10366													
Ocate	40	40	288	300	105	300	400		397	397	118	500	650	75		
Oil Center	225	270	600	750	100	258	107	115	130							
Ojo Caliente	300	500	200	300		632						250				
Ojo Feliz	70	150	190	250	365	312	150									
Ojo Sarco	100	100	184	226	250	106	100									
Organ	500	500	400	500	100	156	130	275								
Oro Grande	60	80	80	75	50		140	80	200							
Padillas													350			

POPULATION HISTORY OF NEW MEXICO CITIES AND TOWNS 1850-1990

COMMUNITY	1990	1980	1970	1960	1950	1940	1930	1920	1910	1900	1890	1884	1880	1870	1860	1850
Paguate	492	400	600	500	520	625	515	400					400			
Pajarito	1400	2000	2500		150		200									
Paradise Hills	5513	5096	2000													
Paraje						312	456	300	400	400	72	600	86			
Pasamonte					100	378	100			35						
Pecos	1012	885	598	584	1241	1148	1029	550	540	536	673	350	241	356	369	
Pena Blanca	300	375	250	203	250	108	250			610	410		504	300		
Penasco	648	900	450	500	627	500	600	600	610	116	116					
Peralta	450	325	325	380	573	486	573	565		72	72	100		50		
Petaca	50	50	84	200	150	253	300	345		50						
Picacho	100	100	125	80	150	128	200	200								
Pinos Altos	200	200	200	250	250	188	233	315	393	1118	870	500	150	246	824	
Placitas	1611	450	150	300	200	316	200						283			
Playas	750	650														
Pojuaque	1037	900	700	330	200		250	400								
Polvadera	200	200	200	150	300	128	300	420		40						
Ponderosa	200	150	200	217	100	252	100									
Portales	10690	9940	10554	9695	8112	5104	2519	1154	1292	115						
Prewitt	400	400	150	135	65											
Pueblo Pintado	300	300														
Puerto de Luna	130	130	250	400	300	110	300	400	750	750	92	100	500			
Quemado	250	250	300	260	375	438	250	48	50							
Questa	1707	1202	1095	1350	600	700	600	675	551	551	72					
Rainsville	170	300	300	220	200		100									
Ramah	600	600	400	250	175	125	298	275	46	46	46					
Ranches of Taos	1779	1411	900	1668	1386	1186	800	1415		1397	1397	2000				
Raton	7372	8225	6962	8146	8241	7607	6090	5544	4539	3540	1255	2000	2250			
Red River	387	332	180	150	150	100	150	210	115	115						
Rehoboth	150	100	300	100	150		150									
Reserve	319	439	400	400	300	275	206		40							
Ribera	100		300	300	213	133	327	310	120							
Rincon	250	195	300	300	310	312	300	280	185	60	147					
Rio Communities	3233	2089														
Rio Rancho	32505	9985	1163													
Rodeo	200	120	100	200	150	250	150	67	50							
Rodey																
Romerville	200								65				159			
Roswell	44654	39676	33908	39593	25738	13482	11173	7033	6172	2049	343					
Rowe	200	100	150	510	365	185	200									
Roy	362	381	476	633	1074	1138	713	564	400							

POPULATION HISTORY OF NEW MEXICO CITIES AND TOWNS 1850-1990

COMMUNITY	1990	1980	1970	1960	1950	1940	1930	1920	1910	1900	1890	1884	1880	1870	1860	1850
Ruidoso	4600	4260	2216	1557	806	165	149	150								
Ruidoso Downs/Green Tree	920	949	702	407	363											
Sabinal												250				
Sabinoso													169			
Salem	200	200	400		300		91		40							
San Acacia												300				
San Antonio	400	500	500	500	400	315	400	375	400	127	127	500	52			
San Cristobal	180	150	275	325	215	265	201									
San Felipe	1557	1465	1187	1034	817	750	618		492	516	554					
San Hilario													300		357	
San Ildefonso	447	120	120	200	400	500	500		363							
San Jon	277	341	308	411	362	250	200	200	200					300		
San Jose	250	250	180	200	175	185	200	310		150			277			
San Juan	900	600	600	700	275	125			362				600			
San Lorenzo	100	230	200	350	340	300	310	340					284			
San Marcial	200					475	400	500	973	973	742	1000	37			
San Mateo	500	200	250	150	230	200	250	325					311			
San Miguel	200	200	200	400	300	300	300		43	43		1000				
San Patricio	200	300	150	375	300		250									
San Pedro									130	130	835					
San Rafael	600	560	400	500	300	135	300	700	300	76						
San Ysidro	233	199	182	144		250			115							
Sandia	6742	5288	6867													
Sandia Park	500	250	200	150												
Sandoval				600	600				625	625						
Sanostee	626	100														
Santa Ana	476	200							212							
Santa Clara	1156	450	400						268							
Santa Cruz	975	600	450	500	600	375	600	675	417	417	110		196			
Santa Fe	55859	48953	41167	33394	27998	20325	11176	7236	5072	5603	6185	8000	6635	4765	4635	4846
Santa Rita	2263	2469	600		2135	4344	3889	3565	1951	1874		500				
Santa Rosa	950	950	2485	2220	2199	2310	1127	1093	531	300	260	500	157		167	
Santa Teresa																
Santo Domingo	2866	2082	1662	900	1169					772	671				263	
Santo Tomas	400	400	400		200											
Sapello	403	200	250	250			169	355	91	91	113		182			
Seama	150	100	150	200			100	225								
Seboyeta					167	520	330		42	42						
Ship Rock	7687	7237	900	900	500	500	188	68	50					80		
Silver City	10683	9887	8557	6972	7022	5044	3519	2662	3217	2735	2102	3000	1800			

POPULATION HISTORY OF NEW MEXICO CITIES AND TOWNS 1850-1990

COMMUNITY	1990	1980	1970	1960	1950	1940	1930	1920	1910	1900	1890	1884	1880	1870	1860	1850
Socorro	8159	7173	5849	5271	4334	3712	2058	1256	1560	1512	2295	3000	1272	921	523	543
South Valley	35701	38916	29389													
Springer	1262	1696	1574	1564	1558	1314	957	915	550	558	614	600	34			
Steins					60		100	167	120	35	35					
Sugarite					300		300									
Sunland Park/Meadow Vista	8179	3377	1402	600												
Taiban									320							
Tajique	200	200	100	200	250	220	200	325								
Talpa	350	500	400	500			50									
Taos	4065	3369	2479	2463	1815	965	1035	785	755	1225	978	1500	850	1302		
Taos Pueblo	1187	1030	1030	900	911		847	832	830	419	509		350		363	
Taos Ski Valley	300															
Tapicitoes				42	100	250	400									
Tatum	768	896	982	1168	688	480	598	312								
Tecolotenos		150			95	250	250						176			
Tererro	70	65			100		500									
Tesuque	1490	1014	600	500	300	300	200	381	409							
Texico	966	958	772	889	691	478	569	67	50							
Thoreau	1099	699	900	700	200	300	250									
Tierra Amarilla	900	800	850	820	782	648	1097	1106	963	844	624	1000	478	559		
Tijeras	340	311	500	500	150	190	50	59	40							
Toadlena	250	300	250	250	250	300										
Tohatchi	661	1011	400	350	300		200									
Tome	400	400	500	400	210		250	500	300	300						
Torreon	225	150	100	100	200	400	400	763	100	100						
Tortugas	500	500	465													
Tramperas					250						81	150	250			
Trementina			80	39	100		300	93	50	50	109	70				
Tres Piedras	200	200	200	150			75	110	90	75						
Truchas	400	400	400	500	694	850	850									
Truth or Consequences/Hot Springs	6221	4219	4656	4269	4563	2940	1336	455								
Tucumcari	6831	6765	7189	8143	8419	6194	4143	3117	2526							
Tularosa	2615	2536	2851	3200	1642	1446	1406	1096	1022	752	572	500	549			
Turn					400		600									
Turquesa												500				
Tyrone	950	950	100	98	200	165	350	4064								
University Park	4520	4383	4165	4387												
Vadito	283	180	335	375	300	300	200									
Vado	200	200	200	170	190	105	225									
Valedon/Shakespeare							1113	1470			238	250	250			

POPULATION HISTORY OF NEW MEXICO CITIES AND TOWNS 1850-1990

COMMUNITY	1990	1980	1970	1960	1950	1940	1930	1920	1910	1900	1890	1884	1880	1870	1860	1850
Valencia	200		500	818	350	400	350	475	410	410	270					
Vallecitos	150	150	150	450	400		275	300	220	220	322					
Van Houten							764	611	798							
Vanadium	200	200	200	300	200	116	87									
Vanderwagen	300	300				110										
Vaughn	633	737	867	1170	1356	1331	968	888	700							
Veguita	200	200	200	170	170		200									
Velarde	400	400	300	650	600	688	600									
Villanueva	350	300	300	400	560		300									
Virden	108	246	151	135	146	206	196									
Wagon Mound	319	416	630	760	1120	979	852	875	983	895	449	300				
Wallace											205	1000				
Waterflow	300	500	475	288	150	300	246									
Watrous	100	150	250	400	350	313	406	435	336	244	365	250	100			
Weed							80	525		63						
White Oaks				27	61		59	157	271	404	385	1000	268			
White Rock	6192	6560	3861													
White Sands	2616	3120	4167													
Willard	183	166	209	294	296	462	482	421	450							
Williamsburg	456	433	367	300	200											
Winston	75	50		40	100	162	100									
Yeso			125	300	250	230	98	60	75							
Youngsville							219	219								
Zia	637	400	600	458					123							
Zuni	5857	5551	3958	3585	2563	2000	1736	1680	1300	1525	558				1300	1294

1884: Colorado, New Mexico, Utah, Nevada, Wyoming, and Arizona Gazetteer and Business Directory. Chicago: R.L. Polk, 1884.

POPULATION HISTORY OF NORTH DAKOTA CITIES AND TOWNS 1870-1990

COMMUNITY	1870	1880	1890	1900	1905	1910	1915	1920	1925	1930	1940	1950	1960	1970	1980	1990
Abercrombie			275	206	357	299	313	266	257	242	215	244	244	262	260	252
Acton		200														
Adams						338	406	404	375	345	355	411	360	284	303	248
Adrian						225	150									
Alamo								310	146	211	214	192	182	124	122	69
Alexander					100	200	274	415	356	386	415	302	269	208	358	216
Alfred						250	85									
Alice					125	400	250	130		169	181	162	124	83	62	62
Almont						450	500	216		216	232	190	190	109	146	117
Alsen						250	125	163	317	358	312	114	228	201	169	113
Ambrose				100	200	320	301	389	364	334	294	286	220	109	60	48
Amenia		75	70			300	100	100		90	104	127	117	80	93	82
Amidon								145	151	141	102	82	84	54	43	24
Anamoose				150	600	669	586	563	484	495	478	542	503	401	355	277
Aneta			61	210	643	654	666	662	687	568	509	469	451	376	341	314
Anselm						160	35									
Antler				298	450	342	294	265	276	318	254	217	210	135	101	74
Ardoch			214	200	219	271	242	153	144	110	119	137	106	70	78	49
Argusville			89		100	200	100	63	106	115	145	126	118	118	147	161
Arnegard							50	216	220	254	222	206	228	141	193	122
Arthur		50	90	140	100	225	200	120	246	322	335	380	325	412	445	400
Arvilla		150	179	199	300	225	160	168		182	106	115	135	115	110	150
Ashley			271	157	474	682	745	1009	962	1033	1345	1423	1419	1236	1192	1052
Auburn			210	142	100	121	50	59		62	79	39	40	48	35	40
Ayr			52	92	100	275	200	368	222	106	107	104	81		42	19
Balfour				209	522	399	292	322		197	193	162	159	93	51	33
Balta							105	110		110	263	196	165	133	139	79
Bantry					200	450	400	375		399	266	125	93	40	28	16
Barlow					250	425	300	269		288	103	43	40		30	40
Barney						300	150	157		170	209	145	115	81	70	79
Bartlett		175	94	199	144	120	106	98	70	67	78	61	39	19	19	20
Barley							235									
Barton			500	160	300	202	176	158	168	170	157	102	80	34	38	24
Bathgate		261	377	641	561	328	376	352	342	292	312	209	175	133	67	75
Bay Center			200	50	50											
Beach					50	1003	1542	1106	1148	1263	1178	1461	1460	1408	1381	1205
Belcourt			49		50			205		205	212	524	524	950	1803	2458
Belfield				208		725	561	526	489	653	870	1051	1064	1130	1274	887
Benedict						250	150	195	121	145	167	127	129	72	68	52
Bentley						200	200									

POPULATION HISTORY OF NORTH DAKOTA CITIES AND TOWNS 1870-1990

COMMUNITY	1990	1980	1970	1960	1950	1940	1930	1925	1920	1915	1910	1905	1900	1890	1880	1870
Bergen	12	24	24	52	51	67	98		319	150	275	40				
Berlin	32	57	76	78	124	132	135	116	130	119	137	150				
Berthold	409	485	398	431	459	428	511	523	498	320	454	150				
Berwick	20	22	33	56	71	92	294		275	450	650	250	119			
Beulah	3363	2908	1344	1318	1501	942	913	626	552	228						
Big Bend				39	207											
Binford	233	293	242	261	309	311	317	288	393	324	275	250	80			
Bisbee	227	257	305	388	365	393	531	449	500	471	444	360	269			
Bismark	49256	44485	34703	27670	18640	15496	11090	9150	7122	6344	5443	4913	3319	2186	1758	
Blabon										150	350	60				
Blaisdell										100	175					
Blanchard										100	160					
Bonnersville												100			195	
Bordulac										125	180	50				
Bottineau	2598	2829	2760	2613	2268	1739	1322	1067	1172	1206	1331	1227	888	493		
Bowbells	498	587	584	687	806	787	695	615	643	639	651	547	150			
Bowdon	196	220	229	259	348	348	303	265	306	316	302	200	175			
Bowesmont										50	200	200	180	125	75	
Bowman	1741	2071	1762	1730	1382	967	888	775	767	744	481					
Braddock	56	86	106	141	175	185	193	179	216	350	400	100	141			
Brierwood	88	47														
Brinsmade	21	54	36	110	136	206	199	164	191	164	203	152	130			
Brocket	81	74	95	153	212	291	276	262	240	214	186	150				
Buchanan										125	250	100				
Bucyrus	22	32	42	60	111	117	124	109	113	100	275					
Buffalo	204	226	241	234	261	245	242	236	268	243	241	237	213	177	219	
Buford										200	300	50				
Burlington	995	762	247	262	240	232	246		219	200	350	100	98			
Butte/Dogden	129	157	193	257	272	261	231	237	252	237	320					
Buttzville										65	200					
Buxton	343	336	235	321	387	404	410	394	315	450	625	375	282	274	200	
Caledonia	80	100	150	150	150	160	145		133	250	250	200	276	267	225	
Calio	43	60	75	101	102	98	152	168	132	75	150					
Calvin	27	61	78	104	152	345	344		400	275	525					
Cando	1564	1496	1512	1566	1530	1282	1164	1055	1111	1117	1332	1328	1061	200		
Cannon Ball	702	400														
Canton City/Hensel	64	68	81	130	139	148	125	101	101	134	115	120	98			
Carpio	178	244	215	199	194	322	344	265	244	457	257	347				
Carrington	2267	2641	2491	2438	2101	1850	1717	1345	1420	1328	1217	1106	492	494	350	
Carson	383	469	466	501	493	473	356	283	277	200	100					

POPULATION HISTORY OF NORTH DAKOTA CITIES AND TOWNS 1870-1990

COMMUNITY	1990	1980	1970	1960	1950	1940	1930	1925	1920	1915	1910	1905	1900	1890	1880	1870
Cassellton	1601	1661	1485	1394	1373	1358	1253	1416	1538	1564	1553	1269	1207	840	361	
Cathay	54	66	110	110	209	189	235	255	185	210	225	200	158			
Cavalier	1508	1505	1381	1423	1459	1105	850	810	819	773	652	744	671	217	100	
Cayuga	60	75	116	195	178	196	219	204	182	206	175	100	52			
Center	826	900	619	476	492	509	293		200	300	100					
Chaffee										250	257					
Christine	140	147	108	125	150	138	235		219	210	375	200	168	83		
Churches Ferry	118	139	131	161	223	244	295	304	353	363	457	376	264	430		
Cleveland	121	130	128	169	181	246	273	277	341	280	325	150	56			
Clifford	51	51	84	109	158	290	240		224	200	350	100	130	72		
Clyde	60	50		100	110	162	287		268	300	375	200				
Coalgate/Colgate				50						250	375					
Cogswell	184	227	203	305	393	430	426	430	445	445	418	350	109	61		
Coleharbor/Coalharbor	88	150	112	210	315	158	320		300	240	300	50	62			
Colfax	80	101	70	98	116	134	124		113	100	225	125	90	150		
Columbus	223	325	465	672	525	506	516	471	332	302	225		216	224	60	
Concrete				50						150	225					
Conway	24	33	57	67	107	120	100	132	148	193	184	256				
Cooperstown	1247	1308	1485	1424	1189	1077	1053	1007	1112	920	1019	1002	648	368	218	
Coteau										125	525					
Coulee	70	110	125	168	229	297	350	328	490	466	539	459	346			
Courtenay	145	139	150	195	235	267	278	244	307	330	279	285	200	84		
Crary										100	225					
Crete										85	200					
Crosby	1312	1469	1545	1759	1689	1404	1271	1100	1147	1101	206	150				
Crystal	199	256	272	372	429	428	314	334	349	301	376	400	385	90	50	
Cumings										100	250	100	100			
Davenport	218	195	147	143	150	147	205	186	214	267	226	250	245	126		
Dawson	78	144	131	206	280	263	306	241	293	200	300	200	288	332	215	
Dazey	129	143	128	226	196	215	251	218	293	233	265	231	310	204		
Deering	99	85	75	117	136	140	192	130	142	170	150	100	168			
Delamere										350	300	150				
Denbigh										150	425	200				
Denhoff	80	80	85	112	170	119	341		334	340	525	318				
Des Lacs	216	212	197	185	180	197	205	151	188	188	450	150				
Devils Lake	7782	7442	7078	6299	6427	6204	5519	5409	5004	4525	5157	2367	1729	846	500	
Dickey	53	74	118	143	165	203	168	74	190	149	187	250	114			
Dickinson	16097	15924	12405	9971	7469	5839	5025	4467	4122	4120	3678	3188	2076	897	414	
Dodge	135	199	121	226	251	234	204	164	172							
Dogden										300						

POPULATION HISTORY OF NORTH DAKOTA CITIES AND TOWNS 1870-1990

COMMUNITY	1990	1980	1970	1960	1950	1940	1930	1925	1920	1915	1910	1905	1900	1890	1880	1870
Donnybrook	106	112	163	196	207	215	259	304	267	295	297	281	71			
Douglas	93	112	144	210	236	313	288	297	284	213	171					
Doyon										160	275	100				
Drake	361	479	636	752	831	654	636	517	508	348	348	150				
Drayton	961	1082	1095	940	875	688	502	600	637	640	587	601	688	318	62	
Dresden	160	150	128	175	225	238	276	304	289	155	325	225	156			
Driscoll	128	170	107	250	246				247	250	725	60				
Dunn Center										369						
Dunseith	723	625	811	1017	713	719	484	382	374	450	478	375	136	162	173	
Durbin				35	34		23		78	40	50	50	69	103	140	
Dwight	83	72	93	101	129	168	104	120	139	160	300	200	141	159		
East Fairview	100	80			202		155	127	175							
Eastedge										25	150					
Eckelson										100	300			80		
Eckman					55	66	79	56	64	87	84					
Edgeley	680	843	888	992	943	803	821	735	803	718	749	415	306	300	50	
Edinburg	284	300	315	330	343	378	284	285	278	264	300	400	286	211		
Edmore	329	416	398	405	458	453	396	402	501	403	344	348				
Edmunds										125	250	50				
Egeland	103	112	96	190	248	275	333	328	306	272	266	150				
Elgin	765	930	839	944	882	583	505	414	429	371						
Ellendale	1798	1967	1517	1800	1759	1517	1264	1094	1334	1361	1389	1099	750	761	701	
Elliott	32	44	50	62	87	118	106	91	95	75	150		22	53		
Embden										75	125	50				
Emerado	483	596	515	328	125	159	340		315	230	350	250	292	212	150	
Enderlin	997	1151	1343	1596	1504	1593	1839	1824	1919	1813	1540	1104	636			
Englevale	64	104	140	151	158	154	183	157	116	150	200	50				
Epping										250	350					
Erie										205	275	100	100			
Esmond	196	337	416	420	475	449	313	314	343	375	353	531				
Everest					14	106	69		64		97	50				
Fairdale	76	97	102	126	131	187	171	191	192	190	140	150	213	172	180	
Fairmount	427	480	412	503	660	705	611	608	706	701	387	368	284	91	75	
Fargo	74111	61383	53365	46662	38256	32580	28619	24921	21961	20549	14331	12512	9589	5664	2693	400
Fessenden	655	761	815	920	917	902	738	757	731	856	713	781	421			
Fingal	138	151	166	190	210	300	324	321	490	500	550	500	376			
Finley	543	718	809	808	671	677	587	572	599	507	516	317	276			
Flasher	317	410	467	515	413	387	346	285	287	303	450	50				
Flaxton	121	182	286	375	436	362	423	385	374	402	301	350				
Flora										60	300	75				

POPULATION HISTORY OF NORTH DAKOTA CITIES AND TOWNS 1870-1990

COMMUNITY	1990	1980	1970	1960	1950	1940	1930	1925	1920	1915	1910	1905	1900	1890	1880	1870
Forbes	56	84	88	138	204	268	265	277	293	245	221	100				
Fordville	299	326	361	367	376	439	442	390	320	378	550					
Forest River	148	152	169	191	236	207	198	231	226	258	233	246	252	84	200	
Forman	586	629	596	530	466	500	386	356	402	358	353	304	257	178	175	
Fort Abercrombie														246		100
Fort Abraham Lincoln																
Fort Buford													42	500	500	454
Fort Clark							92	40	86					410	400	
Fort Pembina															90	168
Fort Ransom	111	99	121	100	200	114	234		218	100	250	100	86	97	300	103
Fort Rice							50		210		75			122	169	215
Fort Stevenson															125	151
Fort Totten	867	750	550	215	250	106	67		61	300	150	136	109	206	200	240
Fort Yates	183	771	1153	825	825	848	491		400	350		300	150	77	450	
Fortuna	53	98	216	185	181	214	196	185	198	125						
Foxholm										200	300	50				
Fredonia	66	82	100	141	268	309	394	354	296	202	350					
Frontier	218	160														
Fullerton	94	107	110	181	206	184	206	218	202	190	206	75				
Gackle	450	456	470	523	604	537	493	472	424	384	600	250				
Galesburg	161	165	134	166	169	290	346		325	250	325	250	198			
Gardar										75	150	50				
Gardena	41	66	84	112	116	125	120	104	99	163	119					
Gardner	85	94	96	107	136	103	108		212	250	266	250	266			
Garfield															150	
Garrison	1530	1830	1614	1794	1890	1117	1024	946	714	535	406	200				
Gascoyne	22	23	34	50	76	48	97	74	60	68	275					
Geneseo										200	280	125				
Gilby	262	283	268	281	350	267	341		420	320	325	300	391	276		
Gladstone	224	317	222	185	224	278	236		220	240	250	200	142	164	195	
Glasston	30	25		75	54	165	153		160	150	75	100	218	137		
Glen Ullin	927	1125	1070	1210	1324	976	950	872	875	887	921	545	215	130		
Glenburn	439	454	381	363	281	190	263	248	228	183	268	199				
Glenfield	118	164	127	129	165	116	110			75						
Golden Valley	239	287	235	286	339	400	294	318	369	243						
Golva	101	101	104	162	174	134	325		325							
Goodrich	192	288	300	392	448	476	468	454	476	479	410	250				
Grace City	103	94	87	104	89		100		130	150						
Grafton	4840	5293	5946	5885	4901	4070	3136	2913	2512	2476	2229	2423	2378	1594	1225	
Grand Forks	49425	43765	39008	34451	26836	20228	17112	15168	14010	13554	12478	10127	7652	4979	1705	

POPULATION HISTORY OF NORTH DAKOTA CITIES AND TOWNS 1870-1990

COMMUNITY	1990	1980	1970	1960	1950	1940	1930	1925	1920	1915	1910	1905	1900	1890	1880	1870
Grand Forks AFB	9343	9390	10474													
Grand Harbor										50	200	50	46	150	250	
Grand Rapids										75	125	50	406	206	200	
Grandin	213	210	187	147	156	158	172		319	330	450	200				
Grano				14	27	57	90	76	112	150	325	150				
Grant										153						
Granville	236	281	282	400	404	443	450	363	394	452	455	500	36			
Great Bend	108	113	86	164	169	198	169	155	142	161	191	100	139			
Grenora	261	362	401	448	525	425	487	456	358							
Grove										249					200	
Gwinner/Forsby	585	725	623	242	197	212	345	329	326	300	350	250	414	50		
Hague	109	127	146	197	328	442	364	278	315	221	183	100	50			
Halliday	288	355	413	509	477	395	305		289	148	50					
Hamar										55	225					
Hamberg	19	41	51	64	124	164	187	175	110	100						
Hamilton	74	109	110	217	241	255	151	179	200	201	213	187	224	257	254	
Hampden	89	126	114	159	203	193	222	197	199	230	425	200				
Hankinson	1038	1158	1125	1285	1409	1420	1400	1390	1477	1625	1503	1047	713	354		
Hanks	11	10	13	78	115	192	213	223	213							
Hannaford	204	201	244	277	313	405	351	439	431	322	340	300	120			
Hannah	49	90	145	253	257	261	262		420	550	600	550	596			
Hansboro	20	43	49	143	134	196	176	204	218	320	400	100	116			
Harlem														106		
Hartland										100	275					
Harvey	2263	2527	2361	2365	2337	1851	2157	2019	1590	1503	1443	803	590			
Harwood	590	326	200	150	126	110	83		79	65	150	60	69			
Hastings										150	375	50				
Hatton	800	787	808	856	991	933	804	768	828	821	666	550	430	257	51	
Havana	124	148	156	206	267	305	271	300	319	321	387	325	198	102		
Haynes	37	58	53	111	145	210	167	161	113	79	350					
Hazelton	240	266	374	451	453	500	446	437	382	426	350	100				
Hazen	2818	2365	1240	1222	1230	662	689	464	520	312						
Heaton										115	275					
Hebron	888	1078	1103	1340	1412	1267	1348	1300	1374	1005	597	307	182	84		
Hensel										200	300	125	160			
Hettinger	1574	1739	1655	1769	1762	1138	1292	1009	817	840	766					
Hickson										75	275	85	100			
Hillsboro	1488	1600	1309	1278	1331	1338	1317	1162	1183	1299	1237	1251	1172	715	500	
Hoople	310	350	330	334	447	346	325	258	250	195	175	183	174			
Hope	281	406	365	390	470	474	535	577	699	633	909	776	606	238	100	

POPULATION HISTORY OF NORTH DAKOTA CITIES AND TOWNS 1870-1990

COMMUNITY	1990	1980	1970	1960	1950	1940	1930	1925	1920	1915	1910	1905	1900	1890	1880	1870
Horace	662	494	226	178	190	265	124		113	104	275	125	115	48		
Hunter	341	369	362	446	417	414	406	387	424	404	365	390	407	194	175	
Hurdsfield	92	113	139	183	223	258	220		275	400	425	50				
Inkster	95	135	198	282	304	310	257	323	368	342	353	432	307	211	40	
Jamestown	15571	16280	15385	15163	16697	8790	8187	7230	6627	5516	4358	5093	2853	2296	393	
Jessie										80	250	75				
Joliette										130		160				
Jud	84	118	110	156	175	202	140	187	178	155	99					
Judson										90	225					
Karlsruhe	146	164	172	221	282	289	258		114	60						
Kathryn	72	95	109	142	200	229	224	229	289	260	550	250				
Kempton										100	200	50				
Kenmare	1214	1456	1515	1696	712	1528	1494	1388	1446	1533	1437	1011	300			
Kensal	191	210	263	334	376	356	420	376	415	462	456		73			
Kensington															200	
Kermit	24	36	46	97	135	23	26	28	37	61	108					
Kief						159	139	171	307	300	375					
Killdeer	722	790	615	765	698	650	495	441	512	322	625	500	348	266	200	
Kindred	569	568	495	580	504	450	429	388	334	310	325					
Kloten										50			107			
Knox	45	69	104	122	190	189	177	204	173	165	330	200	100			
Kramer	51	84	125	175	198	220	190	178	172	211	181			71		
Krem										100	200					
Kulm	514	570	625	664	707	734	742	639	725	628	645	587	463			
La Moure	970	1077	951	1068	1010	990	889	994	1014	1007	929	707	457	309		
Lakewood Park	200															
Lakota	898	963	964	1066	1032	907	860	869	959	873	1023	900	576	227	200	
Landa	38	62	61	110	132	149	140	154	139	100	250					
Langdon	2241	2335	2182	2151	1838	1546	1221	1239	1228	1150	1214	1544	1188	291		
Lankin	152	175	221	303	287	283	267	301	334	325	341					
Lansford	249	294	296	382	352	300	353	348	337	397	456	272				
Larimore	1464	1524	1469	1714	1374	1222	979	865	1089	1255	1224	1635	1235	553	550	
Larson	26	21	35	62	59	79	89	93	114	100	225					
Lawton	63	101	123	159	211	210	233	192	227	216	450					
Leal	35	45	41	70	72	102	105	125	88	200	250	100	50			
Leeds	542	678	626	797	778	782	725	668	704	631	682	520	349	58		
Lehr	191	254	287	381	394	536	458	434	362	156	182	300				
Leipzig										30	225	75				
Leith	43	59	92	100	160	166	174	177	158	150	50					
Leonard	310	289	221	232	325	370	286		189	190	375	125	104	104	50	

POPULATION HISTORY OF NORTH DAKOTA CITIES AND TOWNS 1870-1990

COMMUNITY	1990	1980	1970	1960	1950	1940	1930	1925	1920	1915	1910	1905	1900	1890	1880	1870
Lidgerwood	799	971	1000	1081	1147	1042	1029	1009	1065	1127	1019	749	585	327		
Lignite	242	332	354	355	230	235	217	232	214	150	350					
Lincoln	1132	656														
Linton	1410	1561	1695	1826	1675	1602	1192	1034	1011	730	644	500	109		75	
Lisbon	2177	2283	2090	2093	2031	1997	1650	1626	1855	1553	1758	1362	1046	935	931	
Litchville	205	251	294	345	408	430	410	468	528	476	484	285				
Loma	27	39	85	20	53	256	293		123	200	375					
Loraine	15	21	33	54	70	74	92	75	74	75	300					
Lucca										150	250	150	100			
Ludden	41	47	44	59	96	150	164	154	132	71	109	109	242	427		
Luverne	41	65	84	109	154	187	177	241	225	150						
McClusky	492	658	664	751	850	924	719	625	646	611	517					
McHenry	85	113	152	155	189	250	219	222	299	280	398	417	178			
McKenzie										150	225					
McKinney							22		21			299				
McLeod										125	175					
McVille	559	626	583	551	626	548	513	472	546	401	310					
Maddock	559	677	708	740	741	691	631	583	557	514	374					
Makoti	145	199	159	214	219	212	276	257	283	100						
Mandan	15177	15513	11093	10525	7298	6685	5037	5068	4336	4142	3873	2714	1658	1328	239	
Mandaree	367	300														
Manfred										150	450					
Manning										250	225					
Mantador	77	76	95	98	138	142	229		212	100	100					
Manvel	333	308	265	313	278	209	183		210	200	187	200	218	107	150	
Mapes	30	45		55	30		69		64	60	75	75	60			
Mapleton	682	306	219	180	169	180	195	191	198	215	207	237	322	98	200	
Marion	169	214	215	309	272	242	258	277	294	350	475			119	150	
Marmarth	144	190	247	319	469	626	721	874	1318	708	790					
Martin	117	114	120	146	171	228	211	195	198	350	525					
Max	301	317	301	410	465	423	500	429	473	369	285					
Maxbass	123	141	174	218	259	215	217	180	147	212	240					
Maxwell									285							
Mayville	2092	2255	2554	2168	1790	1351	1199	1345	1218	1154	1070	1212	1106	657	453	
Maza	12	21	20	31	82	66	70	85	64	40	125					
Medina	387	521	488	545	564	500	407	344	415	668	343	100	43			
Medora	101	94	129	133	180	232	228		212	100	150					
Melville										60	200					
Menoken	30	35	132	60	45	262	50		125	187	129					
Mercer	104	134	154	214		291		269		150	325					

POPULATION HISTORY OF NORTH DAKOTA CITIES AND TOWNS 1870-1990

COMMUNITY	1990	1980	1970	1960	1953	1940	1930	1925	1920	1915	1910	1905	1900	1890	1880	1870
Merricourt		17	22	66	105	153	120	114	70	77	78	399				
Michigan City	413	502	478	451	486	491	433	404	491	480	449	529	309	243	130	
Milnor	651	716	645	658	674	677	564	577	680	675	641	437	322	279	331	
Milton	133	195	198	264	322	310	329	370	393	388	410	400	384	202	26	
Minnewaukan/Devil's Lake	401	461	496	420	443	521	480	441	564	518	510	445	432	418	50	
Minot	34544	32843	32290	30604	22032	16577	16099	12245	10476	10053	6188	4125	1277	575		
Minot AFB	9095	9880	12077													
Minto	560	592	636	642	592	630	565	513	602	630	701	950	860	467	450	
Mohall	931	1049	950	956	1073	687	676	598	651	712	493	409				
Monango	53	59	112	133	138	175	211	197	231	177	238	200	133	304		
Montpelier	82	96	116	97	105	133	165	175	186	250	250	50	50	53		
Mooreton	193	216	158	164	161	146	147	141	123	160	425	200	60	147	50	
Mott	1019	1315	1368	1463	1533	1220	1036	810	723	738	725					
Mountain	134	156	146	218	219	205	244		227	150	250	200		50	50	
Munich	610	300	249	213	248	216	260	234	248	256	675	425	146			
Mylo	20	31	51	103	110	89	134	123	140	131	98					
Napoleon	930	1103	1056	1078	1070	982	709	578	554	423	675	300	96	42		
Neche	434	471	451	545	615	565	502	469	528	513	528	613	682	314	200	
Nekoma	63	102	84	143	140	184	191	199	189	159	120					
New England	663	825	906	1095	1117	895	911	709	613	553	550	50	50	152		
New Leipzig	326	352	354	390	447	366	443	385	378	280	150					
New Rockford	1604	1791	1969	2177	2185	2017	2195	2050	2111	1652	1575	800	698	569	128	
New Salem	909	1081	943	986	942	875	804	786	711	652	621	527	229	245	175	
New Town	1388	1335	1428	1586												
Newburg	104	151	125	158	105	119	87	108	110	146	102					
Niagara	73	76	115	157	163	179	207	210	199	132	157	167	201	201		
Niobe										150	250					
Nome	67	67	103	145	217	277	218	255	267	261	218	400			50	
Noonan	231	283	403	625	551	520	423	363	376	290	153					
Norma										150	375					
North Fargo																
North Minot		65							390							
North River	68								432	432	432					
Northwood	1166	1240	1189	1195	1182	1063	971	915	935	968	769	709	697	268		
Norwich										125	325	175				
Oakes	1775	2112	1742	1650	1774	1665	1709	1509	1637	1403	1499	1303	668	379		
Oberon	103	150	151	248	238	238	345		326	320	450	250	269	104		
Olga				50	145	110	191		178	200	200	400	241	79		
Oljata														58		
Omemee				11	60	123	170	147	222	293	332	504	230		200	

POPULATION HISTORY OF NORTH DAKOTA CITIES AND TOWNS 1870-1990

COMMUNITY	1990	1980	1970	1960	1950	1940	1930	1925	1920	1915	1910	1905	1900	1890	1880	1870
Surrey	856	999	361	309	175	197	183		169	120	275	85				
Sutton	110	85	87	110	125		215		115	100						
Sweden															250	
Sykeston	167	193	232	236	272	273	327	326	367	333	276	200	167	167		
Tagus	20	14	14	72	101	140	136	126	133	136	105	50				
Tappen	239	271	294	326	379	323	268	210	182	113	125	100	128	176		
Taylor	163	239	162	215	258	251	263	248	285	136	450	275	79	79	100	
Temvik				50	71	212	175		175	250	350					
Thompson	930	785	291	290	270	276	273	262	364	360	425	250	333	192	100	
Thorne					37	45	38	47	78	53	105	125				
Tioga	1278	1597	1667	2087	456	385	435	365	320	369	203	50				
Tokio	120	100	130	125	100		112		112	45	100					
Tolley	79	103	163	189	248	177	225	284	325	306	250	250				
Tolna	230	241	247	291	281	172	174	192	199	228	209					
Tower City	233	293	289	300	292	364	435	389	447	492	452	461	468	309	159	
Towner	669	867	870	948	955	918	622	531	610	707	691	535	331	211		
Trenton	230	125	150	169	150				310	60	125					
Turtle Lake	681	802	712	792	839	632	579	472	395	550	800	200				
Tuttle	160	202	216	255	368	357	383	351	321	200						
Underwood	976	1329	781	819	1061	613	488	484	453	415	422	450				
Upham	205	227	272	333	403	243	257	217	196	273	296	175				
Valley City	7163	7774	7843	7809	6851	5917	5268	4695	4686	4783	4606	4059	2446	1089	302	
Van Hook					380	329	372	368	331							
Velva	968	1101	1241	1330	1170	1017	870	872	836	858	837	505	156			
Venturia	30	40	77	148	190	257	233	278	207	197	375					
Verona	103	63	140	162	189	201	222	243	258	233	235	102				
Voltaire	63	65	54	70	72	101	61		166	75	150	175				
Wahpeton	8751	9064	7076	5876	5125	3747	3176	3187	3069	2814	2467	2741	2228	1510	400	
Walcott	178	186	166	250	296	396	293		275	250	475	300	126	175		
Wales	48	74	116	151	235	287	517		513	400	550	275	64			
Walhalla	1131	1429	1471	1432	1463	1138	700	633	634	544	592	520	377	207	67	
Walum										100	175	50				
Warwick	80	108	168	204	155	224	249	267	290	180	500					
Washburn	1506	1767	804	993	913	901	753	618	558	622	657	898	268	101	100	
Watford	1784	2119	1768	1865	1371	1073	769	427	260							
Watson				59	63	137	213	209	198							
Webster					159	117					275	100				
Werner															200	
West Fargo	12287	10099	5161	3328												
Westhope	578	741	705	824	575	460	521	416	439	606	592	626				

POPULATION HISTORY OF NORTH DAKOTA CITIES AND TOWNS 1870-1990

COMMUNITY	1990	1980	1970	1960	1950	1940	1930	1925	1920	1915	1910	1905	1900	1890	1880	1870
Wheatland	100	75		119	134	208	556		379	520	400	500	486	472	158	
Wheelock	23	34	21	82	101	94	115	104	220	250	350	50				
White Earth	73	98	128	208	218	272	240	245	247	238	264	250				
White Shield	274	160														
Wildrose	193	214	235	361	430	472	518	494	449	387	125					
Williamsport													62	153	51	
Williston	13131	13336	11280	11866	7378	5790	5106	3948	4178	4678	3124	1125	763	295		
Willow City	281	329	403	494	595	524	577	442	559	648	623	676	476	254		
Wilton	728	950	695	739	769	851	1001	964	1026	713	437	302				
Wimbledon	275	330	337	402	449	357	421	447	521	533	571	450	226			
Wing	208	220	223	303	312	235	237	183	264	344			180			
Winona							65			35		100	136	161		
Wishek	1171	1345	1275	1290	1241	1112	1146	1006	1003	722	432	200				
Wolford	56	76	81	136	140	206	235		219	250	400	100				
Woodworth	102	501	139	221	207	245	261	245	297	300						
Wyndmere	501	550	516	644	627	499	521	511	570	489	439	287	148	107		
York	35	69	102	148	220	444	341		320	300	475	300	142	68		
Zap	287	511	271	339	425	574	406	345	257	50						
Zeeland	197	253	313	427	484	489	419	280	323	200	193	75				

1905: North Dakota Secretary of State. Census of 1905. Senate Journal, 10th Sess., 1907, pp.37-53.
1905: Minnesota, North and South Dakota and Montana Gazetteer and Buniess Directory - Chicago: R.L. Polk, 1906.
1915: North Dakota Secretary of State. Census of 1915.
1915: Minnesota, North and South Dakota and Montana Gazetteer and Business Directory - Chicago: R.L. Polk, 1915.
1925: North Dakota Secretary of State. Inter-decennial Census Enumeration of 1925. Sixteen Biennial Report. Public Documents, 1925-1926,v.2 no.15, pp. 1257-1265.

POPULATION HISTORY OF OKLAHOMA CITIES AND TOWNS 1870-1990

COMMUNITY	1870	1880	1890	1900	1907	1910	1920	1930	1940	1950	1960	1970	1980	1990
Achille							500	383	356	383	294	382	480	491
Acme								275						
Ada				158	3257	4349	8012	11261	15143	15995	14347	14859	15902	15820
Adair			120	268	340	376	369	290	407	299	434	459	508	685
Adamson						165		250	250	250	160	160	150	150
Addington				56	383	493	368	318	250	174	144	123	141	100
Afton			320	606	1071	1279	1518	1219	1261	1252	1111	1022	1174	915
Agra					382	366	272	258	281	302	265	335	354	334
Albany				62		110		250	300	400	150	150	100	150
Albert								300	300	300	135	100	100	150
Albion						200	301	256	240	178	161	186	165	88
Alderson				990	517	786	855	421	340	311	207	215	366	395
Alex				50		240	478	598	544	563	545	492	769	639
Aline					272	303	358	429	405	385	314	260	313	295
Allen				300		645	1377	1438	1389	1215	1005	974	998	972
Alma				40		95		275	150				35	100
Altus				750	1927	4821	4522	8439	8593	9735	21225	23302	23101	21910
Alva				1499	2800	3688	3913	5121	5055	6505	6258	7440	6416	5495
Amber						300	319	300	291	300	250	300	416	418
Ames						500	278	290	332	263	211	227	314	268
Amorita						111	196	194	208	125	74	63	66	56
Anadarko		100	118	124	2190	3439	3116	5036	5579	6184	6299	6682	6378	6586
Antlers					862	1273	1842	2246	3254	2506	2085	2685	2989	2524
Apache				1000	883	950	919	1302	1047	1190	1455	1421	1560	1591
Apperson						125	2040	153	109	21	40	40	30	30
Arapaho				253	610	713	326	414	401	311	351	531	851	802
Arcadia						300	312	312	312	350	410	400	400	320
Ardmore			1000	5681	8759	8618	14181	15741	16886	17890	20184	20881	23689	23079
Arkoma								58	250	1691	1862	2098	2175	2395
Arlington				135		125								
Armstrong											140	150	133	122
Arnett						511	404	426	529	690	547	711	714	547
Arpelar							37	60				150	180	600
Asher					465	381	370	653	507	420	343	437	659	449
Ashland						350	100	131	142	104	87	73	72	56
Atoka		200	316	1215	1660	1968	2038	1856	2548	2653	2877	3346	3409	3298
Atwood						90	213	250	250	125	200	200	300	300
Augusta				350		128								
Autwine						168								
Avant						200	1071	696	501	389	381	439	461	369

POPULATION HISTORY OF OKLAHOMA CITIES AND TOWNS 1870-1990

COMMUNITY	1990	1980	1970	1960	1950	1940	1930	1920	1910	1907	1900	1890	1880	1870
Avard	37	51	59	56	36	126	212	147	170					
Bache									250					
Bacone							225				74			
Barnsdall	1316	1501	1579	1663	1708	1831	2001	1099						
Bartlesville	34256	34568	29683	27893	19228	16267	14763	14417	6181	4215	698			
Bearden	142	78	150	250	250	244	150	93	85					
Beaver	1584	1939	1857	2087	1495	1166	1028	920	326	271	112	413		
Beggs	1150	1428	1107	1114	1214	1283	1531	2327	855	720				
Bennington	251	302	288	226	561	513	492	951	513	427	70			
Berlin	100	45		48	51	125	50	84	75		60			
Bernice	330	318	189	100	91	205	162	198						
Berwyn						227	300				276			
Bessie	248	245	210	226	205	284	415	363	378					
Bethany	20075	22130	22694	12342	5705	2590	2032	485	420					
Bethel	300	250	297	225	765				90		150			
Bethel Acres	2505	2314	1083	225	165									
Beulah									265					
Big Cabin	271	252	198	228	210	270	271	929	220					
Bigheart							2477	2099	307					
Billings	555	632	618	510	520	661	658	846	524	444	406			
Binger	724	791	730	603	773	840	849	482	280	257				
Bison	100	75		200	200	115	228		400					
Bixby	9502	6969	3973	1711	1517	1291	1251	1249	384	283				
Blackburn	110	114	88	129	135	198	219	257	335	330	300			
Blackwell	7538	8400	8645	9588	9199	8537	9521	7174	3266	2644	2283			
Blair	922	1092	1114	893	700	570	585	437	508					
Blanchard	1922	1688	1580	1377	1311	1139	1040	842	629					
Blocker	200	225	100	150	150	200	162		131					
Blue	200	120	120	150	150	150	150		130		50			
Bluejacket	175	247	234	245	274	349	271	442	508	427	303			
Bois D'Arc	300	300	300	150										
Boise City	1509	1761	1993	1978	902	1144	1256	219	200	613	80			
Bokchito	576	628	607	620	643	581	466	627	535					
Bokhoma		50		200	350		200		100					
Bokoshe	403	556	588	431	589	690	715	869	483		153			
Boley	908	423	514	573	646	942	874	1154	1334	824				
Boswell	643	398	755	753	875	962	934	1212	828	836				
Bowden	50	40				158	158							
Bowlegs	398	522	350	300	365	500	500							
Boynton	391	518	522	604	718	842	1204	1204	679	393				

POPULATION HISTORY OF OKLAHOMA CITIES AND TOWNS 1870-1990

COMMUNITY	1990	1980	1970	1960	1950	1940	1930	1920	1910	1907	1900	1890	1880	1870
Braden	166					150	150		100		100			
Bradley	308	284	247	294	248	281	227	186	174		59			
Braggs	251	351	325	279	374	392	400	430	259	330	113			
Braman		355	295	336	392	427	507	396	339	300	249			
Bray	925	591	100	110	40		32	47	35					
Breckenridge	251	261	70	42	67	80	76	132	176					
Bridgeport	137	115	142	139	199	302	432	294	428	462				
Brinkman				14	102	164	252	239	200					
Bristow	4062	4702	4653	4795	5400	6050	6619	3460	1667	1134	626			
Britton					1850	2239	2214	1070	696					
Broken Arrow	58043	35761	11018	5928	3262	2074	1964	2086	1576	1383				
Broken Bow	3961	3965	2980	2087	1838	2367	2291	1983	1576					
Bromide	162	180	231	264	258	312	352	523	200					
Brooksville	69	46	80	175	175	130	360	360	50					
Bryant	70	74	86	72	88	143	156	67	50					
Buck														
Buffalo	1312	1381	1579	1618	1544	1209	990	479	282		510			
Burbank	165	161	188	238	268	329	372	237	225					
Burlington	169	206	165	174	181	177	166	169	135					
Burnett											98	122		
Burneyville	60	60			50	110								
Burns Flat	1027	2431	988	2280	800	800	800		100		57			
Butler	341	388	315	351	250	428	473	332						
Byars	263	353	247	256	284	466	502	629	487	537				
Byng	755	833	250	250	351		46	36						
Byron	57	67	72	82	131	177	197	249	286	193	35			
Cache	2251	1661	1106	1003	677	620	425	382	317	312				
Caddo	918	923	886	814	895	954	933	1421	1143	1280	930	500	350	150
Calera	1536	1390	1063	692	643	597	503	703	575					
Calhoun	45	55		100	200		360							
Calumet	560	469	386	354	339	476	393	479	160		80			
Calvin	251	315	359	331	557	589	626	700	570	389	360			
Camargo	185	264	236	254	312	289	291	310	47		47			
Cameron	327	365	311	211	209	203	233	203	206	183	316	75		
Campbell									316		100			
Canadian	261	279	304	255	277	385	295	373	481	401	522			
Caney	185	147	200	128	252	361	274	432	295	289	125			
Canton	632	854	844	887	959	775	797	582	703					
Canute	538	676	420	370	355	374	366	412	400					
Capron	38	54	80	102	100	147	155	184	196		46			

POPULATION HISTORY OF OKLAHOMA CITIES AND TOWNS 1870-1990

COMMUNITY	1990	1980	1970	1960	1950	1940	1930	1920	1910	1907	1900	1890	1880	1870
Carbon	165	600	800	850	750	424	510		350		350			
Cardin							437	2640	883	708				
Carmen	459	516	519	533	654	818	904	792						
Carnagie	1593	2016	1723	1500	1719	1740	2063	1150	835	491				
Carney	558	622	396	227	227	283	328	367	260	310	117			
Carrier	171	259	197	80	135	320	275	275	315					
Carter	286	367	311	364	406	535	642	389	265					
Carthage											193			
Cartwright	800	200	200	400	150	500			40					
Cashion	430	547	329	221	182	232	291	296	289	256	472			
Castle	94	130	212	149	144	242	283	381	294					
Catoosa	2954	1772	970	638	438	405	364	363	404	303	241	195	150	
Cedar Valley	61	34												
Cement	642	884	892	959	1076	1039	1117	1098	770	618				
Center	100	100	100	200	75	200	551	461	150		590			
Centrahoma	106	166	155	148	154	625	382	892	600		100			
Centralia	35	60	43	80	124	378	192	300	387	405				
Chandler	2596	2926	2529	2524	2724	2738	2717	2226	2024	2234	1430	1140		
Chant								279	882	1232				
Chattanooga	437	403	302	356	333	365	362	507	471	362				
Checotah	3290	3454	3074	2614	2638	2126	2110	2390	1683	1524	805			
Chelsea	1620	1754	1622	1541	1437	1642	1527	1692	1350	1249	566			
Cherokee	1787	2105	2119	2410	2635	2553	2236	2017	2016	964	67			
Cheyenne	948	1207	892	930	1133	1070	826	400	468	288	450	180		
Chickasaw	14988	15828	14194	14866	15842	14111	14099	10179	10320	7862	3209			
Chilocco		500	400				200		280		500			
Choctaw	8545	7520	4750	623	355	289	242	199	242	230	347	316		
Choteau	1771	1559	1046	958	653	400	430	541	483	344	188	100	75	
Cimarron City	71	35									40			
Claremore	13280	12085	9084	6639	5494	4134	3720	3435	2866	2064	855	100		
Clarita	150	180	100	114	200	185	191	232	150					
Clarksville									388		240			
Clayton	636	833	718	615	612	392	127	110	100			112		
Clearview	47	140	350	500	500	275	420	420	115					
Clebit	50	50	200	250	400	300	300							
Cleo Springs	359	514	344	236	310	386	356	377	425	405	275			
Cleveland	3156	2972	2573	2519	2464	2510	2959	2717	1310	1441	211			
Cliff											110			
Clifton											147			
Clinton	9298	8796	8513	9617	7555	6736	7512	2596	2781	1278				

POPULATION HISTORY OF OKLAHOMA CITIES AND TOWNS 1870-1990

COMMUNITY	1990	1980	1970	1960	1950	1940	1930	1920	1910	1907	1900	1890	1880	1870
Eddy									215					
Edmond	52315	34637	16633	8577	6086	4002	3576	2452	2090	1833	965	294		
El Reno	15414	15486	14510	11015	10991	10078	9384	7737	7872	5370	3383	285		
Eldon							150							
Eldorado	573	688	737	708	732	929	1183	967	926	916				
Elgin	975	1003	840	540	428	381	335	181	178					
Elk City	10428	9579	7323	8196	7962	5021	5666	2814	3165	2195	152			
Elmer	132	131	138	120	145	249	288	362	350	276	192			
Elmore/Banner	493	582	653	982	743	494	395	337	266					
Emet	55	75					219	359	500		342			
Empire City	219	13	23		150		80	45						
Enid	45309	50363	44986	38859	36017	28018	26399	16576	13799	10087	3444			
Enterprise	100	100	130	75	200	100	618	315	500		340			
Enville					100		250							
Eram							175							
Erick	1083	1375	1285	1342	1579	1591	2231	971	915	686				
Erin Springs									200		200			
Eschite									232					
Eufala	2652	3159	2355	2382	2540	2355	2073	2286	1307	974	757	500	175	100
Fair Oaks	1133	324												
Fairfax	1749	1949	1889	2076	2017	2327	2134	1342	819	470				
Fairland	916	1073	814	646	699	786	679	818	569	521	499			
Fairmont	129	419	154	115	134	153	169	166	215					
Fairview	2936	3370	2894	2213	2411	1913	1887	1751	2020	887	60			
Fallis	49	22	39	42	105	137	173	239	248	321				
Fame				100	100	163	163	129	135		100			
Fanshawe	331	416	199	150	305	124	129	129	130		52			
Fargo	299	409	262	291	318	291	325	258	341					
Farris	100	100			100	200	300		40					
Faxon	127	140	121	137	135	178	212	163	215					
Fay	200	120	120	150	112	155	155		109		73			
Felt	115	20				100	200							
Fittstown	500	500	325	450	350	1000								
Fitzhugh	196	164	212	122	200	250	250	180	172					
Fletcher	1002	1074	950	884	875	789	739	482	374	220	376			
Flint				100										
Foraker	25	34	52	74	105	222	310	394	415	237				
Forest Park	1249	1148	835	766									150	
Forgan	489	611	496	532	410	428	605	582						
Fort Cobb	663	760	722	687	665	699	827	546	382	462				

POPULATION HISTORY OF OKLAHOMA CITIES AND TOWNS 1870-1990

COMMUNITY	1870	1880	1890	1900	1907	1910	1920	1930	1940	1950	1960	1970	1980	1990
Fort Coffee											200	400	900	150
Fort Gibson	82	500	500	617	1063	1344	1353	1159	1233	1496	1407	1418	2477	3359
Fort Reno		300	110	213			525	150	150	250				
Fort Sill	792	300	300			799	799		4260		22500	21217	15924	12107
Fort Supply/Supply	638	540	100	266	136	169	231	230	414	293	394	550	559	369
Fort Towson					745	697	965	486	501	713	474	430	789	568
Foss					540	525	348	524	306	210	289	150	188	148
Fox/Pike City				54		100	38	38	350	438	300	350	350	350
Foyil				72		250	109	184	170	146	127	164	191	86
Francis				35	872	931	911	607	370	271	286	283	365	346
Frederick					2036	3027	3822	4568	5109	5467	5897	6132	6153	5221
Freedom						90	62	354	364	332	268	292	339	264
Frisco			327	61		60	219	264	219	100				
Gage				130	755	924	804	856	684	648	482	536	667	473
Gans				136	279	351	295	204	198	300	234	238	346	218
Garber				317	334	382	1446	1356	1086	957	905	1011	1215	959
Garden City						60		180	520	763				
Garvin						957	292	263	170	155	138	117	162	128
Gate			98	42		300	309	307	243	197	130	151	146	159
Geary				467	1565	1452	1167	1892	1634	1614	1416	1380	1700	1347
Gene Autry/Berwyn				276	378	378	435	300	227	170	110	120	178	97
Geronimo				186	317	186	161	134	117	103	199	587	726	990
Gerty/Guertie						305	251	137	206	155	135	139	149	95
Glencoe				425	358	373	354	297	337	309	284	421	490	473
Glenpool						1500	428	310	284	260	353	770	2706	6688
Goldsby										100		298	603	816
Goltry					183	320	287	346	330	277	313	282	305	297
Goodland						150		220	220	150		250	150	50
Goodwater														
Goodwell						300	264	501	360	714	771	1467	1186	1065
Gore					295	316	329	297	334	387	334	478	445	690
Gotebo					539	740	737	827	607	574	538	376	457	370
Gould						200	228	367	391	303	240	368	318	237
Gowen				106		106	106	633	400	525	525	350	350	400
Gracemont						220	266	394	328	301	306	424	503	339
Graham				115		115	115	115	200	128	250	250	250	280
Grainola						90	329	197	157	79	67	66	67	58
Grandfield						830	1990	1416	1116	1232	1606	1524	1445	1224
Granite				192	1026	1229	912	1341	1058	1096	952	1808	1617	1844
Grant				100	440	416	395	296	309	351	286	273	270	300

POPULATION HISTORY OF OKLAHOMA CITIES AND TOWNS 1870-1990

COMMUNITY	1990	1980	1970	1960	1950	1940	1930	1920	1910	1907	1900	1890	1880	1870
Grayson	66		142	142	191	304	500	1035	1000					
Greenfield	200	150	143	128		303	436	369	300					
Grove	4020	3378	2000	975	928	1093	804	869	888	694	314			
Guertie									305		132			
Guthrie	10518	10312	9575	9502	10113	10018	9582	11757	11654	11652	10006	5333		
Guymon	7803	8492	7674	5760	4718	2290	2181	1507	1342	839				
Haileyville	918	832	928	922	1107	1183	1801	2067	2024	1452				
Hall Park	1090	577	163											
Hallett	159	186	125	132	120	159	176	279	147					
Hammon	611	866	677	656	621	705	736	440	130					
Hanna	99	157	181	233	325	344	360	460	200					
Hanson	140	100			200	250	235	194	230		182			
Hardesty	228	243	223	187	201	146	244		36		36			
Hardy					17	41	51	78	101	101		40		
Harrah	4206	2897	1931	934	741	620	693	365	356		74			
Harris	190	192	200	210	192	96	137	110	100		60			
Hartshorne	2120	2380	2121	1903	2330	2596	3587	3480	2963	2435	2352			
Haskell	2143	1953	2063	1887	1676	1572	1682	2196	857	720				
Hastings	164	246	184	200	285	352	379	629	727	560				
Haworth	293	341	293	351	254	232	276	400	220					
Hayward	50	30				100			150					
Haywood	300	150	175	150	200		35	35	35					
Headrick	183	223	139	152	144	174	243	280	270	212	104			
Healdton	2872	3769	2324	2898	2578	2067	2017	2157	170					
Heavener	2601	2776	2566	1891	2103	2215	2269	1850	780	473	234		100	
Helena	1043	710	769	580	484	776	735	615	760	521				
Hendrix/Kemp City	108	106	117	142	152	145	84	130	115					
Hennepin	300	300	306	256	300	250	250	230						
Hennessey	1902	2287	2181	1228	1264	1342	1271	1310	1665	1573	1367	1225		
Henryetta	5872	6432	6430	6551	7987	6905	7694	5889	1671	1051	50			
Hester				22	31	44	109	80	220					
Hewitt														
Hickory	77	95	62	112	112	224	157	359	350	468	262			
Hillsdale	96	110	77	60	104	131	173	209	140					
Hinton	1233	1432	889	907	1025	842	1009	744	686	532				
Hitchcock	139	172	160	134	166	222	246	281	275	198				
Hitchita	118	126	160	120	141	206	228	264	150					
Hobart	4305	4735	4638	5132	5380	5177	4982	2936	3845	3136				
Hockerville	75	75	175	300	450	900	550							
Hodgen	250	175	150	100	100	150	150	34						

POPULATION HISTORY OF OKLAHOMA CITIES AND TOWNS 1870-1990

COMMUNITY	1870	1880	1890	1900	1907	1910	1920	1930	1940	1950	1960	1970	1980	1990
Hoffman					344	307	365	375	432	302	248	262	407	175
Holdendale				749	1868	2296	2932	7268	6632	6192	5712	5181	5469	4792
Hollis					524	964	1683	2914	2732	3089	3006	3150	2958	2584
Hollister						250	264	198	200	172	166	105	82	59
Homestead						383		287	100				45	100
Hominy					468	760	2875	3485	3267	2702	2866	2274	3130	2342
Hooker					448	525	946	1628	1146	1842	1684	1615	1788	1551
Howe				626	599	538	711	692	640	486	390	403	562	510
Hoyt				92		125		320	320	320	320	140	120	150
Hugo					2676	4582	6368	5272	5909	5984	6287	6585	7172	5978
Hulbert						450	316	300	311	500	500	505	633	499
Hunter					254	341	443	336	291	279	203	274	276	218
Hydro					524	562	686	948	759	714	697	805	938	977
Idabel					726	1493	3067	2581	3689	4671	4967	5946	7622	6957
Illinois						316								
Indiahoma				155	307	188	195	288	337	319	378	434	364	337
Indianola				265		481	415	378	311	314	234	205	254	171
Ingalls											30	17	20	20
Ingersoll				53	301	253	218	156	134	78				1550
Inola					324	405	498	398	395	254	584	948	1550	1444
Jay						65	216	380	741	697	1120	1594	2100	2220
Jefferson				300	298	281	322	269	229	179	119	128	92	36
Jenks				165	465	290	1508	1110	1026	1037	1734	2685	5876	7493
Jennings					380	361	910	653	453	338	306	338	395	381
Jester						65		550		100				
Jet					213	365	370	389	442	371	339	317	352	272
Johnson						239							306	196
Jones				184		163	214	288	260	476	794	1666	2270	2424
Kansas				88		110	154	163	158	250	400	317	491	556
Kaw City		300		290	486	595	627	1001	809	561	457	283	283	314
Keefeton						150								
Kellyville				221	368	250	520	548	647	528	501	685	960	984
Kemp						336	396	186	204	158	153	153	178	138
Kendrick						280	255	270	256	172	155	126	132	171
Kenefic						200	413	284	227	115	125	153	140	147
Kenton						240	175	250	100		100		50	50
Keokuk Falls			250	198										
Keota						210	494	470	525	619	579	685	661	625
Ketchum						200	265	265	254	254	255	238	326	263
Keyes						90		350	431	431	627	569	557	454

POPULATION HISTORY OF OKLAHOMA CITIES AND TOWNS 1870-1990

COMMUNITY	1990	1980	1970	1960	1950	1940	1930	1920	1910	1907	1900	1890	1880	1870
Keystone				151	228	406	482	300	273	229				
Kiefer	962	912	803	489	275	330	606	1663	1197					
Kildare	94	112	79	124	155	137	160	146	216	162	227			
Kingfisher	4095	4245	4042	3249	3345	3352	2726	2447	2538	2214	2301	2200		
Kingston	1237	1171	710	639	677	481	552	767	439	477		1134		
Kinta	233	303	247	233	283	221	259	393	300					
Kiowa	718	866	754	607	802	802	689	1287	1021	803	406	77		
Knowles	18	44	52	62	91	105	219	218	100					
Konawa	1508	1711	1719	1555	2707	2205	2070	896	761	620				
Koreb											150			
Kosoma									130		112			
Krebs	1955	1754	1515	1342	1532	1436	1375	2078	2884	1508	2600	3000		
Kremlin	243	301	200	128	143	146	124	169	253	273	250			
Kusa						99	266	1069	200					
La Kemp							57	48						
Lahoma	645	537	299	160	190	195	197	262	275	273	275			
Lake Aluma	96	101	124	82										
Lamar	97	121	153	150	180	296	250	520	350					
Lambert	11	20	16	21	55	99	116	130	127					
Lamont	454	571	478	543	594	577	554	586	635	474	251			
Langley	526	582	481	205	204	838	351				48			
Langston	1471	443	486	417	685	514	903	259	339	274	251	175		
Laverne	1269	1563	1373	1937	1269	816	243	476						
Lawrence	97			100	250	243		330	40					
Lawton	80561	80054	74470	61697	34757	18055	12121	8930	7788	5562				
Le Flore	119	322	175	350	400	333	328	328	328					
Leach	60	140			300		184							
Lebanon	400	250	200	150	200	200	250	270	250		185			
Leedey	468	499	465	451	558	574	646	468	50					
Leflore											166			
Leger											750			
Lehigh	303	284	296	296	352	519	497	1898	1880	2188	1500	3000	500	
Lenapah	253	350	325	322	328	395	336	434	412	331	154			
Leon	101	120	112	109	122	178	146	216	197	232	211	97	75	
Leonard	500	150	115	130	115	125	125	110	110					
Lexington	1776	1731	1516	1216	1176	1084	836	950	768	836	861	223		
Liberty	155	19												
Lima	133	256	238	90	99	271	239	146	50					
Limestone	700													
Lindsay	2947	3454	3705	4258	3021	1792	1713	1543	1156	1102	38			

POPULATION HISTORY OF OKLAHOMA CITIES AND TOWNS 1870-1990

COMMUNITY	1870	1880	1890	1900	1907	1910	1920	1930	1940	1950	1960	1970	1980	1990
Little City										101	102	80	250	200
Lockridge						230		65						
Loco				100		350	610	333	268	236	268	193	215	160
Locust Grove					241	45	587	510	545	730	828	1090	1179	1326
Lone Grove				215		222	286	350	284	285	285	1240	3369	4114
Lone Wolf					337	677	657	1023	783	660	617	584	613	576
Longdale						296	308	284	291	277	218	331	405	281
Lookeba						217	240	312	279	206	158	165	221	141
Loveland						310	191	106	101	96	90	36	21	13
Lovell						220	234	218	120	73	27	28	28	40
Loyal							113	113	177	125	87	107	112	76
Lucien						400		150	150	150	100	100	120	150
Lugert						200		200	200					
Lula						100		215	215				40	40
Luther				315	423	310	601	613	425	409	517	836	1159	1560
Lutie						175					300	150	150	
McAlester	100	1200	4200	4125	8144	12954	12095	11804	12401	17878	17419	18802	17255	16370
MacArthur						312								
McBride												44	91	80
McCurtain					528	526	1062	934	870	705	528	575	549	465
McGee				209										
McLemore														
McLoud				498	784	638	651	812	616	718	837	2159	4061	2493
McMillan				166		163								
Macomb					207	166	281	197	201	123	76	41	58	64
Madill					1587	1564	2717	2203	2594	2791	3084	2875	3173	3069
Manchester				158	249	271	237	281	269	190	162	165	146	106
Mangum			202	520	2672	3667	3405	4806	4193	4271	3950	4066	3833	3344
Manitou					394	412	335	323	258	293	269	308	322	244
Mannford						220	315	421	403	426	358	892	1610	1826
Mannsville				198	529	515	639	372	359	311	297	364	568	396
Maramec					272	224	287	376	271	184	169	128	101	110
Marble City					292	342	344	168	214	285	271	299	294	232
Marietta				842	1391	1546	1977	1505	1837	1875	1933	2013	2494	2306
Marland							135	361	257	221	191	236	340	280
Marlow				1016	1648	1965	2276	3084	2899	3399	4027	3995	5017	4416
Marshall/New Marshall			42	250	364	480	434	695	382	336	363	420	372	288
Martha						250	261	327	242	222	243	268	219	217
Maud					575	503	637	4326	2036	1389	1137	1143	1444	1204
May						100	324	258	239	143	114	91	89	42

POPULATION HISTORY OF OKLAHOMA CITIES AND TOWNS 1870-1990

COMMUNITY	1990	1980	1970	1960	1950	1940	1930	1920	1910	1907	1900	1890	1880	1870
Maysville	1203	1396	1380	1530	1294	880	875	627	476	308				
Mazie	100	100	160	100	100	150	200		150					
Mead	109	143	140	200	200	204	200	265	250		48			
Medford	1172	1419	1304	1223	1305	1121	1084	1050	1110	802	551			
Medicine Park	285	437	483	825	650		50							
Meeker	1003	1032	804	664	672	502	562	513	349	320				
Meno	155	171	119	118	76	180	96	92	69					
Meridian	45	78	104	160	187	210	165	201	199					
Merrick							220		396					
Miami	13142	14237	13880	12869	11801	8345	8064	6802	2907	1893	1527			
Midland														
Midway				2292	200	200	255		200		150			
Midwest City	52267	49559	48212	36058	10166									
Milburn	264	376	275	228	350	442	429	496	438	416				
Milfay	150	150	110	130	125	193	193							
Mill Creek	336	431	234	287	299	459	422	620	626	644	115		100	
Millerton	234	262	250	200	250	266	255	168	250					
Milo		30			378		550		55		46			
Minco	1411	1489	1129	1021	978	921	962	606	706	725	879			
Moffett	219	269	312	357	380	538	340							
Monroe	200	250	200	135	349	349	225		185		50			
Moore	40318	35063	18761	1783	942	499	538	254	225	163	129	108		
Mooreland	1157	1383	1196	871	867	811	706	592	493	274				
Moral											137			
Morris	1216	1288	1119	982	1122	1197	1706	1926	470					
Morrison	640	671	421	256	297	333	284	353	327	351	110			
Mounds	980	1086	766	674	560	627	740	1078	701	675	86			
Mountain Park	473	557	458	403	418	441	459	334	449	381				
Mountain View	1086	1189	1110	864	1009	1075	1025	917	855	791	1016			
Moyers	100	100	100	150	150	213	213							
Muldrow	2889	2530	1680	1137	828	638	557	693	671	618	465			
Mulhall	199	301	250	253	320	406	374	385	441	443	564	428		
Muse									168					
Muskogee	37708	40011	37331	38059	37289	32332	32036	30277	25278	14418	4254	2000	500	50
Mustang	10434	7496	2637	198	210	214	107	446	170					
Mutual	68	135	94	84	130	179	177	169	264					
Nalegoney			62		138	174	123	450						
Nardin	75	98	135	142	184	217	180	200	277	238	173			
Nash	281	301	294	230	290	348	412	439	348	167				
Navina				11	15	43	79	126	119					

POPULATION HISTORY OF OKLAHOMA CITIES AND TOWNS 1870-1990

COMMUNITY	1990	1980	1970	1960	1950	1940	1930	1920	1910	1907	1900	1890	1880	1870
New Alluwe/Alluwe	83	129	116	150	200	200	200							
New Prue	272	252	202					619						
New Tulsa							99	86	75					
Newcastle	4214	3076	1271	175	175									
Newkirk	2168	2413	2173	2092	2201	2283	2135	2533	1992	1778	1754			
Nicholls Hills	4020	4171	4478	4897	2606	942								
Nicoma Park	2353	2588	2560	1263	1200	700	250							
Ninnekah/East Ninnekahiah	1016	1085	300	250	250	300	300	410	274		67			
Noble	4710	3497	2241	995	724	536	463	497	403	457	349	210		
Norge	97	87	54		100	108	162	162	150					
Norman	80071	68020	52117	33412	27006	11429	9603	5004	3724	3040	2225	787		
North Enid	874	992	730	286	219	166	165	95	128	109	205			
North Miami	450	544	503	472	485	393	503	483						
Nowata	3896	4270	3679	4163	3965	3904	3531	4435	3672	2223	498			
Oak Grove	200	660							40					
Oak Hill							200							
Oak Lodge									40				250	
Oakhurst	3030	2000	1500	400	200	200	200	159						
Oakland	602	485	317	288	293	311	248	420	366	445	701	77		
Oaks	431	591	219	199	70		57	47	60			45		
Oakwood/Randolph	107	140	129	122	161	233	266	224	199					
Oberlin					100	215	215		215		120			
Ochelata	441	480	330	312	357	333	335	419	550	359	100			
Oconee									258					
Octavia	35	25			100		315							
Oilton	1060	1244	1087	1100	1109	1225	1518	2231						
Okarche	1160	1064	826	584	532	453	482	449	402	414	588	200		
Okay	528	554	419	419	427	322	248	275						
Okeene	1343	1601	1421	1164	1170	1079	1035	1084	920	775	250	200		
Okemah	3085	3381	2913	2836	3435	3811	4002	2162	1389	1027				
Oklahoma City	444719	403213	368164	324253	243504	204424	185389	91295	64205	32452	10037	4151		
Okmulgee	13441	16263	15180	15951	18317	16051	17097	17430	4176	2322	1000	300	350	50
Oktaha	266	376	193	199	207	233	292	335	324	286				
Ola											177			
Olustee	701	721	819	463	455	570	651	665	850	552				
Omega	800								180					
Oneta		75					50	66	35					
Oologah	828	798	458	299	242	236	263	277	255	349	308			
Optima	92	133	103	64	97	69	115	113	200					
Orlando	198	218	202	194	262	332	226	161	340	262	300	268		

POPULATION HISTORY OF OKLAHOMA CITIES AND TOWNS 1870-1990

COMMUNITY	1990	1980	1970	1960	1950	1940	1930	1920	1910	1907	1900	1890	1880	1870
Orr	45			70	70	145	150	254	249		222			
Osage	163	243	170	220	425	628	627	757	450		665			
Otex							225							
Otoe									417		150			
Overbrook									110		110			
Owasso	11151	6149	3491	2032	431	371	416	379	373	379	118			
Paden	400	448	442	417	426	620	595	600	419	272				
Panama	1528	1425	1121	937	1027	880	754	568	310	290	300			
Panola	300	100	100	120	75		65	28						
Paoli	574	573	480	358	353	423	394	363	239	229	234			
Paradise Hill	88	154	87											
Parks Hill	450	170	170	150	150	300	300	320	140					
Pauls Valley	6150	5664	5769	6856	6896	5104	4235	3694	2689	2157	1467		500	
Pawhuska	3825	4771	4238	5141	5331	5443	5931	6414	2776	2408	805	325	125	
Pawnee	2197	1688	2443	2303	2861	2742	2562	2418	2161	1943	1464	75	100	
Pearson	25	45	60											
Peckham				140	140	94	66				147			
Peggs	150	90	82	28	51	93	76	157	263	219				
Pensacola	69	82	56	55	48	109	162	162	40					
Peoria	136	165	179	156	201	227	189	166	135	201	144			
Perkins	1925	1762	1029	769	706	728	606	608	603	670	719	287		
Pernell	200	200	150	150	300	525	525							
Perry	4978	5796	5341	5210	5137	5045	4206	3154	3133	2881	3351			
Pershing	30	30			62	46	76	891						
Phillips	161	178	106	91	181	212	176	972	680	650	75			
Picher	1714	2180	2363	2553	3935	5848	7773	9676						
Pickens	150	100	200	300	150			28						
Pickett	425	300												
Piedmont	2522	2016	269	146	120	151	148	213	255					
Pine Valley					745	1700	1700							
Pink	1020	911	337											
Pittsburg	249	305	282	195	278	689	873	892	400					
Platter	200	200	200	200	200	275	210		120		74			
Pleasant Valley									240					
Pocasset									420					
Pocola	3664	3268	1840		200	200	200		65		50			
Ponca City	26359	26238	25940	24411	20180	16794	16136	7051	2521	2529	2528			
Pond Creek	982	949	903	935	1066	1019	857	965	1113	1155	822			
Pontotoc	200	200	150	100	160	297	325	325	380		366			
Poolville	100	50			150	180	180		152					

POPULATION HISTORY OF OKLAHOMA CITIES AND TOWNS 1870-1990

COMMUNITY	1990	1980	1970	1960	1950	1940	1930	1920	1910	1907	1900	1890	1880	1870
Port									225					
Porter	588	642	624	492	562	562	525	597	637	448	225			
Porum	851	668	658	573	616	502	471	533	548	393				
Poteau	7210	7089	5500	4428	4776	4020	3169	2679	1830	1726	1182			
Prague	2308	2208	1802	1545	1546	1422	1299	1127	1025	998				
Prattville				2530										
Preston/Hamilton	500	400	300	250	525	250	400	520	450					
Proctor	100	65				300	150		44					
Prue	346	554	271	300	60	473	195	164	160					
Pryor Creek	8327	8483	7057	6476	4486	2501	1828	1767	1798	1113	495			
Purcell	4784	4638	4076	3729	3546	3116	2817	2938	2740	2553	2277	2000		
Purdy	50	74	84	83	100		213	213	200		200			
Putnam	44				106	142	140	317	310					
Quapaw	928	1097	967	850	938	1054	1340	1394	350					
Quay	59	50	41	51	70	104	186	225	200					
Quinlan	23	64	81	75	107	188	231	310	355	148				
Quinton	1133	1228	1262	898	951	1245	1804	1557	697					
Ralston	405	495	443	411	416	621	725	703	597	587	155			
Ramona	508	567	600	546	583	574	617	793	725	873	165			
Ranchwood Manor		296	213											
Randlett	458	461	384	356	396	327	257	323	574					
Ratliff City	157	350	250	150		100								
Rattan	257	332	300	300	200		47	47						
Ravia	404	487	373	307	327	424	345	513	556	690	128			
Reagan									200		200			
Red Fork							997	844	350	397	156	65		
Red Oak	602	676	609	453	568	484	460	593	398	277	118	225	170	
Red Rock	321	376	233	262	253	395	375	329	378	314	41			
Redbird	166	199	230	310	411	393	218	336	200					
Redland							150							
Reed									200					
Reeding									167					
Reevesville									200					
Renfrow	19	27	39	38	68	115	125	132	207	159	129			
Reno											222	234		
Rentiesville	66	78	96	122	156	180	154							
Reydon/Rankin	200	252	215	183	331	311	216	255	411					
Rexroat					100	1025	1025							
Richland	390						152	152	140					
Ringling	1250	1561	1206	1170	1092	902	1002	1039						

POPULATION HISTORY OF OKLAHOMA CITIES AND TOWNS 1870-1990

COMMUNITY	1990	1980	1970	1960	1950	1940	1930	1920	1910	1907	1900	1890	1880	1870
Ringwood	394	389	241	232	331	288	265	225	271	225	101			
Ripley	376	451	307	263	292	415	487	406	368	346	474			
Rock Island	478	373	97	120	110									
Rocky	181	242	260	343	366	442	518	322	378		46			
Rocky Point													200	
Roff	717	729	632	638	623	705	772	1138	1044	1079	368			
Roland	2481	1472	827	492	443	311	212	271	228					
Romulus									219					
Roosevelt	323	396	353	495	679	744	721	362	298	173				
Rosedale	48	97	98	88	136	112	268	268	250					
Rosston	54	66	56	58	85	143	185	181						
Roxana							367							
Rush Springs	1229	1451	1381	1303	1402	1422	1340	768	823	588	518			
Rusk									170					
Ryan	945	1083	1011	978	1019	1115	1258	1379	1207	1115	1108			
Sacred Heart	181	109	207	76	30	261	110	90	100		276	276	250	
St. Louis	1153	1115	1024	972	290	326	493	35	250		100			
Salina					905	687	582	411						
Sallisaw	7122	6403	4888	3351	2885	2140	1785	2255	2479	1698	965			
Salt Fork									248					
Sand Point	200	179												
Sand Springs	15346	13246	10565	7754	6994	6137	6674	4076						
Sans Bois									200		130	130	100	
Sapulpa	18074	15853	15159	14282	13031	12249	10583	11634	8283	4259	891			
Sasakwa	169	335	321	253	365	532	781	355	241	237	28			
Savanna	869	828	948	620	900	267	318	264	200	200	238			
Sawyer / Roby	150	175	175	235	200	175	191		210					
Sayre	2881	3177	2712	2913	3362	3037	3157	1703	1881	1119				
Schulter	600	300	300	500	700	500	650	217	40					
Scipio									240					
Scullin			9	27	21	66	55	62	73					
Seiling	1031	1103	1033	910	700	629	568	323	352	333	150			
Selman	30	75			100	126	200							
Seminole	7071	8590	7878	11464	11863	11547	11459	854	476	206				
Sentinel	960	1016	984	1154	1131	1088	1269	723	857	351	47			
Seward	50	49		49	75	168	106	118	159	163	136			
Shady Point	597	235	350	350	315	310	146	119	131		104			
Shamrock	95	218	204	211	263	461	777	1409						
Sharon	108	171	155	97	133	226	227	254						
Shattuck	1454	1759	1546	1625	1692	1275	1490	1365	1231	1009				

POPULATION HISTORY OF OKLAHOMA CITIES AND TOWNS 1870-1990

COMMUNITY	1990	1980	1970	1960	1950	1940	1930	1920	1910	1907	1900	1890	1880	1870
Shawnee	26017	26506	25075	24326	22948	22053	23283	15348	12474	10955	3462			
Shidler	487	708	717	870	840	718	1177	3005					115	
Short							320		150					
Shrewder							315		40					
Silo	249	43			125	148	150	167	153	180	246			
Skedee	96	117	117	128	170	235	272	268	289	277				
Skiatook	4910	3596	2930	2503	1734	1496	1789	1653	606	342	50			
Slaughterville	1843	1953						1540						
Slick	124	187	171	151	151	300	422							
Smith Village	34	82		93	93									
Smithville	125	133	144	110	256	290	319	65	65		65			
Snyder	1619	1848	1671	1663	646	1278	1195	1197	1122	679				
Soper	305	465	322	309	337	481	417	538	233	296				
South Coffeyville	791	873	646	622	527	364	271	179	196					
Southward	100	100	115	385	400	500	500		171					
Sparks	202	772	183	186	233	339	470	472	421	503				
Spavinaw	432	623	470	319	213	255	110	90	90					
Speermoore									180					
Spelter City	200	390	250	250	300									
Spencer	3972	4064	3714	1189	300	229	198	180	240					
Sperry	937	1276	1123	883	665	570	563	487						
Spiro	2146	2221	2057	1450	1365	1041	969	1162	1173	962	543			
Sportsmen Acres	181	218												
Springer	485	679	256	212	325	314	403	325	300		188			
Stanley				50	50	300	210	210	200		350			
Stapp	100				225	225	225		220					
Stecker		50			200	230	230	265	276					
Sterling	684	702	675	562	447	430	361			219				
Sterrett							829	703	575		575			
Stidham	48	60	53	88	46	103	93	62	116					
Stigler	2574	2630	2347	1923	2125	1861	1517	1797	1583	1001	200			
Stillwater	36676	38268	31126	23965	20238	10097	7016	4701	3444	2577	2431	480		
Stillwell	2663	2369	2134	1916	1813	1717	1366	1155	1039	948	779			
Stonebluff	300	150	300	300		155	155							
Stonewall	519	672	653	584	634	761	478	622	494	530	300	100	110	
Straight	75	150	240	300	320	283	286	515						
Strang	141	126	164	176	201									
Stratford	1404	1459	1278	1058	1065	896	950	964	685	445				
Stringtown	366	1047	397	414	499	718	558	360	225		168		400	
Strong City	49	56	40	51	107	245	353	350						

POPULATION HISTORY OF OKLAHOMA CITIES AND TOWNS 1870-1990

COMMUNITY	1990	1980	1970	1960	1950	1940	1930	1920	1910	1907	1900	1890	1880	1870
Stroud	2666	3148	2502	2456	2450	1917	1894	1361	1220	1313	800			
Stuart	228	235	294	271	303	340	535	513	290	237	100			
Sugden	65	76	54	68	105	171	146	218	321		100			
Sulpher	4824	5516	5158	4737	4389	4970	4242	3667	3684	2935	1198			
Summit	170	175	125	260	260			34						
Sumner	250	20	16	27	46	80	64	65	105					
Sutter									360		200			
Swink	250	90	88	86	96	116	122	169						
Taft	400	489	525	386	541	772	690	553	352	250				
Tahlequah	10398	9708	9254	5840	4750	3027	2495	2271	2891	1916	1482	1500	525	
Tahoma					300	300	400							
Talala	206	191	163	147	210	188	198	197	340	307	118			
Talihina	1297	1387	1223	1048	965	1057	1032	690	491	416	548			
Taloga	415	446	363	322	430	533	436	365	468	430	415			
Tamaha	188	145	83	80	117	245	202	501	498	464	237		52	
Tangier									300					
Tatums	176	281	150	319	210	226	466	389	100					
Tecumseh	5750	5123	4451	2360	2275	2042	2419	1429	1626	1621	1193	1375		
Temple	1223	1339	1354	1282	1442	1313	1182	906	852	739				
Terlton	121	155	111	90	122	245	234	426	250					
Terral	469	604	636	585	616	521	593	506	573	583	267			
Texanna									200					
Texhoma	746	785	921	911	1464	577	819	687	372	262	100			
Texmo									300					
Texola	45	106	144	202	265	337	581	298	361					
Thackerville	290	431	257	185	178	207	185	210	190		154			
Thomas	1246	1515	1336	1211	1171	1220	1256	1223	1371	925	400			
Three Sands	875			300	200	500	1698							
Timber Brook			60	100	100	261	250							
Tipton	1043	1475	1206	1117	1172	1470	1459	727	441					
Tishomingo	3116	3212	2663	2381	2325	1951	1281	1871	1408	1300	348	100		
Tom	150	150	200	300		200	200							
Tonkawa	3127	3524	3337	3415	3643	3197	3311	1448	1776	1238	707			
Treece	288	215							288					
Tribbey														
Troy	100	80		100			150							
Tryon	514	435	301	254	285	279	299	225	176	211	117			
Tullahassee	92	145	183	199	209	200	164	189	80					
Tulsa	367302	360919	330350	261685	182740	142157	141258	72075	18182	7298	1390	57		
Tupelo	323	542	485	261	376	391	496	380	387	289				

POPULATION HISTORY OF OKLAHOMA CITIES AND TOWNS 1870-1990

COMMUNITY	1990	1980	1970	1960	1950	1940	1930	1920	1910	1907	1900	1890	1880	1870
Turley	2930	6336	6300	1200	200	267	410		75					
Turpin	450	425	295	195	175	100	90							
Tushka	256	358	230	248	400	236	293	248	300				100	
Tuskahoma	175	200	200	300	325	174	350	213	180		350			
Tuttle	2807	3051	1640	855	715	940	766	590	794	613				
Tuxedo Park					1179									
Tyrone	880	928	588	456	261	257	482	718	235					
Uncas			53	90	100	121	305	96	150					
Union											284			
Union City	1000	558	306	329	301	523	296	459	220		144			
Valley Brook	744	921	1197	1378										
Valliant	873	927	840	477	661	551	608	809	656	419				
Vanoss	100	75		106	125	100	518	518	225					
Velma	661	831	611	775	1034	120	114	165	85					
Vera	167	182	215	125	164	208	206	209	312	175	50			
Verden	546	625	439	405	508	575	587	496	524	312				
Verdigris	900	300	307	120	150	64	140	113	75			77	609	
Vernon	100	100	100	150	600	420	420							
Veterans Village		600	600		3355						296			
Vian	1414	1521	1131	930	927	941	900	1176	794	617				
Vici	751	845	694	601	620	617	593	425	55					
Village	10353	11049	13695	12118										
Vinita	5804	6740	5847	6027	5518	5685	4263	5010	4082	3157	2339	400	600	200
Vinson	60	75	100		100	188	188		250					
Vireton									210		150			
Wade	50	50	150	150	150	200	200		181		41			
Wagoner	6894	6191	4959	4469	4395	3535	2994	3436	4018	2950	2372			
Wainwright	223	182	135	114	138	162	162	254	213					
Wakita	453	526	545	452	440	444	317	338	405	388	275			
Walters	2519	2778	2661	2825	2743	2238	2262	3032	1377	1243				
Wanette	346	473	303	381	594	665	758	782	677	739	87			
Wann	126	156	135	157	99	147	168	404	286	201				
Wapanucka	402	472	425	459	592	730	553	1038	948	789	238			
Wardville	52	61	100	150	89	275	217	100	125		75			
Warner	1479	1310	1217	881	382	391	316	318	370					
Warr Acres	9288	9940	9887	7135	2378	54	255	210	129					
Warwick	160	167	146	95	132	359	400	336						
Washington	279	477	322	278	292				350					
Washita	180	180	180	150		147	147							
Washunga			25	60	91	177	288		190					

POPULATION HISTORY OF OKLAHOMA CITIES AND TOWNS 1870-1990

COMMUNITY	1990	1980	1970	1960	1950	1940	1930	1920	1910	1907	1900	1890	1880	1870
Watonga	3408	4139	3696	3252	3249	2828	2228	1678	1723	1608	427	560		
Watson	300	150	48	60	100		200	396						
Watts	303	316	326	268	267	307	353	125					200	
Wauhillau					48		118		51			200		
Waukomis	1322	1551	842	516	537	397	445	463	533	570	688			
Waurika	2088	2258	1833	1933	2327	2458	2368	3204	2928	696				
Wayne	519	621	618	517	501	401	427	429	332	198	248			
Waynoka	947	1377	1444	1794	2018	1584	1840	1500	1160		253			
Weatherford	10124	9640	7959	4499	3529	2504	2417	1929	2118	1315	1017			
Webb City	99	157	186	233	284	352	493	106						
Webbers Falls	722	461	485	441	489	486	415	480	380	332	211	125		
Welch	499	697	651	557	483	498	448	696	684	481	334			
Weleetka	1112	1195	1199	1231	1548	1904	2042	1588	1229	1020				
Wellston	912	802	789	630	643	607	632	650	590	669	383			
West Guthrie												404		
West Siloam Springs	539	431	210											
Westport	326	265	146											
Westville	1374	1049	934	727	781	716	691	956	802	624	296			
Wetumka	1427	1725	1687	1798	2025	2340	2153	1422	1190	966	150	26		
Wewoka	4050	5480	5284	5954	6747	10315	10401	1520	1022	794	119	100	175	
Wheatland	253	240	250	300	350	341	409	341	165					
Whitefield	275	400	300	150			110	110	350		248			
Whitesboro									50					
Wilburton	3092	2996	2504	1772	1939	1925	1524	2226	2277	1451	1500			
Wildcat	140		142	142	147	188	134	298	411	375				
Williams	125	125	125		300	300	500							
Willis					120	100	390				104			
Willow	142	162	188	187	223	248	347	286	104					
Wilson	1639	1584	1569	1647	1832	1700	2517	2286	175					
Winchester	301	150							100		100			
Wirt				500	500	650	650							
Wister	956	982	927	592	729	763	761	586	498	410	313			
Witcher						280	280		281					
Wolco														
Woodford					150				160		130			
Woodlawn Park	170	167	220	129										
Woodville	31	94	118	98	78	364	353	443	389	390	80			
Woodward	12340	13610	8710	7747	5915	5406	5056	3849	2696	2018	584			
Wright City	836	1168	1068	1161	1121	267	572	1030	255					
Wyandotte	366	336	297	226	242	348	271	274		321	224		100	

POPULATION HISTORY OF OKLAHOMA CITIES AND TOWNS 1870-1990

COMMUNITY	1990	1980	1970	1960	1950	1940	1930	1920	1910	1907	1900	1890	1880	1870
Wybark / Verdark	30	40				212	212		150					
Wynnewood	2451	2615	2374	2509	2423	2318	1820	2200	2002	2032	1907			
Wynona	531	780	547	652	678	810	1171	2749	270					
Yale	1392	1652	1239	1369	1359	1407	1734	2601	685	439				
Yeager	40	138	107	129	180	284	300	286	231	300				
Yukon	20935	17112	8411	3076	1990	1660	1455	1016	1018	830	614	325		
Zincville	30	30			400	500	500							

1907: U.S. Bureau of the Census. Population of Oklahoma and Indian Territory, 1907. Washington: GPO, 1907 (Bulletin 89).

POPULATION HISTORY OF OREGON CITIES AND TOWNS 1850-1990

COMMUNITY	1990	1980	1970	1960	1950	1940	1930	1920	1910	1900	1890	1880	1870	1860	1850
Adair	554														
Adams	223	240	219	192	154	169	178	198	205	263	450				
Adrian	131	162	200	300	500	150	60								
Agate Beach			975	606	379		150								
Albany	29462	26546	18181	12926	10115	5654	5325	4840	4275	3149	3079	1867	1292		
Albina											5129	143			
Alderbrook											442				
Algoma							250								
Alicel							300								
Aloha	34284	28353	6000	675	900	500	500								
Alsea	400	400	600	200	130		100	210	150	108	108	332			
Altamont	18591	19591	15746	10811	9419		200								
Alvadore	300	300	350	230	130										
Amity	1175	1092	708	620	672	545	438	522	407	292	300	215			
Antelope	34	39	51	46	60	90	136	199	175	249	184				
Applegate	800	800	125	300	75				42	42		209	346	514	
Arlington	425	521	375	643	686	609	601	529	317	388	356	300			
Ashland	16234	14943	12342	9119	7739	4744	4544	4283	5020	2634	1784	842	400	327	
Astoria	10069	9998	10244	11239	12331	10389	10349	14027	9599	8381	6184	2803	639	252	
Athena	997	965	872	950	750	513	504	621	586	703	495				
Auburn											60	200	442		
Aumsville	1650	1432	590	300	281	174	153	171	250	178	129	100			
Aurora	567	523	306	274	242	228	215	299	190	122	410	175			
Austin					39		59	149	144	66	28				
Azalea	335	335	200		480		200								
Baker	9140	9471	9354	9986	9471	9342	7858	7729	6742	6663	2604	1258	312		
Ballston	175	200	125	115	115	115	115	125	98			150			
Bandon	2215	2311	1832	1653	1251	1004	1516	1140	1803	645	219	175			
Banks	563	489	430	347	376	247	209	324	375	329					
Barlow	118	105	105	85	75	52	40	42	69						
Barnes				5076											
Barview	1402	1462	1388	75	125										
Battin		1700	1500	700											
Bay City	1027	986	898	996	761	379	427	511	281	203					
Beaver Creek	425	425	708	100		100	100		50						
Beaver Hill								143	149	119					
Beaverton	53310	30582	18577	5937	2512	1052	1138	580	386	249	207	200			
Bend	20469	17263	13710	11936	11409	10021	8848	5415	536	20	76	220			
Bethany	750														
Bly	750	750	500	600	800	800	800	100	100						

POPULATION HISTORY OF OREGON CITIES AND TOWNS 1850-1990

COMMUNITY	1990	1980	1970	1960	1950	1940	1930	1920	1910	1900	1890	1880	1870	1860	1850
Boardman	1387	1261	192	153	120	110	100	113							
Bonanza	323	270	230	297	259	233	141	77							
Bonneville			175	150		500			250	118		100			
Boring	500	500	500	800	800	200	300	150	250						
Bourne					19		30	77	592	386					
Bridal Veil			150		150	204	204	210	200	200					
Brighton							100	310							
Brookings	4400	3384	2720	2637	1000	500	250	515							
Brownsville	1281	1261	1034	875	1175	784	746	763	919	698	580	143	200	222	
Browntown												100			
Bryant						500									
Buena Vista						100	150		139	132	193	193			
Bunkerhill	1242	1555	1549	1655	1409										
Burns	2913	3579	3293	3523	3093	2566	2599	1022	904	547	264				
Butte Falls	252	428	358	384	372	339	298	166	150						
Butter Creek												275			
Butteville	60	60	85	70	50		50		49	127	103	250			
Buxton							120	227	250						
Camas Valley	400	400	665	550	160	302	302	116	76	93	43				
Canby	8983	7659	3813	2168	1671	988	744	852	587	372	207				
Canemah												183			
Cannon Beach	1221	1187	779	495	125	125	125	354	364	345	304	393	250		
Canyon City	648	639	600	654	508	312	268	156	149	245	200	243	288	322	
Canyonville	1219	1288	940	1089	861	255	167	552	386	145	125	72			
Carlton	1289	1302	1126	959	1081	864	749								
Carson									221	221					
Cascade Locks	930	838	574	660	733	703	356	356	248	248	275	200			
Cave Junction	1126	1023	415	248	283	120									
Cedar Hills	9294	9614	2900	1200											
Cedar Mill	9697	3900	1500	215	300		250		76	53	48	150			
Centennial		22118													
Centerville									45	61	534	221	100		
Central Point	7509	6357	4004	2289	1667	906	821	582	761	322		50			
Champoeg	700								112	112					
Charleston		700	500	700	576	250	150								
Chemawa			900	825	850	700	700	625	742	742					
Chemult	425	425	580	310	115	220	55								
Chenoweth	3246	2820	2329	950											
Cherry Grove							250					150			
Chiloquin	673	778	826	945	688	741	481	160							

POPULATION HISTORY OF OREGON CITIES AND TOWNS 1850-1990

COMMUNITY	1990	1980	1970	1960	1950	1940	1930	1920	1910	1900	1890	1880	1870	1860	1850
Clackamas	2578	3250	3600	3141	550	600	500	315	75	119	46	120			
Clarksville												335			
Clatskanie	1629	1648	1286	797	901	708	739	1171	747	311	212	75			
Clatsop									240	176					
Cleone									204	100					
Clifton							150		117	117	84				
Cloverdale		300	151	183	280	150	72								
Coburg	763	699	713	754	693	456	263	270	613	185	210	50			
College Crest			750	1000	1863										
Colton	300	300	305	300	167	125	125								
Columbia City	1003	678	537	423	405	327	310		50	65					
Concord	3600	3600	2000							65					
Condon	635	783	973	1149	968	856	940	1127	1009	230	60				
Coos Bay/Marshfield	15076	14424	13466	7084	6223	5259	5287	4034	2980	1391	1461	642	250		
Copperfield								155	750						
Coquille	4121	4481	4437	4370	3523	3327	2732	1642	1398	728	494	176	100		
Corbett	425	425	140	140			90	90	50						
Cornelius	6148	4055	1903	1146	998	637	487	494	459	246	214	106			
Comucopia						355		355	176	359	182	150			
Corvallis	44757	40960	35153	20669	16207	8392	7585	5752	4552	1819	1527	1128	800	620	
Cottage Grove	7402	7148	6004	3895	3536	2626	2473	1919	1834	974	750	450	75		
Cove	507	451	363	311	282	321	307	399	433	223	223				
Crabtree	300	300	350	550	350	136	136	136	100						
Crane	150	150	63	21	99	145	275	113							
Crawfordsville									212	212	358				
Crescent	700	700	850	400	300		49								
Creswell	2431	1770	1193	760	662	497	345	273	367	224	139	108			
Culver	570	514	407	301	301		62								
Cushman							200	162							
Dalles	9422	8530	6361	5072	4793	3579	2975	2701	2124	1271	848	670	495	450	
Damascus									127	127					
Days Creek	525	525	602	200		138									
Dayton	1526	1409	949	673	719	506	413	448	453	293	304	368	250		
Dayville	144	199	197	234	286	136	106	117	100	52	120				
De Lake				803	644	200									
Deer Island									175						
Depoe Bay	870	723	450	750	750	300									
Detroit	331	367	328	206	300	250	250	111							
Dexter	300	300	450	300	400	100			100	97	103	97			
Dillard	1000	1000	602	500	300					97					

POPULATION HISTORY OF OREGON CITIES AND TOWNS 1850-1990

COMMUNITY	1990	1980	1970	1960	1950	1940	1930	1920	1910	1900	1890	1880	1870	1860	1850
Dilley				201	187	164	150	155	125	93	53	150			
Donald	316	267	231				114	126	50						
Drain	1011	1148	1204	1052	1150	597	497	607	335	193	451	188	75		
Draperville	250	250	250	250	201										
Drewsey	30	30	22	39	64	58	66	83	82	125		100			
Dufur	527	560	493	488	422	392	382	533	523	336		100			
Dundee	1663	1223	588	318	308	209	232	193	196	124					
Dunes	1081	1124	976	629											
Durham	748	707	410	500	250										
Eagle Creek	300	300	250	75	75	200			100	78	110	63			
Eagle Point	3008	2764	1241	752	607	243	211	128	175	128	99	50			
East Portland											10532	2934	830		
Eastside		1601	1331	1380	890	638	556	453	252						
Echo	499	624	479	456	457	280	311	501	400	113	227				
Elgin	1586	1701	1375	1315	1223	997	728	1043	1120	603					
Elkton	172	155	176	146	201		90	99	150	118	118	100			
Ellensburgh												200			
Elmira	500	500	950	500	500	200	200	213	100	72					
Empire				3781	2261	665	493	182	147	185	252	317	350	176	
Englewood				1382											
Enterprise	1905	2003	1680	1932	1718	1709	1379	1895	1242	396	242				
Errol Heights	7800	7800	8400	10700											
Estacada	2016	1419	1164	957	950	526	524	483	405						
Eugene	112669	105624	76346	50977	35879	20838	18901	10593	9009	3236	2958	1117	861	1183	
Fairview	2391	1749	1045	578	438	305	266	184	204						
Falcon Heights	800	800	1389												
Falls City	818	804	745	653	853	715	494	994	969						
Flora							64	159	137	137					
Florence	5162	4411	2246	1642	1026	458	339	317	311	222	185	68			
Forest Grove	13559	11499	8275	5628	4343	2449	1859	1915	1772	1096	668	547	422		
Fort Klamath				672	645	532	200	217	167	167					
Fossil	399	535	511	350	350		538	519	421	288	153	50			
Foster	600	600	850			100	55	63	100	60		100			
Four Corners	12156	11331	6199	4743	1284										
Fox Valley										163	163	175			
Freewater	3982	4733	2655	2158	1439	825	732	664	532	188					
Fruit Dale	6652	6926	2980	2200	1711										
Garden Home					750		60		50	135					
Gardiner	600	600	500	350	600	250	300	400	391	286	229	200	150		
Garibaldi	877	999	1083	1163	1249	500	213	213	74	74					

POPULATION HISTORY OF OREGON CITIES AND TOWNS 1850-1990

COMMUNITY	1990	1980	1970	1960	1950	1940	1930	1920	1910	1900	1890	1880	1870	1860	1850
Gaston	563	471	429	320	368	333	227	221	275	187	182	108			
Gates	499	455	250	189	445		260	260	75	113					
Gearhart	1027	967	829	725	568	319	125	127							
Gervais	992	1144	746	438	457	332	254	268	276	224	532	202	150		
Gesher Corner					2094										
Gilbert	4000	4000	3300												
Gilchrist	600	600	500	500		300									
Gladstone	10152	9500	6237	3854	2434	1629	1348	1069							
Glencullen				1500		1000	400								
Glendale	707	712	709	748	871	557	513	548	646	112					
Gleneden Beach	800	800	400	185	185										
Glenwood	1600	1600	500	750	500	350	200	75	50						
Glide	900	900	470	200	100		50								
Goble	130	130	108	70	73	90	91	117	375	188					
Gold Beach	1546	1515	1554	1765	677	500	500	321	125	112	200				
Gold Hill	964	904	603	608	619	536	502	422	423	385	100				
Grand Ronde	550	550	289	300	400	125	280		60		56	100			
Granite					40	86	45	55	89	245	249	200	448		
Grant										200					
Grants Pass	17488	14977	12455	10118	8116	6028	4666	4200	3897	2290	1432	250			
Grass Valley	160	164	153	234	195	204	208	317	342	196					
Green	5076	3897	1612	500	160		185								
Greenville									144	144	200				
Gresham	68235	33005	9875	3944	3049	1951	1635	1103	540	165					
Haines	405	341	212	331	321	377	431	503	423	148					
Halfway	311	380	317	505	312	416	351	324	186	51					
Halsey	667	693	467	404	388	305	300	339	337	294	270	306	150		
Hammond	589	516	500	480	522	422	244	547	957	70					
Happy Valley	1519	1499	1392												
Harbor	2143	2856	750	600	600	200									
Hardman	20		19	30	58	83	120	193	191	121					
Harney							16	23	58	82					
Harrisburg	1939	1881	1311	939	862	622	575	573	453	502	240	422	200		
Hauser	630	630	400	233	158	126	126								
Haysville	14318	9213	5518	4568	2697										
Hebo	300	300	350	350	250	150	275		54	54					
Helix	150	155	152	148	182	121	193	290	109	112					
Henryville												206			
Heppner	1412	1498	1429	1661	1648	1140	1190	1324	880	1146	675	318			
Hermiston	10040	9408	4893	4402	3804	803	608	655	647						

POPULATION HISTORY OF OREGON CITIES AND TOWNS 1850-1990

COMMUNITY	1990	1980	1970	1960	1950	1940	1930	1920	1910	1900	1890	1880	1870	1860	1850
Hilgard							100	156	148	148	429				
Hillsboro	37520	27664	14675	8232	5142	3747	3039	2468	2016	980	1246	450	396		
Hines	1452	1632	1407	1207	918	677	97								
Hood River	4632	4329	3991	3657	3701	3280	2757	3195	2331	766	201	200			
Houlton						1000			347	187					
Hubbard	1881	1640	975	526	493	387	330	320	283	213	117	141	100		
Humboldt Basin												150			
Huntington	522	539	507	689	733	741	803	666	680	821	321	200			
Idanha	289	319	382	295	442		60								
Imbler	299	292	139	137	149	182	203	206	225	96					
Independence	4425	4024	2594	1930	1987	1372	1248	1143	1160	909	1000	691	400	425	
Ione	255	345	355	350	262	262	283	439	239	223					
Irrigon	737	700	261	232	75		65	115	125						
Irving										78	127				
Island City	696	477	202	158	138	177	116	141	166	249	498	210			
Jacksonville	1896	2030	1611	1172	1193	761	706	489	785	653	743	839	1000	892	
Jefferson	1805	1702	936	716	636	479	391	417	415	273	307	207	150		
Jennings Lodge	6530	3000	3500	2867	3500	800									
John Day	1836	2012	1566	1520	1597	708	432	321	258	282	211	280	179		
Johnson City	586	378	378												
Jordan Valley	364	473	196	204	236	274	306	355	200	110					
Joseph	1073	999	839	788	666	593	504	770	725	237	249	100			
Junction City	3670	3320	2373	1614	1475	1187	922	687	759	506	617	494	428		
Juntura	65	65	56	98	107	167	136	127	55	55					
Keizer	21884	19785	11405	5288											
Kendall	2100	2100	2000				100								
Keno	900	900	500	350	300	300	150								
Kerbyville	550	550	650	800	150	200	400		85	165	143	75	100	132	
Kernville	65	65								62					
King	2060	1853	1427												
Kinzua	300	300	400	900	900	600	450								
Klamath Falls	17737	16661	15775	16949	15875	16497	16093	4801	2758	447	364				
Knappa							74	184	100	32	32	125			
La Grande	11766	11354	9645	9014	8635	7747	8050	6913	4843	2991	2583	400	240		
La Pine	900	900	900	750	250		50								
Lacomb							360			63					
LaFayette	1292	1215	786	553	662	409	350	410	412	359	365	396	200		
Lake Grove						800	800								
Lake Oswego/Oswego	30576	22868	14573	8906	3316	1726	1285	1818	1000	510	544	396	200		
Lakeside	1437	1453	900	350	150	134	92		125			96	150		

POPULATION HISTORY OF OREGON CITIES AND TOWNS 1850-1990

COMMUNITY	1990	1980	1970	1960	1950	1940	1930	1920	1910	1900	1890	1880	1870	1860	1850
Noti	400	400	300	300	310										
Nyssa	2629	2862	2620	2611	2525	1855	821	563	449	315		275			
Oak Grove	12576	11640	6300	3404	2000	1500									
Oakland	844	886	1010	856	829	367	421	516	467	368	339	369	300	357	
Oakridge	3063	3729	3422	1973	1562	520	400	65							
O'Brien	400	400	315	235	265		400								
Oceanlake				1342	700	650	400								
Odell	600	600	450	450	350										
Olney								68	50	134	76	81			
Ontario	9392	8814	6523	5101	4465	3551	1941	2039	1248	445	200				
Oregon City	14698	14673	9176	7996	7682	6124	5761	5686	4287	3494	3062	1263	1382	888	698
Orenco	450	450	200	400	313			335	75						
Orodell												219			
Pacific City	1500	1500	500	200	200										
Paisley	350	343	260	219	214	237	259	257	176	176	69	89			
Park Place	280	280	1200	950	500	250	350	213	55	155					
Parkersburg									109	109	52	200			
Parkrose	21108	21108	22500	9900	3800	500	500								
Pendleton	15126	14521	13197	14434	11774	8847	6621	6837	4460	4406	2506	730	243		
Perrydale							80	314	98	98	98	74			
Philomath	3983	2673	1688	1359	1289	856	694	591	505	343	316	224	100		
Phoenix	3239	2309	1287	769	746	452	439	159	250	268	245	277	100		
Pilot Rock	1478	1630	1612	1695	847	358	275	361	197	137	239	160	100		
Pine									150	100					
Pleasant Home							300			50	86	250			
Pondosa				160		300									
Port Orford	1025	1061	1037	1171	674	755	300	217	227	227	108		100	146	
Portland	437319	366383	382619	372676	373628	305394	301815	258288	207214	90426	46385	17577	8293	2868	821
Powell Butte	600	600	550	580	661	400	400								
Powell Valley		200		700					72	72					
Powellhurst	9000	9000	8100	4300											
Powers	682	819	842	1366	895	647	438	160							
Prairie	1117	1106	867	801	822		210	643	348	213	222	235	100		
Prescott	63	73	105	129	119			34							
Prineville	5355	5276	4101	3263	3233	2358	1027	1144	1042	656	460	400	100		
Prospect	1200	1200	200	500	500	125	125								
Prosper							50			32					
Quinaby					827										
Quincy				200					75						
Rainier	1674	1655	1731	1152	1285	1183	1353	1287	1359	522	238	150	100		

POPULATION HISTORY OF OREGON CITIES AND TOWNS 1850-1990

COMMUNITY	1990	1980	1970	1960	1950	1940	1930	1920	1910	1900	1890	1880	1870	1860	1850
Rajneespuram	600	606													
Raleigh Hills	6066	6517	8000												
Randolph				2800						173	173				
Redmond	7163	6452	3721	3340	2956	1876	994	585	216						
Redwood	3702	3171													
Reedsport	4796	4984	4039	2998	2288	1421	1178	850							
Reedville							75	162	100	65	65	110			
Rhododendron	800	800	350	200			50								
Richland	161	181	133	228	220	254	212	244	334	135					
Riddle	1143	1265	1042	992	634	214	195	268	187	131					
River Road	9443	10370	12000	7000											
Rivergrove	294	314	319												
Rockaway	970	906	665	771	1027	300	300	120							
Rockwood	11000	11000	9700	600	550	208	100		100	67					
Rogue River	1759	1308	841	520	590	383	286	211							
Rooster Rock												206			
Rose Lodge	1257	200	300	150	150										
Roseburg	17032	16644	14461	11467	8390	4924	4362	4258	4738	1690	1472	822	600	835	
Rufus	295	352	317	150	124		70		113	113					
Russelville	6500	6500	4500		500	400	400		50	120					
Rye Valley				100	250	150	150		125	53	29	150			
Saginaw									34	214					
St. Helens	7535	7064	6212	5022	4711	4304	3994	2220	742	258	220	209	100		
St. Johns									4872	348	310	109			
St. Paul	322	312	347	254	226	183	148	160	103	165	143	200			
Salem	107786	89233	68296	49142	43140	30908	26266	17679	14094	4258	3422	2538	2139	902	
Salem Heights				10880	2351										
Sandy	4152	2905	1544	1147	1003	473	284	242	250	96					
Santa Clara	12834	14288	11000	2380	200										
Scapoose	3529	3213	1859	923	659	336	248	215	225	108					
Scio	623	579	447	441	448	351	258	300	295	346	253	193			
Scotts Mills	283	249	208	155	217	227	153	208	164	248					
Seal Rock	800	800	430	500	330										
Seaside	5359	5193	4402	3877	3686	2902	1565	1802	1121	191	87	75			
Seneca	191	285	400	450	760	275	275								
Shady Cove	1351	1097	613	875	500	100									
Shaniko	26	30	58	39	61	55	100	124	495	72					
Shedd	200	200	150	152	165	180	200	130	250	201					
Sheridan	3979	2249	1881	1763	1922	1294	1008	979	1021	466	355	55	50		
Sherwood	3093	2386	1396	680	575	447	382	320	115	111	299	196	75		

POPULATION HISTORY OF OREGON CITIES AND TOWNS 1850-1990

COMMUNITY	1990	1980	1970	1960	1950	1940	1930	1920	1910	1900	1890	1880	1870	1860	1850
Shevlin					600	642	642								
Siletz	926	1001	596	583	570	350	350	113	100	121					
Silverlake	150	150	200	150	100	97	122	126	250	95					
Silverton	5635	5168	4301	3081	3146	2925	2462	2251	1588	656	511	229	200		
Sisters	679	696	516	602	723	500	130	80	100						
Sodaville	192	171	125	145	157	99	77	72	110	178	66	56			
South Lebanon	1203	1309	2229												
South Medford		2898	3497	2306	1226										
Sparta								34	58	58	188	213			
Spray	149	155	161	194	375	110	110	52	125	48					
Springfield	44683	41621	27047	19616	10807	3805	2364	1855	1838	353	371	160	200	198	
Stanfield	1568	1568	891	745	845	241	204	278	318						
Stayton	5011	4396	3170	2108	1507	1085	797	649	703	324	381	226			
Sublimity	1491	1077	634	490	367	280	214	172	138	108	58	40			
Summerville	111	132	76	76	73	80	116	116	237	184	280	163	160		
Sumpter	119	133	120	96	146	420	154	219	643	2216	91	261			
Sunriver	1095	1095	100												
Sutherlin	5020	4560	3070	2452	2230	525	457	515							
Svensen	650	650	800	500	200	280	280	45							
Sweet Home	6850	6921	3799	3353	3603	1090	189	175	202	172	285	90			
Taft				557	450	350			50	97					
Talent	3275	2577	1389	868	739	381	421	278	275	84	207	38	50		
Tangent	556	478	350	220	200	140	140	212	100						
Terrebone	1143	900	521	378	198		75								
The Dalles	11060	10820	10423	10493	7676	6266	5883	5807	4880	3542	3239	2232	942	802	
Tigard	29344	14286	6499	1980	800	600	500	615	125	248					
Tillamook	4001	3981	3968	4244	3685	2751	2549	1964	1352	834	760	200	100		
Tillican	600	600													
Toledo	3174	3151	2818	3053	2323	2288	2137	678	541	302	160				
Trail	300	300	160	88	45										
Tri-City	3585	3439	1039	500											
Troutdale	7852	5908	1661	522	514	211	227	191	309	365					
Troy							200								
Tualatin	15013	7348	750	359	248	180	193	234	137	137		120	100		
Tumalo		500	300	125	50		50	59							
Turner	1281	1116	846	770	610	414	283	289	191	239	208	142			
Tygh Valley	500	500	238	410	449		60	130	225	102					
Ukiah	250	249	375	200	300	100	100	117	150						
Umatilla	3046	3199	679	617	883	370	345	390	198	127	118	149	150		
Union	1847	2062	1531	1490	1307	1398	1107	1319	1483	937	604	416	200		

POPULATION HISTORY OF OREGON CITIES AND TOWNS 1850-1990

COMMUNITY	1990	1980	1970	1960	1950	1940	1930	1920	1910	1900	1890	1880	1870	1860	1850
Unity	87	155	312	288	212	150	34								
Upper Astoria										127	501	713			
Vale	1491	1558	1448	1491	1518	1083	922	935	992	131					
Valsetz	345	345	500	675	500		60								
Veneta	2519	2449	1377	1150	750	200	200	114							
Vernonia	1808	1758	1643	1089	1521	1412	1625	142	69	62	96				
Vida	400	400	175	250	250										
Waldo									76	76		71	100	256	
Waldport	1595	1274	700	667	689	630	367	181	225	85					
Wallowa	748	847	811	989	1055	838	749	894	793	243					
Wamie									175						
Warm Springs	2287	500	550	450	350	150	250	110	150	42					
Warren	800	800	900	500	81		50	159	110						
Warrendale									110	110					
Warrenton	2681	2493	1825	1717	1896	1365	683	730	339	332					
Wasco	374	415	412	348	305	303	400	701	386	322	90	60			
Waterloo	191	221	186	151	180			82	83	59					
Wauna			175	175		500	250	510							
Wedderburn							100	163							
Welches	500	500	100	150	119		75								
Wendling						800	500	315							
West Haven															
West Linn	16367	12956	7091	3933	2945	2165	1956	1628							
West Salem	3400	3400	3000			1490	974	208							
West Seaside									149						
West Slope	7959	5364	6000	4000		2000									
Westfall								92	140	84					
Westfir	278	312	750	492		500	500								
Weston	606	719	660	783	679	498	384	595	499	626	568	446	200		
Westport	500	500	650	300	600	500	450	410	100	48		65			
Wheeler	335	319	262	237	291	259	280	162							
White City	5891	5445	450	200											
Whitney						19	36	97	55						
Wilbur	350	350	476	150	150	138	138	155	100	179	66	49			
Willamette				950		1100	330	330	317	83		278			
Williamina	1717	1749	1193	960	1082	677	360	247	376	163	173	68			
Williams	500	500	750	500	100				46	46					
Wilsonville	7106	2920	1001	229	162	110	75	219	125	80					
Winchester	1900	1900	900	631	300				50						
Winchester Bay	900	900	245	450	500	275	288	62							

POPULATION HISTORY OF OREGON CITIES AND TOWNS 1850-1990

COMMUNITY	1990	1980	1970	1960	1950	1940	1930	1920	1910	1900	1890	1880	1870	1860	1850
Winston	3773	3359	2468	2395	500										
Wolf Creek	600	600	500	500	250	250	139			60					
Wood Village	2814	2253	1533	822											
Woodburn	13404	11196	7495	3120	2395	1982	1675	1656	1616	828	405	175			
Woodville									175	100					
Yachats	533	482	441	500	300	225	320								
Yamhill	867	690	516	407	539	418	390	366	325	254					
Yaquina							88	310	289	268					
Yoncalla	919	805	675	698	626	277	252	232	233	230	110	100			

POPULATION HISTORY OF SOUTH DAKOTA CITIES AND TOWNS 1860-1990

COMMUNITY	1990	1980	1970	1960	1950	1945	1940	1935	1930	1925	1920	1915	1910	1905	1900	1890	1880	1870	1860
Aberdeen	24927	25956	26476	23073	21051	18103	17015	16725	16465	15036	14537	11846	10753	5841	4087	3182	1164		
Ada												30	100						
Agar	82	139	156	139	141	93	142	203	200	128	86	100	114						
Akaska	52	49	46	90	84	72	151		169	116	101	76							
Albee	15	23	26	42	75	82	114	100	94		115	140	131	89	129	125			
Alcester	843	885	627	479	585	499	581	546	460	481	492	477	409	366	381	100			
Alexandria	518	588	598	614	714	570	746	802	688	865	965	936	955	938	680	587	99		
Alpena	251	288	307	407	426	363	440	477	499	521	576	394	417	341	153	150			
Altamont	48	58	54	77	76	90	144	144	123	127	116	103	110	100	162	150	189		
Amherst												150	225				291		
Anchor																			
Andover	106	139	138	224	277	298	350	324	322	353	442	349	446	307	225	232	202		
Antelope	744	400																	
Ardmore		16	14	73	107	97	195	194	261	204	220	140	146	28	90				
Arlington	908	991	954	996	1096	917	1157	1060	1020	977	1011	884	791	788	314	270	200		
Armour	854	819	925	875	900	734	1013	1008	1009	966	1045	953	968	1125	912	482			
Artas	28	43	73	87	172	169	180	209	193	177	143	159	325	42					
Artesian	217	227	277	330	429	311	502	528	556	606	689	586	583	444	339	256	289		
Ashton	148	154	137	182	222	186	240	275	314	365	372	326	430	331	274	359			
Astoria	155	154	153	176	206	227	214	251	231	243	221	110	300	80					
Athol												150	400	105	130	200	200		
Aurora	619	507	237	232	202	209	225	234	166	235	246	277	236	213	182	412	100		
Avon	576	576	610	637	692	577	728	661	670	650	630	525	451	360					
Badger	114	99	122	117	180	141	170	176	163	194	162	100	300		46	75			
Baltic	666	679	364	278	255	269	270	276	272	307	287	306	278	200	166	50	100		
Bancroft	30	41	48	86	100	97	126	154	155	165	141	139	136	100	143	158			
Bangor														25	269	278			
Batesland	124	163	135	100	88		145		300										
Bath	175	175	150	90	90				77		69	100	156	105	156	237			
Bear Gulch															80	200	52		
Belle Fourche	4335	4692	4236	4087	3540	2603	2496	2314	2032	1244	1616	1101	1352	1023	451				
Belvidere	63	80	96	232	172	130	187	193	214	163	170	232	375	80					
Bemis												100	250						
Beresford	1849	1865	1655	1794	1686	1590	1642	1618	1460	1507	1519	1350	1117	1192	1046	404	100		
Big Stone City	669	672	631	718	829	646	681	675	617	581	630	652	551	532	590	471	376		
Bijou Hills					35		120		136		120		300	100	130	127			
Bison	451	457	406	457	457		260		173		155	200	275	150	84	48			
Black Hawk	1995	1608	550	375	91				110		110	200	84		100	218			
Bloomington																			
Blunt	342	424	445	532	423	240	322	428	477	504	512	277	566	214	246	353	227		

POPULATION HISTORY OF SOUTH DAKOTA CITIES AND TOWNS 1860-1990

COMMUNITY	1990	1980	1970	1960	1950	1945	1940	1935	1930	1925	1920	1915	1910	1905	1900	1890	1880	1870	1860
Bon Homme													70		70	100	138	250	
Bonesteel	297	358	354	452	485	501	532	547	564	609	652	532	563	754					
Bonilla												55	175	100	115				
Bowdle	589	644	667	673	788	583	757	818	773	769	818	538	671	481	622	372			
Box Elder	2680	3186	607	190	33										125				
Bradley	117	135	157	188	226	255	311	289	291	310	368	533	351	337	180	168			
Brandon	3543	2589	1431	720	250		168		162		144	150	225	85	62	52	242		
Brandt	123	129	132	148	211	247	271	254	265	307	299	224	158	132	90				
Brentford	69	91	94	96	132	105	161	152	174	173	132	100	425						
Bridgewater	533	653	633	694	748	494	790	808	762	934	976	971	934	822	691	410	287		
Bristol	419	445	470	562	647	607	675	624	666	621	545	457	444	488	282	199			
Britton	1394	1590	1465	1442	1430	1340	1500	1473	1312	1113	1105	907	901	804	519	514	100		
Broadland	40	49	45	33	74	73	73	77	102	115	129	114	300	50	42	102	52		
Brookings	16270	14951	13717	10558	7764	5218	5346	5311	4376	4613	3924	3416	2971	3265	2346	1518	521		
Brooklyn																28	300		
Bruce	235	254	217	272	305	263	394	346	371	310	342	328	262	191	158	152			
Bryant	374	388	502	522	624	535	658	561	656	632	651	687	645	750	405	172			
Buffalo	488	453	393	652	380		180		184		163	150	125						
Buffalo Gap	173	186	155	194	186	124	182	150	183	104	132	137	280	178	160	501			
Bullhead	179	300	449	400	250		70		70		70								
Burbank												150	200	100					
Burke	756	859	892	811	829	584	602	591	605	700	623	421	311	200					
Bushnell	81	76	65	92	96	98	134	146	134	177	350	146	225	100					
Butler	17	22	38	62	109	107	153	170	184	180	156	149	162	155					
Camp Crook	146	100	150	90	122	100	227	186	161	141	163	133	120	200					
Canistota	608	626	636	627	687	562	665	611	590	540	594	511	409	365	263				
Canova	172	194	204	247	340	304	333	305	364	339	338	318	311	233	169	187			
Canton	2787	2886	2665	2511	2530	2538	2518	2542	2270	2562	2225	2316	2103	2279	1943	1101	675		
Capa												50	275						
Carbonate													67	50		173	200	250	
Carlock												35	200	100					
Carlyle												100	200						
Carpenter												85	200						
Carter			17	18	16	23	42	61	89	94	105	103	400						
Carthage	221	274	362	368	458	379	512	537	590	663	667	555	554	370	265	200			
Castalia																			
Castlewood/Keator	549	557	523	500	498	442	493	474	500	559	582	537	594	611	180	318	160		
Cavour	166	117	134	140	154	83	138	196	202	201	249	192	408	145	430	290	247		
Centerville	887	892	910	887	1053	985	1046	1202	1169	1168	1104	1109	971	922	871	410	183		
Central City	185	232	188	247	218	94	302	268	198	189	199	262	296	684	310	519	1008		

POPULATION HISTORY OF SOUTH DAKOTA CITIES AND TOWNS 1860-1950

COMMUNITY	1990	1980	1970	1960	1950	1945	1940	1935	1930	1925	1920	1915	1910	1905	1900	1890	1880	1870	1860
Chamberlin	2347	2258	2626	2598	1912	1529	1626	1506	1364	1521	1303	1055	1275	1007	874	939	755		
Chancellor	276	257	220	214	193	196	232	251	267	270	280	228	160	131	138				
Chelsea	33	41	45	53	41	42	51	72	84	111	110	86							
Cherry Creek	335	300	275	290	140		100		100				400						
Chester	200	200	260	223	200		175		180		200	300	475	75					
Claire City	85	87	100	86	109	112	149	177	193	229	213	122							
Claremont	135	180	214	247	236	210	271	283	285	310	290	279	294	144	120	121			
Clark	1292	1351	1356	1484	1471	1314	1291	1273	1290	1279	1392	1200	1220	985	684	592			
Clear Lake	1247	1310	1157	1137	1105	825	997	929	834	976	835	804	704	630	491	147			
Colman	482	501	456	505	509	380	462	448	488	475	535	399	362	366	213	224			
Colome	309	361	375	398	451	360	509	531	599	630	568	415	700						
Colton	657	757	601	593	521	497	615	564	575	553	608	522	407	300	130				
Columbia	133	161	240	272	270	253	275	307	251	279	327	250	235	142	143	400	133		
Conata												40	200						
Conde/Coral	203	259	279	388	409	361	395	437	431	526	544	483	592	282	195	318			
Corona	118	126	133	150	191	196	177	160	152	147	219	211	350	100	90	68			
Corsica	619	644	615	479	551	372	452	486	516	450	346	300	286	250					
Cottonwood			16	38	102	67	118	150	191	159	121	120	475						
Coulson																212			
Crandall												100	325						
Crandon											38	65	200		216	198	187		
Cresbard	185	221	224	229	235	249	288	298	358	348	349	238	320	100					
Crocker												150	350						
Crooks	671	594	200	200	120		120		114		100	150	275	50					
Custer	1741	1830	1597	2105	2017	1894	1845	1239	1203	802	595	416	602	596	599	790	271		
Cyanide														146					
Dallas	142	199	233	212	244	227	278	308	423	645	705	751	1277	250					
Dante	98	83	88	102	140	106	118	109	132	157	175	113	160						
Davis	87	100	101	124	153	188	230	214	209	236	245	244	164	200	151				
Daviston												50	175						
De Smet	1172	1237	1336	1324	1180	903	1016	988	1017	1009	1035	1014	1063	985	749	541	116		
Deadwood	1830	2035	2409	3045	3288	3412	4100	3662	2559	2432	2403	3313	3653	4364	3498	2366	3777		
Dell Rapids	2484	2389	1991	1863	1650	1470	1706	1636	1657	1582	1677	1538	1367	1339	1255	993	500	250	
Delmont	235	290	260	363	405	368	461	518	472	513	518	494	369	400	210	87			
Dempster												100	150	85					
Dimock	157	140	167	198	120		140		113		113								
Dixon												100	225						
Doland	306	381	430	481	535	455	542	510	538	603	667	515	581	354	235	216			
Doltan	43	47	60	71	93	89	121	132	124	123	147	133	147	120	96				
Draper	123	138	200	215	252	141	190	176	169	157	173	120	211						

POPULATION HISTORY OF SOUTH DAKOTA CITIES AND TOWNS 1860-1990

COMMUNITY	1990	1980	1970	1960	1950	1945	1940	1935	1930	1925	1920	1915	1910	1905	1900	1890	1880	1870	1860
Dupree	484	562	523	548	438	494	460	361	365	269	213	108							
Eagle Butte	489	435	530	495	375	247	374	310	387	251	210	78							
East Sioux Falls											268	268	268	229	232	577			
Eden	97	142	132	136	149	147	171	168	150	165	209								
Edgemont	906	1468	1174	1772	1158	1082	1002	947	1103	1092	1254	743	816	490	479				
Edgerton																277			
Egan	208	248	281	310	347	307	418	445	419	426	569	605	516	540	503	399			
Elbon										109	136	100	159						
Elizabethtown																	316		
Elk Point	1423	1661	1372	1378	1367	1272	1483	1425	1294	1319	1470	1546	1200	1282	1081	1209	719	500	
Elkton	602	632	541	621	657	666	779	807	856	852	872	768	742	532	578	331	67		
Ellsworth AFB	7017	4766	6207																
Emery/Farmington	417	399	452	502	480	439	482	485	542	600	600	545	446	415	247	218	200		
Emmett																	180		
Englewood								77	104	72	78	91	91						
Erwin	42	66	106	157	153	193	182	222	205	264	257	232	230	178	131	212			
Esmond			19	19	49	58	96	96	116	131	145	110	300	100	129	126			
Estelline/Spaulding	658	719	624	722	760	559	627	551	488	585	658	575	509	471	351	210	234		
Ethan	312	351	309	297	319	259	324	301	369	369	416	308	312	260	190	208			
Eureka	1197	1360	1547	1555	1576	1340	1457	1430	1308	1228	1200	968	961	693	961	552			
Evarts															43	75			
Fairburn	62	41	50	47	80	61	120	95	91	130	38	50	70	266	70				
Fairfax	144	225	199	253	301	309	338	393	430	512	530	391	500	386	190				
Fairview	73	90	72	101	155	150	150	177	156	163	174	151	107	97	207				
Faith	548	576	576	591	599	368	522	574	607	506	575	232	325						
Farmer	23	27	58	95	114	101	113	150	132	145	110	550	300	100	76				
Faulkton	809	981	955	1051	827	640	747	713	739	815	709	458	802	655	539	462			
Fedora	75	100	75	145	125		212		165		148	250	475	100					
Ferney	55	80	72	84	100		110		181		163	220	350	140	65	48			
Firesteel	20	35	17	75	110	270	125		148		80	40							
Flandreau	2311	2114	2027	2129	2193	1850	2212	2474	1934	1850	1929	1688	1484	1455	1244	569	471		
Florence	192	190	175	216	226	272	254	286	298	306	290	216	270	75	127	76			
Forest City	150	150	150	200	144				143		127	100	127	56	63	87			
Forestburgh							165												
Fort Bennett									244		219	130	300		60	245	100		
Fort Meade			900	900	860	633	850	777	850			737		618	576	900			
Fort Pierre	1854	1789	1448	2649	951		764		683	759	805	673	792	505	395	360	287		
Fort Randall															130	265	265	207	341
Fort Sisseton													49			134	134		
Fort Sully																134	460	745	

POPULATION HISTORY OF SOUTH DAKOTA CITIES AND TOWNS 1860-1990

COMMUNITY	1990	1980	1970	1960	1950	1945	1940	1935	1930	1925	1920	1915	1910	1905	1900	1890	1880	1870	1860
Fort Thompson	1088	300	750	500	225		106		180		65								
Frankfort	192	209	192	240	331	268	335	346	367	443	438	428	408	313	198	186	125	100	
Frederick	241	307	359	381	408	384	422	458	461	372	424	402	433	304	251	281	125		
Freeman	1293	1462	1357	1140	944	870	976	942	987	917	894	725	615	601	525	408	68		
Friesland																	250		
Fruitdale	43	88	74	79	70	81	89	114	113	80	40	100	550	150	93				
Fulton	70	108	101	135	139		168	141	171	209	214	234	109	129	240	118			
Galena												59					167		
Gannvalley	130	100	80	104	101		180		238		213	250	200	66	100				
Garden City	93	104	126	226	282	251	272	308	257	258	294	254	304	257	98				
Garretson	924	963	847	850	745	575	666	677	655	678	715	819	668	640	500	341			
Gary	274	354	366	471	558	519	566	546	543	533	588	591	477	502	345	277	312		
Gayville	401	407	269	261	271	253	278	269	261	309	305	320	257	291	296	124	130		
Geddes	280	303	308	380	502	607	581	609	680	1002	695	664	701	616	203				
Gettysburg	1510	1623	1915	1950	1555	1264	1324	1414	1400	1047	951	751	936	650	429	377	153		
Glenham	134	169	178	171	168	131	131	164	187	169	135	139	182	82	119	220	113		
Goodwin	126	139	114	113	141	160	152	168	149	148	157	126	145	132		76	111		
Grandview																			
Greenmount														262	139				
Greenwood	100	125	90	200	210		200		344		310	300	100	150	69	100	60		
Gregory	1384	1503	1756	1478	1375	1100	1246	1185	1034	1251	1067	919	1142	400					
Grenville	81	119	154	151	207	190	260	282	247	256	264	100	150						
Groton	1196	1230	1021	1063	1084	953	946	1036	1009	1113	1273	1028	1108	1064	700	684	242		
Hamill													200				125		
Harrisburg	727	558	338	313	274	244	241	217	205	205	193	185	164	145	106	100			
Harrison	60	80	68	95	88		109		131		115	120	291	300	291	322			
Harrold	167	196	184	255	263	202	229	260	309	342	252	173	230	100	57	300	100		
Hartford	1262	1207	800	688	592	509	647	643	628	645	677	703	648	586	423	298	89		
Hawley															12	20	176		
Hayti	372	371	393	425	413	334	370	332	344	327	293	256	650						
Hayward																172			
Hazel	103	94	101	128	161	136	182	177	191	221	247	249	229	210	66	48			
Hecla	398	435	407	444	500	483	555	568	558	533	553	474	462	271	112	84	147		
Henry	215	217	182	276	323	263	322	344	358	425	418	435	441	358	160	457			
Hermosa	242	251	150	126	123	104	121	108	128	93	74	77	114	150	191	194	75		
Herreid	488	570	672	767	633	506	592	594	544	475	460	391	414	224					
Herrick	139	115	126	160	169	152	246	287	339	419	422	445	412	206					
Hetland	53	66	81	107	123	150	199	207	250	233	248	245	223	241	162				
Highmore	835	1055	1173	1078	1158	1004	1136	1002	1034	1224	1022	700	1084	507	376	435	219		
Hill City	650	535	389	419	361	327	400		335		308	271	271	500	507	479	111		

POPULATION HISTORY OF SOUTH DAKOTA CITIES AND TOWNS 1860-1990

COMMUNITY	1990	1980	1970	1960	1950	1945	1940	1935	1930	1925	1920	1915	1910	1905	1900	1890	1880	1870	1860
Milltown		25	28	24	39				34		31	50							
Mina												85	225	150	100	98	150		
Minnesela/Florence																50	200		
Minnesota														50	70	178			
Miranda												100	175						
Mission	730	748	739	611	388	236	452	275	113		114	50							
Mission Hill	180	197	161	165	169	162	195	183	184	189	167	166	300	100	76				
Mitchell	13798	13916	13425	12555	12123	9894	10633	12834	10942	10119	8478	7785	6515	5719	4055	2217			
Mobridge	3768	4174	4545	4391	3753	3127	3008	3425	3464	2822	3517	1551	1200						
Monroe	151	170	134	156	160	150	219	242	221	235	217	170	169	208	170				
Montrose	420	396	377	430	448	423	506	564	471	471	519	552	442	471	375	653	100		
Morristown	64	127	144	219	190		217	235	268	208	269	127	222						
Mound City	89	111	164	144	177	183	195	204	165		58	288	200	99	287	225			
Mount Vernon	368	402	398	379	387	322	405	460	489	601	661	541	614	412	222	127	222		
Murdo	679	723	865	783	739	477	680	625	619	748	500	352	372						
Naples	35	45	38	36	62	75	84	99	89	105	146	130	275	75	107	126			
Nemo	50	40	100	100	100		200		223		223	200	261	261					
New Effington	219	261	258	280	367	251	344	335	337	328	305	348	46						
New Underwood	553	517	416	462	268	181	215	275	311	186	164	119	134						
Newark			25	39	80	64	147	148	168	183	190	192	450	150	226	245			
Newell	675	638	664	797	784	642	683	580	547	387	414	212	150						
Nisland	174	216	157	221	216	183	212	234	187	156	173	128	225						
Norden													525						
Nordland																400	300		
North Eagle Butte	1423	1354	1351																
North Sioux City	2019	1992	860	736															
Northville	105	138	119	153	220	247	223	257	260	275	372	282	392	304	243	624			
Nowlin												100	150						
Nunda	45	60	85	106	102	121	147	171	163	176	206	250	137						
Oacoma	367	289	215	312	231	130	197	175	167	201	224	163	235	300	147	300			
Oakwood																	300		
Oelrichs	138	124	94	132	168	144	212	209	206	194	176	100	150	253	100	308			
Oglala	616	150	250	300					150						140	140			
Oldham	189	222	244	291	349	323	386	431	419	404	364	362	355	393	222	327			
Olivet	74	96	103	135	202	179	242	222	184	197	200	163	133	161	156	265	185	150	
Onaka	52	70	96	85	158	132	139	131	164	157	142	120	275						
Onida	761	851	785	843	822	523	597	605	636	632	455	251	319	200	150	197			
Ordway									51		46	40	125		214	156	100		
Orient	59	87	131	133	206	206	250	301	302	267	189	180	400	300			100		
Ortley	63	80	111	127	144	150	184	168	157	171	187	162	192	300	97				

POPULATION HISTORY OF SOUTH DAKOTA CITIES AND TOWNS 1860-1990

COMMUNITY	1990	1980	1970	1960	1950	1945	1940	1935	1930	1925	1920	1915	1910	1905	1900	1890	1880	1870	1860
Owanka																			
Pactola																			
Palisade												100	175	165		372			
Parker	984	999	1005	1142	1148	1153	1244	1225	1229	1309	1288	1324	1224	1227	893	728	113		
Parkston	1572	1545	1611	1514	1354	1301	1305	1272	1336	1305	1230	1132	970	862	596	262			
Parmalee	450	400	475	302	116		105		245										
Peever	195	232	202	208	221	169	272	262	265	262	386	301	259	137					
Pennington																			
Philip	1077	1088	983	1114	810	745	833	887	786	708	647	404	578						
Pickstown	95	114	300	500	2217														
Piedmont	325	300	650	200	200		200		113		113	100	125	150					
Pierpont	173	184	241	258	326	324	362	378	379	432	400	320	314	308	193	50			
Pierre	12906	11973	9699	10088	5715	4218	4322	4013	3659	3560	3209	3010	3656	2794	2306	3230	1527		
Pine Ridge	2596	3059	2768	1265	1000		471		674		618	100	128	200	207	140	140		
Plankinton	604	644	613	644	754	528	694	715	758	803	803	916	712	606	465	654	569		
Platte	1311	1334	1351	1167	1069	879	1017	1139	1207	1393	1242	939	1115	700	300				
Pleasant Valley																	162		
Pluma	100	100	100								30		105	105					
Pollock	375	255	2	417	395	358	527	520	481	501	437	238	304	195					
Porcupine	783	150	200																
Prairie Farm																	300		
Presho	654	760	922	881	712	430	568	517	487	537	626	355	635	300					
Pringle	96	105	86	145	193	145	273	250	48		42	50	100						
Prospect																	260		
Pukwana	263	234	208	247	302	275	258	283	307	381	192	182	164	126	357	336	100		
Quinn	72	80	105	162	214		189	144	141	137	450	250	650						
Ramona	194	241	227	247	278	224	265	214	279	313	356	324	312	299	172	148			
Rapid City	54523	46492	43836	42399	25310	17262	13844	11346	10404	7465	5777	4268	3854	1797	1342	2128	292		
Rapid Valley	5968	3265																	
Ravinia	79	88	109	164	200	101	155	153	157	161	199	96	81						
Raymond	96	106	114	168	174	178	206	229	200	268	330	241	241	125	88	250	300		
Redfield	2770	3027	2943	2952	2655	2248	2428	2573	2664	2751	2755	3122	2856	1591	1015	796	321		
Ree Heights	91	88	183	188	254	205	258	307	339	312	167	250	250	75	68	100	300		
Reliance	169	190	204	201	215	183	219	247	287	291	317	350	192	50	28				
Revillo	152	158	142	202	249	291	325		274	365	338	293	332	254	187	387			
Richland	50	50	70	30	30		100		79		99		99		136	123	100		
Riverside												50	200						
Rochford			50									75	150	300	88	100	315	150	
Rockerville													28	100	28	87	321		
Rockford		50	50	102	50		139		100		89				39	48			

POPULATION HISTORY OF SOUTH DAKOTA CITIES AND TOWNS 1860-1990

COMMUNITY	1860	1870	1880	1890	1900	1905	1910	1915	1920	1925	1930	1935	1940	1945	1950	1960	1970	1980	1990
Rockham				32	41	150	286	283	347	371	288	258	220	110	113	197	60	52	48
Rockport		100	140	150															
Roscoe			159	114	92	134	357	320	459	427	497	540	608	596	726	532	398	370	362
Rosebud			300	82	200	150	108	110	120		136		200		600	537	650	600	1538
Rosholt								154	301	314	327	369	362	335	387	423	456	446	408
Roslyn				220	72	94	167	150	211	255	237	253	253	182	222	256	250	261	251
Roswell						457	50	50	180	148	116	143	96	60	69	39	32	19	19
Roubaix									479		84		110						
Rowena				126	100	75	92	100			126				70	68	76	100	60
Running Water			152	150	196	100	94				238				23				
Rutland							400	225	164		250		125		100	100	100	60	75
St. Charles							200	100											
St. Francis			100	320	115	149	305	253	260		300		273	273	241	421	300	766	815
St. Lawrence									390	343	413	356	297	224	261	290	249	223	223
St. Onge						50	225	250	156		174		211	214	104	108	200	100	120
Salem			350	429	741	810	1097	1132	1187	1104	1115	1171	1185	1219	1119	1188	1391	1486	1289
Scenic							200	100	121		150	349	300		75	125	56	50	75
Scotland		75	150	1083	964	1120	1102	1249	1234	1186	1163	1203	1204	1054	1188	1077	984	1022	968
Selby						349	558	646	564	568	548	613	599	568	706	979	957	884	707
Seneca				193	125	100	321	182	264	259	318	295	243	198	204	161	118	103	81
Sheridan			142	50	107		27												
Sherman			75	42	106	130	138	211	206	193	192	205	158	113	120	116	82	100	66
Silver City				200															
Sinai							275	145	216	230	217	203	182	177	181	166	147	129	120
Sioux Falls		1000	2164	10177	10266	12283	14094	20929	25202	30127	33362	33644	40832	42343	52696	65466	72488	81343	100814
Sisseton			1500	500	928	1375	1397	1386	1431	1468	1569	1840	2513	2056	2871	3218	3094	2789	2181
Smithwick							160	35											
South Bend			209																
South Shore				175	210	270	335	331	305	299	322	305	296	255	269	259	199	241	260
South Sioux Falls					114	103	132	171	195	256	306	442	591	669	1586				
Spearfish			170	678	1166	1158	1130	921	1254	1349	1577	1738	2139	2354	2755	3682	4661	5251	6966
Spencer				325	332	393	506	572	637	599	561	608	617	485	552	460	385	380	317
Spring Creek																		60	112
Springfield		150	235	302	525	717	675	695	719	689	881	661	667	545	801	1194	1566	1377	834
Stamford							200	50											
Stickney						75	310	312	386	426	412	348	361	305	388	456	421	409	323
Stockholm						175	275	200	219	116	130	121	114	119	114	155	116	95	89
Strandburg						120	325	117	169	124	113	154	177	124	144	105	98	79	74
Stratford							625	400	297	261	202	203	205	173	164	109	106	82	85
Strool							325	200											

POPULATION HISTORY OF SOUTH DAKOTA CITIES AND TOWNS 1860-1990

COMMUNITY	1860	1870	1880	1890	1900	1905	1910	1915	1920	1925	1930	1935	1940	1945	1950	1960	1970	1980	1990
Sturgis			400	668	1100	1329	1739	1029	1250	1448	1747	2591	3008	2517	3471	4639	4536	5184	5330
Summit				200	237	373	545	536	556	490	431	503	459	471	431	283	332	290	267
Swan Lake		100	200	100															
Tabor					129	301	273	441	428	422	397	391	391	355	373	378	388	460	403
Tea			117	118	118	175	134	177	165	168	148	180	165	132	151	188	302	729	786
Terraville			775	696	517	633	483	491	664		190		186					100	
Terry				900	988	483	225	600	507	174	562						200		
Thomas								60							70				
Tigerville			150																
Timber Lake							425	238	555	537	572	560	512	352	552	624	625	660	517
Tinton						108													
Tolstoy							142	148	183	244	210	204	171	111	180	142	99	97	69
Toronto			50	148	447	411	424	438	380	392	341	341	362	330	322	268	216	236	201
Trail City								100	46		300		275		200	150	75	70	75
Trent				42	80	200	375	274	295	263	256	235	240	198	213	232	177	197	211
Tripp				226	366	496	675	903	970	927	939	901	913	697	913	837	851	804	664
Trojan							262		164		100		242		200		25		
Troy			110	62	40	100		110	148		60				44	44	13		
Tulare				218	137	100	250	250	324	359	305	257	244	179	212	225	211	238	244
Turton				67	100	180	240	263	243	265	323	249	180	170	201	140	121	101	76
Twin Brooks			100	257	166	175	190	177	141	157	138	135	121	106	113	86	122	87	54
Tyndall			200	509	1167	1171	1107	1302	1405	1370	1287	1303	1289	1177	1292	1262	1245	1253	1201
Utica			75	70	100	73	103	133	141	160	98	106	95	76	84	70	89	100	115
Vale							250	100											
Valley Springs		100	200	308	388	362	331	372	374	403	393	411	396	399	389	472	566	801	739
Vayland							200	60	72		550		497		24	75			
Veblen					99	146	173	340	530	524	520	505	486	436	476	437	377	368	321
Vega					180	50	50												
Verdon			200	94	118	121	136	89	90	81	69	59	65	32	34	28	18		
Vermillion	225	1000	714	1496	2183	2147	2187	2376	2590	3410	2850	2906	3324	3608	5337	6102	9128	10136	10034
Vermont City				175															
Viborg				250	222	329	410	484	618	709	719	721	659	615	644	699	662	812	763
Vienna				100	171	371	453	458	477	425	443	373	313	260	306	191	119	90	93
Vilas				220	118	156	157	141	144	131	106	108	91	65	71	49	33	28	28
Villa Ranchaero																	3171	1666	1666
Virgil				48	50	100	350	220	189	182	166	131	145	146	124	81	43	37	33
Vivian							425	150											
Volga			278	298	396	552	568	616	600	601	604	557	632	545	578	780	982	1221	1263
Votin				68	207	245	286	333	314	304	283	269	292	200	197	171	157	156	175
Wagner					96	513	964	906	1236	1444	1420	1350	1319	1122	1528	1586	1655	1453	1462

POPULATION HISTORY OF SOUTH DAKOTA CITIES AND TOWNS 1860-1990

COMMUNITY	1990	1980	1970	1960	1950	1945	1940	1935	1930	1925	1920	1915	1910	1905	1900	1890	1880	1870	1860
Wakonda	329	383	290	382	454	444	451	461	453	441	451	403	326	246	220	350			
Wakpala	235	250	500	424	350		200		200		69	50	225						
Wall	834	770	786	629	556	376	500	325	326	209	224	128	167						
Wallace	83	90	95	132	188	125	193	161	189	209	235	218	207						
Walworth																25	200		
Wanblee	654	350	500	300	325		300		300										
Ward	35	43	57	74	96	80	84	98	90	93	118	102	72	74	51				
Warner	336	322	57	150	115		141		154		136	250	275	200	476	375			
Wasta	82	99	127	196	144	95	153	131	175		145	250	375						
Waterbury															25	150	103		
Watertown	17592	15649	13388	14077	12699	10984	10617	10246	10214	10319	9400	8313	7010	5164	3352	2672	746		
Waubay	657	675	696	851	879	777	882	976	903	1007	979	879	803	540	430	75			
Webster	2017	2417	2252	2409	2503	2076	2173	2033	1805	1687	1800	1640	1713	1918	1506	618	200		
Wecota												125	225						
Wentworth	181	193	193	211	270	279	303	300	310	309	360	350	329	296	181	500			
Wessington	265	327	380	378	467	324	516	564	681	717	728	526	576	350	220	150	149		
Wessington Springs	1083	1203	1300	1488	1453	1222	1352	1408	1401	1414	1618	1142	1093	722	320	200			
Westport	112	122	136	150	116		284		180		215	100	325						
Wetonka	12	22	31	46	115	113	109	92	111	134	164	300	325	175	206	200	75		
Wewela												100	200						
Wheeler															107	75			
White	536	474	418	417	525	471	559	522	533	521	594	581	468	479	454	137	125		
White Butte												60	175						
White Lake	419	414	395	397	395	368	496	506	530	570	610	504		250			246		
White River	595	561	617	583	465	284	562	431	471	320	417	400	507	366	264				
White Rock	7	10	35	76	113	114	220	253	281	319	353	384	368	337	170				
Whitewood	891	821	689	470	304	210	267	421	392	300	339	295	390	352	311	443			
Willow Lake	317	375	353	467	484	404	427	472	514	514	477	398	437	298	210	240			
Wilmot	566	507	518	545	590	538	628	604	566	567	617	520	427	391	352	350	257		
Winfred	54	81	110	137	171	126	245	251	290	310	328	301	243	228	147	225			
Winner	3354	3472	3789	3705	3252	2306	2426	2136	2220	2203	2000	923	675						
Witten/New Witten	87	134	102	146	198	117	211	210	307	221	204	400	550						
Wolsey	442	437	436	354	391	295	410	445	455	454	510	439	436	182	122	100	300		
Wood	73	134	132	267	260	192	414	285	257		210	200							
Woonsocket	766	799	852	1035	1051	1039	1050	1128	1108	1203	1368	1201	1027	929	648	687	385		
Worthing	371	388	294	304	272	228	291	276	262	274	238	191	179	220	213	75	48		
Wounded Knee	270	250	500	500	150			63								48			
Yale	128	136	148	171	164	129	156	163	190	184	319	250	425						
Yankton	12703	12011	11919	9279	7709	6843	6798	6579	6072	5507	5024	4771	3787	4189	4125	3670	3431	737	358
Yorkville																	161		

POPULATION HISTORY OF SOUTH DAKOTA CITIES AND TOWNS 1860-1990

COMMUNITY	1990	1980	1970	1960	1950	1945	1940	1935	1930	1925	1920	1915	1910	1905	1900	1890	1880	1870	1860
Zell												200	200	150	90	125			

1905: South Dakota Superintendent of the Census. Second Census of the South Dakota, Taken in the Year 1905. Aberdeen: News Printing, 1905.
1905: Minnesota, North and South Dakota and Montana Gazetteer and Business Directory. Chicago: R.L. Polk, 1906.
1915: Minnesota, North and South Dakota and Montana Gazetteer and Business Directory. Chicago: R.L. Polk, 1915.
1915: South Dakota Department of History. Third Census of the State of South Dakota Taken in the Year 1915. Sioux Falls: Press of M.D. Scott, 1915.
1925: South Dakota Department of History. Fourth Census of the State of South Dakota Taken in the Year 1925. Sioux Falls: Press of M.D. Scott, 1926.
1935: South Dakota Department of History. Fifth Census of the State of South Dakota Taken in the Year 1935. Pierre:1936.
1945: South Dakota Department of History. Sixth Census of the State of South Dakota Taken in the Year 1945. Pierre:1947.

POPULATON HISTORY OF TEXAS CITIES AND TOWNS 1840-1990

COMMUNITY	1990	1980	1970	1960	1950	1940	1930	1920	1910	1900	1890	1880	1870	1860	1850	1840
Abbott	314	359	375	289	345	264	326	303	475	322	106					
Abernathy	2720	2904	2625	2491	1692	847	858	310	160							
Abilene	106654	98315	89653	90368	45570	26612	23175	10274	9204	3411	3194	1000				
Abram	700	900	500	400	319	319	319	319	60							
Ace	400	400			150	400	400			75						
Ackerly	243	317	348	450	550	220	250									
Acme				200	200	250	250		75							
Acre Homes		19500	5000													
Acton	200	130	130	100	100	158	157	157	112	168						
Addicks	70	150	150		500	500	500	47								
Addison	8783	5553	593	308	258	110	110	75	65							
Adkins	200	380	150				218	218	183	183						
Adrian	220	222	228	258	205	119	119	119	225							
Atton	100	100		98		150	62	62	45							
Agnes									78	78		300				
Agua Dulce	794	934	742	867	660	224	112	100	40							
Alameda												280				
Alamo	8210	5831	4291	4121	3017	1944	1018	500				200				
Alamo Heights	6502	6252	6933	7552	8000	5700	3874									
Alanreed	75	60		250	200	220	263	263	250							
Alba	489	568	555	472	547	675	662	1352	625	376		129				
Albany	1962	2450	1978	2174	2241	2230	2422	1469	999	983	857	500	150			
Albuquerque																
Aldine	11133	12623			101	110	155		72	72						
Aldridge								809								
Aledo	1169	1027	620	648	260	302	517	400	300	286		300				
Alexander					96	125	519	381	381	381	381					
Alfred							319	319	60							
Algoa	600	500	400	500	250		75	75	80							
Alice	19788	20961	20121	20861	16449	7792	4239	1880	2136	887						
Alief		1400	100	300	330	200	161	161	112	112	115	96				
Allen	18309	8314	1940	659	500	550	500	360	260	193	351	189	150			
Alleyton	300	400	375	400	200	220	264	264	251	300						
Allison	250	135	120	200	150	330	150									
Alma	205	171	101	125	250	275	263	263	158	158						
Almeda				1800	1000	300	300	275	63	63						
Alpine	5637	5465	5971	4740	5261	3866	3495	931	800	768	396					
Alta Loma		1530	1536	1020	500	440	350	550	150	98						
Altair							219		150	116						
Alto	1027	1203	1045	869	1021	1141	1053	1081	672	426	210	88	61			

POPULATON HISTORY OF TEXAS CITIES AND TOWNS 1840-1990

COMMUNITY	1840	1850	1860	1870	1880	1890	1900	1910	1920	1930	1940	1950	1960	1970	1980	1990
Altoga							76	120	169	169	168	80	130	100	269	250
Alton					181	108								961	2732	3069
Alum Creek				250	326											
Alum Spring																
Alvarado					377	1543	1342	1155	1284	1210	1324	1656	1907	2129	2701	2918
Alvin						261	986	1453	1519	1511	3087	3701	5643	10671	16515	19220
Alvord					100	560	1172	1023	1376	754	821	735	694	791	874	865
Amarillo						482	1442	9957	15494	43132	51686	74246	137969	127010	149230	157615
Amelia									119		350	609				
Ames									64	64	100	100	500	920	1155	989
Amherst					42	111	181	181	217	964	749	922	833	825	971	742
Ammamsville							40	300	500	217	330	217	217		42	
Anahuac	300	100	677	495	412	572	647	572	600	513	550	1284	1985	1881	1840	1993
Anderson							42	42	200	723	540	600	500	500	320	600
Andrews										401	611	3294	11135	8625	11061	10678
Angleton							584	896	1043	1229	1763	3399	7312	9906	13929	17140
Angleton South													800	1017	1350	1017
Angus									59	72		100		93	244	363
Angus Valley															855	904
Anna						163	273	402	538	467	509	525	639	736	855	904
Annaville													900		454	672
Anneta															281	265
Anneta North															115	413
Anneta South															471	329
Annona					150	267	357	429	775	426	446	392	369	373		
Anson						495	759	1842	1425	2093	2338	2708	2890	2615	2831	2644
Antelope							166	166								
Anthony							78	78		112	548	800	1082	2154	2640	3328
Anton												934	1068	1034	1180	1212
Apache Shores															360	500
Apple Springs							63	63	312	270	200	250	200	150	120	250
Appleby					42	115	166	208	500	495	550	495	200	280	453	449
Aquilla					100		142	450	500	668	557	450	400	150	130	136
Aransas Pass		50				1069	790	1197	1569	2482	4095	5396	6956	5813	7173	7180
Arcadia							268	200	319	158	330	600	950	800	215	500
Archer City					60	135	316	825	689	1512	1675	1901	1974	1722	1862	1748
Arcola					50		76	76	76	76		268	240	300	661	666
Argyle					200	148	173	197	268	268	261	268	170	443	1111	1575
Arinosa																
Arlington					163	664	1079	1794	3031	3661	4240	7692	44775	90229	160113	261721

POPULATION HISTORY OF TEXAS CITIES AND TOWNS 1840-1990

COMMUNITY	1990	1980	1970	1960	1950	1940	1930	1920	1910	1900	1890	1880	1870	1860	1850	1840
Armstrong																
Arneckville						240	240	814	62	171	56	150				
Arp	812	939	816	812	909	1139	1000	369	300	59	62	75				
Arroyo City	500															
Artesian Forest	800	800														
Arthur City	500	500	400	400	400	220	212	163	163	217						
Arvana					750											
Asherton	1608	1574	1645	1890	2425	1538	1858	1000	500							
Ashland									180			600				
Ashwood							163									
Aspermont	1214	1357	1198	1286	1062	1041	769	436	600	250	205					
Atascosa	500	300		100	100	100	100	122	115	115	116					
Athens	10967	10197	9582	7086	5194	4765	4342	3176	2261	2088	1035	368	545	240	177	
Atlanta	6118	6272	5007	4076	3782	2453	1665	1469	1604	1301	1764	396				
Aubrey	1138	948	731	534	491	472	439	800	575	340						
Augusta	623				635	275	121	121	120	187	121	119	150			
Aurora		376								336	372	100				
Austin	465622	345496	253539	186545	132459	87930	53120	34876	29860	22258	14575	11013	4428	3494	2000	400
Austiino							312									
Austwell	189	280	284	287	228	301	233	213								
Avalon	350	130	250	300	310	330	385	310	226	226						
Avery	430	520	491	343	442	477	1540	1540	100							
Avinger	478	671	642	730	546	624	519	505	600	296	123	63				
Avoca							262		200	49						
Avondale	300	250														
Axtell	300	300	200	200	300	242	290	220	220	221						
Azle	8868	5822	4493	2969	770	231	146	146	250	189						
Bacliff	5549	4851	2000	1707												
Bagdad													150			
Bagwell	250	300	300	300	420	275	420	420	320	235	161	314				
Bailey	187	185	197	176	198	223	313	313	360	207	237	250				
Baileys Prairie	634	353	228													
Baileyville									175	175						
Baird	1658	1696	1538	1633	1821	1810	1965	1902	1710	1502	850	400				
Balch Springs	17406	13476	10464	6821												
Balcones Heights	3022	2556	2504	950	376											
Balcones Village	950	950														
Bald Prairie	950															
Ballinger	3975	4207	4203	5043	5302	4472	4187	2767	3536	1128	213	500				
Balmorhea	765	568	655	604	448	500	283	263	200	138	1390					

POPULATON HISTORY OF TEXAS CITIES AND TOWNS 1840-1990

COMMUNITY	1840	1850	1860	1870	1880	1890	1900	1910	1920	1930	1940	1950	1960	1970	1980	1990
Bammel												102		350	450	500
Bandera				150	254	372	419	419	700	470	1100	1036	950	891	947	877
Bangs							136	512	709	717	756	935	967	1214	1716	1555
Bankersmith									2041	232						
Bannister										50						
Barquette									319	211	500	750	450	600	600	700
Bardwell							71	400	358	303	266	229	220	277	335	387
Barksdale							384	300	200	219	221	125	400	175	175	200
Barnhart									65	250	250	600	357	200	200	190
Barrett													2364	2750	3183	3052
Barrington Oaks															900	
Barry							373	350	350	319	385	450	178	149	192	175
Barstow					150	206	322	500	490	468	558	683	707	614	637	535
Bartlett							957	1815	1731	1873	1668	1727	1540	1622	1567	1439
Bartonville							48	84	317	333	333		100	119	441	849
Bassetts	400						63	63		200						
Bastrop			1107	1199	1546	1634	2145	1707	1828	1895	1976	3176	3001	3112	3789	4044
Batesville							136	150	200	625	224	500	850	700	800	1313
Batson								400	700	817	1100	850	722	650	650	600
Bay City							437	3156	3454	4070	6594	9427	11656	13445	17837	18170
Bay Oaks													200	150	250	200
Bayou Vista															1030	1320
Bayside									75	308	300	300	350	350	381	400
Bayside Terrace													250	360	500	200
Baytown									1006	5194	5720	22983	28159	43980	56923	63850
Bayview					100	93	218	117	131		100	350	200	312	291	231
Bazette											275	300		100	60	60
Beach City					450	56	56	56					250	363	977	852
Bear Creek							70	70								
Beasley									217	217	217	217	240	343	410	485
Beaumont			151	300	1650	3296	9427	20640	40422	57732	59061	94014	119175	117548	118102	114323
Beaumont Place													1176	1600	3800	8600
Beauxart Gardens											400	300	600	1000	900	850
Beckville				100	125	307	606	606	606	435	453	550	632	582	945	783
Bedford							96	84	84	100	84	100	2706	10049	20821	43762
Bedias				100	100	116	63	400	500	536	560	509	575	300	350	500
Bee Cave				70	300				44	44					200	241
Beeville				75		1311	2705	3269	3063	4806	6789	9348	13811	13506	14574	13547
Belcherville					208	516	305	305	192	85	94	31				
Belden					350											

POPULATON HISTORY OF TEXAS CITIES AND TOWNS 1840-1990

COMMUNITY	1990	1980	1970	1960	1950	1940	1930	1920	1910	1900	1890	1880	1870	1860	1850	1840
Bon Weir	550	500	350	350	450	330	400	113	100							
Bonanza	600	950	150		250		59	59	59	59						
Bonham	6666	7338	7698	7357	7049	6349	5655	6008	4844	5042	3361	1880	928	477	211	
Bonita					150	239	218	400	375	375						
Bonney	339	94	112		82	75	82		50							
Bonus					100	100	200	610	100	65						
Booker	1236	1219	904	817	619	386	495	823								
Boonsville	80	50			50	204	217	217	186	168						
Booth	135	120	120		500	110	319	319	50							
Borderland	600	600	200													
Boren										239						
Borger	15675	15837	14195	20911	18059	10018	6532									
Bosqueville	700	700	700	100	300	148	224	94	94	94	77	250				
Boston			500					135	140	76		257	273			
Bovina	1549	1499	1428	1029	612	450	350	175	200	36						
Bowie	4990	5610	5185	4566	4544	3470	3131	3179	2874	2600	1486	1000				
Boyce							275		160	99						
Boyd	1041	889	695	581	550	496	342	410	500	273						
Brackettville	1740	1676	1539	1662	1858	2653	1822	1630	1500	1594	1649	1126	232			
Bradshaw				77	105	311	311	157	120							
Brady	5946	5969	5557	5338	5944	5002	3983	2197	2669	682	560	115				
Branch	350	300	310													
Branchville																
Brandon	100	140	100		100	114	200	418	300	86	86	40				
Brantley				121	180	236	260	307	401	457	58					
Brashear	300	300	300	250	350	330	500	319								
Brazoria	2717	3025	1681	1291	776	880	816	816	633	633	432	676	725			500
Brazos						200	317	113	175	175						
Breckenridge	5665	6921	5944	6273	6610	5826	7569	1846	750	734	462	497				
Bremond	1110	1025	822	803	1141	1106	1025	1250	808	808	387	758	400			
Brenham	11952	10966	8922	7740	6941	6435	5974	5066	4718	5968	5209	4101	2221	920	500	
Brewer										216	303					
Briar		1810	630							303						
Briarcliff	335	129														
Briaroaks	535	592	277													
Bridge City	8034	7667	8164	4677												
Bridgeport	3581	3737	3614	3218	2049	1735	2464	1872	2000	900	498	39				
Briggs	95	230	100	125	250	330	520	520	220	134						
Bristol	260	240	240	150	100	336	361	361	308	321	303	98				
Britton	100	100	150	200	250	340	370	260	260	202						

POPULATON HISTORY OF TEXAS CITIES AND TOWNS 1840-1990

COMMUNITY	1990	1980	1970	1960	1950	1940	1930	1920	1910	1900	1890	1880	1870	1860	1850	1840
Broadus	212	225	174	200	630	440	300	510	120							
Bronson	259	254	500	500	500	400	600	1025	550							
Bronte	962	983	925	999	1020	754	671	529	635	213						
Brookland	400	400	250	500	500	553	813	813	500	144	144	150				
Brookshire	2922	2175	1683	1339	1015	565	600	1050	700	242						
Brookside	1470	1453	1507	560												
Brooksmith									150							
Brookston	250	250	250	250	400	334	375	375	360	419	237	100				
Browndell	192	228	243		150	660	519	519	300							
Brownfield	9560	10387	9647	10286	6161	4009	1907	821	275							
Brownings	545	582	474	507	518	640	416	168	160		67	300				
Brownsboro											133	48				
Brownsville	98962	84997	52522	48040	36066	22083	22021	11791	10517	6305	6134	4938	4905	2734	2000	
Brownwood	18387	19396	17368	16974	20181	13398	12789	8223	6967	3965	2176	725	75			
Bruceville	1075	1038	250	250	300	552	460	612	500	521	236					
Bruni	375	400	400	400	800	350	200	119	48	48						
Brunner										482						
Brushy Creek	1200								131	131						
Bryan	55002	44337	33719	27542	18102	11842	7814	6207	4132	3589	2979	2710	1000			
Bryans Mill	125	100	100	100	125	113	94	84	180	212	109					
Bryson	520	579	455	545	588	806	641	263	350	162						
Buchanan					400	300				274	274					
Buchanan Dam	1099	2500	400		400											
Buchanan Lake	500	500														
Buckeye							219									
Buckholts	335	388		700	700	880	515	800	500	182	64	50				
Buckingham	102	159	218	239												
Buda	1795	597	498	45?	483	336	400	300	450	268	268					
Buena Vista												150				
Buffalo	1555	1507	1242	1108	970	737	470	510	310	310	310	190	100			
Buffalo Gap	499	387	320	316	350	250	250	249	249	249						
Bullard	890	681	573	364	317	233	413	212	300	218	568	300				
Bulverde	800	700							129	129						
Buna	2127	1900	1649	950	395	440	414	519	300							
Bunavista		1500	1402	2067											60	
Bunker Hill	3391	3750	3977	2216	75											
Burkburnett	10145	10668	9230	762	4555	2814	3281	5300	625							
Burke	314	322	188	400	350	210	210	300	161	116						
Burkett	120	160	160	150	325	217	325	167	198	107						
Burkeville	500	600	450	600	750	890	350	300	410	321	314	109	175		50	

POPULATON HISTORY OF TEXAS CITIES AND TOWNS 1840-1990

COMMUNITY	1990	1980	1970	1960	1950	1940	1930	1920	1910	1900	1890	1880	1870	1860	1850	1840
Burleson	16113	11734	7713	2345	791	573	591	241	368	273	249	50				
Burlington			200	150		250	250	413	600			312				
Burnet	3423	3410	2864	2214	2394	1945	1055	966	981	1003	1484	490	280			
Burrow	100	100	100			75				532						
Burton	311	325	347	500	478	558	425	500	425	384	384	125				
Butler	150	80	250	200	300	300	300	115	115	119	115	300	150			
Byers	510	556	553	497	542	427	487	850	475							
Bynum	192	232	170	270	300	350	250	158	300	163						
Cactus	1529	898	644	900	200		159	169	113	113						
Caddo	200	120	120	60	319	385	319	319	149	149	85	100				
Caddo Grove										142		500	150			
Caddo Mills	1068	1060	935	732	509	390	450	600	550	343	234	50				
Calallen				400			319	319	60							
Calaveras						115	110	369	396	396	369					
Caldwell	3181	2953	2308	2204	2109	2165	1724	1689	1476	1535	1250	301	200			
Caldwell's Store																
Call	400	350	200	500	565	750	997	1018	300	358						
Callisburg	344	281	131	125	110	128	110	110	110	110	110					
Calvert	1536	1732	2072	2073	2548	2366	2103	2099	2579	3322	2632	2280	600			
Cambridge												285				
Camden	300	200	350	1131	1001	800	818	500	66	66						
Camelot	4000	4000														
Cameron	5580	5721	5546	5640	5052	5040	4565	4298	3263	3341	1608	441	200			
Camilla							219									
Camp Wood	595	728	660	879	785	778	265					500				
Campbell	683	549	350	356	428	428	416	583	508	708	508	100				
Campbellton	275	279	279	271	368	118	419	419	100							
Campo Alto	300	230	200													
Camps				500	500											
Canadian	2417	3491	2292	2239	2700	2151	2068	2187	1648	444	486					
Candelaria	75	90		250	200	300	300	519	300	200						
Caney City	170	312	117		150	164		218	200		185	214	150			
Canton	2949	2845	2283	1114	881	715	704	583	600	421	421	331	183			
Canutillo	4442	2000	1588	1377	1326	907	700	112								
Canyon	11365	10724	8333	5864	4364	2622	2821	1618	1400	386						
Canyon Lake	9975	6000														
Caps									180							
Carbon	255	281	264	309	444	459	463	741	479	307						
Carbondale					263	250	263	410	300							
Carey							200									

POPULATION HISTORY OF TEXAS CITIES AND TOWNS 1840-1990

COMMUNITY	1990	1980	1970	1960	1950	1940	1930	1920	1910	1900	1890	1880	1870	1860	1850	1840
Carlisle	100				125	519	519	519	300							
Carlsbad	500	500	400	350	250	300	200	113								
Carlton	200	300	300	300	400	300	400	161	350	294	161	50				
Carmine	192	239	350	400	500	556	500	500	400	246	114					
Carmona					200	250	175	212	42							
Caro				220	86	161	165	1275	1000	113	243	200				
Carrizo Springs	5745	6886	5374	5699	4316	2494	2171	954	500	491	289	400				
Carroll Prairie										39	231	120				
Carrollton	82169	40595	13855	4242	1610	921	689	573	525	137	110	100				
Carthage	6496	6447	5392	5262	4750	2178	1651	1366	1350	956	554	290	200			
Casa Piedra							200	80	60							
Cash			100	200	266	266	266									
Cason	500	500	500	500	500	558	515	515	300	329	205	125				
Cassin				100	350	75										
Castle Heights					319	319										
Castle Hills	4198	4773	5311	2622												
Castlewood	1000	700														
Castroville	2159	1821	1893	1508	985	746	865	600	679	679	679	731	515	458	366	
Cat Spring	130	100	100	150	350	375	320	350	406	406	607	800	50			
Catarina	120	170		160	380	403	592									
Cayuga	400	400	300	450	650	450										
Cedar Bayou				800	1000	300	300	415	79	79						
Cedar Creek	125				400	334	150	300	296	296	296	386				
Cedar Hill	19976	6849	2610	1348	732	476	400	318	242	242	242	50	137			
Cedar Lane	250	250														
Cader Mill									84	84	146		75			
Cedar Park	5161	3474			100	150	250									
Celeste	733	716	736	588	729	730	803	1022	821	671	250					
Celina	1737	1520	1272	1204	1051	994	948	1126	724	211						
Celotex					400											
Cement					249	249	609	878	503							
Center	4950	5827	4989	4510	4323	3010	2510	1838	1684	856	856	177	120			
Center City					100			109	119	119	215	500				
Center Mill											207	500				
Center Point	900	600	600	600	800	660	613	543	500	532	543	134				
Centerville	812	799	831	836	961	900	388	760	400	332	288	223	221			
Central	600	600	140	140	200											
Central Gardens	4026	1300	1700													
Central Heights	1500	1100	800													

POPULATON HISTORY OF TEXAS CITIES AND TOWNS 1840-1990

COMMUNITY	1840	1850	1860	1870	1880	1890	1900	1910	1920	1930	1940	1950	1960	1970	1980	1990
Chalk Mountain					250	196	81	150								
Champions																14692
Chanayville						609										
Chandler							266	341	341	630	687	666	715	765	1308	1630
Channelview											1000	7500	10000	9000	17471	25564
Channing							278	300	475	531	522	450	351	336	304	277
Chapel Hill		600	1720	602	675	813	749	813	675	600	600	500	500	400	450	500
Charco							113	200	250	163	150	163	190	150	90	60
Charleston					150	58	221	183	218	218	250	300	190	160	150	200
Charlotte									610	610	1000	1272	1465	1329	1443	1475
Chase					300		64							1221	590	641
Chateau Woods														75	60	100
Chatfield				50	84	100	114	200	97	211	212	82				
Cheapside					100		150	150								
Cherokee				50	100	153	209	250	500	450	287	500	190	260	450	350
Chester					50	176	278	250	319	319	500	500	700	260	305	285
Chico					292	323	642	642	1023	850	700	475	654	723	890	800
Chicota						321	342	212	212	129	233	500	370	350	200	300
Chief														350		
Childress						621	692	3818	5003	7163	6464	7619	6399	5408	5817	5055
Chillicothe							219	1207	1351	1610	1423	1415	1161	1116	1052	816
Chilton							285	400	516	884	500	400	750	400	500	600
China								174	175	432	386	400	700	1255	1351	1144
China Grove													200	329	434	872
China Spring					150	163	214	214	314	285	235	225	150	250	350	500
Chireno					125	276	267	200	262	521	558	800	500	308	371	415
Chisholm							102	102	268	268	125	145	100	100		
Choice										211						
Chriesman							78	150	219	750	700	250	150		100	100
Christine								100	259	524	286	289	276	289	392	368
Christoval								80		500	604	700	512	600	700	700
Churchhill Bridge							250	250						150	400	300
Cibolo						58	58	250	250	262	275	325	325	440	549	1757
Cincinnati	200															
Circleville						62	62	100		163						400
Cisco					1000	1063	1514	2410	7422	6027	4868	5230	4499	4160	4517	3813
Clairmont							65	150	210	210	150					
Clairette							58	120		219						
Clarendon					150	949	1494	1946	2456	2756	2431	2577	2172	1974	2220	2067
Clareville								120	419	419	419					

POPULATON HISTORY OF TEXAS CITIES AND TOWNS 1840-1990

COMMUNITY	1990	1980	1970	1960	1950	1940	1930	1920	1910	1900	1890	1880	1870	1860	1850	1840
Clarksville	4311	4917	3346	3851	4353	4095	2952	3386	2065	2069	1588	764	613	400	700	
Clarksville City	720	525	398	359							446					
Clarkwood				500	400	300	119	119								
Claude	1199	1112	992	895	820	761	1041	770	692	298	285					
Clawson							262		82	82						
Clay	200	220	220	250	500	500	500	120	120	48						
Clayton	130	150	150	150	150	192	163	163	200	218	163	96	75			
Clear Lake City			9000													
Clear Lake Shores	1096	755	721	500	350											
Cleburne	22205	19218	16015	15381	12905	10558	11539	12820	10364	7493	3278	1855	686			
Clermville							250									
Cleveland	7124	5977	5627	5838	5183	1783	1422	1500	800	302						
Clifton	3195	3063	2578	2335	1837	1732	1367	1327	1137	1000	204	113	50			
Clint	1035	1314	900	975	802	500	500	250	40							
Clinton (De Witt)												190				
Clinton (Harris)						100	55					202				
Clinton (Hunt)				100	250	88	88	96	100	138		190	217			
Cloverleaf	18230	17317	4000	3000												
Clute	8910	9577	6023	4501	2200	250	75	62	495							
Clyde	3002	2562	1635	1116	908	800	706	610		81						
Coahoma	1133	1069	1158	1239	802	574	620	500	500							
Coal										276						
Coalville												500				
Cockrell Hill	3746	3262	3515	3104	2207	1246	800	459								
Coffee City	216	254	157													
Coffeyville					150				200	163	153	67				
Cold Hill												175				
Coldspring	538	569	488	400	500	562	550	619	439	373	439	300				
Coleman	5410	5960	5608	6371	6530	6054	6078	2868	3046	1362	906	311	100			
College Station	52456	37272	17676	11396	7925	2184	1500	459	500	441	300					
Collegeport						100			200							
Colleyville	12724	6700	3342	1491	1150											
Collins										887						
Collinsville	1033	860	768	560	561	653	670	837	791	666	332	200	200			
Colmesneil	569	553	531	550	750	665	719	632	632	632	1016					
Colorado City	4749	5405	5227	6457	6774	5213	4671	1766	1840	1847	1582	1500				
Cotharp								167	113	113	285	250				
Columbia								525	612	983	515	739	426			300
Columbus	3367	3923	3342	3656	3878	2422	2054	1720	1824	1824	2199	1959	750			250
Comaltown						113	113	113							286	

POPULATON HISTORY OF TEXAS CITIES AND TOWNS 1840-1990

COMMUNITY	1990	1980	1970	1960	1950	1940	1930	1920	1910	1900	1890	1880	1870	1860	1850	1840
Comanche	4087	4075	3933	3415	3840	3209	2435	3524	2756	2070	1226	704	300			
Comanche Harbor	370	350														
Combes	2042	1488	689	605	400	400	400	24								
Combine	1329	688	249													
Comfort	1477	1226	950	1200	823	880	713	800	560	498	307	177	75			
Commerce	6825	8136	9534	5789	5889	4699	4267	3842	2818	1800	810	148				
Como	563	554	474	300	356	412	392	827	650	359						
Comstock	350	350	250	300	300	224	319	319	63	63						
Concepcion	175	150	150	150	100	106	319	75	150	224	612	719	75			
Concord	200	175			400	280	163	163	100	48			50			
Concret									58	58	58	225	50			
Conroe	27610	18034	11969	9192	7298	4624	2457	1858	1374	492						
Content					175	166	175	57		317	136	64	150			
Converse	8887	4907	1383	800				78	63	63	63	80				
Cooks Point					437	437	437	437	87	87	87	75				
Cookville	350	450	300	300	150	462	518	518	425	285	285					
Cool	214	202	237													
Coolidge	748	810	786	913	1062	1102	1169	880	505							
Cooper	2153	2338	2258	2213	2350	2537	2023	2563	1513	1518	629	294	100			
Copeville	350	300	250	300	235	264	224	304	204	173						
Coppell	16881	3826	1728	666	250	228	400	419	118	118						
Copper Canyon	978	465														
Copperas Cove	24079	19469	10818	4567	1052	356	406	509	600	486						
Corinth	3944	1264	461		74	105	74	74	41	41						
Corlena									200							
Corn Hill									239	242	239	108				
Corpus Christi	257453	231999	204525	167690	108287	57301	27741	10522	8222	4703	4387	3257	2140	175	533	
Corral City	46	85														
Corrigan	1764	1770	1304	986	1417	1402	1200	1000	461	461	298					
Corsicana	22911	21712	19972	20344	19211	15232	15202	11356	9749	9313	6285	3373	80		250	
Coryell	150	120	100	100	100	335	225	225	266	123	266	250				
Cotton Center	200	300	300	400		400										
Cotton Gin					150	226	113	113	100	217	125	126	200			
Cotton Mill					450											
Cottonwood	156	117		100	250	290	264	264	250	336	78					
Cottonwood Shores	548	348														
Cotulla	3694	3912	3415	3960	4418	3633	3175	2058	1880	794	672	500				
Coupland	300	300	200	150	241	170	200	250	200	183						
Courtney			250	150	250	275	317	250	228	307	228	186	150			
Cove	402	645	250	150	260	163	300	52				126				

POPULATON HISTORY OF TEXAS CITIES AND TOWNS 1840-1990

COMMUNITY	1990	1980	1970	1960	1950	1940	1930	1920	1910	1900	1890	1880	1870	1860	1850	1840
Covington	238	259	300	300	400	570	413	413	300	267	57	46				
Coyanosa	250	300	225	100												
Craft Prairie										184	163	257				
Crafton	75	60														
Crandall	1652	831	774	640	727	825	750	616	500	306	251	99				
Crane	3533	3622	3427	3796	2154	1420	2000									
Cranfills Gap	269	341	350	450	400	400	400	127	140	97	39	150				
Crawford	631	610	477	480	423	471	491	573	516	443	476	226				
Creedmoor	194	188	200	200	221	160	160	145	145							
Cresson	200	200	175	350	300	316	279	300	279	314						
Crockett	7024	7405	6616	5556	5932	4536	4441	3061	3947	2612	1445	599	538	350	150	
Crosby	1811	1533	1118	1200	411	335	500	300	159	83						
Crosbyton	2026	2289	2251	2088	1879	1615	1250	428	120							
Cross					428	428	428		125							
Cross Cut				150	350	100	86	86	79	79	79	200				
Cross Plains	1063	1240	1192	1168	1305	1229	1507	700	200	156	59	175				
Cross Roads	361	302	125	50	150	125	57									
Cross Timbers				150									300			
Crowell	1230	1509	1399	1703	1912	1817	1946	1175	1341	283						
Crowley	6974	5852	2662	583	500	300	318	250	275	150						
Crystal Beach/Patton	750	776	595	300												
Crystal City	8263	8334	8104	9101	7198	6529	6609	1137	350							
Cuero	6700	7124	6956	7338	7498	5474	4672	3671	3109	3422	2442	1333	700			
Cumby	571	647	628	447	504	642	646	945	800	867						
Cuney	170	184	250	220	350	260	260									
Cunningham	150	125	125	300	250			413								
Curry's Creek											210					
Cushing	587	518	396	388	479	473	800	1213	600							
Custer City										47	148	86				
Cut and Shoot	903	568	451	150												
Cypress	800	700	400		500		100		125							
Cypress Bend	400	400	250													
Cypress Mill							400			38	138	157				
Cyril										39						
Dabney				500												
Dacus						114	100	127	100	207						
Daingerfield	2572	3030	2630	3133	1668	1032	818	843	1100	699	553	395	272		200	
Daisetta	969	1177	1084	1500	1764	2000	1200	75								
Dalby Springs	100	100		200	300	450	400	226	200	186	186	72				
Dale	220	200	260	200	500	225	300	319	100	142						

POPULATON HISTORY OF TEXAS CITIES AND TOWNS 1840-1990

COMMUNITY	1840	1850	1860	1870	1880	1890	1900	1910	1920	1930	1940	1950	1960	1970	1980	1990
Dalhart								2580	2676	4691	4682	5918	5160	5705	6854	6246
Dallas		250	2000	4500	10358	38067	42638	92104	158976	260475	294734	434462	679684	844401	904078	1006877
Dalworth Park																
Dalworthington Gardens													430	757	1100	1758
Damon							84	84	363	363	332	560	750	400	700	800
Danbury								40	521	500	556	600	600	807	1357	1447
Danevang							66	66	261	300	200	250	300	100	100	250
Daniel							52	52	264	264		150				
Danville														300	100	200
Darrouzett						105			96	266	467	328	375	396	444	343
Davenport								44		300						
Davilla				200	285	241	249	421	400	421	440	421	400	300	300	250
Dawson					200	365	463	803	950	1131	1155	1107	911	848	747	766
Dayton					348	239	106	200	787	1207	1279	1820	3367	3804	4908	5151
Dayton Lakes															159	191
De Berry					100	127	127	125	183	350	500	350	350	200	420	450
De Cordova Bend															1300	1350
De Kalb				75	200	420	554	650	910	1023	1287	1928	2042	2197	2217	1976
De Leon					100	364	807	1015	3302	1766	1971	2241	2022	2170	2478	2190
De Soto							96	97	97	97	106	298	1969	6617	15538	30544
Deadwood							68	120	312	312	137	50			212	277
Dean														100	200	150
Deanville					70	106	106	106	207	250	250	190	150	100		
Dearborn								300								
Decatur				200	579	1746	1562	1651	2205	2037	2578	2922	3563	3240	4104	4252
Decker Prairie												100		400	600	600
Deer Park										350	350	736	4865	12773	22648	37652
Del Mar Hills														1000	1200	
Del Monte														400	500	
Del Rio				50	150	1980	2164	4000	10589	11693	13343	14211	18612	21330	30034	30705
Del Valle					150	410	64	200					125	500	1200	1300
Delba							54	41	41	41						
Dell City												400	600	383	495	569
Delmita										150	650	200				
Denison				1000	3975	10958	11807	13632	17065	13850	15581	17504	22748	24923	23884	21505
Denton				361	1194	2558	4187	4732	7626	9587	11192	21372	26844	39874	48063	66270
Denver City					100	147	147	47	62	62	709	1855	4302	4133	4704	5145
Depot					50	242	447	700	821	819	822	734	639	761	724	746
Derby									62	62	250	500	100	198		
Desdemona					121	410	431	340	3008	609	179	198	198	198	198	180

POPULATON HISTORY OF TEXAS CITIES AND TOWNS 1840-1990

COMMUNITY	1990	1980	1970	1960	1950	1940	1930	1920	1910	1900	1890	1880	1870	1860	1850	1840
Detmold					400											
Detroit	706	805	668	576	679	1064	1350	1530	1056	1130	604					
Devers	318	507	366	800	687	213	213	213	187	143	187	80				
Devine	3928	3756	3311	2522	1672	1398	1093	995	1042	472	310					
Deweyville	1218	1171	850	600	600	1650	1500	519	100	51						
Dexter				135	317	387	317	350	226	262	226	200	100			
D'Hanis	650	550	650	645	750	445	700	513	400	308	266	210	213		84	
Dialville							219		250							
Diana	350	300	175	500												
Diboll	4341	5227	3557	2506	2391	1499	1363	500	100	38						
Dickens	322	409	295	302	420	465	265	250	375	237						
Dickenson	9497	7505	10776	4715	2704	1100	810	1000	250	149						
Dido												250				
Dilley	2632	2579	2362	2118	1809	1244	929	600	500	51						
Dime Box	300	300	300	750	500	506	219	219	129	127						
Dimmitt	4408	5019	4327	2935	1461	943	829	162	140	39						
Dimple	300			100												
Dittinger							230									
Dobbin	300	300	500	250	375	200	317	158	180							
Dodd City	350	286	302	239	329	308	370	495	289	369	333	300				
Dodge	300	250	160	250	507	552	467	467	350	206	206	137	75			
Dodson	113	185	239	308	336	357	426	513								
Dogwood		500	500													
Doke					357											
Dolores					609	500		525								
Domino	101	249	147		300	150	218	218	100							
Donie	200	250	250	300	100	100			400							
Donna	12652	9952	7365	7522	7171	4712	4103	1579								
Donnybrook Place				2537												
Doole		130			500	250	100	36								
Dorchester	137	205	221	100	100	100	162	100	100							
Doss	150	250	100													
Double Bayou	100	120	120	120	150	330	263	263	151	216						
Double Oak	1664	836	129													
Doucette	600	600	500	400	314	554	519	519	160	193						
Douglass	200	200	150	400	300	336	314	114	169	169	205	168	100			
Douglassville	192	228	282	172	450	187	328	328	176	176	350	230	150			
Drasco							75		300							
Dresden					60	139	165	165	150	127	150	122				
Dripping Springs	1033	606	250	235	300	166	167	167	180	317	109	100	200			

POPULATON HISTORY OF TEXAS CITIES AND TOWNS 1840-1990

COMMUNITY	1990	1980	1970	1960	1950	1940	1930	1920	1910	1900	1890	1880	1870	1860	1850	1840
Ennis	13883	12110	11046	9347	7815	7087	7069	7224	5669	4919	2171	1351	400			
Eola	200	250	250	150	350		116	116	100							
Era	300	300	300	150	350	289	263	263	210	210						
Escobares	1705	500	400	300		350										
Eskota									160							
Estacado	194	258	301	346	464	68	83	83	68	68	238					
Estelline					50	603	950	394	400	109						
Ethel		45				100	100	75	81	243						
Etoile	350	500	800	100	100	100	100	36	40							
Eubank Acres	1600	2300														
Euless	38149	24002	19316	4263	110	100	150	162	200	104						
Eureka	242	233	140			162	162									
Eustace	662	541	491	351	650	440	513	400	250	54						
Evadale	1422	1601	900	750	515	515	515	515	300							
Evansville							261									
Evant	444	425	575	500	850	556	350	500	300	252	56					
Evergreen	650	650			200	150	500	217	112	112	72					
Evergreen Park																
Everitt					150	335	320	320	99	99						
Everman	5672	5387	4570	1076	451	300	200	136	120							
Eylau	300	300	500													
Ezzell				100	400		50	63	44	44	200					
Fabens	5599	4285	3241	3134	3089	3000	1623									
Fair Oaks	1860															
Fairbanks					388	282	148	84	71	71						
Fairfield	3234	3505	2074	1781	1742	1047	712	629	629	605	499	358	800	609		
Fairgreen	3300	1600														
Fairlie	100	75	120	200	350	272	362	362	248	248						
Fairview (Collin)	206	893	463	175												
Fairview (Wise)	1554	180				50	44	44	83	66	110		50			
Falcon Heights	500	500	225													
Falfurrias	5788	6103	6355	6515	6712	2540	2641	1825	750							
Falls City	478	580	442	462	422	564	521	500	300	142						
Fannett	250	250	200	180	600	250	264	264	80							
Fannin	150	100	100	75	250	114	150	300	200	58						
Farmer									261	261						
Farmers Branch	24250	24863	27492	13441	915	331	317	274	205	205	205	150				
Farmersville	2640	2360	2311	2021	1955	2206	1878	2167	1848	1856	1093	230	114			
Farmington	80	45			150	171	171	171	171	171	206	142	75			
Farnsworth	175	230	150	100	100											

POPULATION HISTORY OF TEXAS CITIES AND TOWNS 1840-1990

COMMUNITY	1990	1980	1970	1960	1950	1940	1930	1920	1910	1900	1890	1880	1870	1860	1850	1840
Farwell	1373	1354	1185	1009	400	558	647	509	500							
Fashing		80			200	250	350									
Fate	475	263	329	191	141	127	194	299	212	331						
Fayetteville	283	356	400	394	462	445	437	390	274	296	269	400	319			
Faysville	350	300	300													
Fentress	300	300	300	350	220	275	269	269	208	208						
Ferguson					1741	125										
Ferris	2212	2228	2180	1807	1735	1436	1438	1586	1233	904	311	106				
Fieldcreek				61	63	110	111	111	111	217						
Fieldton	35	100	100	250	70	105	105									
Fincastle					50	100	100	36		350	350	142	75			
Fiskville				225	500					43						
Fitz Williams Mills												2283				
Flat	250	325	250	200	250	200	113	113	80							
Flatonia	1295	1070	1108	1009	1098	1024	966	995	886	1210	1304	866	300			
Fleig	800				870											
Fletcher	600	800	800	160	90	175	90	65								
Flint		600	350	150	250		260	260	200	65						
Flomont							212									
Florence	829	744	672	610	561	476	421	650	363	405	263	159	100			
Floresville	5247	4381	3707	2126	1949	1708	1581	1518	1398	895	913	275	100			
Flower Mound	15527	4402	1685													
Floyd	150	200	100	150	250	330	250	231	231							
Floydada	3896	4193	4109	3769	3210	2726	2637	1384	664	362						
Fluvanna	150	200	250	600	350	412	265	375	450	332						
Flynn	200	125	170	170	300	340	419	419	180							
Foard City			100			100	120	120	60							
Follett	441	547	522	466	540	431	658	150								
Fordtran					400	75	65	65	65							
Forest	50	50		100	250	500	500	162	123	123						
Forest Glade	300	300	250													
Forest Hill	11482	11684	8236	3221	1519											
Forest Home						500	100					300				
Forestburg	150	125	125	150	250	198	264	372	372	317	372	100				
Forney	4070	2483	1745	1544	1425	1295	1216	1345	1114	1165	811	317				
Forreston	250	250	250	250	250	256	400	420	233	233						
Forsan	256	239	237	400	500	440	275									
Fort Belknap													67			
Fort Bliss	13915	12687	13288								100	100	50	60	91	
Fort Brown						500	350				150	415	437	249	107	

POPULATON HISTORY OF TEXAS CITIES AND TOWNS 1840-1990

COMMUNITY	1840	1850	1860	1870	1880	1890	1900	1910	1920	1930	1940	1950	1960	1970	1980	1990
Fort Chadbourne																
Fort Clark			107	395	1030	821										
Fort Concho			92	913	716											
Fort Croghan		98														
Fort Davis			138	615	1162	1061	593	1061	525	666	734	1000	900	900	850	1100
Fort Duncan		216	88	294	156											
Fort Elliott					200											
Fort Ewell					150											
Fort Gates		92														
Fort Graham		91				107		56						363	777	818
Fort Griffin				297	179	306	63			133	102	50				
Fort Hancock								34		250	385	475	600	600	550	650
Fort Hood														32597	31250	35580
Fort Inge		98	47													
Fort Lancaster			79													
Fort Lincoln		141														
Fort Mcintosh		133	81	184	200	180					200					
Fort Mckavett			124	332	275	536	132	132	140	110	149	100	120	110	110	
Fort Mason																
Fort Merrill		118														
Fort Quitman			32	361												
Fort Richardson				593												
Fort Sam Houston							750	200						10553		
Fort Stockton				458	600	439	329	439	1297	2695	3294	4444	6373	8283	8688	8524
Fort Wolters				593										3743		
Fort Worth		100		1000	6663	23076	26688	73312	106482	163447	177662	278778	356268	393455	385164	447619
Fosterville					600	731		38								
Fostoria									1518	1518	1650	666	666		450	
Fountain View																1300
Fowlerton								150	2021	1021	660	300	180	110	110	100
Fox Run															1500	1500
Francitas									521	521	330	200	150	120	110	100
Franklin					311	665	869	869	1131	961	1087	1209	1065	1063	1349	1336
Frankston								550	818	1109	1216	1050	953	1056	1255	1127
Fred									68	175	175	450	500	160	500	500
Fredericksburg		754		1164	1085	1532	1632	2100	2500	2416	3544	3854	4629	5326	6412	6934
Fredonia						273	173	173	200	184	190	200	200	100	40	60
Freeport									1798	3162	2579	6012	11619	11997	13444	11389
Freer										100	2346	2280	2724	2804	3213	3271
Freisburg				150		403	356	356	328	75	101		100			50

POPULATON HISTORY OF TEXAS CITIES AND TOWNS 1840-1990

COMMUNITY	1990	1980	1970	1960	1950	1940	1930	1920	1910	1900	1890	1880	1870	1860	1850	1840
Fresno	1000	900	300	350	350	300	50									
Friday							250									
Friendswood	22814	10719	5675	850	400	300	300	142	50							
Frio							67	67			115	334	75			
Friona	3688	3809	3111	2048	1202	803	731	200	200							
Frisco	6141	3499	1845	1184	736	670	618	733	332							
Fritch	2335	2299	1778	1617	700	550	500									
Front				150	350											
Fronton	500	300	300	400	400				204	204						
Frosa Lim											109	300				
Frost	579	564	548	508	585	671	748	913	702	621						
Fruitdale				1418	876	515	300									
Fruitvale	349	367	206	180	300	300	150	175	50							
Fulbright	100	100	150	200	300	342	225	330	178	217						
Fuller Springs	1470	1470	707													
Fulshear	557	594	300	300	200	116	200	263	249	249						
Fulton	763	725	1101	900	600	200					81	79	50			
Fuqua							670	670	400							
Gabion												300				
Gail	120	150	150	130	356	138	200	263	275	179	100					
Gainesville	14256	14081	13830	13083	11246	9651	8915	8648	7624	7874	6594	2667	500			
Gainor							400									
Galena Park	10033	9879	10479	10652	7186	1562	1200	165								
Gallatin	368	132	210	150	400	330	300		125							
Galleon Bay		300														
Galveston	59070	61902	61809	67175	66568	60862	52938	44255	36981	37789	29084	22248	13818	7307	4177	3000
Ganado	1701	1770	1640	1626	1258	717	626	716	558	407						
Gap	500	500	100	125					160							
Garceno	450	400	350					219	68	68						
Garcias				900	750	650	650									
Garden City	315	300	300	300	274		315	315	200	82						
Garden Oaks					797											
Garden Ridge	1450	647	110			207										
Garden Valley	40	30					214	214	218	218	172	200	75			
Gardendale	1103	950	700		200	175	162									
Garfield	1336	200	150				63	63	63	63						
Garland	180650	138857	81437	38501	10571	2233	1584	1421	804	819	478					
Garner									200							
Garrett	340	220	225	167	300	178	162	162	162	162		86				
Garrison	883	1059	1082	951	699	770	527	603	627	530	252					

POPULATON HISTORY OF TEXAS CITIES AND TOWNS 1840-1990

COMMUNITY	1990	1980	1970	1960	1950	1940	1930	1920	1910	1900	1890	1880	1870	1860	1850	1840
Garvin																
Garwood	600	600	650	625	568	600	600	462	116	116	204					
Gary City	271	322	202	600	575	535	530	514	341	341						
Garza								517	250	179	79					
Gatesville	11492	6260	4683	4626	3856	3177	2601	2499	1929	1865	1375	434	200			
Gause	500	500	500	500	500	500	428	428	289	280	88	88				
Gay Hill		75	100	100	150	278	240	159	216	216	71					
Geneva	225	200		300	125	100	200	84	84	84		200				
Genoa				500	750	1000	610	267	100	61						
Gent										173						
George																
George West	2586	2627	2022	1878	1533	200	327	327								
Georgetown	14842	9468	6395	5218	4951	3682	3583	2871	3096	2790	2447	1354	479	107		
Germantz		240					500	267								
Geronimo	250	150	150	110			178	127	123	123						
Gholson	692															
Gibbs		263	594		315	315	213									
Gibtown					50	182	163	200	216	242						
Giddings	4093	3950	2783	2821	2532	2166	1835	1650	1375	1451	1203	624	500			
Gilchrist	700	600	300	300			50									
Gillette						267	267	267	250							
Gilmer	4822	5167	4196	4312	4096	3138	1963	2268	1484	1758	591	386	200		300	
Girard	250	160	125	150	500	554	500	156	60							
Gladewater	6027	6548	5574	5742	5305	4454	5000	560	550	231	259	163	75			
Gladstell						413	413	413								
Glazier									475							
Glen Garden					500	125	125	313								
Glen Rose	1949	2075	1554	1422	1254	1050	983	1036	890	767	400	132				
Glendale				100			200	120	120							
Glenfawn					250	286	135	267	267	267	267	200				
Glenflora	400	400	400	500	700	770	500	419	500	62						
Glenn Heights	4564	1033	257													
Glenwood	200	200	350	150	150	135	131	131	131	131						
Glidden	200	350	350	400	360	440	360	400	184	219						
Gober	250	210	280	300	250	335	319	319	211	217						
Godley	569	614	533	401	424	317	378	600	500	220						
Golden	400	200	200	150	450	440	163	400	350	136						
Golden Acres				2500	800											
Goldsboro							150		150							
Goldsmith	297	409	387	670	444	935										

POPULATON HISTORY OF TEXAS CITIES AND TOWNS 1840-1990

COMMUNITY	1840	1850	1860	1870	1880	1890	1900	1910	1920	1930	1940	1950	1960	1970	1980	1990
Goldthwaite					250	1066	1282	1129	1214	1324	1414	1566	1383	1693	1783	1658
Goliad	100			300	885	885	1261	1261	2000	1424	1446	1584	1782	1709	1990	1946
Golinda							68	68	68		68	100		310	335	347
Gonzales	100	307	1103	1255	1581	1641	4297	3139	3128	3859	4722	5659	5820	5854	7152	6527
Goodlow														345	343	319
Goodlow Park														500	500	500
Goodnight								150	218	240	180	125	75	100	200	250
Goodrich								100	137	500	500	800	800	600	350	239
Goose Creek									1025	5208	6924					
Gordon					300	378	684	609	675	510	532	404	349	457	516	465
Gordonville					128	182	182	182	168	300	335	250	250	200	100	130
Goree							66	675	614	457	425	640	543	538	524	412
Gorman							583	963	3200	1154	1157	1317	1142	1236	1258	1290
Goshen				50		129		275	162	200	308	230				
Graceton																
Graford								300	163	481	804	655	448	613	495	561
Graham					576	667	1410	1596	2544	4981	5175	6742	8505	7477	9170	8986
Granbury				150	524	1164	878	1336	1364	996	1166	1683	2227	2473	3332	4045
Grand Prairie					75	123	427	994	1263	1529	1595	14594	30386	50904	71462	99616
Grand Saline				50		864	1081	1065	1528	1799	1641	1810	2006	2257	2709	2630
Grandfalls							107	250	134	134	653	995	1012	622	635	583
Grandview				50	287	257	713	1018	1084	892	823	886	961	935	1205	1245
Granger						261	841	1708	1944	1703	1723	1637	1339	1256	1236	1190
Grangerland														100	300	500
Granite Mountain							267	134		133	138					
Granite Schoals														342	634	1378
Grape Creek																800
Grapeland				50	88	216	331	350	936	1027	1327	1358	1113	1211	1634	1450
Grapevine				75	199	442	762	681	821	936	1043	1824	2821	7049	11801	29202
Gray Rock					75	152	84									
Grayburg								750	1406	474	520	533	400	200	194	257
Grays Prairie/Peedes Mill															171	286
Great Northwest																750
Green Pastures														900	950	600
Greenfield Acres														300		
Greenview Hills																245
Greenview Manor															500	
Greenville			246	275	1200	4330	6860	8850	12384	12407	13995	14727	19087	22043	22161	23071
Greenvine						182	120	182	148	148	114	50				
Greenway							64	64							450	400

POPULATION HISTORY OF TEXAS CITIES AND TOWNS 1840-1990

COMMUNITY	1840	1850	1860	1870	1880	1890	1900	1910	1920	1930	1940	1950	1960	1970	1980	1990
Greenwood					49	210	316	316	314	314	334	110	110		70	100
Greenwood Acres															300	200
Greenwood Village															4650	5000
Greggton										2000	1992	2168				
Gregory							122	200	517	517	440	932	1970	2246	2739	2458
Gresham												100		100	200	250
Grey Forest														385	442	425
Griffing Park											1344	2096	2267	2075	1802	
Groesbeck				300	402	663	1462	1454	1522	2059	2272	2182	2498	2396	3373	3185
Groom								150	100	564	475	678	679	808	736	613
Groves										1000	3500	5600	17304	18067	17090	16513
Groveton					100	1076	1570	1570	1103	1046	940	805	1148	1219	1262	1071
Grow											750	750				
Grulla								344	518	1800	1000	1013	1436	1194	1442	1335
Gruve										330	350	813	1030	1265	1216	1172
Guadelupe Heights																550
Guffey								200	600	216	330					
Guion												550				
Gulf									725	500	1650					
Gum Springs														150	150	400
Gun Barrel City														327	2118	3526
Gunsight						255	255	255	68	91						
Gunter							255	300	575	475	481	463	593	647	849	898
Gustine							212	212	750	368	409	421	380	357	416	430
Guthrie							188	200	318	318	318	318	200	250	250	190
Guy						158	119	119	75	89	101	70	100	100	200	250
Hackberry						149					220	200			120	200
Haines										500					100	200
Hale Center							116	400	250	1007	836	1626	2196	1964	2297	2067
Halesboro					103	159	159	159	159	105	105					
Hallettsville				431	588	1011	1457	1379	1444	1406	1581	2000	2808	2712	2865	2718
Hallsburg														314	455	450
Hallsville				400	179	203	236	700	695	542	528	617	684	1038	1556	2288
Haltom City											221	5760	23133	28127	29014	32856
Hamilton				100	277	726	987	1548	2018	2084	2716	3077	3106	2760	3189	2937
Hamlin								1978	1633	2328	2406	3569	3791	3325	3248	2791
Hammond					100	56	115	115		183						
Hampton							84	84	375	375	200	200				
Hamshire										200		350	350	450	500	600
Handley					72	156	156	156	905	2000	2000					

POPULATON HISTORY OF TEXAS CITIES AND TOWNS 1840-1990

COMMUNITY	1840	1850	1860	1870	1880	1890	1900	1910	1920	1930	1940	1950	1960	1970	1980	1990
Hankamer								100	310	195	200	675	400	500	700	700
Happy								250	250	724	576	690	624	672	674	588
Harbin				75	100	207	186	83	80	80	80					
Hardin							113			216	222	500	500	400	779	563
Hargill	100									350	494	600	900	800	1030	1030
Harker Heights							238	350	513	513	393		200	4216	7345	12841
Harleton												300	300	150	250	300
Harlingen								750	1784	12124	13306	23229	41207	33503	43543	48735
Harper							136	136	145	335	340	750	300	300	400	400
Harpers Mill					300											
Harrisburg			1863	571	942	431	563	563	1461	1461						
Harrisdale					500											
Harrold							366	375	362	200	138	250		160	180	135
Hart								75	319	300	271	200	577	905	1008	1221
Hartley					50		87	200	98	250	250	400	375	185	280	300
Hartzo							58					500				
Harvest Acres															600	500
Harvest Heights															700	700
Harwood					155	215	219	300	200	225	222	157		112	112	150
Haskell						745	781	2436	2300	2632	3051	3836	4016	3655	3782	3362
Haslam									1027	527	527					
Haslet							67	175	169	300	168	350	100	100	262	795
Hasse								350	350	258	272	200	200	276	250	135
Hastings											400	350	400			
Hatchel								40		180						
Havana							48				300	300	250	250	500	
Hawkins				75	142	227	297	350	300	250	554	493	868	977	1302	1309
Hawley							38	300	200	200	200	200	300	422	679	606
Hays							54	54	54		100	200		206	286	251
Hayward										600	800	900				
Hazy Hollow															900	900
Hearne				500	1421	1532	2129	2352	2741	2956	3511	4872	5072	4982	5418	5132
Heath							136	198	327	327	164	100	150	520	1459	2108
Hebbronville							109	150	600	2742	2640	4302	3987	4079	4684	4465
Hebron								190	100	131	150	125	150	336	385	1128
Hedley								325	594	807	637	588	494	439	380	391
Hedwig Village						162							1182	3255	2506	2616
Hedwigs Hill							62									
Heidenheimer					285	354	249	249	249	166	273	166		150	150	350
Helena				200			296	184	120	120	106	120	180	100	100	30

POPULATON HISTORY OF TEXAS CITIES AND TOWNS 1840-1990

COMMUNITY	1990	1980	1970	1960	1950	1940	1930	1920	1910	1900	1890	1880	1870	1860	1850	1840
Helmic					150	330	380	380	371	371	371	475				
Helotes	1535	1100	900	300	300	150										
Hemphill	1182	1353	1005	913	972	739	731	2000	279	386		300	100			
Hempstead	3551	3456	1891	1505	1395	1674	1942	2515	1849	1942	1671	1612	600			
Henderson	11139	11473	10187	9666	6833	6437	2932	2273	1750	1563	1536	1656	918	705	400	
Henrietta	2896	3149	2897	3062	2813	2391	2020	2563	2104	1614	2100	438	100			
Hereford	14745	15853	13414	7652	5207	2584	2458	1696	1750	532						
Hermleigh	325	300	500	350	671	404	544	613	400							
Herty				900												
Hester									171	171						
Hewitt	8983	5247	569	280	185	104	162	162	100	79						
Hi Ho	300	240														
Hickory Creek	1893	1422	218		200	100		112	100	100	76					
Hickson					400											
Hico	1342	1375	975	1020	1212	1242	1463	1635	1437	1480	649	200				
Hidalgo	3292	2288	1289	1078	500	693	630	1019	389	398	389	259	300			
Hidden Echo	500															
Hidden Forest		600														
Hidden Valley			1200													
Higgins	464	702	582	711	675	741	812	688	769	361	213					
High Hill	30	30			32	75	110	110	134	134						
High Island	550	550	300	800	661	800	500	219	78	78	397	300	200			
Highbank				100	500	400	212	62	100							
Highland Acres	750	750														
Highland Bayou		1163	700													
Highland Oaks		500														
Highland Park	8739	8909	10133	10411	11405	10288	8422	2321								
Highland Village	7027	3246	516													
Highlands	6632	6467	3462	4336	2723	1000	500									
Highpoint	750	520														
Highway Village	700			1927												
Hiland Shores	1038	700														
Hill Country Village	695	972	636	418	2826	250	150									
Hillcrest	600	771	650	850			180									
Hillister		600	400		500											
Hillsboro	7072	7397	7224	7402	8363	7799	7823	6952	6115	5346	2541	550	313	153		
Hilshire Village	665	621	627	543												
Hitchcock	5868	6655	5565	5216	1105	700	500	667	300	216						
Hobson							210		82	82						
Hochheim	150	100	100	100	100	115	273	273	261	216	261	100				

POPULATION HISTORY OF TEXAS CITIES AND TOWNS 1840-1990

COMMUNITY	1990	1980	1970	1960	1950	1940	1930	1920	1910	1900	1890	1880	1870	1860	1850	1840
Hockley	900	500	220	200	450	410	410	410	296	269	296	308	250			
Holiday Lakes	1039	583	107													
Holiday Oaks	200	500														
Holland	1118	863	723	653	674	741	738	690	778	678	368					
Holland Quarters	400	400	125													
Holliday	1475	1349	1048	1139	1007	798	786	300	140	217						
Hollywood	600	600	500													
Hollywood Park	2841	3231	2299	783												
Homer	300	315	316			100		130	166	666	682	244	216			
Hondo	6018	6057	5487	4932	4188	2750	2106	2000	1325	684	592	200				
Honey Grove	1681	1973	1853	2071	2340	2456	2475	2642	2300	2483	1828	884	382	284		
Honey Island	200	250	250	250	400	200	63	63								
Honey Springs						342										
Hood						100	65	265	161	161						
Hooks	2684	2507	2545	2048	2319	120	160	421	98	98						
Hooks Switch										382						
Hoover's Valley												250				
Horizon City	2308	1956	350													
Hortense							523	523	346	346						
Hortontown															139	
Houghton									167	167						
Houmont Park	2500	4000	1000	1300												
Houston	1630553	1595138	1232802	938219	596163	384514	292352	138276	78800	44633	27557	16513	9382	4845	2396	1500
Houston Heights								9800	6984	800						
Howard								110	110	110		150				
Howardwick	211	165	50						175							
Howe	2173	2072	1359	680	572	546	565	583	581	531	284	200				
Howland	40	80		160	160	118	145	415	226	226						
Hoxie										322						
Hoyt				419			419	419								
Hubbard	1589	1676	1572	1628	1768	1871	1855	2072	1843	1608	894	400				
Huckaby									174	172						
Hudson	2374	1659	670	500												
Hudson Oaks	711	309	118													
Huffman	1650	1500	600	400	200											
Hufsmith	200	300	300	100	150	275	250	158	175							
Hughes Springs	1938	2196	1701	1813	1445	767	736	831	600	469	296	69				
Hull	850	950	900	888	684	900	727	1000								
Humble	12060	6729	3272	1711	1388	1371	3527	1500	1250	61						
Hungerford	550	550	550	500	750	320	128	128	183	183						

POPULATON HISTORY OF TEXAS CITIES AND TOWNS 1840-1990

COMMUNITY	1990	1980	1970	1960	1950	1940	1930	1920	1910	1900	1890	1880	1870	1860	1850	1840
Hunt	600	400	400	400	116	116	116	116	162	162						
Hunter							178									
Hunters Creek	3954	4215	3959	2478												
Hunters Retreat	200	180														
Huntington	1794	1672	1192	1009	1039	969	1000	515	350	276	276					
Huntsville	27925	23936	17610	11999	9820	5108	5028	4689	2072	2485	1509	2536	1599	939	750	
Hurwood	150	150	300	200	100											
Hurst	33574	31420	27215	10165	743	560	400	368	68	168	116	116	50			
Hutchins	2719	2837	1755	1100	529				204	297	106					
Hutto	630	659	545	442		597	538	571	563	749						
Huxley	335	341	208					121	100							
Huxley Bay	100	250														
Hyatt							200			722	429					
Hylton							212		187	187						
Iago	450	500	200	300	320	115	115		100	100						
Iatan									125							
Idalou	2074	2348	1729	1274	1014	503	538	95								
Illinois Bend				100	150	68	75	68	112	219						
Impact	25	54	61	200												
Imperial	600	750	750	950	750	75	75									
Independence	150	200	200	200	250	319	319	319	373	337	373	424	100	1400		
Independence Heights								715	150							
Indian Gap																
Indian Harbor	1200	1200														
Indian Lake	390	190														
Indian Oaks	100				681											
Indian Rock					400											
Indian Shores	800															
Indianola	300	300	100													
Industry			185	500	500	660	518	518	485	321	485	931	1900	1150	250	
Inez	1371	900	300	400	152	210	210	210	93	93						
Ingersoll											215					
Ingleside	5696	5436	3763	3022	1424	1180	1000	178	36							
Ingram	1408	1921	900	800	300	300	200	104	97	97						
Inwood Place	500	840														
Iola	300	300	300	451	318	318	318	318	121	219	109	100				
Iowa Colony	675	585	100	150	90			60								
Iowa Park	6072	6184	5796	3295	2110	1980	2009	2041	603	842	424					
Ira	350	350	350	250	118	150	150	217	150							
Iraan	1322	1358	996	1255	1196	1603	1458									

POPULATON HISTORY OF TEXAS CITIES AND TOWNS 1840-1990

COMMUNITY	1990	1980	1970	1960	1950	1940	1930	1920	1910	1900	1890	1880	1870	1860	1850	1840
Iredell	339	407	316	366	394	483	377	780	571	415	251	171	75			
Ireland	135	135		65	135	385	357	251				174				
Irene	135	135	250	200	400	294	267	264	400	132						
Irving	155037	109943	97260	45985	2621	1089	731	357	350							
Italy	1699	1306	1309	1183	1185	1224	1230	1350	1149	1061	370					
Itasca	1523	1600	1483	1383	1718	1759	1665	1599	1356	1277	548	185				
Ivanhoe									216	216						
Jacinto City	9343	8953	9563	9547	6856											
Jacksboro	3350	4000	3554	3816	2951	2368	1837	1373	1480	1311	751	387	150			
Jacksonville	12765	12264	9734	9590	8607	7213	6748	3723	2875	1568	970	349	300			
Jamaica Beach	624	365	200													
Jarrell	700	600	400	430	500	350	250	215								
Jasper	6959	6959	6251	4889	4403	3497	3393	2019	473	472	473	377	360		150	
Jayton	608	638	703	649	635	770	623	750								
Jean	100	100	150	125	150	300	310	83								
Jeddo					150	75		57		595	559					
Jefferson	2199	2643	2866	3082	3164	2797	2329	2549	2515	2850	3072	3260	4190	988	750	150
Jermyn	100	90		230	250	213	213	213								
Jersey Village	4826	4084	765	493												
Jewell										88	118	150				
Jewett	668	597	447	445	598	515	516	460	586	433	363	227	200			
Joaquin	805	917	819	528	579	487	407	300	400	148						
Johnson City	932	872	767	611	648	378	400	400	344	344	259	200				
Johntown	180	200	100	200	500	500	157	2136								
Joinerville	300	350	250	200	360	300										
Jolly	201	174	100	100	96	63	96	50	42	59						
Jollyville	800	500	200	300	300											
Jonah									210	210						
Jones Creek	2160	2634	1763	950												
Jonesboro	125	200	125	200	500	415	462	378	378	278	207	300				250
Jonestown	1250	850	100													
Jonesville	200	150	150	150	250	150	88	100	239	239	239	200				
Josephine	503	416	296	296	400	400	360	519	274	207						
Joshua	3828	1470	924	764	750	891	810	810	482	482	285					
Josserand					125	120	300	317	538	331	461					
Jourdanton	3220	2743	1841	1504	1481	950	767	682	500							
Judson	200	900	900	800	250				89	89						
Juliff	100	60		200	400				63	63						
Junction	2654	2593	2654	2441	2471	2086	1415	1269	536	594	449	175				
Justiceburg							200									

POPULATON HISTORY OF TEXAS CITIES AND TOWNS 1840-1990

COMMUNITY	1840	1850	1860	1870	1880	1890	1900	1910	1920	1930	1940	1950	1960	1970	1980	1990
Justin							476	476	493	450	542	496	622	741	920	1234
Kamay									163	163	800	600	500	500	250	250
Kanawha										275						
Karnack							72	72	113	250	250	450	400	600	600	600
Karnes City							635	635	787	1141	1571	2588	2693	2926	3296	2916
Katy							119	350	228	375	440	849	1569	2923	5660	8005
Kaufman				250	490	1282	2378	1959	2501	2279	2654	2714	3087	4012	4658	5238
Keenan							172	172	515	150	150	150	100	100	90	100
Keene							500	500	420	500	800	700	1532	2440	3013	3944
Keller						79	257	294	259	400	330	782	827	1474	4156	13683
Kellyville						279	297	150	163	163	250	60			75	90
Kelsey										200	200	400	140	100	50	
Kellys							496	590	1054	399	880	1091	1056			
Kemah								150	216	250	500	850	950	1144	1304	1094
Kemp					300	335	1139	925	1213	990	1000	881	816	999	1035	1184
Kemp City												500				
Kemp Newby												1324				
Kempner							353	150	169	200	200	150	250	250	280	300
Kendleton							116	116	68	168	150	600	440	450	606	496
Kenedy							437	1147	2015	2610	2891	4234	4301	4156	4356	3763
Kenefick													100	205	763	435
Kennard								425	600	610	664	450	300	448	424	341
Kennedale							172	216	312	350	700	1046	1521	3076	2594	4096
Kenneth								600								
Kenney							202	202	202	202	160	160	100	190	190	200
Kentuckytown				200	106	112	112	112	112	112						
Kerens					100	503	735	945	1343	1435	1287	1198	1123	1446	1582	1702
Kermit								100		300	2584	6912	10465	7884	8015	6875
Kerrville				226	156	1044	1423	1843	2353	4506	5572	7691	8901	12672	15276	17384
Kickapoo				50		82	82		510	510	510	510				
Kildare					500	366	352	214	261	261	500	550	400	250	250	270
Kilgore				50	82	248	404	700	725	850	6708	9638	10092	9495	10968	11066
Killeen					100	285	780	1265	1298	1260	1263	7045	23377	35507	46296	63535
Kimball					219	312	193	321	221							
Kings Point																750
Kingsbury					100	185	346	346	350	300	380	300	200	200	200	400
Kingsland							194	194	194	200	165	150	375	950	2241	2725
Kingston					150	338	383	278	337	337	305	155	150	150	100	125
Kingsville (Bowie)					300											
Kingsville (Kleburg)								3450	4770	6815	7782	16898	25297	28915	28808	25276

POPULATON HISTORY OF TEXAS CITIES AND TOWNS 1840-1990

COMMUNITY	1990	1980	1970	1960	1950	1940	1930	1920	1910	1900	1890	1880	1870	1860	1850	1840
Kingwood	37397	2100	1800	2530	600	149	121	121	100							
Kirby	8326	6385	3238	630	964	1088	1184	1165	1000	336						
Kirbyville	1871	1972	1869	1660	1150											
Kirk									172	172						
Kirkland	50	75	250	150	350	668	524	600	425							
Kirvin	107	107	65	31	152	231	238	288	160	112						
Kleberg						385	115	115	100							
Klein	12000	9000	4768	3572												
Klomatia								1010								
Klondyke	175	150	150	220	300	500	350	418	220	154						
Knickerbocker	150	150	100	150	200	215	215	150	172	172						
Knippa	400	400	280	350	345	250	200									
Knolwood	205	228														
Knox City	1440	1546	1536	1805	1489	1127	906	698	925							
Kopperl	250	230	230	230	235	350	350	329	329	267	229					
Kosciuko	50	80			500											
Kosse	505	484	471	354	566	881	805	872	764	717	647	476	300			
Kountz	2056	2716	2173	1768	1651	1248	1500	342	342	613	295	50				
Kress	739	783	578	438	350	232	325	200	225			180	150			
Krohne						115										
Krugerville	735	469	180													
Krum	1542	917	454	517	525	475	475	600	550	231						
Kyle	2225	2093	1629	1023	888	874	606	744	742	1183	779					
La Blanca	300	450	250													
La Casita	300	300														
La Coste	1021	862	768	650	720	521	521	521	250	79						
La Feria	4360	3495	2642	3047	2952	1644	1594	236	80							
La Grange	3951	3768	3092	3623	2738	2531	2354	1669	1850	2392	1626	1325	1165			400
La Grulla			1194	900		800	800									
La Hacienda Heights	900															
La Joya	2604	2018	1217	500	300	175										
La Marque	14120	15372	16131	13969	7359	740	740	210	200	107						
La Paloma	550	150	150		300	500	500									
La Porte	27910	14062	7149	4512	4429	3072	1280	889	678	537						
La Pryor	1343	1257	900	900	968	702	702	415	60							
La Puerta	350	100														
La Vernia	639	632	425	700	600	522	480	500	342	316	298	300	150			
La Villa	1388	1442	1255	1261	848	300	200									
La Ward	162	218	247	175	150											
Labelle					350											

POPULATON HISTORY OF TEXAS CITIES AND TOWNS 1840-1990

COMMUNITY	1990	1980	1970	1960	1950	1940	1930	1920	1910	1900	1890	1880	1870	1860	1850	1840
Lackland AFB	9352	14459	19141													
Lacy/Lakeview	3617	2752	2558	2272	150	100	100									
Ladonia	658	761	757	890	1104	1279	1199	1713	1293	1409	765	223	516			
Lafayette	100	80			250	245	263	263	225	173	107					
Lagarto					100	110	184	184	178	178	266	199	70			
Lago Vista	2199	500	100													
Laguna Heights	1671	600	600	550												
Laguna Park	350	600	600	175												
Laguna Vista	1166	632	287	141												
Laird Hill	800	800	700	842	770	550										
Lajitas	90						417	417								
Lake Barbara	300		605	477												
Lake Bonanza	300	285														
Lake Bridgeport	322	271	118													
Lake Brownwood	1403	950	900													
Lake Cherokee	300	300														
Lake City	465	431	165													
Lake Conroe Forrest	400	400														
Lake Dallas	3656	3177	1431	800	500	537	517									
Lake Gardens	1200															
Lake Jackson	22776	19102	13376	9651	2897											
Lake June	500	500	300		1517											
Lake Kiowa	600	500														
Lake Meredith	600	80														
Lake Placid	300	350														
Lake Ransom Canyon	750	561	110													
Lake Shore Gardens	300	400														
Lake Tanglewood	637	485														
Lake Victor									200							
Lake Wildwood	435	300														
Lake Worth	4591	4394	4958	3833	2351											
Lakehills	2147	1500														
Lakeport	710	835	411													
Lakeside (San Patricio)	292	276														
Lakeside (Tarrant)	816	957	988	651												
Lakeside City	865	515	187													
Lakeside Heights	250	500	350													
Lakeside Village	600	220	300													
Lakeview (Dallas)		500	500	500	500											
Lakeview (Hall)	202	244	214	219	287	330	375	311	120							

POPULATON HISTORY OF TEXAS CITIES AND TOWNS 1840-1990

COMMUNITY	1990	1980	1970	1960	1950	1940	1930	1920	1910	1900	1890	1880	1870	1860	1850	1840
Lakeview (Jefferson)	500															
Lakeview (McLennan)		500														
Lakeview (Orange)	4044	790	212													
Lakeway				1882												
Lakewood (Harris)			3567	3849	3091	852	350									
Lakewood (Montgomery)	350	300														
Lakewood Village	169	165														
Lamar	150	150	150	150	200	100			118		118	129				
Lamasco			100				317	317	179	179						
Lamesa	10809	11790	11559	12438	10704	6038	3528	1188	500							
Lamkin	75			125	200	276	189	189	97	97	97					
Lampasas	6382	6165	5922	5051	4869	3426	2709	2107	2119	2107	2408	653	420			
Lamplight Village	950	950														
Lanark												200	250			
Lancaster	22117	14807	10522	7531	2632	1151	1131	1190	1115	1045	741	497				
Lane City	400	400	350	530	200	150	150	47	150							
Laneville	250	200	375	430	600	500	320	240	171	171						
Langtry	30	50		93	125	325	325	138	68	68						
Lanier											68	500				
Laredo	122899	91449	69024	60678	51910	39274	32618	22710	14855	13429	11319	3521	2046	1256	500	
Larissa	150				150	150		163	138	138	159	173				
Larue		110	100	200	150	300	300	145	100				200			
Las Milpas	600	450	400	400	400	400	400									
Lasara	500	500	100	100	175	175	263	268	100	103	103	150				
Lassater																
Latexo	289	312	300	400	500	440	225	144	60							
Laughlin AFB	2556	2994	3458													
Laurel										527						
Laurelia									500							
Lavon	303	185	213	160	200	222	300	315	178	178						
Lawn	358	390	344	310	311	306	339			64						
Lawndale											264					
Lawrence			98	100	130	159	159	159	176	176	176	300	75			
Lazbuddie	450	1000	352	300	300	200	60									
Leachville	150	200				112						200				
League City	30159	16578	10818	2622	1341	880	781	800	525							
Leakey	399	468	393	587	550	400	400	326	318	318	318					
Leander	3398	2179	300	350	300	225	240	283	283	482	329	100				
Leary	395	253	352	300	300	200	57	57								
Lebanon						112	100	267	272	274	218	100	50			

POPULATION HISTORY OF TEXAS CITIES AND TOWNS 1840-1990

COMMUNITY	1990	1980	1970	1960	1950	1940	1930	1920	1910	1900	1890	1880	1870	1860	1850	1840
Ledbetter	100	100	130	140	186	200	200	300	310	336	310	147	75			
Ledbetter Hills			500													
Leesburg	150	200		150	150	300	325	325	318	318	238	224	100			
Leesville	150	175	175		250	340	250	400	246	248	345	200	150			
Lefors	656	829	816	864	577	809	952									
Leggett	350	300	300	300	400	400	250	300	300	185	185					
Legion				1691	800	200	100									
Lelia Lake	150	160		150	105	342	360	125								
Leming	700	500	500	600	600	250	100	82								
Leon Springs					100	100	57	72	158	178	158	130				
Leon Valley	9581	8951	2487	536												
Leona	178	165	96	250	500	500	218	138	150	79	58	94	50			
Leonard	1744	1421	1423	1117	1211	1331	1131	1383	990	750	392	100				
Leroy	292	253	215	220	193	193	126	150	250							
Levelland	13986	13809	11445	10153	8264	3091	1661	35								
Lewisville	46521	24273	9264	3956	1516	873	853	815	900	898	498	466				
Lexington	953	1065	719	711	603	531	519	600	525	460	215	179	157			
Lexington Woods	650	700														
Liberty	7733	7945	5591	6127	4163	3087	2187	1117	980	865	512	497	458	584		150
Liberty City	1607	1121	250	150												
Liberty Hill	750	700	500	600	750	550	604	500	500	637	309	153	47			
Lillian	250	200	150		150	275	275	315	150							
Lincoln									148							
Lincoln Park	287	39	100													
Lindale	2428	2180	1631	1285	1015	820	743	701	658	489	237	100				
Linden	2375	2443	2264	1832	1744	1168	718	702	675	316	444	304	200			
Lindsay	610	581	435	236	340	154	140	140	151	151						
Lingleville	100	100	100	100	100	264	240	242	242	212						
Linn	30	100	200	155					84	84	84					
Linwood										176						
Lipan	354	435	333	309	475	350	375	300	550	305	286	100				
Lipantitlan																150
Lipscomb	40	125	100	100	125	200	250	261	110	110	68					
Lisbon							300	168	68	68						
Lissie	200	200	100	150	150	100	100	60	60							
Littig							264		168	168						
Little Cypruss	600		600	800												
Little Elm	1255	926	363		150	122	107	120	194	194	125	116				
Little Mexico	600	600														
Little River/Academy	1155	1155	300	350	250	200	200	236	123	123						

POPULATON HISTORY OF TEXAS CITIES AND TOWNS 1840-1990

COMMUNITY	1840	1850	1860	1870	1880	1890	1900	1910	1920	1930	1940	1950	1960	1970	1980	1990
Littlefield										3218	3817	6540	7236	6738	7409	6489
Live Oak														2779	8183	10023
Liverpool									100			100	325	319	602	396
Livingston				200	135	986	973	1024	928	1165	1851	2865	3398	3965	4928	5019
Llano			77	188	213	812	879	1687	1645	2124	2658	2954	2656	2608	3071	2962
Locke Hill					300						125	250				
Lockett					100											
Lockhart			423	560	718	1233	2306	2945	3731	4367	5018	5573	6084	6489	7953	9205
Lockney							307	750	1118	1466	1231	1692	2141	2094	2334	2207
Lodi					45	106	133	200	162	250	150	250	150	150	180	200
Lodwick							48	80	85			120				
Loeb										200	200	100	200	600	600	600
Log Cabin															148	487
Lohn									83	360	250	150			150	150
Lolita									215	215	330	300	450	700	700	700
Lomax												200	439	894	2991	625
Lometa							507	550	995	865	915	951	817	633	666	
London				75			86	160	178	200	200	175	200	200	200	150
Lone Oak					79	443	496	756	1017	720	735	571	495	518	467	521
Lone Star							158	236	250		275	900	1513	1760	2036	1615
Long Branch					200	53	53	180	318	250	315	250				
Long Point						146	146	146		250	200	200				
Longhorn														300		
Longview				500	1525	2034	3591	5155	5713	5036	13758	24502	40050	45547	62762	70311
Longview Heights													130	450	450	500
Lonoke Place															830	900
Loop											80	500	385	200	450	500
Lopeno									518	518	500		400	150	200	250
Lopezville															300	800
Loraine								633	610	750	700	1045	837	700	929	731
Lorena					50		266	675	342	400	376	460	277	406	619	1158
Lorenzo									69	739	616	939	1188	1206	1394	1208
Los Ebanos									1028	500	500	700	750	300	400	400
Los Fresnos										500	500	1113	1289	1297	2173	2473
Los Indios									162	162	200	500	500	400	400	800
Los Saenz									50	600	700	500				83
Los Ybanez															300	
Lott						416	614	1021	1093	921	1021	956	924	799	865	775
Louise					200		279	500	300	327	340	800	850	900	900	950
Lovelady				100			432	525	625	502	542	541	466	388	509	587

COMMUNITY	1990	1980	1970	1960	1950	1940	1930	1920	1910	1900	1890	1880	1870	1860	1850	1840
Loving	250	250	250	200	200	200	200	199	225							
Lowry Crossing	865	443	285													
Loyal Valley	500	400	350	350	70	100			194	194	119	120				
Lozano					600											
Lubbock	186206	173979	149101	128691	71747	31853	20520	4051	1938	117						
Lucas	2205	1371	540	203	140	145	158	132	132	132						
Luckenbach							175	175	200	492	345					
Lueders	365	420	511	624	708	715	328	200	425							
Luella	559	371	195				50	63				150				
Lufkin	30206	28562	23049	17641	15135	9567	7311	4878	2749	1527	529					
Luling	4661	5039	4719	4412	4297	4437	5970	1502	1404	1349	1792	1114	300			
Lull	700	400	400													
Lumberton	6640	2480	1054													
Luna									146	146						
Lusk						100	300		50							
Lyford	1674	1618	1425	1554	1473	891	795	200	75							
Lyle		350														
Lynchburg	700	490	400		115	100	100	84	178	178	178	152	79			
Lynch's Creek												255				
Lyons	400	360	400	500	525	500	359	218	459	459						
Lyra		50	250	1227	1194	1000	1000	1227	1194	132						
Lytle	2255	1920	1298	798	650	550	423	525	212	131						
Lytton Springs							300		200							
Mabank	1739	1443	1239	944	896	988	963	1512	750	412						
McAdoo	150	100	150	100	108	250	360									
McAllen	84021	66281	37636	32728	20067	11877	9074	5331	500							
McCamey	2493	2436	2647	3375	3121	2595	3446									
McCaulley	200	180	100	180	500	228	350	715								
McCulloch										216						
McDade	475	400	400	400	500	495	400	462	418	367	310	140				
McFaddin	200	200		300	600	300	89									
McGregor	4683	4513	4365	4642	2669	2062	2041	2081	1864	1435	774	400				
McKinney	21283	16256	15193	13763	10560	8555	7307	6677	4714	4342	2489	1479	503	315	192	
McLairnsboro												200				
McLean	849	1160	1183	1330	1439	1489	1521	741	633							
McLendon-Chisholm	646									122						
McLeod	400	403	150	200	350	250										
McNair	1800	850	2039	1880	1313											
McNeil		400							132	132						
McQueeney	2063	1332	900	900	750	400	400	512	40							

POPULATON HISTORY OF TEXAS CITIES AND TOWNS 1840-1990

COMMUNITY	1840	1850	1860	1870	1880	1890	1900	1910	1920	1930	1940	1950	1960	1970	1980	1990
Macdona							123	123	123	123	125	300	300	300	200	300
Machovec												735				
Mackay										300						
Madero													400	400	400	600
Madisonville		118		98	250	418	672	833	1079	1294	2095	2393	2324	2881	3660	3569
Madras								54	276	276						
Magnolia							117	175	400	500	440	400	500	315	867	940
Magnolia Bend															300	600
Magnolia Gardens														200	1100	700
Magnolia Park									4080							
Magnolia Springs					55	77	77		77		500	400	400	200	200	200
Mahl								80				400				
Mahon							141	141								
Malakoff					100	239	305	376	310	1020	2384	1286	1657	2045	2082	2038
Malone								550	488	481	429	352	240	305	315	306
Malta							243	243		150						
Manchaca						118	118	118	114	114	125	200	200	200	950	1500
Manchester							142	142	155	500	156	350			75	100
Mangum								300								
Manning								100	715	715	715	715	715			
Manor				75	120	405	572	900	827	654	688	820	766	940	1044	1041
Mansfield				200	249	418	694	627	719	635	774	964	1375	3658	8102	15607
Mantua				86												
Manvel							142	113	208	208	167	350	540	106	3549	3733
Maple Springs				200												
Maragret										264	200	100				
Marathon							218	300	826	826	831	782	747	750	750	800
Marble Falls						587	875	1061	639	865	1021	2044	2161	2209	3252	4007
Marfa					40	316	494	600	3553	3909	3805	3603	2799	2647	2466	2424
Margaret								200	264	220	200	100				
Marienfeld						208	56									
Marietta							53	120	318	250	350	400	350	177	169	161
Marine							252									
Marion					99	372	321	525	540	400	373	439	557	655	674	984
Markham								250	518	400	440	400	800	850	1554	1206
Marlin				602	1350	2058	3092	3878	4310	5338	6542	7099	6918	6351	7099	6386
Marnells									964							
Marquez				75	200	482	392	482	700	518	381	287	194	185	231	270
Marshall		1189		1920	5624	7207	7855	11452	14271	16203	18410	22327	23846	22937	24921	23682
Marshall Cooks															419	315

POPULATON HISTORY OF TEXAS CITIES AND TOWNS 1840-1990

COMMUNITY	1990	1980	1970	1960	1950	1940	1930	1920	1910	1900	1890	1880	1870	1860	1850	1840
Marshall Meadows	900	900														
Mart	2004	2324	2183	2197	2269	2856	2853	3105	2939	227						
Martindale	904	500	500	500	550	550	517	517	350	497	95					
Martinsburgh												203				
Martinsville	150	100		175	250	115	350	56	46	46	46					
Maryneal									275							
Marysville					80	178	162	300	236	236	254	214	50			
Mason	2041	2153	1806	1910	2456	1250	1535	1200	1137	1000	1137	575	296			
Massey									163	163						
Masterson	35	35	300	500	500											
Matador	790	1052	1091	1217	1335	1376	1302	692	600	158						
Matagorda	850	850	700	750	700	1100	805	1000	482	482	399	438	386		750	450
Matagorda Beach		350														
Mathis	5423	5667	5351	6075	4050	1950	915	500	250	82						
Matthews									136	136						
Maud	1049	1059	1107	951	713	550	430	378	375	74						
Mauriceville	800	800	600	750	500	400	400	68								
Maxville		300	300													
Maxwell	325	300	300	300	450	275	395	421	225	113						
May	300	300	300	400	700	454	413		400	324						
Maydell	250	250	250	350	350	500	400	79								
Mayhill	350	300	300	100												
Maypearl	781	626	462	359	373	377	410	417	500	114	124	153	150			
Maysfield	130	100	120	200	159	136	159	159	138							
Meadow	547	571	491	484	490	408	324	72								
Meadow Lakes	514	134														
Meadowood Acres	500	800														
Meadows	4606	4321														
Medicine Mound		50		100	300	210	210	210	150							
Medina	350	400	400	650	300	278	300	264	117	117						
Megargel	244	381	373	417	347	531	813	521	275	236						
Melissa	557	604	341	405	500	412	350	260	350	268	207	57	50			
Mellwood Place	900	670														
Melody Hills			450													
Melrose	1600	1500		150		170		216	216	216	316	400	50			
Melvin	184	202	290	401	696	495	262	300	80							
Memphis	2465	3352	3227	3332	3810	3869	4257	2839	1936	880	800					
Menard	1606	1697	1740	1914	2685	2375	1969	1164	450	321	185	67				
Mentone	70	50	50	226	145	118	100									
Mercedes	12694	11851	9355	10943	10081	7624	6608	3414	1209							

POPULATON HISTORY OF TEXAS CITIES AND TOWNS 1840-1990

COMMUNITY	1990	1980	1970	1960	1950	1940	1930	1920	1910	1900	1890	1880	1870	1860	1850	1840
Mercury				60	100	111	101	450	375							
Meridian	1390	1330	1162	393	1146	1016	759	1024	718	923	1037	395	150			
Merit	150	150	150	340	340	496	340	340	322	263	189					
Merkel	2469	2493	2163	2312	2338	2005	1848	1810	2008	857	353					
Mertens	104	133	109	104	210	251	338	342	400	375						
Mertzon	778	687	513	584	768	869	684	400								
Mesquite	101484	67053	55131	27526	1696	1045	729	674	687	406	135	150				
Mexia	6933	7094	5943	6121	6627	6410	6579	3482	2694	2393	1674	1298	600			
Meyersville	150	100	100			166	256	256	244	157	244	175	250			
Miami	675	813	611	656	646	713	953	935	400	286						
Mico	175	220	100	250	250	150	60									
Midkiff	150	100			500											
Midland	89443	70525	59463	62625	21713	9352	5484	1795	2192	1453	722	100				
Midlothian	5141	3219	2322	1521	1177	1027	1168	1298	868	832	297	100				
Midway	274	300	300	150	500	530	530	500	217	216	56	100	250			
Mikeska	125			60	60	110	518	518								
Milam		90			100	114	134	134	134	134	202	158				
Milano	408	468	500	600	500	550	300	500	481	481	416	100				
Milburn					100	100	100	309	283	283						
Mildred	176	282								61						
Miles	793	720	631	626	739	814	972	853	1302	56						
Milford	711	681	664	590	690	767	747	940	766	653	353	164	500			
Miller Grove	100	100		100	250	600	600	320	112	112						
Millers Cove	75	61														
Millersview							263		100							
Millett	25	25	150	150	300	330	300	515	150							
Millican	250	250	165	200	150	332	300	613	613	372	613	500	200			
Mills					2233											
Millsap	485	439	300	325	815	815	815	800	475	386						
Millwood								31		192	87	56	75			
Milton	175					200	200	164		67						
Minden		150	125	125	250	500	250	510	227	206	142					
Mineola	4321	4346	3926	3810	3626	3223	3304	2299	1706	1725	1333	1175	250			
Minera									750	1100						
Mineral City						201	400	195	183	183	149	50				
Mineral Heights					552											
Mineral Wells	14870	14468	18411	11053	7801	6303	5986	7890	3950	2048	577	250				
Mingus	215	212	273	253	310	570	1032	1032	500	63						
Mirando City	400	450	500	500	800	1342	981									
Mission	28653	22589	13043	14081	10765	5982	5120	3847	1000							

POPULATON HISTORY OF TEXAS CITIES AND TOWNS 1840-1990

COMMUNITY	1990	1980	1970	1960	1950	1940	1930	1920	1910	1900	1890	1880	1870	1860	1850	1840
Missouri City	36176	24533	4136	604	300	400	200	144	144	144						
Mobeetie	154	291	207	500	500	660	667	200	250	159	508	200				
Moffat	275	250		200	200	161	221	221	147	112	147	124				
Monahans	8101	8397	8333	8567	6311	3944	816	218	150	89		100				
Monkstown	100	125		150	150	189	150	172	172	218						
Monroe City	200	180	150	450	450	625	300									
Mont Belvieu	1323	1730	1144	1350	800	800	1800	263	100							
Montague	350	1253	1265	420	550	312	300	317	284	579	795	328	100			
Montalba	200	200	100	250	100	150	300	125	200	114						
Monte Alto	1319	1319	900	700	100	100										
Montgomery	356	258	216	850	850	550	428	428	672	586	921	414	400			
Montgomery Gardens	550	550	700													
Montopolis					600				142	142						
Moody	1329	1385	1286	1074	1084	931	1014	1106	983	848	432	250				
Moore	400	330	420	600	500	385	575	575	325	173						
Moore Station	256	335	150	300	400	100										
Mooreville		50			300	165	182	182	182	226	110					
Moran	285	344	335	392	610	710	907	1055	400	231						
Morgan	451	485	415	381	424	503	509	672	831	766	426					
Morgan Hill							261		225	143		347				
Morgan's Point	341	428	593	560	656											
Morgan's Point Resort	1766	1082	214													
Morse	200	280	200	150	103	100										
Morton	2597	2674	2738	2731	2274	1137	725									
Morton Valley			100		400	100										
Moscow	300	300	300	225	350	220	263	263	263	372	563	288	250			
Mosheim							265		171	171						
Moss Bluff	500	500		100	55		55		211	211	452	400				
Moulton	923	1009	968	646	692	643	850	762	900	733	231	109				
Mound	150	290	145	130	140	100	53									
Mount Calm	303	393	363	379	456	525	603	626	575	529	276	175	100			
Mount Enterprise	501	485	425	550	504	622	625	655	650	172	118	100	50			
Mount Houston	1450	2300	2000	2500												
Mount Pleasant	12291	11003	9459	8027	6342	4528	3541	4099	3157	1096	963	452	275	227		
Mount Selman	300	300	150	250	250	330	200	123	168	206						
Mount Sylvian	50	30	125		100	199	181	181	181	181	277	75				
Mount Vernon	2219	2025	1806	1338	1433	1443	1222	1212	1200	972	589	311	223			
Mountain City	377	58										100	100		100	
Mountain Peak										154	154					
Mountain Valley	500	500	150													

COMMUNITY	1990	1980	1970	1960	1950	1940	1930	1920	1910	1900	1890	1880	1870	1860	1850	1840
Muenster	2219	1408	1411	1190	896	599	459	450	600	467						
Muldoon	200	200	135	135	300	600	600	215	160	84						
Muleshoe	4571	4842	4525	3871	2477	1327	779	45								
Mullin	194	213	203	219	326	404	459	558	475	261	58	114				
Mumford	200	200	150	300	300	165	215	215	193	141						
Munday	1600	1738	1726	1978	2280	1545	1318	998	956	59						
Murchison	510	513	432	400	500	408	407	517	120	87						
Murphy	1547	1150	261	135	150	118	200	134	92	128		200				
Murvaul									141	141		200				
Mustang	35	12			200	200	150	93	93	93						
Mustang Ridge	576															
Myra	200	200	200	190	250	412	400	417	325	204						
Myrtle Springs	300	300	250	300	350	385	300	163	214	328						
Nacodoches	30872	27149	22544	12674	12327	7538	5687	3546	3369	1827	1138	333	400	485	468	500
Nada	170	150	300	250	500	250	158	158	149	149						
Naples	1508	1908	1726	1692	1346	821	843	887	1178	906						
Naruna												269				
Nash (Bowie)	2162	2022	1961	1124	500	532	500	481	487	217	212					
Nash (Ellis)									212							
Nashland										174						
Nashville																300
Nassau Bay	4320	4526	4462													
Natalia	1216	1264	1296	1154	1000	450	278	515								
Navarro	193	170		100	135	100	100	50								
Navasota	6296	5971	5111	4937	5188	6138	5128	5060	3284	3857	2997	1611	1509			
Nazareth	293	299	250	200	100	106	78	78								
Nechesville	450	400	300	350	350	440	325	325	325	261	265	150	150			
Nederland	16192	16855	16810	12036	3805	1650	1800	175	250	43						
Needville	2199	1417	1024	861	609	557	218	215	80							
Nelsonville	25	60			150	110	184	184	158	113	158	175	150			
Nesbitt	327	129	274		100	75		150	218	218	218					
Neuville	90	80			500	330	275	275								
Nevada	456	317	225	340	450	425	386	578	510	356	247					
New Baden							185		103	103						
New Berlin	188	253	161			114	190	190	175	78	78					
New Birmingham										271	668					
New Boston	5057	4628	4034	2773	2688	1111	949	869	950	762	382	100				
New Braunfels	27334	22402	17859	15631	12210	6976	6242	3590	3165	2097	1608	1938	2261	1740	1298	
New Caney	3000	2500	500	300	250											
New Chapel Hill	439	618	595			157	157	157	127	127						

POPULATION HISTORY OF TEXAS CITIES AND TOWNS 1840-1990

COMMUNITY	1840	1850	1860	1870	1880	1890	1900	1910	1920	1930	1940	1950	1960	1970	1980	1990
New Deal												500	400	404	637	521
New Fountain								100				75				
New Home				100	500	537	502			150	220	200	100	252	274	175
New Hope							106	214			110	150		244	331	523
New London									115	100	600	691	850	899	942	926
New Philadelphia					150	103									50	50
New Salem				100	86	289	206	175	321	321	321	321			319	521
New Summerfield											138	500	525	344	250	250
New Ulm				75	104	247	556	444	344	400	556	500	300	230	824	936
New Waverly					70	206	307	311	600	411	665	755	426	496		
New Willard								300	518	518	770	625	625		50	70
Newark							182	300	359	300	375	285	392	407	466	651
Newcastle								550	1452	1157	1044	743	617	624	688	505
Newgulf										500	1744	1803	1419	900	940	950
Newlin							61	125	78	211	260	160	160			
Newport (Clay)					50	76	176	220	280	280	308	450	100	100	100	50
Newport (Harris)									500	150					400	600
Newsome								160		300			265			
Newton				150	68	85	150	575	800	1000	886	929	1233	1529	1620	1885
Neylandville							107	107	68	70	200	200	200	186	168	94
Nickleberry												300				
Niederwald															164	233
Nigton							67	67		300						
Niles									716							
Nixon								850	1124	1037	1835	1875	1751	1925	2008	1995
Nockenut						147	52					250				
Nocona					250	381	961	1338	1422	2352	2605	3022	3127	2871	2992	2870
Nolanville							117	138	133	157	146	157	300	902	1308	1834
Nome								100	300	310	440	468	450	521	550	448
Noonday							56	100	113			150			385	466
Nordheim							122	400	443	400	411	477	407	369	369	344
Norfolk							78	78	48	50	750					
Normangee								675	662	869	535	657	718	657	636	689
Normanna							85	175		225						
North Abilene												830	277	404	750	
North Baytown																176
North Cleveland															259	
North Galveston							583									
North Gate															850	
North Houston														2700	8700	12800

POPULATON HISTORY OF TEXAS CITIES AND TOWNS 1840-1990

COMMUNITY	1990	1980	1970	1960	1950	1940	1930	1920	1910	1900	1890	1880	1870	1860	1850	1840
North Houston Heights	1700															
North Oaks	800	1500	1000													
North Pleasanton				1018	832	673	369	364								
North Richland Hills	45895	30592	16514	8662												
North Rusk						2500	1800									
North San Pedro	953	2553	2229													
North Texarkana					1328	500	500	500								
North Uvalde	550	500	500		500	442	413	413	250							
North Zulch	950	950		400	550											
Northampton																
Northcliff	1200															
Northcrest	1725	1944	1669	625	150	265	400									
Northfield	30	60		108												
Northlake	250	143														
Northline Terrace	2700	3200	1000													
Northpark					1239											
Northview Hills		680														
Northwest Park	1800															
Northwood		630														
Norton									150							
Notrees	65	120	220	300	200	200	200	200	275							
Novice	183	201	191	227	252			47	90	68						
Nubia					50	50		150								
Nuecestown										177	158	145				
Nursery	300	250	150	400	215	476	476	476	177							
Oak Cliff										3630	2470					
Oak Crest	800															
Oak Flat	200				375					72						
Oak Forest		950														
Oak Grove	557	319	100	125	200		219	219	100	62	72	50				
Oak Island					3930											
Oak Knoll		200														
Oak Leaf	984															
Oak North	500															
Oak Point	645	387	75													
Oak Ridge (Cooke)	180	82	135													
Oak Ridge (Kaufman)	268	247	200				200									
Oak Ridge North	2454	2504	595													
Oak Trail Shores	1750	1800														
Oak Valley	388	192														

POPULATON HISTORY OF TEXAS CITIES AND TOWNS 1840-1990

COMMUNITY	1990	1980	1970	1960	1950	1940	1930	1920	1910	1900	1890	1880	1870	1860	1850	1840
Oakalla	800	800	150	100	500	400	94									
Oakhill	219		150	328	300	80		150	200	115						
Oakhurst	150	150	150		300	300	500	250		200						
Oakland	150	150	150	160	225	224	225	250	264	264	250	167	150			
Oakland Estates			900	650												
Oaks North	500															
Oakview	350	350														
Oakville	75	60	150	400	350	474	400	450	431	392	329	235	150			
Oakwilde	1350	1680														
Oakwood	527	606	547	716	759	1086	888	1100	906	407	231	96				
O'Brien	152	212	258	287	300	330	300	300	150							
Ochiltree								600	450							
Odell	130	131	131	131	238	301	424	317	250							
Odem	2366	2363	2130	2088	1680	1147	842									
Odessa	89699	90027	78380	80338	29495	9573	2407	1055	400	214						
O'Donnell	1102	1200	1148	1356	1473	1187	1026	150								
Oenaville		40			200	213	126	184	300	200	176	98	100			
Oglesby	452	470	440	414	450	396	390	360	283	320						
Oil City								505								
Oilfield							1000									
Olla	300		250													
Oilton		250	300	500	549	500	500									
Ojuelos	475	450							178	178						
Oklahoma					100	150	300									
Oklaunion	175	138	138	138	129	223	254	200	75	37						
Olcott					982											
Old Brazoria	300	900	900													
Old London		300	250													
Old Ocean	950	1000	950	950	755											
Old River-Winfree	1233	1058	228													
Old Round Rock			170	150	150	175	175				385	400				
Old Salem		500			500											
Olden	500	500	500	500	524	554	1026	1026	96							
Olive									383	433	383	300				
Olmito	1400	1500	675	600	500	125	300	62								
Olmos Park	2161	2069	2250	2457	2841	1822										
Olney	3519	4060	3624	3872	3765	3497	4138	1164	1095	58						
Olton	2116	2235	1782	1917	1201	782	687	184	150							
Omaha	833	960	898	854	735	623	506	492	750	377	219					
Omen	150	120	100	100	150	165	150	231	230	368	508					

POPULATON HISTORY OF TEXAS CITIES AND TOWNS 1840-1990

COMMUNITY	1840	1850	1860	1870	1880	1890	1900	1910	1920	1930	1940	1950	1960	1970	1980	1990
Onalaska								125	163	263	263	200	300	146	386	728
Oplin								140	96	96	100		100			
O'Quinn					200		88	88			125	125			50	60
Oran								200	210	210	210	200	100			
Orange				250	2000	3173	3835	5527	9212	7913	7472	21174	25605	24457	23628	19381
Orange Grove (Harris)															1680	2350
Orange Grove (Jim Wells)									219	219	906	935	1109	1075	1212	1175
Orangefield										930	1100	900	950	700	800	800
Orangeville				75			127	127								
Orchard								200	216	216	225	325	285	292	408	373
Ore City											552	400	619	830	1050	898
Orient												1788				
Osage							142	220	265	300						
Osceola					699	105	105	325	418	500	442	200	200			
Otay											150				75	80
Ottine							89	200	219	219	200	100	100	100	100	100
Otto								250	158	200	200	115				150
Ovalo								500	612	400	335	250	140	150	150	150
Overton				250	353	401	568	675	528	426	2313	2001	1950	2084	2430	2105
Ovilla				50	56	139	178	183	210	150	125	150	100	339	1067	2027
Owentown					1500	78	78	78								
Owlet Green													150	175	110	110
Oyster Creek												550	500	500	1473	912
Ozona							427	427	440	2128	2365	2885	3361	2864	3766	3181
Paducah							205	1350	1357	2802	2677	2952	2392	2052	2216	1788
Paige					337	513	439	467	400	450	513	350	235	200	200	200
Paint Rock					200	323	323	800	750	590	562	500	400	193	256	227
Palacios		212						1389	1335	1318	2288	2799	3676	3642	4667	4418
Palestine				750	2997	5838	8297	10482	11039	11445	12144	12503	13974	14525	15948	18042
Palito Blanco										400	200	250	200		50	100
Palm Valley														50	798	1199
Palmer				50	63	250	480	605	748	758	697	647	613	601	1187	1659
Palmetto								250	415							
Palmhurst														120	364	326
Palmview														172	683	1818
Palo Pinto				100	352	610	482	482	500	482	530	439	500	525	525	500
Paluxy					500	108	164	164	164	164	180	50				35
Pampa								300	987	10470	12895	16583	24664	21726	21396	19959
Pandora									261	261	220	250	250	125	120	80
Panhandle							468	521	638	2035	978	1406	1953	2141	2226	2353

POPULATON HISTORY OF TEXAS CITIES AND TOWNS 1840-1990

COMMUNITY	1840	1850	1860	1870	1880	1890	1900	1910	1920	1930	1940	1950	1960	1970	1980	1990
Panna Maria					49	105	105	105	105	150	100	500	500		90	90
Panola									63	63				170	200	200
Panorama City														301	1186	1556
Pantego												646	950	1779	2431	2371
Pantex												655	238			
Paradise					50	57	364	500	500	500	572	600	500	325	400	450
Paris			1003	2000	3980	8254	9358	11269	15040	15649	18678	21643	20977	23441	25498	24699
Park							487									
Park Place									430	430	352					
Park Springs							127	200	319	200		150			50	80
Parker							86	120	110	84	122	75		367	1098	1235
Parks					75					750	770	750				
Parkview Estates															600	600
Parkwood Estates															500	500
Pasadena								100	315	1647	3436	22483	58737	89957	112560	119363
Patroon							396	221	100	100	275	500	500		100	150
Patterson						218	188	179								
Pattison										200	116	100	100	260	318	327
Patton					50	105	120	105	105	200	275	275		667	1050	1155
Pattonville					58		105				200	275	250	200	220	260
Pawnee										250	300	300	175	200	300	300
Payne Springs								68	43	175	175	125		122	422	606
Peach Tree					200											
Peacock								175	263	263	216	165	130	131	131	60
Pear Ridge										1500	1198	2029	3470	3697		
Pearl							62	160	186	149	126	148				
Pearland							136	136		500	500	569	1497	6444	13248	18697
Pearsall					100	766	1543	1799	2161	2536	3164	4481	4957	5545	7383	6924
Peaster									310	220	150	100	125	200	150	200
Pecan Acres															1113	1587
Pecan Gap							383	625	625	625	409	319	278	291	250	245
Pecan Hill															342	564
Pecan Plantation																700
Pecos					50	393	639	1856	1445	3304	4855	8054	12728	12682	12855	12069
Peerless							84	84	264	200	264	200	300	175	600	
Pelham									319	150	319	150	100			
Pelican Bay															518	1271
Pella					300	206	206		216	216						
Pelly									2015	3452	3712					
Pendleton						87	210	210	260	225	210	300		155	155	125

POPULATON HISTORY OF TEXAS CITIES AND TOWNS 1840-1990

COMMUNITY	1990	1980	1970	1960	1950	1940	1930	1920	1910	1900	1890	1880	1870	1860	1850	1840
Penelope	210	235	212	226	243	240	211	428	275							
Peniel					800	405	367	571	467							
Penitas	1077	450	450	700	400	400	600	413				150				
Pennington	125	90		214	400	275	223	223	272	248	372	263	193			
Penwell	75	100	150	335	800	600										
Peoria	150	120	120			141	100	86	129	394	349		234			
Perezville	500	700														
Pernitas Point	174	207														
Perrin	250	400	400	400	500	475	475	220	214							
Perry	100	150	150	150	250	440	214	214	214	152	85	62				
Perryton	7607	7991	7810	7903	4417	2325	2824	2025								
Petersburg	1292	1633	1300	1400	777	496	548	200	200		206					
Petrolia	762	755	584	631	606	597	806	914	517							
Petronila	155	164														
Pettus	650	600	750	800	643	335	200	100	100	48						
Petty	135	135	175	250	250	275	315	315	375	239						
Pflugerville	4444	745	549	650	500	550	500	250	575	64	206					
Pharr	32921	21381	15829	14106	8690	4784	3225	1565								
Phelan							80	760	250							
Phelps	400	400	250	250	250	200	84	84	67	67	58					
Phillips	1729	1729	2515	3605	4105	3300	260									
Philrich				2067												
Phoenix													115			
Pickettsville												150				
Pickton	250	230	275	300	635	556	500	213	200	228						
Pierce	170	150	150	250	200	150	80		65	65						
Pike									172	172						
Pilot Grove	100	55			75	212	250	264	193	193	193	134	100			
Pilot Knob	400	400	200									200				
Pilot Point	2538	2211	1663	1254	1176	1122	1108	1499	1371	1168	1090	790	400			
Pin Oak												250				
Pine Crest	400	400														
Pine Forest	709	639	512		72	101	50		72	72						
Pine Hill	250	150		150	250	276	250	218	250	276	315	250				
Pine Island	571	350														
Pine Lake	200	400	100													
Pine Mills				200	200	200			222	222	158	600	150			
Pinehurst (Montgomery)	3284	1500														
Pinehurst (Orange)	2682	3055	2198	1703			70									
Pineland	882	1111	1127	1236	1454	1650	1619	220	100							

POPULATON HISTORY OF TEXAS CITIES AND TOWNS 1840-1990

COMMUNITY	1990	1980	1970	1960	1950	1940	1930	1920	1910	1900	1890	1880	1870	1860	1850	1840
Pinewood	1174															
Piney Point	3197	2958	2548													
Pioneer	50	50							73	73						
Pioneer Trails	300	300														
Pittsburg	4007	4245	3844	3796	3142	2916	2640	2540	1916	1783	1203	745	250			
Placedo	500	450	450	300	400	100	65	65								
Plains	1422	1457	1087	1195	550	224	125	150	125							
Plainview	21700	22187	19096	18735	14044	8263	8834	3989	2829	673						
Plano	128713	72331	17872	3695	2126	1582	1554	1715	1258	1304	842	556	155			
Plantersville	200	150	150	125	350	225	362	162	207	207	407	300	75			
Pleak	746	626	365													
Pleasant Valley (Dallas)	378	335	323													
Pleasant Valley (Potter)					1648											
Pleasanton	7678	6346	5407	3467	2913	2074	1154	1036	426	420	367					
Pledger	300	350	350	300	200	224	350	265	150	81						
Plum	300	300	300	125		100	68	68	182	182						
Plum Grove	480	455	411													
Poetry							57	310	234	234						
Point	645	468	419	350	350	338	300	219	325	158						
Point Blank	443	325	149		164	105	164	164	100	72						
Point Breeze																
Point Comfort	956	1125	1446	1453	100		750									
Point Enterprise			250	250												
Point Isabel									249	249			75			
Pollock	300	300	250		300	600	162	162	200							
Polytechnic								4338								
Ponder	432	297	208	200	250	275	201	184	250							
Ponta	100	100	125	125	128	300	400	128	175							
Pontotoc	75	120	100	195	101	215	210	300	196	247	274	50				
Poolville	250	200	450	500	305	278	515	515	300	221						
Port Aransas	2233	1968	1218	824	551	495	416	416								
Port Arthur	58724	61251	57371	66676	57530	46140	50902	22251	7663	900						
Port Bolivar	1600	1600	750	700	475	350	350	115	83	83						
Port Isabel/Isabel	4467	3769	3067	3575	2372	1440	1177			500	479					
Port Lavaca/Lavaca	10886	10911	10491	8864	5599	2069	1367	1213	1699	1192	365	200	768	526	315	
Port Mansfield	350	350	100	100												
Port Neches	12974	13944	10894	8696	5448	2487	2327	2450								
Port O'Connor	1031	1031	900	800	500	385	362	362	250							
Porter	7000	5000	1900	950	650	500										
Porter Heights	1448	1331														

POPULATON HISTORY OF TEXAS CITIES AND TOWNS 1840-1990

COMMUNITY	1990	1980	1970	1960	1950	1940	1930	1920	1910	1900	1890	1880	1870	1860	1850	1840
Porters Springs	100	100			50	112	200	69		69	350	300				
Portland	12224	12023	7302	2538	1292	600	300	515	182	182						
Porvenir						300	300									
Post	3768	3961	3854	4663	3141	2046	1668	1436	350	321						
Post Oak	75	55		56	150	112	112	200	212		76	100				
Post Oak Bend City	264	230														
Poteet	3206	3086	3013	2311	2487	2315	1231	1024								
Poth	1642	1461	1296	1119	1089	509	263	300	175							
Potosi									200							
Pottsboro	1177	895	748	640	383	342	358	454	313	400	286	105				
Pottsville	70	90	100	150	200	193	176	176	176	237	216					
Powderly	250	250	250	375	380	125	125	63	63	63						
Powell	101	111	121	250	450	550	521	240	248	248						
Poyner	237	272	200	150	250	220	250	119	100							
Praesel	150	180	225													
Praha	50	30				100	400	112	121	128						
Prairie Hill	200	150	175	300	300	554	262		152	248	152	200				
Prairie Lea	300	250	250	225	250	266	230	260	242	242	167	129	200			
Prairie Plains									262	216	208	100	642			
Prairie View	4004	3993	3796	2326	2200	200	140	150	100	100						
Prairieville					100	100	136	136	206	187	206	111	100			
Premont	2914	2984	3282	3094	2916	1080	1100	1025	125	281	286	147	439			
Presidio	3072	1723	950	1062	735	1320	1202	2045	250							
Preston Hollow	600	590	588		800	887										
Preston Shores																
Price	650	650	600	800	835	500	50									
Priddy	160	200	200	300	250	300	200									
Primera	2030	1380	902	1066	500	200										
Princeton	2321	3408	1105	594	540	564	459	500	450	183						
Pritchett	230	200	100	100	175	269	250	213	250	66						
Proctor	200	200	150	150	100	200	200	325	325	171	42					
Progresso	1951	1456	900	900	350	500	500		200							
Progresso Lakes	154	197														
Prosper	1018	675	501	344	243	271	287	343	500							
Provident City					320	320			175							
Pruitt																
Pulva	100											365				
Purdon		133	133	151	203	262	308	346	220	136						
Pursley					60				86	86	180	200				
Putnam	103	116	134	203	289	487	601	363	450	330	310					

POPULATON HISTORY OF TEXAS CITIES AND TOWNS 1840-1990

COMMUNITY	1990	1980	1970	1960	1950	1940	1930	1920	1910	1900	1890	1880	1870	1860	1850	1840
Pyote	348	382	166	420	201	201	1097	100	150							
Quail	60	85		100	200	250	162	162	150							
Quanah	3413	3890	3948	4564	4589	3761	4464	3691	3127	1651	1477					
Queen City	1748	1748	1227	1081	511	353	321	398	388	627	672	301				
Quemado	500	350	300	800	314	314	400	411	100							
Quigg Switch												450				
Quihi												106				
Quinlan	1360	1002	844	621	599	677	512	519	537	362						
Quintana	51	30	58	100	100	100	100	63	301	301	475	47				
Quitaque	513	696	601	586	647	763	945	580	63	63						
Quitman	1684	1893	1494	1237	927	880	1027	1027	465	303	307	151	320			
Raccoon Bend/Cochran		60	150		500	225										
Ragley								154	150							
Rainbow Hills		3780			70											
Ralls	2172	2422	1962	2229	1779	1512	1365	1042	300							
Ramona	300	250														
Ranchito	200	300	200													
Ranchland Acres																
Rancho																
Rancho Alegre	800	1908							291	291	318	150				
Rancho Viejo	885	208														
Randolph	250	300	300	300	275	242	400	421	221	157						
Randolph AFB			5329		2768	1320	1200									
Ranger	2803	3142	3094	3313	3989	4553	6208	16205	586	687	527	100				
Rangerville	280	80			100	200										
Rankin	1011	1216	1105	1214	1139	672	935	415	80	121						
Ratcliff	200	290	140	200	203	320	320	530	500							
Ravenna	150	186	186	145	185	248	254	412	280	290	237	300				
Rayburn					400				80							
Rayland	100			120	400	150	82	82								
Raymondville	8880	9493	7987	9385	9136	4050	2050	415	300							
Rayner											284					
Raywood	450	400	230	225	130	150	150	122	122	122						
Reagan	200	180	200	225	353	353	428	500	428	428	298	220	100			
Realitos	360	250	250	400	639	445	417	417	184	241						
Red Cut Heights					2563											
Red Oak	3124	1882	767	415	700	440	400	367	210	247	210	100	250			
Red Rock	75	30		150	225	334	315	350	300	187	99	64	50			
Redbank	225	250	100	250	200											
Redfield										166						

POPULATON HISTORY OF TEXAS CITIES AND TOWNS 1840-1990

COMMUNITY	1990	1980	1970	1960	1950	1940	1930	1920	1910	1900	1890	1880	1870	1860	1850	1840
Redford	200	250	250	200			210	210								
Redland	700	700	400	400	100											
Redwater	824	750	500	450	451	283	319	258	260	128						
Reeds					400	400										
Reedsville	50	200			90		90		107	107						
Reese AFB	1263	1934	2545													
Reese Village		1700	1470	1433	250	200										
Refugio	3158	3898	4340	4944	4666	4077	2019	933	773	600	582	465	100			
Reilly Springs	150	100			100	330	300	98	98	98	74	50				
Reinhardt						118	216	87	87	87						
Reklaw	266	305	171	150	200	275	109	48								
Remlig							761	761	500	61						
Rendon	950	900	500													
Renner			339	212	150	220	200	211	161	136						
Reno (Lamar)	1784	1059	487	300	50	80	50	75								
Reno (Parker)	2322	1174	688		70	60	50	60	94	94	98	100				
Retreat	334	255	263	150					98	84						
Retrieve					500	250	50	42	50							
Rhome	605	478	393	412	461	340	415	400	486	350		50				
Rhonesboro	65	50				280	263	263	250							
Rice	564	439	284	295	396	489	591	611	325	268	68	53				
Richards	300	300	500	500	850	600	800	225	225	126	147	50				
Richardson	74840	72496	48405	13810	1289	720	629	610	400	181	63					
Richland	244	260	309	287	308	369	541	750	425							
Richland Hills	7978	7977	8865	7804												
Richland Springs	344	420	425	331	584	541	492	600	475	212	143	100				
Richmond	9801	9692	5777	3668	2030	2026	1432	1273	1371	1187	993	1156	816		323	100
Richwood	2732	2591	1452	649												
Ridge	50	50			250											
Ridgecrest	400	350	350			165										
Ridgeway	175	150	150	200	250	300	300	64	110	73						
Rienzi									161	100						
Riesel	839	691	503	503	409	433	567	561	575	268						
Ringgold	325	300	250	350	480	465	415	400	500	484	200	375	377	127	112	
Ringgold Barracks																
Rio Frio											59	501				
Rio Grande City	9891	8930	5676	5835	3992	2511	2283	3035	2086	1986	1968	2109	150		500	
Rio Hondo	1793	1673	1167	1344	1125	804	713	510								
Rio Medina		100			250	250	250	78								
Rio Vista	541	509	370	284	518	515	518	518	375	363						

POPULATON HISTORY OF TEXAS CITIES AND TOWNS 1840-1990

COMMUNITY	1840	1850	1860	1870	1880	1890	1900	1910	1920	1930	1940	1950	1960	1970	1980	1990
Rios											100	365				
Rising Star							520	640	906	1160	1198	1289	997	1009	1204	859
Rita Santa										400		100			100	100
River Oak Lake															600	600
River Oaks											2000	7097	8444	8193	6890	6580
River Plantation															2000	2000
River Woods															1700	2050
Riverby										300						
Riverside					150	178	186	128	169	318	330	350	350	226	425	451
Riviera								250	400	272	440	600	800	400	600	650
Roanoke					150	292	364	364	410	410	485	511	585	817	910	1616
Roans Prairie						52	52	135	268	268	268	250	125			100
Roaring Springs									300	405	514	435	398	308	315	264
Robert Lee							582	582	815	490	662	1069	990	1119	1202	1276
Robinson						85	100	85	67	100	104	85	2111	3807	6074	7111
Robstown								275	948	4183	6780	7278	10266	11217	12100	12849
Roby							569	712	635	801	904	1051	913	784	814	616
Rochelle							46	275	700	515	566	450	312	310	310	200
Rochester								375	750	562	611	773	625	529	492	458
Rock Creek							507	860	63	86		40				
Rock Island									540	200	200	400	400	350	400	400
Rockdale				500	1185	1505	2515	2073	2323	2204	2136	2321	4481	4655	5611	5235
Rockland					50	405	305	305	600	216	334	216	235	150	200	130
Rockport				400	552	1069	1153	1382	1545	1140	1729	2266	2989	3879	3686	4753
Rocksprings							389	389	1001	998	1339	1436	1182	1221	1317	1339
Rockwall				200	215	843	1245	1136	1388	1071	1318	1501	2166	3121	5939	10486
Rockwood								150		213	200	300	200	100	120	75
Rocky Mound														102	123	53
Rodgers							888						390			
Rogansville							127	200	220	300	300	300	240	240	240	200
Rogers						286	664	1275	1256	1032	911	948	936	1030	1242	1131
Rogers Prairie					48	239	216									
Rolling Hills															300	150
Rolling Hills West															900	
Rolling Meadows														153	252	291
Rolling Oaks															750	750
Rollingwood															1027	1386
Roma/Los Saenz		200		50	100	521	521	521	621	700	1414	1576	1496	2154	3384	8059
Roman Forest															929	1033
Romayor								50	58	300	300	200	200	100	500	600

POPULATON HISTORY OF TEXAS CITIES AND TOWNS 1840-1990

COMMUNITY	1990	1980	1970	1960	1950	1940	1930	1920	1910	1900	1890	1880	1870	1860	1850	1840
Roosevelt			250	600	391	669	371		51	51						
Ropesville	494	489	483	423												
Rosalie						100	521	521	150	82						
Rosanky							205		117	117						
Roscoe	1446	1628	1580	1490	1584	1166	1250	1079	941	126						
Rose City	572	663	737	500												
Rose Hill				220	150	200	200	162	236	247	236					
Rose Hill Acres	468	460	431													
Rosebud	1638	2076	1597	1644	1730	1842	1565	1516	1472	1083						
Rosedale					250	1200	500									
Roseland						100	300									
Rosenberg	20183	17995	12098	9698	6210	3457	1941	1279	1198	481	217	100				
Rosewood	500	500	350	280	150	280	300	255	250							
Rosharon		200	100	100	375	300		112								
Ross	188	200	100	100	200	100	51		60	52	52					
Ross City				100	100	100										
Rosser	366	350	350	300	350	385	350	350	128	128						
Rosston	75	60	100	100	150	333	330	300	229	207	229	114				
Rossville						345	345	345	345	345	750	175				
Rotan	1913	2284	2404	2788	3163	2029	1632	1000	1126							
Round Mountain	59	70			215	215	215	215	158	115	158					
Round Rock	30923	11812	2811	1878	1438	1240	1173	900	1138	1138	1438	628	300			
Round Timber	81	87	94	124	126	120	132	150	98	98	93	325	200			
Round Top	450	465	350	411	500	568	500	345	136	169	238	250				
Rowena									525							
Rowlett	23260	7522	2243	1015	300	300	300	108	108	108						
Roxton	639	735	640	670	887	990	997	641	750	381	226	75	100			
Royal Forest	300	300														
Royal Oaks	300	270														
Royalty		125	200	200	200	335	100									
Royalwood	700	650														
Royse City	2206	1156	1535	1274	1266	1190	1128	1289	1210	503	299					
Royston					400	205	205	205	200							
Ruidosa	90			200	280	530	530	530								
Rule	783	1015	1024	1347	1251	1195	1094	890	891							
Runaway Bay	700	504	113													
Runge	1139	1244	1147	1036	1055	1001	1136	1070	1100	573						
Runnells									76	416	416	50				
Rural Shade										76	76	400				
Rushwood	3600															

POPULATON HISTORY OF TEXAS CITIES AND TOWNS 1840-1990

COMMUNITY	1990	1980	1970	1960	1950	1940	1930	1920	1910	1900	1890	1880	1870	1860	1850	1840
Rusk	4366	4681	4914	4900	6598	5699	3859	2348	1558	846	1383	626	545	395	355	
Rutersville	35	50	100	150	150	300	150	103	231	231			100			
Rye	350	250	100	100	100		300	312								
Rylie				300												
Sabinal	1584	1827	1554	1747	1974	1768	1586	1458	1640	284	172	100				
Sabine City	50	50							673	673			457			
Sabine Pass	900	900	650	816	400	399	400	363	400	363	368	460	50			
Sachse	5346	1640	777	359	125	103	100	63	81	81						
Sacul	500	250	200	250	200	275	300	115	300							
Sadler	316	329	309	300	450	444	400	420	250	115						
Sage	65								242	242						
Sagerton		200	200	250	300	336	300	425	375							
Saginaw	8551	5736	2382	1001	561	300	300	103	83	78						
St. Elmo					950	150		149	136	136						
St. Francis	500	500	500													
St. Hedwig	1443	970	690	589	96	225	96	96	89	89	85	64				
St. Jo	1048	1071	1054	977	1147	1010	960	985	822	825	710	342	100			
St. Louis			400													
St. Mary	415								111	111	111	350	311			
St. Paul		363	160		75	106	108									
Salado	1216	1035	250	300	450	518	415	471	471	386	471	443	300			
Salinero	450	450	400	575	500	330	330	330								
Salt Creek												200				
Saltillo	250	240	250	300	400	276	300	169	220	69	39	200				
Sam Rayburn	350	300														
San Angelo	84474	73240	63884	58815	52093	25802	25308	10050	10321	3851	2615	2000				
San Antonio	935933	785880	654153	587718	408442	253854	231542	161379	96614	53321	37673	20550	12256	8235	3396	2000
San Augustine	2337	2930	2539	2584	2510	1516	1247	1268	1204	261	744	503	920		600	1500
San Benito	20125	17988	15176	16422	13271	9501	10753	5070								
San Carlos	600	200	200		400	50										
San Diego	4983	5225	4490	4351	4397	2674	2262	3525	1897	1787	1877	1572				
San Elizario	4385	1548	950	1064	750	917	550	550	834	1426	1397	910	1120	1050		
San Felipe de Austin	618	532	422	367	296	305	313	451	206	241	177	156	238			150
San Isidro	750	700	500	300	300	100										
San Jacinto												175	172	511		
San Jose					500	108	100	108								
San Juan (Hidalgo)	10815	7608	5070	4371	3413	2264	1615	1203	100							
San Juan (Nueces)	600	600	450	400												
San Leanna	325	290	318													
San Leon	3328	1745	1500	500	300	150			125							

POPULATON HISTORY OF TEXAS CITIES AND TOWNS 1840-1990

COMMUNITY	1990	1980	1970	1960	1950	1940	1930	1920	1910	1900	1890	1880	1870	1860	1850	1840
San Marcos	28743	23420	18860	12713	9980	6006	5134	4527	4071	2292	2335	1232	742			
San Patricio	369	241	84			263	263	263	322	351	315	238	50			150
San Pedro		5294	5294	7634	8127											
San Perlita	512	475	352	348	300	200	137									
San Saba	2626	2847	2555	2728	3400	2927	2240	2011	1200	846	697	598	168			
San Solomon												430				
San Ygnacio	1000	900	800	900	925	217	200	200	198	198	164	175				
Sanatorium				975	700	1475	1040									
Sand							500	115								
Sand Hill					407											
Sand Springs	600	600	600	250												
Sanderson	1128	1241	1229	2189	2047	2062	1850	1254	450	121						
Sandia	250	250	250	450	600	277	250	200	125							
Sandy Corner	200	350	350													
Sandy Point	250	200	200		400	220	168	100	189	186	213	125				
Sanford	218	249	181	400	600	332	200									
Sanger	3508	2574	1603	1190	1170	1000	1119	1204	950	624						
Sansom/Uvalde Junction									478							
Sansom Park	3928	3921	4771	4175	1611											
Santa Ana	1249	1535	1310	1320	1605	1661	1883	1407	1453	736	468					
Santa Cruz	100						215		65							
Santa Elena	150	150		250	950	400	200	86								
Santa Fe	8429	6172	4365													
Santa Maria	500	600	281	281	485	500	250	215	120	142		453			600	
Santa Rita		1000														
Santa Rosa	2223	1889	1466	1572	400	224	737	524		312						
Santo	500	500	350	500	524	445	524	616	400							
Saragosa	400	600	400	620	216	216	216	630	550							
Saratoga	1200	1000	900	800	670	1100	1525	1525	350							
Sarco Creek																
Sargent	700	600				200	250									
Sarita	200	250	250	250	250	100	600	309	300							
Saron					50					89						
Saspamco	150	300	250	300	300	225	225		125							
Satin	150	160	200	170	200	125	75	75								
Savoy	877	855	756	493	314	298	284	378	328	343	344	348	100			
Scenic Hills	600															
Schertz	10555	7262	4061	2281	784	385	315	350	200	47						
Schulenberg	2455	2469	2294	2207	2005	1970	1604	1246	1091	1149	816	719				
Schwertner	60	100				400	300	519								

POPULATON HISTORY OF TEXAS CITIES AND TOWNS 1840-1990

COMMUNITY	1990	1980	1970	1960	1950	1940	1930	1920	1910	1900	1890	1880	1870	1860	1850	1840
Scotland	490	367	257	300	250	347	250	316	175	49						
Scottsville	283	245	259	200	500	500	113	113	50		75	100				
Scranton							250		150	151						
Scurry	400	400	400	500	500	440	300	264	200	182	81	100				
Scyene													175			
Sea Isle	300	260														
Seabrook	6685	4670	3811	2000	900	600	475	108	250	86						
Seadrift	1277	1277	1092	1082	567	437	413	321	50							
Seagoville	8969	7304	4390	3745	1927	760	604	296	400	296		50				
Seagraves	2398	2596	2440	2307	2101	3225	505	80								
Sealy	4541	3875	2685	2328	1942	2200	1640	1640	1225	1084	837					
Sebastian	1200	800	600	424	424	375	424	219	65	65						
Seclusion	1000	800	200	200	50	50										
Seco Mines							300	146	65	65	65	150				
Sedwick																
Segno		300				216	200	216	216							
Seguin	18853	17854	15934	14299	9733	7006	5225	3631	3116	2421	1716	1363	988	856		
Selma	520	528	207	100	60	113	519	519	37	38	96	80	50			
Seminary Hill				600	950	1000	550									
Seminole	6342	6080	5007	5737	3479	1761	262	329	325	31						
Sempronius												160				
Senteritt												150				
Sequoia Estates	600	600														
Serenada Country	1500															
Seth Ward	1402	1186	950	1328	1035											
Seven Oaks	171	300	224		300	150	114		61	61						
Seven Points	723	647	186													
Seymour	3185	3657	3469	3789	3779	3328	2626	2121	2029	1541	1125	183				
Shady Hollow	900															
Shady Shores	1045	813	543	100	975	577										
Shafter	30	60		259			300	124	750	1125						
Shallowater	1708	1932	1339	1001	600	226	150									
Shamrock	2286	2834	2644	3113	3322	3123	3780	1227	725							
Shamrock Shores	1000	150														
Shannon							168		80							
Sharpsburg								236	236	236	371					
Shavano Park	1708	1448	881	343												
Shawnee Shores	500															
Sheffield	425	450	350	500	500	124	100	100	142	126						

POPULATION HISTORY OF TEXAS CITIES AND TOWNS 1840-1990

COMMUNITY	1990	1980	1970	1960	1950	1940	1930	1920	1910	1900	1890	1880	1870	1860	1850	1840
Shelby	85	40			50	248	248	248	248	248	165		50			
Shelbyville	350	300	250	325	300	336	250	216	400	383	272	350	100		250	200
Sheldon	1653	2031	1665	1200	250	106	150	113								
Shell Camp				500	1573											
Shenandoah (Montgomery)	1718	1793	154													
Shenandoah (Williamson)	900															
Shepherd	1812	1674	1037	1094	350	557	513	513	278	273	210					
Sheridan	500	450	250	500	500	218	218	163	175							
Sherman	31601	30413	29061	24988	20150	17156	15713	15031	12412	10243	7335	6093	1439		50	
Sherwood Place	1000	1030	500	249	200	339	339	339	339	582	264					
Shiner	2074	2213	2102	1945	1778	1520	1372	1300	1096	845	340					
Shiro	250	250	250	225	250	574	700	513	325							
Shive									150							
Shore Acres	1316	1260	1872	518	183							150				
Shovel Mount																
Sidney	75			100	300	200	200	122	140	73						
Siep Springs												172				
Sierra Blanca	900	900	800	786	1000	795	725	723	150							
Siesta Shores	800	100														
Silsbee	6368	7684	7271	6277	3179	2525	3060	3500	300	162						
Silver	45															
Silver Lake	65	80														
Silver Valley			500	500	300	300	200	121	250							
Silverton	779	918	1026	1098	857	684	873	416	525	241						
Simmons						400	150	126	60							
Simms	250	250				172	172	172	47	84						
Simonton	717	603	100	100	215	116	49	49	214	214	173	200	200			
Simpsonville						40	100					160				
Sims Creek																
Singleton							200		60							
Sinton	5549	6044	5563	6008	4254	3770	1852	1058	975	492	377					
Sipe Springs	20	40			500	632	350	400	377							
Sisterdale									114	114	114	160	50			
Sivel's Bend									79	79	79	300				
Skellytown	664	889	716	967	529	575	250									
Skidmore	800	800	700	700	529	932	1217	1217	450	238						
Slaton	6078	6804	6583	6568	5036	3587	3876	1525	104	104						
Slidell	100	100	115	120	100	302	250	321	275	175						
Slocum	200	100	100	125	300	160	160	56								
Smeltertown						1260										

POPULATON HISTORY OF TEXAS CITIES AND TOWNS 1840-1990

COMMUNITY	1990	1980	1970	1960	1950	1940	1930	1920	1910	1900	1890	1880	1870	1860	1850	1840
Smiley	463	439	440	455	503	568	515	600	400	141						
Smithfield					950	148	250	166	137	132	74	52				
Smithland			100	100	300	150	150	317	200	76						
Smiths Bluff							300									
Smithsons Valley					300		50		42	42	42					
Smithville	3196	3470	2959	2933	3379	3100	3296	3204	3167	2577	616	50				
Smithwick							318	318	47	48	79	300				
Smyer	442	455	265	100	120	125	76									
Snook	489	408	333	150	200	120			40		500					
Snyder	12195	12705	11171	13850	12010	3815	3008	2179	2514	688						
Socorro	22995	1600	800	950	900	827	600	827	1147		801	600	627	723		
Soda							318	318								
Somerset	1144	1102	861	900	500	550	450	113	200			500				
Somerville	1542	1814	1250	1177	1425	1621	2287	1879	950	384						
Sonoma			678	503	210											
Sonora	2751	3856	2149	2619	2633	2528	1942	1009	783	783						
Sour Lake	1547	1807	1694	1602	1630	1504	1199	3032	800	273	99	75				
South Bend	130	150	150	200	500	554	400	590	60							
South Groveton				619	619	619	1088	614								
South Houston	14207	13293	11527	7523	4126	982	612	750	550							
South Mountain	301															
South Padre Island	1677	791	250													
South San Antonio			3065			2978	2708									
South San Pedro								163								
South Texarkana		1688	600	343	317											
Southlake	7065	2808	2031	1023												
Southland	100	200	168	153	210	280	400	183								
Southmayd	634	318	222	200	300	275	300	261	132	116						
Southside Place	1392	1366	1466	1282	1436	1263										
Southton	50			100	300		89	89								
Spanish Camp	400	400	100	150	200	100	100		79	79						
Spanish Fort	50	50		152	275	278	350	258	247	247	179	300				
Spanish Trail	275	300														
Spearman	3197	3413	3435	3555	1852	1105	1580									
Spicewood (Burnet)	200	150		370	400	125	130	130	48	48						
Spicewood (Travis)	600	600														
Spindle Top						300										
Splendora	745	721	194	350	450	118	150	66	89	89						
Spofford	68	77	69	138	246	319	319	319	79	118						
Spooner					1264											

POPULATON HISTORY OF TEXAS CITIES AND TOWNS 1840-1990

COMMUNITY	1990	1980	1970	1960	1950	1940	1930	1920	1910	1900	1890	1880	1870	1860	1850	1840
Spring	700	1000	950	975	1000	660	400	175	550	46	46					
Spring Branch									74	74	74	175				
Spring Hill (Gregg)	950	900	900													
Spring Hill (Guadalupe)	750	600	700													
Spring Hill (Navarro)									92	92		152	175			
Spring Hills	450															
Spring Valley	3392	3353	3170	3004												
Springlake	132	222	209	245	50	50	50									
Springtown	1740	1658	1194	859	800	770	500	715	700	518	657	166				
Spur	1300	1690	1747	2170	2183	2136	1899	1100	1050							
Spurger	650	650	400	600	700	554	500	121	97	97						
Stafford	8397	4755	2906	1485	465	175	122	89	57	57	57	500				
Stagecoach	340	349	161													
Stagecoach Hills	400	1500														
Stamford	3817	4542	4558	5259	5819	4810	4095	3704	3902	732						
Stanton	2576	2314	2117	2228	1603	1245	1384	1421	650	331						
Staples	300	300	200	175	175	145	250	212	272	272						
Star									171	171						
Star Harbor	368	310	83													
Stargas					400											
Starrville	50				50	112	122	122	122	128	122	115	200			
Startzville			200													
Station Belden											309	50				
Steeles Store						330	213	213	160	59	206	350				
Stephenville	13502	11881	9277	7359	7155	4768	3944	3891	2561	1902	909	725	162			
Sterley						250	250									
Sterling City	1096	915	780	854	865	974	867	867	532	444						
Stewart Heights					600	545	545									
Stiles							161		150							
Stinnett	2166	2222	2014	2695	1170	635	337									
Stockdale	1268	1265	1132	1111	1105	926	696	1031	725	331	115	97				
Stone Point									77	77	97	600				
Stoneburg									173	173						
Stoneham	80	60	170	135	102	224	400	265	100							
Stonewall	300	300			96	230	96	96	84	84	268					
Stowell	1419	1498	650	650	650	275	176	176	176	176						
Stratford	1781	1917	2139	1380	1385	877	873	472	520							
Strawn	709	694	786	817	922	1107	1429	2457	612	741	514					
Streetman	260	415	286	300	419	392	509	478	300			100				
Stribling					450											

POPULATION HISTORY OF TEXAS CITIES AND TOWNS 1840-1990

COMMUNITY	1990	1980	1970	1960	1950	1940	1930	1920	1910	1900	1890	1880	1870	1860	1850	1840
Stringtown	150															
Stuebner									74	74		78	200			
Sublime		130	175	100	100	164	250	210	210	210	210	200				
Sudan	983	1091	976	1235	1348	974	1014									
Sugar Land	24529	8826	3318	2802	2285	2400	1840	2019	1000	1000						
Sullivan City	600	450	450	500	600	250	215	215								
Sulpher Bluff	200	200	200	250	500	570	300	264	164	216	74	63				
Sulpher Prairie												200				
Sulpher Station											246	100				
Sulphur Springs	14062	12804	10642	9160	8991	6742	5417	5558	5151	3635	3038	1854	921	621	441	
Summerfield					100		150	336	75							
Sumner							200		138	138			145			
Sumpter																
Sun Valley	60	76														
Sundown	1759	1511	1129	1186	1492	1500										
Sunny Side	50	60		300	500	450	125		178	178						
Sunnyvale	2228	1404	995	969												
Sunray	1729	1952	1854	1967	1530	1650	150									
Sunrise	1000	1000	1213	1708	1616											
Sunrise Beach	497	420	300													
Sunset	500	500	500	500	665	695	665	665	632	632	375	50				
Sunset Heights		1450	1500													
Sunset Ridge	600	600														
Sunset Valley	327	773	292	179												
Surfside Beach	611	577	600	800												
Sutherland Springs	500	300	250	300	400	400	400	400	550	141	164	101	100			
Swan	400	400	200	300	150	138	300	219	102	188						
Swarthout						115	115	115								
Swearingen					600	800	510	510							150	50
Sweeney	3297	3538	3191	3087	1393											
Sweet Home	250	200	300	400	500	338	400	414	274	333						
Sweetwater	11967	12242	12020	13914	13619	10367	10848	4307	4176	670	614	300				
Swenson		70		150	150	250	190	94	80							
Sylvester	275	250	250	250	405	405	382	200	300							
Taft	3222	3686	3274	3463	2978	2686	1792	313	100							
Taft Southwest	2012	2133	2026	1927												
Tahoka	2868	3262	2956	3012	2848	2129	1620	786	575							
Talco	592	751	837	1024	917	912	400	421								
Talpa	110	122	121	195	234	254	233	425	425							
Tamina	950	900	300	130	500	500	128	128	128	128						

POPULATION HISTORY OF TEXAS CITIES AND TOWNS 1840-1990

COMMUNITY	1840	1850	1860	1870	1880	1890	1900	1910	1920	1930	1940	1950	1960	1970	1980	1990
Tanglewood							97	97	97	97	104	250	100		75	60
Tarkington Prairie					58	45	43	43								
Tarleton			364									950				
Tarrant								100	103	150			200			
Tarzan													100	100	250	300
Tascosa					120	271	192	192	68	68			125			
Tatum							154	425	428	425	427	599	542	684	1339	1289
Taylor (Red River)					152											
Taylor (Williamson)					700	2584	4211	5314	5965	7463	7875	9071	9434	9616	10619	11472
Taylor Lake														990	3669	3394
Taylors Bayou					250	213	66									
Teague								3288	3306	3509	3157	2925	2728	2867	3390	3268
Teepee															550	
Tehuacana				100	100	268	382	425	614	412	408	389	316	285	265	322
Telephone							99	99	99	350	350	250	350	270	250	250
Telferner								200		200		500	350	320	650	500
Tell								100		418	418	500	100		75	75
Temple					1500	4047	7065	10993	11033	15345	15344	25461	30419	33431	42483	46109
Tenaha						613	684	491	577	591	608	715	1097	1094	1005	1072
Terlingua								200		850	350					
Terrell				500	2003	2988	6330	7050	8349	8795	10481	11544	13803	14182	13225	12490
Terrell Hills				150	152						1236	2708	5572	5225	4644	4592
Texana	250			500												
Texarkana					1833	2852	5256	9790	11480	16602	17019	24753	30218	30497	31271	31656
Texas City							236	650	2509	3534	5748	16620	32065	38908	41403	40822
Texhoma								100	313	300	191	299	350	356	358	291
Texla									517	517						
Texline						185	144	350	762	711	385	437	430	387	477	425
Texon										1200	1235	500	250	250	35	35
Thalia								60	60	200	291	300	223		200	100
Tharp						214	172									
The Colony															11586	22113
The Meadows															600	
The Woodlands															8443	29205
Thicket										255		215	200		300	300
Thomas									195	195	220	300	100	100	250	200
Thomaston					161	494	347	347	175	358	358	300	300	150	250	167
Thompsons							104	104	104	104	104	710	150	150	240	250
Thornberry								80								250
Thorndale						47	448	1100	1100	1002	898	855	995	1031	1300	1092

POPULATON HISTORY OF TEXAS CITIES AND TOWNS 1840-1990

COMMUNITY	1990	1980	1970	1960	1950	1940	1930	1920	1910	1900	1890	1880	1870	1860	1850	1840
Thornton	540	498	433	504	623	745	739	733	678	621	466	182				
Thorntonville	693	717	629													
Thorp Spring	200	100	100	200	200	456	308	415	485	512	485	450				
Thrall	550	573	619	631	585	436	422	272								
Three Rivers	1889	2133	1761	1932	2026	1337	1275	516								
Thrift					500	500										
Throckmorton	1036	1174	1105	1299	1320	1133	1135	686	500	689	240					
Thurber						150	500	6017	3000	1453	978					
Tiffin								1536								
Tiki Island	537	200														
Tilden	450	450	450	325	600	350	500	506	506	561	506	200				
Timber Ridge (Bexar)	700															
Timber Ridge (Montgomery)		1500														
Timberlake	400	200														
Timpson	1029	1164	1254	1120	1455	1494	1545	1526	1528	884	518					
Tioga	625	511	456	403	529	638	591	777	797	542	267	50				
Tira	237	249	177			221	264	264	80							
Tivoli	700	600	500	750	900	750	300	139	50							
Toco	127	164														
Tolar	523	415	312	283	338	320	318	416	455	171						
Tolbert									200							
Toledo Village	300	250					225									
Tom Bean	827	811	540	403	286	274	333	367	288	299	206					
Tomball	6370	3996	2734	1713	1065	668	261	149								
Tool	1712	1591	258	121	50	75	115	115								
Tornillo	650	600	500	700	600	350	217									
Tow	300	250	250	200	250	350	40									
Towash	1400											184	150			
Town Bluff					317	317	317	317	65	65	65	73				
Towne West	1400															
Toyah	115	165	245	294	409	464	553	1218	1052	113						
Tradewinds	150	250														
Travis	50	75		100	200	150	118	118	148	148		200	75			
Trawick				100	150	150	309	390	160							
Trent	319	313	333	298	296	366	412	500	400	46						
Trenton	655	691	599	712	603	634	490	616	550	420	276	100				
Tres Palacios										47			226			
Trevat					100	150										
Trickham								200	79	97	250					
Trinidad	1056	1130	1079	786	850	848	1000	75	75	75						

POPULATON HISTORY OF TEXAS CITIES AND TOWNS 1840-1990

COMMUNITY	1990	1980	1970	1960	1950	1940	1930	1920	1910	1900	1890	1880	1870	1860	1850	1840
Trinity	2648	2620	2512	1787	2054	2217	2036	1363	856	865	856	150	75			
Trophy Club	3922	1040														
Troup	1659	1911	1668	1667	1539	1526	1318	1258	1126	724	465	352	100			
Troy	1395	1353	542	400	500	650	509	509	400	391	219	193				
Truscott	90	120	120	550	475	475	500	261	250							
Tucker	75	100	292			275	275		97	97						
Tuleta	300	300	450	300	400	162	150	162	100							
Tulia	4699	5033	5294	4410	3222	2055	2202	1189	1216	184	187					
Tunis	150	160	160	100	100	118	150	218	187	187	187	100				
Turkey	507	644	680	813	1005	930	975	100	125							
Turnersville	75	125	110	95	100	178	178	178	275	162	56	40				
Turnertown					300	350										
Turney							200		100							
Turtle Bayou						50	50	125	127	127	77		75			
Tuscola	620	660	497	414	497	345	418	418	49	49						
Tuxedo									200							
Twin Sisters									51	51	34	350				
Twin Valley	600															
Tye	1088	1394	857	521	150	100	200	263	125							
Tyler	75450	70508	57770	51230	38968	28279	17113	12085	10400	8069	6908	2423	1080		1024	
Tynan	200	300	300	300	500	233										
Uhland	368	272					250		50							
Umbarger	80	50	120	150	200	150	62		100							
Uncertain	194	176	202													
Union	500	100			150	200	200	215	123	123	73					
Union Grove	271	344	200	300	150											
Universal City	13057	10720	7613	800												
University Park	22259	22254	23498	23202	24275	14458	4200									
Utley					140	275										
Utopia	350	400	300	500	865	282	260	250	147	146						
Uvalde	14729	14178	10764	10293	8674	6679	5286	3885	3998	1889	1265	794	163	192		
Valda										468						
Valentine	217	328	213	420	510	499	350	250	175	231						
Valera	125	135	200	150	325	340	310	125	225							
Valley Creek										209	216	250				
Valley Lodge		500	100													
Valley Mills	1085	1236	1022	1061	1037	803	936	855	708	519	300	113				
Valley Spring	40	50		75	500	112	115	100	131	231	244	250				
Valley View	640	514	650	650	750	770	700	762	575	378	263	250	100			
Van	1854	1881	1593	1103	610	983	1000	84	66	66						

POPULATON HISTORY OF TEXAS CITIES AND TOWNS 1840-1990

COMMUNITY	1840	1850	1860	1870	1880	1890	1900	1910	1920	1930	1940	1950	1960	1970	1980	1990
Van Alstyne						737	1940	1441	1588	1453	1650	1649	1608	1981	1860	2090
Van Horn				200	213			175	614	853	939	1161	1953	2889	2772	2930
Van Vleck							78	200	219	275	275	500	900	1051	1157	1534
Vanderbilt									50	250	192	310	670	750	750	750
Vanderpool										100	100					
Vansickles					150											
Vashti								119	261	250	135	76	120	125	90	75
Vaughn					150		108	108								
Veals Station					71	47	279					75				
Vega	300							275	513	519	515	620	658	839	900	840
Velasco					55	475	542	942	621	755	660	2260	324	414	518	977
Venus							337	495	842	570	321	357			120	100
Vera								120		250	250	500	400			
Vernon						2857	1993	3195	5142	9137	9277	12651	12141	11454	12695	12001
Vickery					50				427	813	1000					
Victoria	500	806	1986	2534	3000	3046	4010	3673	5957	7421	11566	16126	33047	41349	50695	55076
Victory Gardens															400	500
Vidor												2136	4938	9738	12117	10935
Vienna								300		300	400	400				
View										75	100	125			60	40
Villa												325				
Village Mills						316	450	316	416	416		250	315	200	500	450
Vineyard								250							271	605
Vinton										141	141		300		200	750
Virginia Point					403								300	150	200	
Voca								160								
Volente													300	150	500	750
Von Ormy							42	42	213	350	350		350	350		850
Voss								150	117	117	120	41				
Votaw								100			200	300	350	250	280	300
Voth								125	68	600	825	900				
Waco			749	3008	7295	14445	20686	26425	38500	52848	55982	84706	97808	95326	101261	103590
Wadeville				75	152			60	144	200	255	500	300	250	300	300
Wadsworth																
Waelder					200	388	583	694	894	1048	1018	1275	1270	1138	942	745
Wake Village												1066	1140	2408	3865	4757
Walburg														100	200	140
Walden							216	200	218	300	300	300			600	600
Walden Place																
Waldrip						47	127	127	264	250	290	100			1280	1300

POPULATON HISTORY OF TEXAS CITIES AND TOWNS 1840-1990

COMMUNITY	1840	1850	1860	1870	1880	1890	1900	1910	1920	1930	1940	1950	1960	1970	1980	1990
Walker Station					300											
Waller							383	383	450	518	495	715	900	1123	1241	1493
Wallis					150	106	226	675	885	690	880	1000	990	1028	1138	1001
Wallis Station					200	83	284	500								
Wallisville								128			250	400	200	200	300	350
Walnut						682										700
Walnut Forest																
Walnut Springs							894	1340	1449	765	723	626	490	495	613	716
Warda						181	116	200	50	100	50				50	75
Waring						82	92	92	326	269	269	200	80		75	90
Warren						833	1471	833	679	679	440	500	360	450	600	600
Warren City					46	218	306	306	406	406	406	406	167	150	281	250
Warrenton					200	224	186	224	324				185			50
Washington	400	750	1000	200	300	207	207	207	204	200	300	300	300	300	300	300
Waskom										500	564	719	1336	1460	1821	1812
Wasson							58	58			275					
Watauga							132	132		150		100	150	3778	10284	20009
Water Valley								476	489	50	157	500	230	200	300	300
Waterman												50				
Watsonville														120	350	400
Waukegan					92	103	232	300	515	200	104					
Waverly								232	232							
Waxahachie					1354	3076	4215	6205	7958	8042	8655	11204	12749	13452	14624	18168
Wayland					50		89	125		250						
Weatherford		175	700	1823	2046	3369	4786	5074	6203	4912	5924	8093	9759	11750	12049	14804
Weaver							79	79		300	300	300		150	60	65
Webberville				330	311	382	382	382	320	300	165	200		100	100	100
Webster							112	112	318	250	224	500	329	2231	2405	4678
Weesatche										212						
Weimar				300	626	1443	1337	906	1171	1256	1353	1663	2006	2104	2128	2052
Weinert								779	472	414	414	288	251	255	253	235
Weir								175	149	257	240	100			207	220
Welch											245	300	500	250	400	350
Welcome					225	246	247	242	242	242	230	200				
Weldon					150	128	159	139	518	500	500	250	300	180	180	200
Wellborn						53	442	300	415	500	500	600	200	300	100	150
Wellington							87	576	1968	3570	3308	3676	3137	2884	3034	2456
Wellman										50	200	225	225	150	239	239
Wells							152	162	162	475	696	718	544	671	926	761
Weser								153								

POPULATON HISTORY OF TEXAS CITIES AND TOWNS 1840-1990

COMMUNITY	1990	1980	1970	1960	1950	1940	1930	1920	1910	1900	1890	1880	1870	1860	1850	1840
Weslaco	21877	19331	15313	15649	7514	6883	4879	500								
Wesley		75			50	222	200	223	150	370	370	300				
West	2515	2485	2406	2352	2130	1979	1807	1629	1645	851						
West Carlisle		980	1200	600								100				
West Columbia	4372	4109	3335	2947	2100	1573	3525	3525	100							
West Dallas						300					474					
West End																
West Fort Hood	1253	1253	1265													
West Lake Hills	2542	2166	1488	714												
West Liberty													230			
West Mineola	400		300													
West Mountain		395	194													
West Odessa	3000															
West Orange	4187	4610	4820	4840	2539											
West Point	225	150	150	150	400	450	400	300	200	289	382					
West Tawakoni	932	840	465													
West University Place	12920	12010	13317	14628	17074	9221	1322									
West Vernon					955	955	955									
Westbrook	237	298	298	214	512	563	512	519	375			50				
Westfield	500	500	900	350	294	200	106	62	48	48	48					
Westfield Estates	2400	2180		110												
Westgate	150	240	240													
Westhoff	200	450	450	450	450	560	375	500	425							
Westlake	185	214	128	112												
Westland				800												
Westlawn	700	700	700													
Westminster	388	278	257	194	192	290	268	631	375							
Weston	362	405	221	100	110	347	300	263	316	316	285	166	157			
Westover		3480	700		150		89	89								
Westover Hills	672	671	374	307	266	197										
Westphalia	150	300	200		400	225		107	107	107						
Westpoint		600	400					289	289							
Westway	2381															
Westworth	2350	3651	4578	3321	529	750										
Wharton	9011	9033	7881	5734	4450	4386	2691	2346	1505	1172	1239	312	150			
Wheeler	1393	1584	1116	1174	904	848	931	315	200							
Wheelock							218		86	86	86	85	50			
Whispering Pines	300	300														
White City						40	325	325								
White Deer	1125	1210	1092	1057	629	733	1010	115	50							

POPULATON HISTORY OF TEXAS CITIES AND TOWNS 1840-1990

COMMUNITY	1990	1980	1970	1960	1950	1940	1930	1920	1910	1900	1890	1880	1870	1860	1850	1840
White Hall									100	112	143	100				
White Mound					75						163	50				
White Oak	5136	4415	2300	1250	880		100									
White Oak Valley		400														
White Rock	450				200	110		132	100	150	158	128				
White Settlement	15472	13508	13449	11513	10827							100				
White Wright																
Whiteface	512	463	394	535	579	121	81									
Whitehouse	4032	2172	1245	842	650	500	500	367	150	114						
Whitemound									89	89	163					
Whitesboro	3209	3197	2927	2485	1854	1560	1535	1810	1219	1243	1110	773	300			
Whitewright	1713	1760	1745	1315	1372	1537	1480	1666	1563	1804	880	100				
Whitheral	250	250	250	400	260	100	100									
Whitney	1626	1631	1371	1050	1383	824	751	1011	766	892	897	526				
Whitt	150	150	150	176	150	168	527	527	300	378	278	130				
Wichita Falls	96259	94201	96265	101724	68042	45112	43690	40079	8200	2480	1987					
Wickett	560	689	598	850	619	450										
Wiergate	325	310	300	450	485	1100	1521	1521								
Wild Peach	2440	2385														
Wildorado	2000	160	160	160	105	105	189	189	200							
Wildwood	850	900	150									250				
Wilkins										331						
Willard	660	660	500													
William Spear																
Williams Ranch											236	253				
Williamsburg									58	60	218	200				
Willis	2764	1674	1577	975	1164	904	1020	1020	832	942	832	656	300			
Willow City									175							
Willow Park	2328	1113	230													
Willow Springs					100	2000	2000									
Wills Point	2986	2631	2636	2281	2030	1976	2023	1811	1398	1347	1025	860	200			
Wilmer	2479	2367	1922	1785	465	278	263	263	200	107						
Wilson	568	578	433	403	265	272	250	134	100	88						
Wimberley	2403	1200	350	500	400	175	124	124	114	114	114					
Winchell						100	275	275	300							
Winchester	150	150	150	200	410	335	410	410	375	375	258	245	100			
Windcrest	5331	5332	3371	441												
Windom	269	276	247	218	297	290	317	389	312	312						
Windthorst	367	409	377	205	375	500	500	159	150	147						
Winfield	345	349	268	251	319	500	500	1025	625	134						

POPULATON HISTORY OF TEXAS CITIES AND TOWNS 1840-1990

COMMUNITY	1990	1980	1970	1960	1950	1940	1930	1920	1910	1900	1890	1880	1870	1860	1850	1840
Winfree	150															
Wingate		200	200	200	600	300	300	317	275							
Wink	1189	1182	1023	1863	1521	1945	3963									
Winkler					250	168	300	213	200							
Winnie	2238	2496	1543	1114	750	228	321	321	125							
Winnsboro	2904	3458	3064	2675	2512	2092	1905	2184	1741	899	388	700	150			
Winona	457	443	155	303	450	388	600	550	550	149	283					
Winters	2905	3061	2907	3266	2676	2335	2423	1509	1347	138						
Wixon Valley	186															
Woden	300	230	100	100	135	200	200		60							
Wolfe City	1505	1594	1433	1317	1345	1339	1405	1859	1402	1549	867					
Wolfe's Crossing											29	179				
Wolfforth	1941	1701	1090	597	450	200	108									
Wood					400											
Woodbine	70	60			50	124	112	113	113	113	183					
Woodbranch	1312	720	378													
Woodbury	100	60			50	162	214	214	150	148	148	120	100			
Woodcreek	894															
Woodcrest	500	200														
Woodhaven	400	400														
Woodlake	800	1000	250	250	300	70										
Woodland	100	60			319	319	319	159	169	218	112	64				
Woodland Hills	200	100	366	339												
Woodlawn		200	200	100	265	265	265	265	104	104	104	85				
Woodlawn Lakes	370	360														
Woodloch	291	351														
Woods							60			98	135	100				
Woods of Shavano	950															
Woodsboro	1731	1974	1839	2081	1836	1426	1286	519	325							
Woodson	262	291	340	337	450	440	275	225	225							
Woodville	2636	2821	2662	1920	1863	1521	969	1218	659	1109	518	390	100			
Woodway	8695	7091	4819	1244												
Woodworth Mills											267					
Wooster				2000		125			198	198	268					
Wootan Wells																
Wortham	1020	1187	1036	1087	1170	1267	1404	1100	899	679	401	245				
Wright City	200	250	200	300	200	555	125									
Wrightsboro	50	100	100	240	300	112	240	540	122	266	122		100			
Wylie	8716	3152	2675	1804	1295	914	771	945	620	773	239					
Yancey	200	150	100	300	450	180	100	64	58	58						

POPULATON HISTORY OF TEXAS CITIES AND TOWNS 1840-1990

COMMUNITY	1990	1980	1970	1960	1950	1940	1930	1920	1910	1900	1890	1880	1870	1860	1850	1840
Yantis	210	210	223	300	300	250	250	181	250	126						
Yarrellton							300		86	86	58					
Yoakum	5611	6148	5755	5761	5231	4733	5656	6184	4657	3499	1745					
Yorktown	2207	2498	2411	2527	2596	2081	1882	1723	1180	846	522	430	400			
Yowell							250		68	68						
Ysleta	7119	3831	2102	2031	4782	2250	2446	2000	1362	1682	1528	1453	799	605		
Zapata	701	762	700	956	1409	1041	1041	1527	250	113						
Zavalla	300	350	200	200	690	500	300	390	715				200			
Zephyr					325	330	500	600	350	178	150					
Zionsville												208	50			
Zodiac															160	

POPULATION HISTORY OF UTAH CITIES AND TOWNS 1850-1990

COMMUNITY	1850	1860	1870	1880	1884	1890	1895	1900	1910	1920	1930	1940	1950	1960	1970	1980	1990
Abraham								75	100	105	250	160	100	111	50		40
Adamsville			179	181	200	128	200	200	100	150	98		50	50	30	35	
Alpine		135	208	319	350	466	423	520	496	470	509	444	571	775	1047	2649	3492
Alta		135	400	414	250	210		110	150	150	150	150	100	100	93	381	397
Altamont													150	102	129	247	167
Alton										170	174	200	154	116	62	75	93
Altonah										250	300	300	300	175	60	50	35
Amalga										210	229	246	225	198	207	323	366
American Fork/Lake City		695	1145	1825	2000	1942	2347	2732	2797	2763	3047	3333	5126	6373	7713	12417	15696
Annabella						100	338	189	189	150	180	321	263	177	221	463	487
Antimony/Coyoto					100			145	150	275	288	245	187	161	113	94	83
Arcadia							236			200	200	200	168	185			
Argenta					400												
Aurora					200	150	360	250	300	500	568	607	614	465	493	874	911
Avon								111	150	150							
Axtell								102	180	237	250	250	155	160	50	50	65
Bacchus									150	213	166	166	94				
Ballard																558	644
Bear River City			389	317	350	340	461	362	463	490	436	429	438	447	445	540	700
Beaver			785	1732	2200	1652	2043	1701	1899	1827	1673	1808	1685	1548	1453	1792	1998
Belmont Heights																600	650
Benjamin						100		200	200	200	200	200	150	150	100	100	100
Bennion														200	800	975	950
Bicknell/Thurber								200	200	220	228	362	373	366	264	296	327
Bigwater/Glen Canyon																154	326
Bingham Canyon			276	450	1000	524	1313	1193	2881	2676	3248	2838	2569	1516	31		
Blanding										875	555	1111	1177	1805	2250	3188	3162
Bloomington						63		75	50	48						350	500
Bluebell									200	200	200	200	218	120	120	50	65
Bluff				107	200	100	194	160	190	150	100	100	150	150	300	120	250
Bluffdale													450	500	600	1300	2152
Boneta										200	200	100	134				
Bothwell/Point Lookout									200	200		282	317	302	300		
Boulder									200	110	150	195	185	108	93	113	126
Bountiful	100	866	1115	1825	2000	1650	2438	1442	1677	2063	2571	3357	6004	17039	27751	32877	36659
Brian Head																77	109
Brigham City		975	1315	1877	2500	2139		2859	3685	5282	5093	5641	6790	11728	14007	15596	15644
Brighton									62						150	150	200
Caineville								150	150	100							
Camp Floyd		284															

POPULATION HISTORY OF UTAH CITIES AND TOWNS 1850-1990

COMMUNITY	1990	1980	1970	1960	1950	1940	1930	1920	1910	1900	1895	1890	1884	1880	1870	1860	1850
Cannonville	131	134	113	153	205	250	329	250	200	150		200		137			
Carbonville		500	500														
Castle Dale	1704	1910	541	617	715	841	713	715	693	559	533	303	450	250			
Castle Gate			205	521	701	851	923	1120	787	1109	843	599					
Castle Rock									200								
Castle Valley	211	239															
Cedar City	13443	10972	8946	7543	6106	4695	3615	2462	1705	1425	1208	967	500	691	547	301	
Cedar Fort	284	269	188	190	213	220	273	215	200	115		100		280			
Cedar Hills	769	571															
Center Creek	425	300	250														
Centerfield	766	653	419	475	601	598	554	566	495	400							
Centerville	11500	8069	3268	2361	1262	691	670	500	540	500	589	450	600	450	400	275	250
Central	250	150	150	200	200	250	250	150									
Charleston	336	320	196	223	201	323	343	361	283	234	421	250	275	246			
Chester	50	50	50	155	153	182	182	200	200	200		100	250	150			
Circleville	417	445	443	478	603	683	436	400	350	300	496	300	100	150			
Clarkston	645	562	420	490	526	579	570	528	564	400	535	400	500	464	153		
Clear Creek	35	30	35	100	168	202	254	578	806	300							
Clear Lake									200								
Clearfield	21435	17982	13316	8833	4723	1053	799	400	210	187							
Cleveland	498	522	244	261	343	447	294	244	350	314	507						
Clinton	7945	5777	1768	1025	670	581	625			74							
Clover	150	100	100	100	110	100	128	150	150								
Coalville	1065	1031	864	907	850	949	938	771	976	808	515	1166	1300	911	626		
Collinston	50	40	70	70	75	150	122	250	300	300		200	200				
Colton							50	60	300	100							
Columbia	70	100	380	412	412	422	646										
Consumers					69	144	475										
Copperfield					878	500											
Copperton	800	850	900	850	790												
Corinne	639	512	471	510	427	411	352	394	231	323	308	297	200	277	783		
Cornish	205	181	173	157	181	221	150	300	260	150							
Cottonwood	12500	11554	8431	1500													
Cottonwood Heights	28766	22665	4500														
Cove						300	310	300	200	300							
Coyoto		50	80						145	160		100	125				
Croydon	250	150	100	78	90	107	179	160	200	180	334	150	125	152	150		
Daniel		150															
Delta	2998	1930	1610	1576	1703	1304	1183	939									
Deseret	250	200	200	300	310	375	375	400	400	300		105	500	197			

POPULATION HISTORY OF UTAH CITIES AND TOWNS 1850-1990

COMMUNITY	1990	1980	1970	1960	1950	1940	1930	1920	1910	1900	1895	1890	1884	1880	1870	1860	1850
Devils Slide	318																
Deweyville		45	55	200	250	252	320	305	300	119	200	200	200	222			
Diamond		311	248	265	233	256	181	250	210		198		200	206			
Dividend																	
Dover					30	347	499					98	210	124	200		
Dragon							60	186	200								
Draper	7257	5530	4000	2000	2000	1080	1190	1054	1000	900	937	700	650	540			
Duchesne	1308	1677	1094	770	804	907	590	700	500								
Dugway	1761	1646	2357	3049	1500												
Dutch John	250	285	250	800													
East Carbon/Dragerton	1270	1942	1614	2959	3453												
East Layton		3531	763	444	217	124											
East Midvale		6500															
East Millcreek	3800	24150	26579	6000	950	1000					2008						
Eastwood Hills	1200	1200	1200														
Echo	50	60	60	130	160	160	160	150	220	250		212	207	124	100		
Eden	200	225	200	200	235	200	200	300	300	400		203	200	150			
Elberta	100	100	100	135	138	149	98	100	150								
Elgin	40	50						200	100								
Elk Ridge	771	381															
Elmo	267	300	141	175	170	198	207	200									
Elsinore	608	612	357	483	657	674	654	843	656	625	809	400	200	50			
Elwood	575	481	294	345	393	535											
Emery	300	372	216	326	488	618	637	650	525	400	481	150					
Enoch	1947	678	420	465	250	250	161	150	100								
Enterprise	936	905	844	859	790	619	464	598	300	100							
Ephriam	3363	2810	2127	1801	1987	2094	1966	2287	2296	2086	2213	1800	1500	1698	1167	910	
Erda								298	150				200				
Escalante	818	652	638	702	773	1106	862	1032	846	650	866	506	500	623			
Eureka	562	670	753	771	1318	2292	3041	3608	3416	3085	1908	1733	750	122			
Ewell																	
Fairfield	100	90	90	85	100	145	170	163	170	108	170	126	122	105		303	
Fairview	960	916	696	655	974	1314	1120	1423	1218	1119	1494	844	900	863	531	303	
Farmington	9028	4691	2526	1951	1468	1211	1339	1170	1231	968	980	950	1200	1073	896	591	
Farr West	2178	1451				100			115	100							
Fayette	183	165	93	161	200	247	81	100	100	91	251	100	150	125	100		
Ferron	1606	1718	663	386	478	515	508	453	651	450	549	270	147	60			
Fielding	422	325	254	270	249	329	333	374	450	78							
Fillmore	1956	2083	1411	1602	1890	1785	1374	1490	1191	1037	1077	838	1000	987	905	715	250
Forest Dale									1549								

POPULATION HISTORY OF UTAH CITIES AND TOWNS 1850-1990

COMMUNITY	1990	1980	1970	1960	1950	1940	1930	1920	1910	1900	1895	1890	1884	1880	1870	1860	1850
Fort Cameron							1071							179			
Fort Douglas	655	200	200	250	200	104	104	100	250	150	100	500		250	173	92	
Fort Duchesne	578	578	467	544	767	988	982	1169	875	755	929	677					
Fountain Green	381	371	268	252	276	300	150						800	650	562		
Francis																	
Freedom								120	200	150							
Fremont	200	150	150	200	224	150	150	211	178	200		251	200	290			
Frisco								50	300	400	457	224	800	751			
Fruit Heights	3900	2728	800	175													
Fruitland				100	127	100	68	84									
Garden City	193	259	134	158	164	261	331	304	300	147	262	200	200	127			
Garfield					2079	1620	2270	2500	600	100							
Garland	1637	1405	1187	1119	1008	926	824	999	600								
Genola	803	630	424	380	314	250	200	210									
Glendale	282	237	200	226	250	300	446	410	250	250	297	152	225	172	200		
Glenwood	437	447	212	277	338	385	350	364	359	422	452	314	627	300			
Gold Hill							75	167	200		50						
Gold Springs																	
Goshen	578	582	459	426	525	616	669	526	470	645	553	298	600	344	300	294	
Grafton							23	46	106	120		100		71	38	150	
Granger			9029	1300	900		325	300		384	606				300		
Granite	650	650	350	300													
Granite Park	5554	5554	9573														
Grantsville	4500	4419	2931	2166	1537	1242	1201	1213	1154	1058	992	1000	600	1007	755	451	
Green River	866	1048	1033	1075	583	470	474	645	628	73							
Greenville	100	115	100	110	173	173	173	200	210	100		109	240	138			
Grouse Creek	100	105	100	136	167	300	300	300	250	200		154	100	100			
Gunlock	100	80	85	81	90	105	127	115	112	100		90		72	30		
Gunnison	1298	1255	1073	1059	1144	1115	1057	1115	950	829	1367	154	300	100	475		
Gusher/Moffat	150	125	100	100	125	100	250	150	200								
Hanksville	200	100	90	100	100	100	80	150	100	100							
Hannah	70	100	100	130	160	150	150	100									
Harrisburg												26					
Harrisville	3004	1371	749	500	425	425	300	200	250	200			100	103	105	120	
Hatch/Asays	103	121	139	198	244	294	212	200	170	140				150			
Hayden	30				52												
Heber	4782	4362	3245	2936	2936	2748	2477	1931	2031	1534	1672	1538	1200	1291	658		
Hebron										200		151	500	75			
Heiner																	
Helper	2148	2724	1964	2459	2850	2843	2707	1606	816	302	258						

POPULATION HISTORY OF UTAH CITIES AND TOWNS 1850-1990

COMMUNITY	1990	1980	1970	1960	1950	1940	1930	1920	1910	1900	1895	1890	1884	1880	1870	1860	1850
Henefer	554	547	446	408	346	335	400	300	300	250	347	291		262	172		
Henrieville	163	167	145	152	114	241	207	196	250	100			100				
Herriman	750	600	450	350	289	300	289	289	250	150		106					
Hiawatha	43	249	166	439	1421	858	939	1408	330								
Highland	5002	2435															
Highland Boy						400				100							
Hildale	1325	1009	480	290	290							179					
Hinckley	658	464	400	397	589	637	678	821	553	327	453						
Holden	402	364	351	388	476	500	485	550	480	450	437	363	300	355	266		
Holladay	26200	22189	23014	20000	3100	1000	715	500	537	537							
Honeyville	1112	915	640	646	599	596	494	436	300	129		150	100				
Hooper	3000	2000	1705	1243	950	1000	911	1000	800	772	905	500	300	400	100		
Howell	237	176	146	188	176	265	170	150	250								
Hoytsville				200	300	300	300	300	350	300			300				
Hunter								510									
Huntington	1875	2316	857	787	1029	997	877	1285	800	653	987	513	400	100			
Huntsville	561	577	553	552	494	496	520	550	890	890	1144	704	1000	500	500		
Hurricane	3915	2361	1408	1251	1271	1524	1197	1021	366								
Hyde Park	2190	1495	1025	696	644	696	723	721	699	550	647	450	600	433	343		
Hyrum	4829	3952	2340	1728	1704	1874	1869	1858	1833	1652	1800	1423	1500	1234	708		
Ibapah	50	50	50	65	150	213	213	200	250	200							
Indianola					50	75	108	136	150	100		97					
Ioka				85	138	225	225	200									
Iosepa							33	150	300	200							
Ivins	1630	600	137	77	95	83											
Jacob City															300		
Jensen	450	400	300	581	350	350	350	350	300	200	556	250	280	150			
Joseph	198	217	125	117	208	297	243	244	227	343		110	100	95			
Juab									198	198			120	71			
Junction	132	151	135	219	285	393	352	389	400	200	206	157					
Kamas	1061	1064	806	749	721	683	491	563	400	300	638	300	300	260			
Kanab	3289	2148	1381	1645	1287	1365	1195	1102	733	710	613	409	350	394	73		
Kanarraville	228	255	204	236	263	309	317	386	290	159		260	400	200	280		
Kanosh	386	435	319	499	476	526	570	573	513	500	685	400	400	406	520		
Kaysville	13961	9811	6192	3608	1898	1211	992	809	887	1708	1759	548	1500	487	100		
Kearns	28374	21353	17071	17172													
Kelton								50	110	76		121	200	135	101		
Kenilworth	250	350	500	560	932	879	858	806	542								
Kimberly						50		50	300	104							
Kingston	134	146	114	143	138	63	150	100	100	100	130	178	100	138			

POPULATION HISTORY OF UTAH CITIES AND TOWNS 1850-1990

COMMUNITY	1990	1980	1970	1960	1950	1940	1930	1920	1910	1900	1895	1890	1884	1880	1870	1860	1850
Knightville								200	200	50			75				
Koosharem	266	183	141	148	300	375	319	300	300	200	419	125	50				
La Sal	300	100	100	160	150	100	200	200	150	75			75				
La Verkin	1771	1174	463	365	387	349	236	150	100								
Lake Point					300	250	250	200	100	150							
Laketown	261	271	208	211	217	200	278	250	255	258	274	302		170	127		
Lapoint	300	250	200	200	200	250	250	200									
Lark		500	728	850	750	430	349	500	450								
Latuda					200	275	316	343	150								
Lawrence										150							
Layton	41784	22862	13603	9027	3456	646	597	500	810	759	905	500					
Laytona					405	356											
Leamington	253	113	112	150	214	279	333	300	300	170	318	253	250	200			
Leeds	254	218	151	109	160	232	165	152	150	190	267	200		200	104		
Lehi	8475	6848	4659	4377	3627	2733	2826	3078	2964	2719	2591	1600	1000	1497	1058	831	
Levan	416	453	376	421	521	621	611	634	722	500	531	350	600	395	320		
Lewiston	1532	1438	1244	1336	1533	1804	1783	1645	989	900	969	600		125			
Liberty			200	225	196	200	125	200	200	200							
Lindon	3818	2796	1644	1150	801	587	589	450	400	300							
Linwood				100	122		100	200	130								
Loa	444	364	324	359	437	396	343	499	400	216		160	250	160			
Logan	32762	26844	22333	18731	16832	11868	9979	9439	7522	5451	5756	4565	4000	3396	1757		
Lyman	198	170	170	250	255	276	200	150	150	100							
Lynndyl	120	90	111	145	241	369	322	360	200								
Maeser	2598	2216	1248	929	643	428	207	300	200								
Magna/Pleasant Green	17829	13138	5509	6442	3502	3780	1604	1515	250								
Mammoth	50	50	50	52	184	492	750	970	1771	1500	389	286		200			
Manila	207	272	226	329	300	214	164	200	230	150							
Manti	2268	2080	1803	1739	2051	2268	2200	2412	2423	2408	2328	1950	1800	1748	1237	916	100
Mantua/Geneva	665	484	413	275	271	319	314	354	300	250		200	300	190			
Mapleton	3572	2726	1980	1516	1175	907	663	586	534	278	536						
Marion	100	100	100					200	150	100							
Martin	200	175	200														
Marysvale	364	359	289	354	520	626	471	624	250	250	546	250	200	250			
Mayfield	438	397	267	329	390	473	467	550	485	400		250	390	150			
Meadow	250	265	238	244	378	422	395	405	331	300	376	349	200	212			
Menden	684	663	345	345	369	454	434	404	459	494	532	500	600	543	100		
Mercur/Lewiston						358		75	1047	2351	303			125			
Mexican Hat	259	100	100	85	80												
Midvale	11886	10144	7840	5802	3996	2875	2451	2209	1760								

POPULATION HISTORY OF UTAH CITIES AND TOWNS 1850-1990

COMMUNITY	1850	1860	1870	1880	1884	1890	1895	1900	1910	1920	1930	1940	1950	1960	1970	1980	1990
Midway			378	288	725	627	944	719	838	805	745	801	711	713	804	1194	1554
Milford				250	200	181	277	298	1014	1308	1517	1393	1673	1471	1304	1293	1107
Millcreek			200	270	2000	375		1500	2300						26579	24150	32230
Millville			402	539	650	500	576	400	353	409	403	439	401	364	441	848	1202
Milton				159													
Minersville			350	450	500	475	523	437	591	675	537	570	593	580	448	552	608
Moab				150		333	525	500	615	856	853	1084	1274	4682	4793	5333	3971
Mohrland										691	620						
Mona			315	397	500	350	418	300	300	250	338	357	328	347	309	536	584
Monroe			200	700	500	880	1151	1057	1227	1719	1247	1292	1214	955	918	1476	1472
Montezuma Creek														200		300	345
Monticello							149	180	375	768	496	667	1172	1845	1431	1929	1806
Morgan			200	433	500	333	800	600	756	995	953	1078	1064	1299	1586	1896	2023
Moroni		703	633	838	1000	958	1406	1224	1223	1355	1218	1158	1076	879	894	1086	1115
Mount Carmel						77		100	120	134	133	125	158	110	100	75	75
Mount Emmons										100	280	250	176		100	100	100
Mount Olympus															5909	6068	7413
Mount Pleasant		746	1346	2004	1500	2254	2481	2372	2280	2415	2284	2382	2030	1572	1516	2049	2092
Mountain Home										200	200		150	143	75	50	100
Murray			200	500	800	1000	2510	2137	4057	4584	5172	5740	9006	16806	21206	25750	31282
Mutual											213	213	213			500	468
Myton									300	479	395	437	435	329	322		
Naples											250				100	250	1334
National										300	300	300	300	52			
Neola									300	300	300	200	300	300	400	550	511
Nephi		715	1286	1797	2000	2034	2515	2208	2759	2603	2573	2835	2990	2566	2699	3285	3515
New Harmony					50	103		139	170	99	107	170	126	105	78	117	101
Newcastle									300	150	100	100	100	129	150	150	200
Newhouse									300	89	115	115					
Newton			145	304	200	300	554	429	515	529	555	549	497	480	444	623	659
Nibley											271	271	304	333	367	1036	1167
North Logan											325	423	535	741	1405	2258	3768
North Ogden			250	450	500	410	787	820	820	820	932	687	1105	2621	5257	9309	11668
North Salt Lake										500	515	515	1255	1655	2143	5548	6474
Oak City				175	175	140	245	200	200	326	340	391	334	312	278	389	587
Oakley						100	279	167	120	250	271	305	264	247	265	470	522
Oasis						100		150	275	400	325	240	240	190	100	125	150
Ogden	500	1464	3127	6069	7000	14889	15828	16313	25580	32804	40272	43688	57112	70197	69478	64407	63909
Ophir				149	186	200	205	259	254	522	170	300	199	36	76	42	25
Orangeville					500	313	672	392	648	553	532	652	589	571	511	1309	1459

POPULATION HISTORY OF UTAH CITIES AND TOWNS 1850-1990

COMMUNITY	1990	1980	1970	1960	1950	1940	1930	1920	1910	1900	1895	1890	1884	1880	1870	1860	1850
Orderville	422	423	399	398	371	420	346	300	300	290	499	289	600	514			
Orem	67561	42399	25729	18394	8351	2914	1915	600	500	150							
Panguitch	1444	1343	1318	1435	1501	1979	1541	1473	1338	883	977	850	600	664	200		
Paradise	561	542	399	368	401	500	433	505	620	596	530	550	200	512	346		
Paragonah	307	310	275	300	404	365	384	449	350	327	314	234	400	256	211		
Park City	4468	2823	1193	1366	2254	3739	4281	3393	3439	3759	4491	2850	2500	1542	164		
Park Terrace	850	850	850														
Park Valley	50	85	100	100	162	162	167	200	250	156		108	135	130			
Parowan	1873	1836	1423	1486	1455	1525	1474	1640	1156	1039	1084	950	950	957	861	526	
Payson	9510	8246	4501	4237	3998	3591	3045	3031	2397	2636	2644	2135	2000	1788	1436	830	
Peerless					105	97	207	171									
Peoa	150	130	130	200	203	200	125	247	260	236		231	350	200	200		
Perry	1211	1084	909	587	449	383	341	367	250	146							
Peruvian Park	750	600	600														
Peterson	120	130	130	150	175	175	156	175	280	200		129					
Pine Valley	150	50	50	54	16	33	49	58	118	251	243	253	250	234	326		
Plain City	2722	2379	1543	1152	829	800	750	800	815	845	295	248	200	230	100		
Pleasant Grove/Battle Creek	13476	10883	5327	4772	3195	1941	1754	1682	1618	2460	2301	1926	1500	1775	930	526	
Pleasant View	3603	3983	2021	927	420	214	100	150	150			146					
Plymouth	267	238	203	231	228	292	304	250	250	190			80	150			
Portage	218	196	144	189	254	342	331	250	250	250	407	300	175	282	100		
Price	8712	9086	6218	6802	6010	5214	4084	2364	1021	539	604	209	100	85			
Promontory								50	75	100		78		140	400		
Providence	3344	2675	1608	1189	1055	1110	1088	1132	1020	877	944	650	700	578	481		
Provo	86835	74108	53131	36047	28937	18071	14766	10303	8925	6185	5992	5159	4500	3432	2384	2030	500
Rains					312	363	271	430	160	160			100				
Ranch																	
Randlett	283	140	125	250	350	350	300	200									
Randolph	488	659	500	537	562	656	447	586	533	600	593	300	600	263	76		
Redmond	648	619	409	413	600	641	577	649	547	451	402	250					
Redwood	1850	2000	2000														
Richfield	5593	5482	4471	4412	4212	3584	3067	3262	2559	1969	1817	1531	1500	1197	250		
Richmond	1955	1705	1000	977	1091	1131	1140	1396	1562	1111	1295	1100	1000	1198	817		
River Heights	1274	1211	1008	880	468	288											
Riverdale	6419	6031	3704	1848	871	600	316	300	300	156	284						
Riverside	270	240	200	195	190	190	190	175	150	100							
Riverton	11261	7293	2820	1993	1666	1404	1130	600	700	318	636						
Robinson									500	400							
Rockport									94	94		184	133	146			
Rockville	182	130	110	138	180	193	226	200	230	142	242	227	190	218	225		

POPULATION HISTORY OF UTAH CITIES AND TOWNS 1850-1990

COMMUNITY	1990	1980	1970	1960	1950	1940	1930	1920	1910	1900	1895	1890	1884	1880	1870	1860	1850
Roosevelt	3915	3842	2005	1812	1628	1264	1051	1054	500								
Rosette					68		77	150	200								
Roy	24603	19694	14356	9239	3723	998	557	500	250	195							
Royal				195	250												
Rush Valley/Onaqui	339	356	541	511	333	374											
Sahara Village					1636												
St George	28502	11350	7097	5130	4562	3591	2434	2215	1737	1600	1661	1377	1500	1384	1142		
St John					140	125	125	175	125	200		153	300	278			
Salem	2284	2233	1081	920	781	659	610	609	693	894	811	527	600	510	353		
Salina	1943	1992	1494	1618	1789	1616	1383	1451	1082	847	1022	601	450	147			
Salt Lake City	159936	163033	175885	189454	182121	149934	140267	118110	92777	53531	48076	44843	25000	20768	12854	8236	6157
Sandy	75058	50546	6438	3322	2095	1487	1436	1208	1037	1030	1195	749	600	400	300		
Santa Clara	2322	1091	271	291	319	283	249	305	293	258	223	202	150	195	233	158	
Santaquin	2386	2175	1236	1183	1214	1297	1115	976	915	889	953	624	200	715	602		
Scipio	291	257	264	328	491	595	544	543	546	578	687	518		500	465		
Scofield	43	105	71	158	236	259	254	678	746	642	593	600	500				
Sego					20	50	200	250									
Sevier				65	110		200	125	130	100							
Sigurd	385	386	291	339	431	364	201	200	150	70							
Silver City					30	111	278	689	549	918	187	224	200	300			
Silver Reef	50											177	1500	1046			
Slaterville												88	75				
Smithfield	5566	4993	3342	2512	2383	2461	2353	2421	1865	1494	1448	1080	1000	1177	744		
Snowbird	130	100															
Snowville	251	237	174	159	199	195	169	245	150	62		127	100	100			
Soldier Summit						97	319	250	50								
South Cottonwood		11117	4800														
South Jordan	12220	7492	2942	1354	1048	869	480	480				302		300			
South Ogden	12105	11366	9991	7405	3763	1407								242			
South Salt Lake	10129	10561	7810	9520	7704	5701											
South Weber	2863	1575	1073	382	244	259	250										
Spanish Fork	11272	9825	7284	6472	5230	4167	3727	4036	3464	2735	3157	2214	2000	2304	1450	773	
Spring Canyon/Starrs					458	691	869	656									
Spring City	715	671	456	463	703	839	992	1106	1100	1135	1226	1044	750	989	623	243	
Spring Glen/Ewell	950	800	700	500	400	350	337	298	200								
Spring Lake	200	300	250	250	310	310	240	230	180	140	115	70		100	100		
Springdale	275	258	172	248	174	268	217	230						50			
Springville	13950	12101	8790	7913	6475	4796	3748	3010	3356	3422	3168	2849	2500	2312	1661	1357	
Spry							50	300	200								
Standardville				250	307	257	504	545									

POPULATION HISTORY OF UTAH CITIES AND TOWNS 1850-1990

COMMUNITY	1990	1980	1970	1960	1950	1940	1930	1920	1910	1900	1895	1890	1884	1880	1870	1860	1850
Stansbury Park	1049																
State Line		300															
Sterling	191	199	144	137	188	223	200	50	250	175	347	85	190				
Stockton	426	437	469	362	414	332	251	238	258	300	358	219	200	350	150		
Storrs								656									
Sugarhouse									1000	800			500				
Summit	175	175	150	158	150	146	146	150	180	150			120	123			
Sunnyside	339	611	485	1740	1881	424	749	2072	1811	240							
Sunset	5128	5733	6268	4235	993	276	600	200									
Syracuse	4658	3702	1843	1061	837	732	419	415	500	234	227						
Tabiona	120	152	125	167	160	211	170	200	100	50							
Talmage	30	50	75	100	160	174	160	100	300	150							
Taylorsville	17448	17448	12522	3340				600	550	470		269	250	79			
Teasdale	200	175							150	150							
Terrace				196	237	200		200	50	150	274	300	200	350	125		
Thatcher				150	250		125	100	100	50							
Thistle		45	50	36	150	216	217	300	300	150	196	250	150	50			
Thurber													150				
Tintic													300				
Tod Park			500	700	1836												
Tooele	13887	14335	12539	9133	7269	5001	5315	3602	2753	1200	1154	1000	1500	918	958	416	
Topliff							58	150	102								
Toquerville	488	277	185	197	219	263	288	331	250	250	349	374	250	371	264	79	
Torrey	122	140	84	128	241	231	217	200	100	64							
Tremonton	4264	3464	2794	2115	1662	1443	1009	937	303								
Trenton	464	447	390	448	451	553	286	400	300	224	241	200	50	50			
Tridell	100	50	80	310	310	347	290	250									
Tropic	374	338	329	382	483	514	447	474	358	300	490	150					
Tucker								25	150	200	187	150	300				
Uintah	760	439	400	344	317	264	250	280	230	212	287	251		250			
Union/East Midvale	5800	9665	2500	1000	811	300	213	213	350	300		100					
Upalco	45		75	110	200	200	300	50									
Upton	125	100	100	125	112	112	112	200	200	189	237	195		174			
Val Verda	3712	6422	1200														
Venice	200	150	200	220	250	305	238	300	140								
Vernal/Ashley	6644	6600	3908	3655	2843	2119	1744	1309	836	644	471	264	300	300			
Vernon	181	181	175	160	175	192	189	200	150	185	194	160	175	100			
Veyo	125	100	100	125	115	100	150	79									
Vineyard	151	197			113	150	160										
Virgin	229	169	119	124	147	143	198	200	200	200	285	208	200	199	224	79	

POPULATION HISTORY OF UTAH CITIES AND TOWNS 1850-1990

COMMUNITY	1990	1980	1970	1960	1950	1940	1930	1920	1910	1900	1895	1890	1884	1880	1870	1860	1850
Wales	189	153	89	130	179	223	243	280	294	250	305	123	100				
Wallsburg	252	239	211	180	207	233	240	300	350	350	468	259	400	198			
Wanship	200	200	175	150	173	215	205	118	118	118	225	223	300	338	315		
Washakie								150	200	200		75					
Washington	4198	3092	750	445	435	507	435	464	424	529	484	415	200	483	463	196	
Washington Terrace	8189	8112	7141	6441	5841												
Wattis				63	283	200	249	262									
Weber									500	500		100					
Wellington	1632	1406	922	1066	845	674	348	361	358	311	429	200		88			
Wellsville	2206	1952	1267	1106	1241	1402	1270	1298	1195	908	1390	850	1300	1193	885		
Wendover	1127	1099	781	609	250	300	192	200	100								
West Bountiful	4477	3556	1246	945	682												
West Jordan	42892	27192	4211	3009	2107	1220	1220	1220	1500	1337	1561	1271					
West Point	4258	2170	1020	599	433	236	630						400	300			
West Portage													350				
West Valley City	86976	72378															
West Weber	6506	7188	6402														
White City	312	200	300	500	276	150	250	50									
Whiterocks				295	170	100	86	100	100	58		100					
Widtsoe					25	103	103	500									
Willard	1298	1241	1045	814	548	541	561	651	577	580	936	492	750	412	552	627	
Wilson	400	300	200														
Winter Quarters						100		623	770	696							
Woodland					200		50	150	162	162							
Woodland Hills	301	60															
Woodruff	135	222	173	169	175	241	332	339	200	300	445	200	300	150	150		
Woods Cross	5384	4263	3124	1098	273	211	500	600	700	400				165			
Woodside							50	100	150	50							
Yost		67	51	87	107	172	201	172	150	56							

1884: Colorado, New Mexico, Utah, Nevada, Wyoming, and Arizona Gazetteer and Business Directory. Chicago: R.L. Polk, 1884.
1895: Utah. Bureau of Statistics. First Triennial Report of the Bureau of Statistics of Utah for the Year Ending December 31, 1894, With Census of 1895. Salt Lake City: 1895.

POPULATION HISTORY OF WASHINGTON CITIES AND TOWNS 1860-1990

COMMUNITY	1990	1980	1970	1960	1950	1940	1930	1920	1910	1900	1890	1880	1870	1860
Aberdeen	16565	18739	18489	18741	19653	18846	21723	15337	13660	3747	1638			
Academy	350	350	400											
Acme	300	250	300	250	200	230	100	317	100	80				
Addy	220	200	200	245	325	300	300	325	375	93				
Adelaide		450	350											
Adrian							75		175					
Ahtanum	400	120	100	200	164	164	164	164						
Airway Heights	1971	1730	744	708	400	450								
Ajune							450	59						
Albion	632	631	687	291	256	206	236	252	276	196				
Alder			300		150	349	265	162	100			65		
Alderton				300	350	350	350	525						
Alderwood	1760	1900												
Alderwood Manor	4350	3950	3800	2500	600	500	500	362						
Alger														
Algona	1694	1467	1276	1311	1500	1329	1000	416	250					
Allen	150	150	135	300		550		82						
Allentown	660	950	900	600	400	250	250							
Allyn	1100	900	750	500	300	258	125	192	100					
Almira	310	330	376	414	395	466	339	450	368	198				
Aloha	100	150	140	200	150	240	200	133						
Alpine								283						
Amanda Park	800	800	350	142	225	200	67	67	112	112				
Amboy	370	300	350	275	360	800	800	134						
American Lake														
American River							300							
Anacortes	11451	9013	7701	8414	6919	5875	6564	5284	4168	1476	1131			
Anatone	90	70	70	75	75	150	300	250	500	109	93			
Angle Lake		3500												
Annapolis				1472	800	500	500	216						
Appleyard		1500	950	950	1479	200	200							
Ardenvoir	120	100	200	150	250	292								
Ariel							300							
Arletta	500	500	300		75		63	63						
Arlington	4037	3282	2261	2025	1635	1460	1439	1418	1476	340	852			
Arlington Heights	500	800	1000											
Armar	850	1250	1100											
Arrowhead	1400	1500												
Ashford	600	500	350	325	300	190	165	136	300	470	200			
Asotin	981	943	637	745	740	686	697	852	820					

POPULATION HISTORY OF WASHINGTON CITIES AND TOWNS 1860-1990

COMMUNITY	1990	1980	1970	1960	1950	1940	1930	1920	1910	1900	1890	1880	1870	1860
Attalia							100		200					
Auburn	33102	26417	21817	11933	6497	4211	3906	3163	957	489	740			
Ault Field	3795	3553												
Avon				150		125	200	125	193	193	142			
Bainbridge Island	3081	2196	1461	919										
Baldi														
Ballard							30	268		4568	1173			
Bangor	240	200	120	124	124	157	157	268						
Baring				155	150		95	214	94	94				
Barneston								412						
Battleground	3758	2774	1438	888	858	440	540	318	200	72	68			
Bay Center	380	350	300	343	250	201	200	264	225	116	132			
Bayne							100	314						
Bay View							135	324	189	189	111			
Beach								241						
Beacon Hill	1496	1500	1263	1019	310									
Beaux Arts	303	328	475	351										
Beaver	930	900	450	300	125				79	79				
Beebe							200							
Belfair	750	450	400	450	300	300	250							
Bellevue	86874	73903	61102	12809	7658	1177	1071	1213	150					
Bellingham/Whatcom/Fairhaven	52179	45794	39375	34688	34112	29314	30823	25585	24298	11062	8135	1300	258	77
Benson Hill	1300	1240												
Benton City	1806	1980	1070	1210	863	165	150	84						
Bethel	500	500	350	300										
Beverly	250	250	215	175	75	103	40		100					
Beverly Park				1950	1700	1208	1000							
Bickleton	150	150	110	125	125	220	215	168	300	116	96			
Biglake	250	150	100	210	220	330	80	515	210	210				
Bingen	645	644	671	636	736	600	365		125	80				
Birch Bay	1050	900	300	350	200	100	100							
Birdsview	400	500	400			357	200							
Black Diamond	1422	1170	1160	1026	769	1559	1400	2246	570	631	561			
Blaine	2489	2363	1955	1735	1693	1524	1642	2254	2289	1592	1563			
Blanchard							150	314						
Blewett							54	367		56				
Blockhouse									164	164				
Blyn				376	200	357	300		60					
Boistfort									40	40		197		
Bonney Lake	7494	5328	2700	645	275									

POPULATION HISTORY OF WASHINGTON CITIES AND TOWNS 1860-1990

COMMUNITY	1990	1980	1970	1960	1950	1940	1930	1920	1910	1900	1890	1880	1870	1860
Bordeaux														
Bossburg						388	500	321	247	347				
Boston Harbor	270	250	200	200										
Bothell	12345	7943	4883	2237	1019	794	818	613	599	342				
Bow	180	400	300	250	100	125	215	121						
Brady							57	319						
Bremerton	38142	36208	35307	26681	27678	15134	10170	8918	2993					
Brewster	1633	1337	1059	940	851	447	413	394	296	220				
Briarwood	4800	1440								194				
Bridgeport	1498	1174	952	876	802	320	305	337	431	110				
Bridle Trail	5633	600												
Brier		2915	3093											
Brinnon	600	600	300	200	150	130	130	213						
Brookdale						500	500							
Brookfield									80	80	76	150		
Brooklyn				85	100	230	230							
Browns Point	1950	1900	700	400		250	250							
Brownstown	50	45	80	80	65									
Brownsville	250	200	100	150	150	120	50	44						
Brush Prairie	620	500	100	175	65	198	100	118	180	63				
Bryant	50			100	150	652	150	214	100	68				
Bryn Mawr	1500	2100	2300	2000	2000	800	600	261						
Buckeye							300		75					
Buckley	3516	3143	3446	3533	2705	1170	1052	1119	1272	1014	878			
Bucoda	536	519	421	390	473	541	703	442	425	777	945			
Buena	800	800	630	640	600	400	400	47						
Burbank	710	700	650	600	175		100	45	60					
Burbank Heights	510	500	200											
Burien/Lake Burien	17000	14250	15000	9000	4387	1325	1030							
Burley	300	300	200	160	198	150	150	317	100					
Burlington	4349	3894	3138	2968	2350	1632	1407	1360	1302	227				
Burnett			150	100			356	215	117	117				
Burton	250	200	300	350	300	250	250	410	76	76				
Byron							80	217						
Camas	6442	5681	5790	5666	4725	4433	4239	1843	1125	439	417			
Camelot	4900	3880												
Cape Horn							150		80					
Carbonado	495	456	394	424	412	450	400	864	730	1309	705			
Carlisle	250	200					75	416						
Carlsborg	420	350	250	250	200	450	560	263						

POPULATION HISTORY OF WASHINGTON CITIES AND TOWNS 1860-1990

COMMUNITY	1990	1980	1970	1960	1950	1940	1930	1920	1910	1900	1890	1880	1870	1860
Carlton	60	100	120	100	200	110	100	49	120					
Carlyle		500	600											
Carnation/Tolt	1243	913	530	490	446	460	360	536						
Carrolls	200	400	250	150	200	200	160	48	94	94				
Carson	990	950	600	500	600	550	276	267	300					
Cascade Vista	7800	7800												
Cascades										62	164	149		
Cashmere	2544	2240	1976	1891	1768	1465	1473	1114	625					
Castle Rock	2067	2160	1647	1424	1255	1182	1239	829	998	750	681			
Cathcart	950			125	175	175	75							
Cathlamet	508	635	647	615	501	621	537	422	352	280	116	133		
Catlin									148	148				
Cedarhome	200	200	400	100	100				116	116				
Centerville	120	95	100	400	125	125	200	225						
Central Park	2669	2900	2720	1622	900				300	300	168	150		
Centralia	12101	10809	10054	8586	8657	7414	8058	7549	7311	1600	2026			
Charleston								3338	1062	197				
Chattaroy	400	400	200	200	200	125	65	117	150	80				
Chehalis	6527	6100	5727	5199	5639	4857	4907	4558	4507	1775	1309			
Chelan	2969	2802	2684	2402	2445	1979	1403	896	682	483				
Chelan Falls	300	250	200	300	350	100	100	78	40	45				
Cheney	7723	7630	6358	3173	2797	1551	1335	1252	1207	781	647			
Cherokee Bay	650	250												
Cherry Point	1000													
Cherry Valley							200		100	205	42	58		
Chesaw	80	40	32		45	100	202	267	300					
Chewelah	1945	1888	1365	1525	1683	1565	1315	1288	823	487	376			
Chico	420	750	700	318	500	589	589	62				90		
Chimacum	750	600	250	300	200	250	364	110	100	49				
Chinook	710	650	430	350	380	550	500	518	218	218				
Church Lake	500													
Clallam Bay	850	600	300	500	450	211	200	162	100	68	68			
Claquato														
Clarkston	6753	6903	6312	6209	5617	3116	2870	1859	1257	480		100		
Clarkston Heights	1150	1100	1000											
Clayton	220	200	180	240	280	357	200	319	200	127				
Cle Elum	1778	1773	1725	1816	2206	2230	2508	2661	2749	296	243			
Clearlake	1100	900	700	600	500	727	1019	719	153	153				
Clearview	240	600	400	200			75							
Clearwater	250	250	250	77	100	200	70							

POPULATION HISTORY OF WASHINGTON CITIES AND TOWNS 1860-1990

COMMUNITY	1990	1980	1970	1960	1950	1940	1930	1920	1910	1900	1890	1880	1870	1860
Cleveland														
Cliffs									170	170	100			
Clift							400		180					
Clinton	1564	2000	500	800	800	150	62	62	62	62				
Clipper							200							
Clyde Hill	2972	3229	2987	1871	1116									
Coalfield	400	300	200	200	150									
Colbert/Dean									160					
Colby	170	180	150	321	200	140	55	520	350	92	44			
Colchester	450	400		230										
Coleman							300							
Colfax	2713	2780	2664	2860	3057	2853	2782	3027	2783	2121	1649	444		
College Place	6308	5771	4510	4031	3174	1505	1505	813	79	79				
Cotton	325	307	279	253	207	262	269	382	393	251	410			
Columbia City										337				
Columbia Heights	2515	1700	1572	2227										
Columbia Valley	900	900												
Colville	4360	4510	3742	3806	3033	2418	1803	1718	1533	594	534	67		
Conconully	153	157	122	106	141	187	102	270	357	369	232			
Concrete	735	592	573	840	760	859	736	924	945					
Connell	2005	1981	1161	906	465	365	321	311	575					
Copalis Beach	900	800	450	450	300	400	400	75	55	55				
Cosmopolis	1372	1575	1599	1312	1164	1207	1493	1512	1132	1004	287			
Cottage Lake	2500	300	300	300										
Coulee City	568	510	558	654	977	744	420	472	276	183				
Coulee Dam	1087	1412	1425	1344	2100	600								
Country Homes	5126	1800	2000	700										
Coupeville	1377	1006	678	740	379	325	277	343	310	540	513	90	100	
Cove				150	110	241	241	416						
Coveland													200	
Covington	450	350	350			150								
Cowiche	350	160	125	155	150	133	500	34						
Cowlitz										137	375	80	100	
Creosote	150			275	275	275	250	162						
Creston	230	309	325	317	268	281	216	317	308	135				
Crewport			120	750	700									
Crimea										250				
Cromwell								163						
Cumberland	130	95	250	150	250	273	225	1247	54	54				
Cunningham							37	89	153					

POPULATION HISTORY OF WASHINGTON CITIES AND TOWNS 1860-1990

COMMUNITY	1990	1980	1970	1960	1950	1940	1930	1920	1910	1900	1890	1880	1870	1860
Curlew	220	200	100	100	100	100	100	127	250					
Cusick	195	246	257	299	360	404	380	184	200	77				
Custer	500	500	400	325	200	200	250	314	350	114	43			
Daisy									200	100				
Dalkena	80	75		125	125	302	350	314	314					
Dallesport	590	500	300											
Danville				150			75	163						
Darrington	1042	1064	1094	1272	921	982	400	376	180					
Dash Point			500	380	297	326	297	226						
Davenport	1502	1559	1363	1494	1417	1337	987	1112	1229	1000	396			
Dayton	2468	2565	2596	2913	2979	3026	2528	2695	2389	2216	1880	996		
Deception											206		100	
Deep Creek									68	68	201			
Deep River					450	715	301	121						
Deer Harbor				375			75	147	61					
Deer Park	2278	2140	1295	1333	1167	1170	1009	1103	875	180				
Delta													500	
Deming	450	450	450	250	250	278	250	268	400	157				
Denny Park	2500	800												
Des Moines	17283	7378	4099	1987	911	1104	600	619	215	278	212			
Desert Aire	600													
Dewey	550	550	500											
Dieringer						266	143	56	56	56				
Dishman	9671	9900	9079	7381	2500	440	406	100						
Dixie	230	200	200	280	250	200	200	314	85	85	42			
Dockton	300	300	200	400	200	257	200	253	125					
Doty	320	280	225	250	300	330	287	624	250					
Douglas						275	60	75		58				
Downs									200					
Driftwood Point	900													
Dryad	100		184	400	400	300	300	319	169	148				
Dryden	480	400	320	646	300	335	250							
Du Pont	592	559	384	354	353	578	400	600						
Dungeness/New Dungeness	160	150	150	290	300	165	150	118	162	162	127			
Duvall	2770	729	607	345	236	234	200	258						
Duwamish	100	500	500							243				
Eagledale	650	550	500	500										
Earlington					595	603	250	320						
East Farms	1400	500					86							
East Olympia/Chambers Prairie	800	700	500	350	300	200	200	163				100	100	104

POPULATION HISTORY OF WASHINGTON CITIES AND TOWNS 1860-1990

COMMUNITY	1860	1870	1880	1890	1900	1910	1920	1930	1940	1950	1960	1970	1980	1990
East Port Orchard													4631	5409
East Spokane					575									2200
East Stanwood							327	600	359	387	300	400		
East Wall Walla								800	330					
East Wenatchee								500	268	389	383	913	1640	2701
Eastgate											3000	5000	5300	4434
Eastmont													1250	1450
Easton					58	58	251	266	275	300	250	400	250	270
Eastsound					138	92	314	256	276	250	200	400	900	1100
Eastview Hills													1500	750
Eatonville					107	754	861	912	996	1048	896	852	998	1374
Edgecomb					70	70		150	150					
Edgewater				191										
Edgewick							217	30						
Edgewood								999	1098	800	700	900	1800	2650
Edison				118	216	350	218	250	250	300	250	250	250	300
Edmonds				63	474	1114	936	1165	1288	2057	8016	23998	27526	30744
Edwall					250	450	275	150	145	143	150	110	110	110
Eglon												100	300	300
Egypt				149	58	58			125					
Elbe					94	180	217	175	175	350	225	150	300	300
Elberton				86	297	330	244	125	151	145	66	75		
Electric City						100	515	250	750	698	404	651	927	910
Elk		150	150						200	93	265	100	50	50
Ellensburg				2768	1737	4209	3967	4621	5944	8430	8625	13568	11752	12361
Ellisport							412	125				1000	1700	1820
Ellsworth						76	34	60						
Elma		250		345	894	1532	1253	1545	1370	1543	1811	2227	2720	3011
Elmer City										513	265	324	312	290
Eltopia						300	219	85	750					
Endicott				210	224	474	634	512	495	397	369	333	290	320
Enetai											2533	2878	2638	
English							110	50	300					
Entiat					248	160	214	290	176	420	357	355	445	449
Enumclaw				65		800	1378	2089	2627	2789	3269	4703	5427	7227
Ephrata						323	628	516	951	4589	6548	5255	5359	5349
Erlands Point											800	1017	1220	1254
Esperance								150	150		100		11120	11236
Ethel					58	42	39	300	300	350	150	100	150	170
Everett					7838	24814	27644	30567	30224	33849	40304	53622	54413	69961

POPULATION HISTORY OF WASHINGTON CITIES AND TOWNS 1860-1990

COMMUNITY	1990	1980	1970	1960	1950	1940	1930	1920	1910	1900	1890	1880	1870	1860
Everson	1490	898	633	431	345	292	295	618	550	118				
Ewan							150							
Factoria		400					50							
Fair Lakes			250			300								
Fairchild AFB	4854	5353	6754		5000	263								
Fairfax	446			50	70	200	200	520	120	56				
Fairfield	6997	582	469	367	369	364	381	413	308	413				
Fairmont	1730	6997	1600	1227	200	200	212	212						
Fairview	2000	2300	2111	2758										
Fairwood		1020			500									
Fall City	1582	1600	1300	950	800	450	400	375	400	369	78			
Fargher Lake						275	100							
Farmer				100	125	278	81	63						
Farmington	126	176	140	176	239	341	344	479	489	434	418	76		
Federal Way	45165	17850	18500	7000										
Felida	1250	2000					260							
Fern Prairie						500		49			46			
Ferncliff														
Ferndale	5398	3855	2164	1442	979	717	752	759	691	248				
Fernhill							250		300	300				
Fernwood		220												
Fidalgo City										44	297	191		
Fife	3864	1823	1458	1463	950	150	135							
Fife Heights	1050	950												
Fir/Conway							200		200	152	280			
Fircrest	5258	5477	5651	3565	1459	486	441							
Firgrove	1300	950												
Fisher	360	360	200	100			50	134	84	84	42			
Florence	50	35		60			300	283	142	142	46			
Fords Prairie	2480	2000	2250	1404	300	300								
Forest Hills	800	900												
Forks	2862	3060	1682	1156	1120	720	600	80						
Fort Casey							35	415	80					
Fort Colville													56	166
Fort Lewis	22224	23761	38054		35000	3773								
Fort Spokane						300	2080				200			
Fort Steilacoom														254
Fort Vancouver											600	300		428
Fort Walla Walla											300	350	83	320
Fort Warden						750	387							

POPULATION HISTORY OF WASHINGTON CITIES AND TOWNS 1860-1990

COMMUNITY	1990	1980	1970	1960	1950	1940	1930	1920	1910	1900	1890	1880	1870	1860
Fortson						200	200	159	100					
Foster		250	250	200	400	412	412	520	100					
Four Lakes	380	1000	600	150	200	125	125	69						
Fox Island	2017		175	175	108	145	300	217	280	248				
Francis					200	165	150							
Franklin	1278	1300	500	200	250	150	300	158	102	688	647	50	50	
Freeland		150	100	175	200	220	100	219	175					
Freeman														
Freeport										998	144			
Fremont											802			
Friday Harbor	1492	1200	803	706	783	658	601	522	400	282	80			
Fruitvale	4125	3600	3275	3345	3654									
Galvin	200	180	150	220	150	220	400	319						
Gardiner	300	300	120	100	150		86	57						
Garfield	544	599	610	607	674	674	703	776	932	697	317			
Garrett	1004	1586	1586	1641										
Gate			75	112	102	133	133	113	113	135				
Geiger Heights		1500	1424											
Geneva	1423	1423	800	500										
George	253	261	273	291										
Georgetown										243				
Gertrude							265	163	97	97				
Getchell		300	230				150	110						
Gibraltar						100								
Gifford									160					
Gig Harbor	3236	2429	1657	1094	803	1203	1200	216	180	334	321			
Gilberton	300	250	100	100	150									
Gillies										700				
Gilman										700				
Gleed	500	500	300	300			50	45						
Glenoma	320	300	200	300		400	450							
Glenrose	400	600	600	550										
Glenwood	300	300	200	300	400	118	96	96						
Gold Bar	1078	794	504	315	305	307	304	353						
Goldendale	3319	3414	2484	2536	1907	1584	1116	1274	1203	738	702	545		
Gore	470	900	500	950	900		300							
Gorst							30	214						
Govan							250	63	200					
Graham	180	150			125	125	450							
Grand Coulee	984	1180	1302	1058	2741	3659	450							

POPULATION HISTORY OF WASHINGTON CITIES AND TOWNS 1860-1990

COMMUNITY	1990	1980	1970	1960	1950	1940	1930	1920	1910	1900	1890	1880	1870	1860
Grand Mound	250	200	100	55	55	100	200		80			80		
Grandview	7169	5615	3605	3366	2503	1449	1085	1011	320					
Granger	2053	1812	1567	1424	1164	752	568	412	453					
Granite Falls	1060	911	813	599	635	683	495	632	714	157				
Grapeview	600	500	250	250	153	123	100	95						
Gravelly Falls						100	200							
Grayland	900	600	550	550	406	100	250							
Grays Harbor	300	220	200					64			523			
Grays River	250	300	300	310	300	300	50	118	200					
Greenacres	4250	3650	2324	2074	1287	770	500	100	100					
Greenbank	800	600	300	250	200	165	100	67						
Guemes	370	300	200											
Guy									276	198	100			
Hadlock/Port Hadlock	2742	1752	500	350	300	168	200	417		238	237			
Hamilton	228	268	196	271	294	229	252	462	405	392	203			
Hanford						471	250	110						
Hangmans Creek												250		
Hansville	1600	900	300	200	125	115	105							
Happy Home												150		
Harper	230	270	250	350	477	250	250	214	80					
Harrah	341	343	305	284	297	500	650	37						
Harrington	449	507	489	575	620	545	519	882	661	362				
Hartford					250	200	170	60	325	141				
Hartline	176	165	189	206	205	168	170	282	237	154				
Harvard					500	500								
Hatton	71	81	60	65	42	43	65	87	161	75				
Hayford			100	350			50							
Hazel Dell	4900	6000	3500	4000		330	125							
Hazelwood	1000	600	500			100	100	36						
Heather Downs		350												
Herron Island			400											
High Point		75	150			150	150	119						
Hillyard								3942	3276					
Hobart	350	300	350	300		125	125	110	60	575				
Hockinson					150	300	100	113	94	94	46			
Holcomb	40													
Holden					601	475	175							
Hollywood	800	800	400				350	114						
Home	950	800	600		175	125	200		80					
Hoodsport	1100	900	500		580	644	500	113	69	129				

POPULATION HISTORY OF WASHINGTON CITIES AND TOWNS 1860-1990

COMMUNITY	1990	1980	1970	1960	1950	1940	1930	1920	1910	1900	1890	1880	1870	1860
Hoquiam	8972	9719	10466	10762	11123	10835	12766	10058	8171	2608	1302			
Houghton				2426	2350	350	260	314	50	78				
Humptulips	290	250	200	200	100	100	100	264	78	78				
Hunters		150	150	300	300	168	200	214	200	132				
Hunts Point	513	480	578	428										
Huntsville							150	230	99	99	78			
Husum							200							
Illahee	400	300	100											
Iwaco	815	604	506	518	628	656	750	787	664	584	517	85		
Incholium	393	200	206	180	97									
Independence						266	381	412	417	56	69			
Index	139	147	169	158	211	217	154	62		162				
Indianola	1729	650	400	500				261						
Inglewood	6500	4000	3700											
Innis Arden	1800													
Ione	507	594	529	648	714	681	594	541	634					
Irby									150					
Irvin							300							
Irondale									425	100				
Issaquah	7786	5536	4313	1370	955	812	763	791	628	1007				
Johnson	100	100		200	200	213	150	125	190	200				
Joyce	140	130	375	350	350			162						
Juanita		10500	9450	4565	900	400	400							
Junction City							166	216						
Kahlotus	167	203	308	131	151	163	164	151	132					
Kalama	1210	1216	1105	1088	1121	1028	940	1228	816	554	325	129	200	
Kamilche								515	66	66				
Kapowsin	350	230	200	408	500	300	400	419	400					
Keller									152	152				
Kellogg Marsh	1250	1050	900											
Kelso	11820	11129	10296	8379	7345	6749	6260	2228	2039	694	354			
Kendall						100	289	289						
Kenmore	8917	7900	7500	2500	1750	500	400	116						
Kennewick	42155	34397	15212	14244	10106	1918	1519	1684	1219	183				
Kennydale		1000	900	1200	1200	544	400	520						
Kenroy	2900	1950	900											
Kent	37960	23152	16275	9017	3278	2586	2320	2282	1908	755	853			
Kettle Falls	1272	1087	893	905	714	560	414	276	377	297				
Keyport	300	900	350	390	250	190	190	319	50					
Kingsgate	14259	12652	1600											

POPULATION HISTORY OF WASHINGTON CITIES AND TOWNS 1860-1990

COMMUNITY	1990	1980	1970	1960	1950	1940	1930	1920	1910	1900	1890	1880	1870	1860
Kingston	1270	750	700	475	500	250	175	319	150	48				
Kiona	50	50	200	200	300	192	150		175	69				
Kirby							300							
Kirkland	40052	18779	15249	8451	5718	2084	1714	1354	532	264				
Kitsap	1260	950	900		325	220	100							
Kittitas	843	782	637	536	586	501	244	200	150					
Klickitat	820	700	700	847	800	913	620	34				85		
Knappton				750	800	275	300	146	146	301	113	132		
Kosmos				99	98	115								
Krupp/Martin	53	83	52			94	101	106	425	75				
Kruse	550	400	400											
La Center	451	439	300	244	204	193	219	167	288	204	105	100		
La Conner	656	633	639	638	594	624	549	516	603	564	398	140	300	
La Crosse	336	373	426	463	457	475	471	400	500	57				
La Push	600	600	450	300	250	243	270	217	75	75				
Lacey	19279	13940	9696	6630	2800	550	600							
Lake City	700	300					200	100	100	100				
Lake Dolloff	8002													
Lake Forest North		7995												
Lake Forest Park	4031	2485	2530	1991	2000	1786								
Lake Heights	2600	2400	600											
Lake Kathleen	1000	950												
Lake Lucerne	400	400												
Lake Meridian	900	770												
Lake Sawyer	1100	900	700	300										
Lake Stevens	3380	1660	1283	1538	2586	1142	375	415						
Lakebay	600	600	300		300	250	250	216		51				
Lakedale	500													
Lakeland South	9027	5225												
Lakeridge	1950	2500	2500											
Lakes District	58412	54533	48195											
Lakeshore	3000	2300	1000											
Lakeside		250	225	900	264	241	238	199	222	58				
Lakeview		250		500	800	600	300	189	185	300	256			
Lakewood	500	500	250			300	110	110	60					
Lamont	91	101	88	111	101	135	130	165	275	118				
Langley	845	650	547	448	427	338	268	274	300	77				
Larchmont					400	803	77		77					
Latah	175	155	169	190	244	270	284	330	339	253	232			
Laurel Heights							500							

POPULATION HISTORY OF WASHINGTON CITIES AND TOWNS 1860-1990

COMMUNITY	1990	1980	1970	1960	1950	1940	1930	1920	1910	1900	1890	1880	1870	1860
Leavenworth	1692	1522	1322	1480	1503	1608	1415	1791	1551	548				
Lebam	260	240	250	400	400	440	400	413	400	88				
Lester			100	150	250	220	199	413	90	90				
Lexington	1907	500	300	110	150	200	200							
Liberty Lake	2015	900	800	650	300		200							
Lilliwaup	80	75	80	50	200		75					250		
Lincoln														
Lind	472	567	622	697	796	679	730	724	831	235				
Littell							314		125					
Little Boston	100	200												
Little Falls/Sopenah									631	201				
Littlerock	390	300	325	300	200	250	250	317	350	95				
Lochloy	120	120				165	420	420	175					
Lone Oak	1121	1121												
Long Beach	1236	1199	968	565	783	620	396	419	350	159				
Long Lake	800	600		150										
Longbranch	900	900	400	495	495	465								
Longview	31499	31052	28373	23349	20339	12385	10652	62	50	50				
Loomis	220	150	150	200	200	245	180	218	428	428				
Loon Lake	750	650		400	250	172	200	193	161	161				
Lopez	600	500	100	100	150	108	151	214	99	99				
Loveland	50	40				180	50	36						
Lowden				125	130	550	503	45						
Lowell				1086	1754	1489	740	852	478	478		50	50	
Lummi Island	400	300	150	150	232		250							
Lyle	850	700	400	475	250	222	250	169	300	102				
Lyman	275	284	324	400	378	376	441	492	441	97	62			
Lynden	5709	4022	2808	2542	2161	1696	1564	1244	1148	365	560			
Lynnwood	28695	21937	16919	7207	650									
Lynwood Center	750	600					50							
Mabton	1482	1248	926	958	831	485	423	547	666	110				
Machias	300	300	150	100	200	275	200	167	350	148				
McChord AFB	4538	5746	6515											
McCleary	1235	1419	1265	1115	1175	1200	1200	1320	180					
McCormick							50	217	90					
McKee	300						300							
McKenna	210	300	200	200	250	250	200	416						
McMillan		180	130	100	100	378	300	136	92	92				
McMurray		320	150	125		289	224	243	377	205				
Malaga	400			65	64	55	80	110	50					

POPULATION HISTORY OF WASHINGTON CITIES AND TOWNS 1860-1990

COMMUNITY	1990	1980	1970	1960	1950	1940	1930	1920	1910	1900	1890	1880	1870	1860
Malden	189	200	219	292	332	325	375	1005	798					
Malone	300	250	200	200	300	330	300	514						
Malott	380	350	150	350	250	381	381	42						
Maltby	650	500	200	150	150	125	125	68	106	106				
Manchester	800	900	500	700	700	150	100	83						
Manett	1600					1000	400							
Manito		950	800						80					
Manor									70	70				
Mansfield	311	315	272	385	414	349	288	478	600					
Manson	700	500	500	390	350	385	300	63						
Maple Falls	300	200	100	100	105	220	150	216	400					
Maple Hills	1000	540												
Maple Valley	1211	900	350	800	800	122	250	225	112	112				
Maple Valley Heights	900	800												
Maplewood Heights	3300	1100												
Marblemount	200	350	350	300	300	155	55	55	55	55				
Marcus	135	174	142	126	149	393	583	551	481	381	311			
Marietta	560	200	250	300	350	176	200	412	118	156				
Marine Hills		1000												
Markham							260							
Martin							101	273						
Martha Lake	10155	7022		900										
Marysville	10328	5080	4343	3117	2259	1748	1354	1244	1239	728	262			
Mason City					2606	3000								
Matlock	100	150	250	150	100	100	136	136	136	136				
Mattawa	941	299	180	394										
Mays Pond	2400	1300												
Maytown							75	214						
Mead	2150	1400	1099	498	520	190	103	160	160	59				
Meadow Glade	520	400	350	100	100	100								
Meadowdale							150	319	70					
Medical Lake	3664	3600	3529	4765	4488	2114	1671	2545	1730	516	617			
Medina	2981	3220	3455	2285	650	590	358	261						
Menlo	250	200	200	250	400	165	400	35						
Mercer Island	20816	21522	19819	12692	6000	1100	1069							
Meridan Heights	600	500	500	150										
Mesa	252	278	274	263	260	275	45	57	250					
Metaline	198	190	197	299	563	127	125	125	150					
Metaline Falls					547	453	316	153						
Meyers Falls	210	296	307	469			200	361	260	212				

POPULATION HISTORY OF WASHINGTON CITIES AND TOWNS 1860-1990

COMMUNITY	1990	1980	1970	1960	1950	1940	1930	1920	1910	1900	1890	1880	1870	1860
Mica							150		100					
Midland	2900	3450	3000	1000	1000	1083	100	84	100					
Midway	300			1000	600	500								
Milan	70	65	90	81	100	100	115	217	119	125				
Mill Creek	7172	900												
Milltown	1559	1717	1770	1776	1240	717	493	164	250					
Millwood	4995	3162	2607	2218	1374	671	559	50						
Milton	530	500	500	500	600	500	500	484	448					
Mineral								461	325					
Minnehaha	2400	2750	2000	2000										
Mirror Lake	2360				750									
Mirrormont		900												
Mission										190				
Misty Meadows	800	950												
Moclips	700	700	600	500	500	400	300	169	500					
Mohler							150	214	172	172				
Molson							165	30	400	238				
Monitor	100	70	100	200	350	176								
Monroe	4278	2869	2687	1501	1556	1590	1570	1675	1552					
Monte Cristo							30	30	100	500				
Monte Vista			1500	1530										
Montborne								259				70		
Montesano	3064	3247	2847	2486	2328	2242	2460	2158	2488	1194	1632	100	100	
Monticello														
Moorlands	2000	2200	1800											
Moran Prairie	480													
Morgan Acres	1500	1750	2500	2500										
Morton	1130	1264	1134	1183	1140	778	461	522	60					
Moscow										159				
Moses Lake	11235	10629	10310	11299	2679	326								
Moses Lake North	3677	3348	2672											
Mossyrock	452	463	409	344	356	220	169	169	78	78	64			
Mount Pleasant	1200	900	650	400										
Mount Vernon	17647	13009	8804	7921	5230	4278	3690	3341	2381	1120	770	40		
Mountlake Terrace	19320	16534	16600	9122	7000									
Moxee City	814	687	600	499	543	335	283	297	400					
Mukilteo	7007	1426	1369	1128	826	1134	618	618		79	52	56		
Munson Point	450													
Naches	596	644	666	680	633	536	423	325	200					
Nagroom							415	415						

POPULATION HISTORY OF WASHINGTON CITIES AND TOWNS 1860-1990

COMMUNITY	1990	1980	1970	1960	1950	1940	1930	1920	1910	1900	1890	1880	1870	1860
Napavine	745	611	377	314	242	220	181	340	290	290	284			
Naselle	1000	900	500	700	750	200	100	213						
National	50	50			500	300	300	264						
Navy Yard City	2905	2827	2827	3341	3030									
Neah Bay	916	1000	600	800	663	750	550	52	40	40	32	200		
Neppel														
Nespelem	187	284	323	358	425	300	125	34	80		78			
Newaukum			350				400	80						
Newcastle							348	819	125	683	109		172	
Newhalem	300	300	300	400		100								
Newman Lake	620	300	100	113	56		100							
Newport	1691	1665	1418	1513	1385	1174	1080	950	1199	100				
Newport Hills	6000	6000	6000											
Newport Shores		900												
Nisqually			500	350	250	200	150	63						
Nooksack	584	429	322	318	323	302	293	283	250	148	159			
Nordland	500	500	500	300	200		100							
Norma Beach	600													
Normandy Park	6709	4268	4202	3224	1790									
North Bend	2578	1701	1625	945	787	646	548	387	299	280				
North Bonneville	411	394	459	494	564	643								
North City	8200	6200	6500	2000										
North Hill	5706	10170												
North Lynwood	1250	1250	1100											
North Marys	4050	2400												
North Puyallup	1300	1150	600	680	275	300								
North Richland					3067									
North Yakima									14082	3154	1535			
Northport	308	368	423	482	487	427	391	906	476	787				
Novelty						233		110	50	50				
Oak Harbor	17176	12271	9167	3942	1193	376	362	337	350	132				
Oak Park						600						70		
Oakesdale	346	444	447	474	576	590	637	816	882	928	528			
Oakville	493	537	460	377	372	418	469	396	465	276	86	40		
O'Brien							400	317	105	105				
Ocean Beach	2108	2108												
Ocean City	500	500	500	325	225									
Ocean Park	1650	1500	825	750	650	250	250	50						
Ocean Shores	2301	1692	918											
Ocosta				100	157	173	157	160	166	127				

POPULATION HISTORY OF WASHINGTON CITIES AND TOWNS 1860-1990

COMMUNITY	1990	1980	1970	1960	1950	1940	1930	1920	1910	1900	1890	1880	1870	1860
Odessa	935	1009	1074	1231	1127	816	830	1050	885	122				
Okanogan	2370	2302	2015	2001	2013	1735	1519	1015	611					
Olalla	570	450	400	800	850	350	200	200	200	106				
Olympia	33840	27447	23111	18273	15819	13254	11733	7795	6996	4082	4698	1232		
Omak	4117	4007	4164	4068	3791	2918	2547	525	600					
Onalaska	600	560	200	230	210	1200	1200	826						
Opportunity	22326	17600	16604	12465	8000	1500	1500	415						
Orcas								212	56	56				
Orchards	3450	3950	9500	1800	600	200	165	164	100					
Orient	60	50	200	200	200	200	175	267	350					
Orillia					200	127	127	89	180	107				
Orondo	400	350	130	250	250	200	200	182	50	50				
Oroville	1505	1483	1555	437	1500	1206	800	1013	495	128				
Orting	2106	1763	1643	1520	1299	1211	1109	972	799	728	623	110		
Osborne					357	550								
Oso	200	200	150	250	250	200	65	125	225					
Ostrander	100				75	275	275	164	181	181				
Othello	4638	4454	4122	2669	526	332	397	649	475					
Otis Orchards	3200	1000	900	750	500	200	200	60						
Outlook	320	300	300	308	300	476	150	239	250					
Oysterville	100	100	86	140	140	126	138	118	150	164	197	125	104	
Pacific	4622	2261	1831	1577	755	357	347	320	413	50				
Pacific Beach	1200	1000	900	820	500	275	200	58	50					
Packwood	1010	1150	900	450	350	185	200							
Paha									150	100	100			
Palisades	40	50	90	120	150	238	185	34						
Palmer	250	250	170	80	200	160	160	98	98	98				
Palouse	915	1005	948	926	1036	1028	1151	1179	1549	929	1119	148		
Park Orchard	3800	2700												
Park Place												150		
Parker	370	550	400	300	250	118	125	110	60	44				
Parkland	20882	22355	21012	15000	5500	1989	750	517	150	150				
Parkwater	4300	4850	4500		1000	125	125							
Parkwood	6853	4599	900											
Pasadena Park	1700	2000	2200	2000										
Pasco	20337	17944	13920	14522	10228	3913	3496	3362	2083	254	320			
Pataha	70	75	97	100	60		50	165	176	157	212	160		
Pateros	570	555	472	673	866	484	486	412						
Paterson							150	162	838					
Pe Ell	547	617	582	593	787	825	891	861		217				

POPULATION HISTORY OF WASHINGTON CITIES AND TOWNS 1860-1990

COMMUNITY	1990	1980	1970	1960	1950	1940	1930	1920	1910	1900	1890	1880	1870	1860
Peach	1750													
Pearcot		900	700											
Pearson							150	210						
Penn Cove Park	600	600	600	175										
Peshastin	900	900	700	600	250	385	250	150	150					
Pilchuck							50		50					
Pine Lake	1000		800											
Pinehurst				3989	4260	1839	1200	817						
Pioneer	600	600								26	18	200		
Pipe Lake	600	600												
Plaza			50	50	55	116	250	110		97	97			
Pleasant Beach							450			100				
Plymouth	190	190	89	65			100							
Point Roberts	750	750	400	265	260	200	281	261	100	108				
Pomeroy	1393	1716	1823	1677	1775	1723	1600	1804	1605	953	661	200		
Ponder	600				200	230								
Ponderosa Estates	1450	800												
Pontius Park		1500	1300											
Port Angeles	17710	17311	16367	12653	11233	9409	10188	5351	2286	2321	316			
Port Angeles East	2672	2786	1523											
Port Blakely	110	110	110	200	100	100	100	240	750	1000	643	100	61	
Port Crescent									40		364			
Port Discovery							100	34	75		39	100	152	70
Port Gamble	380	300	425	400	500	182	500	320	420	590	420	421	326	
Port Ludlow	630	500	200	225	275	200	200	375	236	348	236	212	259	124
Port Madison	250	200	185	343	100	100	100	63			269	228	249	188
Port Orchard	4984	4787	3904	2778	2320	1566	1145	1393	682	254	226	100	80	47
Port Stanley							162	162						
Port Townsend	7001	6067	5241	5074	6888	4683	3970	2847	4181	3443	4558	917	593	264
Portage									150					
Porter	60			200	200		200	200	180					
Potlach		50	100				60	110						
Poulsbo	4848	3453	1856	1505	1014	639	584	546	364	69				
Prairie						407	50	219	53	53				
Prairie Ridge	1250	900												
Prescott	267	341	242	269	244	324	275	559	502	410	313			
Preston	600	500	400	500	500	555	405	413	59	59				
Prosser	4476	3896	2954	2763	2636	1719	1569	1697	1298	229	142			
Puget Island					735	1100								
Pullman	23478	23579	20509	12957	12022	4417	3322	2440	2602	1308	868			

POPULATION HISTORY OF WASHINGTON CITIES AND TOWNS 1860-1990

COMMUNITY	1990	1980	1970	1960	1950	1940	1930	1920	1910	1900	1890	1880	1870	1860
Purdy	600													
Puyallup	23875	18251	14742	12063	10010	7889	7094	6323	4544	1884	1732	297	312	
Queensborough	4850	2800	1500											
Queensgate		700	1200											
Queets	300	300	180	250	250	220	60							
Quilcene	1200	950	900	700	280	400	250	415	200	105				
Quillayute	350	350	300	370	300	220	220	64	52	52		250		
Quinault	3738	3525	3237	3269	804	318	266	285	264	40				
Rainier	991	891	382	245	331	932	500	264	150	121				
Rainier Terrace	600													
Ralston									220					
Randle	800	600	300	200	250	230	160	80	80					
Ravensdale	600	500	250	300	250	143	109	159	250					
Raymond	2901	2991	3126	3301	4110	4045	3828	4260	2450					
Reardon	482	498	389	474	410	422	422	420	527	241				
Redmond	35800	23318	11031	1426	573	530	460	438	450	116				
Redondo	700	600	700	600	500	127	116	114	60					
Regents Park														
Reintree	500						319	319						
Renton	41688	30612	26686	18453	16039	4488	4062	3301	2740	412	406	200		
Republic	940	1018	862	1064	895	922	710	781	999	2050				
Retsil	1524	800	750	950	900	700	700	659						
Rhododendron Park	1160	900												
Richland	32315	33578	26290	23548	21809	247	208	279	350					
Richmond Beach	5000	6700	2550	3000	1900	780	780	262	180					
Richmond Highlands	26037	24463	6854	6000	2300	664	600							
Ridgecrest	5500	7000	4500	3000										
Ridgefield	1297	1062	1004	823	762	643	607	620	297	249				
Riffe				670	450	175	100	40						
Riparia							150	162	50					
Ritzville	1725	1800	1876	2173	2145	1748	1777	1900	1859	761	619			
Rivercrest	650	730												
Riverside	223	243	228	201	149	192	218	209	400	57				
Riverton Heights	15337	14182	15000	9000	3060			818						
Riverview Hills	400													
Roche Harbor	300	250	175	98	98	277	200	319	254	312	247			
Rochester	1250	900	350	345	350	300	300	259	180	185				
Rock Island	524	491	191	260	152	130	90	435	663	433				
Rockford	481	442	327	369	360	377	381				644			

POPULATION HISTORY OF WASHINGTON CITIES AND TOWNS 1860-1990

COMMUNITY	1990	1980	1970	1960	1950	1940	1930	1920	1910	1900	1890	1880	1870	1860
Rockport	300	200	150	250	185	266	200	125	180					
Rocky Point	1495	1000	1733	1000										
Rocky Woods	550	400												
Rollingbay	700	700	600	600	600	585	530	514						
Ronald	250	200	200	250	500	545	496	718						
Roosevelt									150					
Rosalia	552	572	569	585	660	596	633	714	767	379	248			
Rosario								213						
Rosburg	80	90	250	150	300	300	400							
Rose Hill		3900	3000						80					
Rose Valley	1400	1400												
Rosedale	360	300	300			200	200	58	58	58				
Roslyn	869	938	1031	1283	1537	1743	2063	2673	3126	2786	1484			
Ross	258	417	381	264	263	261	284	287	315	220	248			
Roy										188	108			
Royal City	1104	676	477	301										
Ruby											207			
Ruff				75	75	150	100	75						
Ruston	693	612	668	694	838	739	818	1128	780					
Ryderwood	370	360	350	400	851	450	400							
St. John	499	529	575	545	542	526	471	597	421	219				
Salkum	320	300	298	250	250	200	200			42				
Salmon Creek	2100	1900	350	350	500	500	500	45						
Saltwater	2200	1800												
Samish Island	620	500	250	250	150	150			108	108	82	160		
Samish Lake	900	900												
Sappho						130	130							
Satsop	350	300	250	283	250	300	300	219	250	118		144		
Sauk				60	250	165		63	46	46				
Scatchet Head	3500				75									
Schwarder	70	65	400	200										
Scotia														
Seabeck	500	500	300	400	300	150	264	134	108	108	118	266	150	107
Seahurst	1900	1500	3000	3000	2305	300	150	219	62	62				
Seatac	23027													
Seattle	516259	493846	530831	557087	467591	368302	365583	315312	237194	80671	42837	3533	1107	
Seaview	600	500	600	600	600	400	200							
Sedro-Woolley	6031	6110	4598	3705	3299	2954	2719	3389	2129	885	106			
Seguin	600								150	177				
Sekiu	600	600	475	572	371	330	150							

POPULATION HISTORY OF WASHINGTON CITIES AND TOWNS · 860-1990

COMMUNITY	1990	1980	1970	1960	1950	1940	1930	1920	1910	1900	1890	1880	1870	1860
Selah	5113	4372	3311	2824	2489	1130	767	827	350					
Selleck	200	200	200	275	300	385	415	415	150					
Semiahmoo									40	208		50		
Sequim	3616	3013	1549	1164	1044	676	534	402	300					
Sequoia	1140	880												
Shelton	7241	7629	6515	5651	5045	3707	3091	984	1163	833	648			
Sheridan Beach	6518	1500	1250	1500										
Shorewood	3100	1300												
Shoultes		2400	2000	3159	1973									
Sidney										254	226			
Sifton	770	2000	300	150	150	200	300	329	160	160				
Silvana	160	150		150										
Silver Brook	500	50												
Silver Creek	50		382	262	216	114	114	114	87	87	84			
Silverdale	1100	1500	900	950	500	500	300	262	62	62				
Silverlake	1550	1600	1300	500	750	200	300	45	45	45				
Silverton							75	110	89	89				
Skamania				325		150								
Skamokawa	220	250	300	466	562	336	750	367	450	346	118	184		
Skykomish	273	209	283	366	497	479	562	267	238	129				
Skyway	8500	12500	9000											
Slaughter											740	100	150	
Smokey Point	2620	200	100											
Snohomish	6499	5294	5174	3894	3094	2794	2688	2985	3244	2101	1993	149		
Snoqualmie	1546	1370	1260	1216	806	775	752	450	279	196	99			
Snoqualmie Falls			250	800	758			362	200					
Soap Lake	1149	1196	1064	1531	2091	662	282	352						
South Aberdeen							3000							
South Bend	1551	1686	1795	1671	1857	1771	1798	1948	3023	711	68			
South Broadway	2735	3620	3298	3661	3229									
South Cle Elum	457	449	374	383	442	340	338	587						
South Colby	260	500	400	268	300	280	280	615						
South Hill	4550	3650												
South Prairie	180	202	206	214	207	226	204	215	264	361				
South Snohomish	400	400	150											
South Wenatchee	1207	1376			479	338	300			560				
Southpark														
Southworth	360	500	300	250	200	100	100							
Spanaway/Lakepark	15001	5940	5768	2500	1400	1240	400	520	250	346				
Spangle	229	276	179	208	242	203	218	291	299	331	303	36		

POPULATION HISTORY OF WASHINGTON CITIES AND TOWNS 1860-1990

COMMUNITY	1990	1980	1970	1960	1950	1940	1930	1920	1910	1900	1890	1880	1870	1860
Spokane	177196	171300	170516	181608	161721	122001	115514	104437	104402	36848	19922	350		
Sprague	410	473	550	597	598	641	639	822	1110	695	1689	94		
Springdale	260	281	215	254	268	227	215	184	251	259				
Stanwood	1961	2744	1347	1123	710	600	715	704	544	438	407			
Star Lake	1100	1350	800	100			150							
Starbuck	170	198	216	161	194	251	346	524	761	588	42			
Stark's Point												200		
Startup	620	450	400	350	386	350	450	316	200					
Steilacoom	5728	4886	2850	1569	1233	832	722	564	430	284	270	250	314	
Steptoe	190	200	200	100	110	291	172	120	120					
Stevenson	1147	1172	916	927	584	563	400	348	387	142				
Stillwater							30	364						
Streeters	560													
Sultan	2236	1578	1119	821	814	961	830	687	576	348				
Sumach	650	500	500	1345	500									
Sumas	744	712	722	629	658	650	647	854	902	319				
Summit	2700	2400	2000	900						76				
Sumner	6281	4936	4325	3156	2816	2140	1967	1499	892	531	580	116		
Suncrest	1500													
Sunnydale	2800	2750	2000	1296	1296	1050		514						
Sunnyside (Snohomish)	2150	2500	1000											
Sunnyside (Yakima)	11238	9225	6751	6208	4194	2368	2113	1809	1379	122				
Sunnyslope (Chelan)	1907	700	350											
Sunnyslope (Kitsap)	520	700	500											
Suquamish	3105	1500	900	900	500	691	691	927						
Swan Trail	400	200			100	155	50	87						
Sylvan					350									
Tacoma	176664	158501	154581	147979	143673	109408	106817	96965	83743	37714	36006	1098	73	
Tacoma Point	500													
Taholah	788	800	400	350	350	350	450	134						
Tahuya	370	300	100	150	60	100								
Tanglewald	3280	3850	2000											
Taylor						350	250	319	100					
Tekoa	750	854	808	911	1189	1383	1408	1520	1694	717	301			
Tenino	1292	1280	962	836	969	952	938	850	1038	343	339	100	100	
Terrace Hights	4223	3199	1033				350	218	100					
Thomas	180	900	900	350	300	250								
Thompson Place	2500	1750	1200	150	250		180							
Thornton	120	100	100	225	250	275		325	400	205				
Thorp	350	350	275	430	350	300	500	317	192	248				

POPULATION HISTORY OF WASHINGTON CITIES AND TOWNS · 860-1990

COMMUNITY	1990	1980	1970	1960	1950	1940	1930	1920	1910	1900	1890	1880	1870	1860
Three Lakes								516						
Tieton	693	528	415	479	620	350	350	417						
Tillicum	600		1900	1500	1500	412	450	36						
Timber Lakes		3000												
Timberlane	3000													
Tokeland	450	400	350	150	200	175	89	89	69	69				
Toledo	586	637	654	499	602	523	530	324	375	285	276	250	250	159
Tolt							360		120	50				
Tonasket	847	985	951	958	957	643	513	530						
Tono						200	200	46	80					
Toppenish	7418	6517	5744	5667	5265	3683	2774	3120	1598	50				
Touchet	410	400	350	275	600	385	500	263	250	45	58			
Toutle	300	250	200	200	100		50							
Town and Country/Linwood	4921	5578	6484											
Tracyton	2621	2304	1413	600	550	250	150	274	76	76				
Trend		3600												
Trentwood	4060	2600	1800											
Trinidad				135	150		210	61	50					
Trout Lake	650	550	250	500	450	300	300	70	70	70				
Tukwila	11874	3578	3496	1804	800	521	424	453	361					
Tulalip							146	620	160					
Tumtum	370	350	100	75	100	100	100	100	40					
Tumwater	9976	6705	5373	3885	2725	955	793	472	490	270	410	171	206	
Twisp	872	911	756	750	776	477	335	289	227	78				
Two Rivers							100	214	50					
Tyler							55	160						
Underwood	400	350	350	350	370	275	200	100	79	79				
Union	700	600	500	500	550	182	175	79		287	196		124	
Union Gap	3120	3184	2040	2100	1766	976	586	332	263					
Union Mills	4623	4623	150	150			165	165						
Union Ridge	277	286	310	242	254	332	360	404	426	404	279	100	200	
Uniontown														
University Place	27701	20381	13230	7200										
Usk	210	200	200	300	225	221	221	157	250	67				
Utsalady				150						293	207	187		
Vader	414	406	387	380	426	479	465	500	631	96				
Valley	250	165	145	225	250	302	500	128						
Valleyford	200	150	250	213	213	250	250	100	100					
Vancouver	46380	42834	42493	32464	41664	18788	15766	12637	9300	4006	3545	1722	500	
Vashon	1000	800	800	850	850	638	583	514	350	120				

POPULATION HISTORY OF WASHINGTON CITIES AND TOWNS 1860-1990

COMMUNITY	1990	1980	1970	1960	1950	1940	1930	1920	1910	1900	1890	1880	1870	1860
Vashon Heights	700													
Vaughn	700	300	300	400	300	200	300	213	108	108				
Veradale	7836	600	2400	2450	750	180	50							
Vineland								114						
Waitsburg	990	1035	953	1010	1015	936	869	1174	1237	1011	817	248	107	
Walla Walla	26478	25618	23619	24536	24102	18109	15976	15503	19364	10049	4709	3588	1394	722
Walla Walla East	2959	3285	2840	1557										
Wallula	150	150	150	150	200	150	150	319	160	348	518	148	150	
Walnut Grove	1850	1700	1000	100										
Walville							500							
Wapato	3795	3307	2841	3137	3185	1483	1222	1128	400					
Warden	1639	1479	1254	949	322	78	100	173	500					
Warm Beach/Birmingham	400	300	250	300	314	314	314							
Washougal	4764	3834	3388	2672	1577	1267	1206	765	456	203	103			
Washtucna	231	266	316	331	316	285	261	359	300	110				
Waterman	380	300	200	200	200	100	100	150						
Waterville	995	908	919	1013	1013	939	856	1198	950	482	293			
Wauna	360	300	200	200	100	117	50							
Waverly	37	99	48	108	120	131	151	234	318	562	99	50		
Wellington/Tye									148	148				
Wellpinit	350	250	100	100	100		72							
Wenatchee	21756	17257	16912	16726	13072	11620	11627	6324	4050	451				
West Clarkson	2600	2500	2000											
West Pasco	7312	5729	3809	2851	1100									
West Richland	3962	2938	1107	1347										
West Seattle										1206				
West Sound							75	219	54	54				
West Spokane							500							
West Tapps	2200													
West Wenatchee	2220	2700	2134	2518	2690									
Westlake			258	298										
Westport	1892	1954	1364	976	731	443	272	114	164	164				
White Bluffs						600	600	225	250					
White Center	15700	19700	18600	15000	15000									
White Salmon	1861	1853	1585	1590	1353	985	798	619	682	176	62	100		
White Swan	650	600	220	300	200	232	200	114	200	136				
Wickersham	120	100	120	120	140	105	127							
Wilbur	863	1122	1074	1138	1043	1011	737	870	757	595	410			
Wiley	280	100	300	350	300			110						
Wilkeson	366	321	317	412	386	369	448	803	899	896	109	104		

POPULATION HISTORY OF WASHINGTON CITIES AND TOWNS 1860-1990

COMMUNITY	1990	1980	1970	1960	1950	1940	1930	1920	1910	1900	1890	1880	1870	1860
Willapa	350	300	300	230	250	400	175	259	107	103	207	100		
Wilson Creek	148	222	184	252	337	210	216	300	405					
Winlock	1027	1052	890	808	878	861	864	832	1140	655	284			
Winona							159	318	350	80				
Winslow	3081	2196	1461	919	637	500	669	314	200					
Winthrop	302	413	371	359	396	365	270	89	113	113				
Wishram	670	675	650	750	678	440	300							
Wollochet	800	800	300	150	150	100	150							
Woodinville	1500	950	400	550	650	607	425	310	250		43			
Woodland	2500	2341	1622	1336	1292	980	1094	521	384	241	41			
Woodmont Beach	3550	1250	900	200										
Woodway	914	832	879	713										
Wooster							400							
Yacolt	600	544	488	375	411	297	295	520	435					
Yakima	54827	49826	45588	43284	38486	27221	22101	18539	196	287	263	267	150	
Yardley	180			300	500	200	89	68						
Yarrow Point	962	1064	1103	766										
Yelm	1337	1294	628	479	470	378	384	118	180	99	53		73	
Zenith	1100	300	800	720	600	326	214	214						
Zillah	1911	1599	1138	1069	911	803	728	647	250	169				

POPULATION HISTORY OF WYOMING CITIES AND TOWNS 1860-1990

COMMUNITY	1990	1980	1970	1960	1950	1940	1930	1925	1920	1915	1910	1905	1900	1890	1884	1880	1870	1860
Acme		150	100	100	125	220	200	153	153									
Afton	1394	1481	1290	1337	1319	1211	807	850	796	673	570	733	449	54				
Aladdin	120	128	118				110		110		150	150	106					
Albin	70	75	250	172	208	160	125				50							
Allendale									41									
Almy	200				140	140	140		262		268	268	250	450	300	725		
Alpine		154				150	50				53							
Arapaho	393		95	193	193	111	150		53									
Arminto				30	35	100	100		54									
Arvada	50	80	50	100	125	133	100		80									
Atlantic City	40	35	25		20	113	83		105		213	213	235	156		82	325	
Auburn	150	200	240	270	400	327	275		183				100					
Baggs	272	433	146	199	206	221	192	111	200	157	425		188	100				
Bairoil	228	150	350	250	250	333	250											
Bar Nunn	835	782																
Basin	1180	1349	1145	1319	1220	1099	903	1009	1088	728	763	370	489					
Battle													168					
Bedford	65	65		334	265	265	265											
Beulah			63	60	100	100	174		114		100	75	117	100				
Big Horn	220	225	200	181	144	165	144		132		154		154	227	100	100		
Big Piney	454	530	570	663	206	241	184		173	141	80		80					
Blairtown						185	100											
Blazon						175	175											
Bondurant	110	100	100				86		86									
Broadmoor			500															
Bryan																27		
Buffalo	3302	3799	3394	2907	2674	2302	1749	1650	1772	1246	1368	1307	710	1087	600	300	239	
Buford	30	25	36	30	28	94	46		46		80							
Burlington	184	158	100	150	150	172	250		472		175		70					
Burns	254	268	185	225	216	253	216	190	300		250							
Burnt Fork																		
Byron	470	633	397	417	350	388	250	141	326	232	50							
Cambria							783		675	1023	442	491	538	329				
Carbon											1033	737	634	1140	1000	600	244	
Carbonate							220				117	94						
Carter																		
Casper	46742	51016	39361	38930	23673	17964	16619	23288	11447	4040	2639	1690	883	544	150	386		
Centennial	100	60	100	50	68	114	165		215						100	40		
Chatham/Winchester					200		200									61		
Cheyenne	50008	47283	41254	43505	31935	22474	17361	13202	13829	9661	11320	13656	14087	11690	6000	3456	1450	

POPULATION HISTORY OF WYOMING CITIES AND TOWNS 1860-1990

COMMUNITY	1990	1980	1970	1960	1950	1940	1930	1925	1920	1915	1910	1905	1900	1890	1884	1880	1870	1860
Chugwater	192	282	187	287	283	245	286	237	315		49		49	53	50			
Clark				59	100		150											
Clearmont	119	191	141	154	225	215	214	225	162		154		154					
Clearview			500															
Cody	7897	6790	5161	4838	3872	2536	1800	1017	1242	1035	1132	1200	170					
Cokeville	493	515	440	545	440	452	431	388	430	305	305	305	138	90	75	62		
Columbine					40	86	200											
Cowley	477	455	366	459	463	491	526	560	687	630	574							
Crosby							303	476	494									
Cumberland							1225		227		500	1891						
Cummins													23	253	300	253		
Dana																		
Daniel	100	100	125	125	75	100	44											
Dayton	565	701	396	333	316	240	348	97	136	177	313		137	77				
Deaver	199	178	112	121	118	111	85	71	142									
Dewey													246					
Diamondville	864	1000	485	398	415	586	812	864	726	1018	696	840	897					
Dietz						100	800		413		150							
Dillon												208						
Dines					237	150	225	353										
Dixon	70	82	72	108	124	94	145	106	170	111	175	124	139	99		75		
Douglas	5076	6030	2677	2822	2544	2205	1917	1758	2294	1845	2246	1255	734	491				
Downer	100	300	250				250											
Du Noir					67													
Dubois	895	1067	898	574	279	412	177		243	142	142		57					
East Thermopolis	221	359	316	281	246													
Eden	230	250	220	250	200	200	200											
Edgarton	247	510	350	512	203	232	269	453										
Elk Basin							125	210										
Elk Mountain	174	338	127	190	196	107	54	91	89	177	98		58					
Elkol									132									
Elmo			53	91	213	134	68		58									
Emblem			250	280	250		250		59									
Encampment	490	611	321	333	288	331	209	284	230	218	421	1021	579					
Ethete	70	70	50	40	150	109	200											
Etna	200	400	200	300	400	329	60		45									
Evanston	10903	6421	4462	4901	3863	3605	3075	3507	3479	2756	2583	2741	2110	1995	1700	1277	77	
Evansville	1403	2652	832	678	393	206	174	280										
Fairview	150	100	100	255	360	445	425		216		200		231					
Farson	100	75	210	250	150	141	124	124										

POPULATION HISTORY OF WYOMING CITIES AND TOWNS 1860-1990

COMMUNITY	1990	1980	1970	1960	1950	1940	1930	1925	1920	1915	1910	1905	1900	1890	1884	1880	1870	1860
Fontenelle																125		
Fort Bridger	200	175	150	150	100	165	138		113		129		129	295		44	236	
Fort D.A.Russell														553		508	828	143
Fort Fetterman																166	338	
Fort Francis						890									150			
Fort Halleck															200	250		360
Fort Laramie	243	356	197	233	300	311	245	164					230	735	500	531	493	
Fort McKinney														291	200	279		
Fort Sanders																401	228	
Fort Steele		20	15	50	40		168		139		100				300	381	252	
Fort Stambaugh																	154	
Fort Washakie	250	250	300	250	150	200	150						248	162	150	191		
Fox Farm	2850	2850	1329	1371	800		150	105	62									
Foxpark	100	100	135	150	110	113	162		162		100							
Frannie	148	138	139	171	180		37		32									
Freedom	450	450	497	504	510	627	522		452		100							
Frontier	150	250	246	377	671	885	1757		1575		700	656						
Garland				80	61	61	88		88		129	129						
Gas Hills		100	400	400														
Gebo			15	200	260	975	894	774	689		75							
Gillette	17635	12134	7194	3580	2191	2177	1340	770	1157	505	448	285	151					
Glenco						200	599		510		200							
Glendo	195	367	210	292	215	162	201	208			43		43					
Glenrock	2153	2736	1515	1584	1110	1014	819	1170	1003	220	427	427	297	492				
Gramm									213									
Granger	126	177	137	159	122	163	135	135	136	134	134		62		50			
Grass Creek	30	75	115	253	300	525	482	482										
Green River	12711	12807	4196	3497	3187	2640	2589	2326	2140	1219	1313	1014	1361	723	500	327	106	
Greybull	1789	2277	1953	2286	2262	1828	1806	2047	2692	421	258							
Grover	100	60	120	175	250	220	350				53		53					
Guernsey	1155	1512	793	800	721	603	656	412	372	239	274	168	640					
Gunn						36	74	313	227	220	220							
Hamilton Dome	80	100	100	202	187	117												
Hanna	1076	2288	460	625	1326	1127	1720	1483	1575	1347	1347	1209	930	260		260		
Hartville	78	149	246	177	229	179	189	180	138	105	235	152	843					
Hawksprings	80	80	100	128	149													
Hiawatha					236													
Hilliard																		
Hillsdale	60	60	160	125	125	145			97		75		56	54	75	73	150	
Hudson	392	514	381	369	293	330	328	368	977	428	319							

POPULATION HISTORY OF WYOMING CITIES AND TOWNS 1860-1990

COMMUNITY	1990	1980	1970	1960	1950	1940	1930	1925	1920	1915	1910	1905	1900	1890	1884	1880	1870	1860
Hulett	429	291	318	335	236	197	150	332	126		150	206	157					
Hyattville	90	100	73	210	125	109	243	395	206	204	206		59					
Jackson	4472	4511	2688	1437	1244	1046	533		307		204							
Jamestown	280	275	150															
Jeffrey City	1882	400	700	800														
Kaycee	256	271	272	284	211	210	161	166	217	57	75		39					
Kemmerer	3020	3273	2292	2028	1667	2026	1884	1993	1517	1481	843	655	832					
Kendall						172	173	183	174		70		70					
Kirby	59	129	75	82	99	107					50							
Kleenburn					500		1450		1450									
Kooi							350		256		50							
La Barge	493	302	375	400	110	218	44											
La Grange	224	232	189	176	221	211	250				32		32	41				
Lance Creek	100	150	175	400	501	545	100											
Lander	7023	9126	7125	4182	3349	2594	1826	1739	2133	1726	1812	956	737	525	200	193		
Laramie	26687	24410	23143	17520	15581	10627	8609	9629	6301	4962	8237	7601	8207	6388	4000	2696	828	
Linch	200	250	300	635	300		75											
Lingle	473	475	446	437	403	428	62	277	363									
Lionkol							161	241	320									
Lost Cabin	30		25	47	73	34	34		49	55	130			27				
Lost Springs						38	65	76	121	80	75		52					
Lovell	2131	2447	2371	2451	2508	2175	1857	1575	1686	640	699	717						
Lucerne							150				80							
Lusk	1504	1650	1495	1890	2089	1814	1218	929	2092	434	414	274	180	253				
Lyman	1896	2284	643	425	483	378	377	274	577	182	50							
Lysite	70	75	50	75	50	113	75		62									
McFadden	80	100	135	160	170	222	62											
McKinnon							161											
Manderson	83	174	117	167	107	130	96	104	225		225							
Manville	97	94	92	124	154	240	201	207	584	133	241	241	106	89				
Marbleton	634	537	223	189		43	26		89	67								
Medicine Bow	389	953	455	392	328	338	264	250	210	170	127	236	168	84	250	97	105	
Meeteetse	368	512	459	574	404	373	296	400	300	226	207	318	245	56				
Midwest	495	638	743	850	2000	2180	1021	2122	415									
Mills	1574	2139	1724	1477	866	379	357	1277	796									
Miners Delight																		
Monarch/Alger											380		56	29	150	42	50	
Moorcroft	768	1014	981	826	517	270	543	278	1010	131	178							
Mountain View (Natrona)	1345	1500	1641	1721	250	387	341		420									
Mountain View (Uinta)	1189	628	500	400	400	223	107		89		75							

POPULATION HISTORY OF WYOMING CITIES AND TOWNS 1860-1990

COMMUNITY	1860	1870	1880	1884	1890	1900	1905	1910	1915	1920	1925	1930	1940	1950	1960	1970	1980	1990
Natrona												150	113	15				
Newcastle					1715	756	1008	975	651	1003	944	1201	1962	3395	4345	3432	3596	3003
Node												200	25	13	15		15	
Oakley										558		558	545					
Opal						127		127	65	210	94	110	78	67	55	34	128	95
Orchard Valley														1000	1449	1015	3321	3327
Orin							54			165								
Osage										709		200	128	284	325	346	350	350
Osmond													177	200	150	150	150	100
Otto						134		134				300	300	400	400	75	50	50
Paradise Valley																1764	2300	
Parkerton												150		90				
Parkman						115		175		124		260	103	75	30	30	20	20
Pavillion										113		175	176	241	190	181	287	126
Piedmont		150	79	75	77	109		109				34		29	29	25		
Pine Bluffs		147	47	100	156	135		246	650	618	424	670	771	846	1121	937	1077	1054
Pine Haven																	81	141
Pinedale									83	94	250	219	647	770	965	948	1066	1181
Powell								406	406	2463	1065	1156	1948	3804	4740	4807	5310	5292
Prospector-Rawhide																	1100	1100
Quealy										480	257	227	150	147	42			
Ralston														64	160		125	130
Rambler							106	106								100		
Ranchester						172	172	172		147	86	155	189	251	235	208	655	676
Rawlins		612	1451	1500	2235	2317	3617	4256	2975	3969	5587	4868	5351	7415	8968	7855	11547	9380
Reliance										416	808	600	872	700	405	425	500	500
Riverside			28	100	28	33		49	57	29		34	68	50	87	46	55	85
Riverton								483	803	2023	1168	1608	2540	4142	6845	7995	9588	9202
Rock River								123	195	281	270	260	349	424	497	344	415	190
Rock Springs		100	763	1500	3406	4363	5343	5778	5699	6456	6875	8440	9827	10857	10371	11657	19548	19050
Rolling Hills																	443	330
Salt Creek										515	513	75						
Saratoga			274	100	274	672	766	557	425	449	504	567	810	926	1133	1181	2410	1969
Sheridan			40	150	281	1559	4937	8408	8906	9175	8436	8536	10529	11500	11651	10856	15146	13900
Shirley Basin																300	450	100
Shoshoni								604	278	561	250	263	226	891	766	562	879	497
Sinclair/Parco											564	727	604	775	621	445	586	500
Smoot								150		210		251	355	280	250	200	175	200
South Laramie																250	1500	1500
South Pass City		460	37	100	33	69	83	150		157		191		15	25		10	

POPULATION HISTORY OF WYOMING CITIES AND TOWNS 1860-1990

COMMUNITY	1860	1870	1880	1884	1890	1900	1905	1910	1915	1920	1925	1930	1940	1950	1960	1970	1980	1990
South Superior								265	265	419	728	751	885	780	401	197	586	300
South Torrington														930	500	250	300	300
Stansbury														200				
Story								347	524	83		175	300	335	500	637	700	700
Sublet/Quealy										408	481	462	462	462				
Sundance					515	294	300	281	341	328	325	369	685	893	908	1056	1087	1139
Sunrise							672	672		787	636	736	981	450	345	80	200	100
Superior								1382	1382	1034	1676	1156	1240	1580	241	241		273
Sweetwater						200		290										
Ten Sleep								170		175		208	345	289	314	320	407	311
Teton																100	200	250
Thayne								100		115		140	269	229	214	195	256	267
Thermopolis						299	534	1524	1191	2095	1606	2129	2422	2870	3955	3063	3852	3247
Tie Siding/Hermosa			110	50	71	182		182		262		108		50	50			
Torrington								155	443	1301	874	1811	2344	3247	4188	4237	5441	5651
Trabing				200														
Ulm										181								
Upton						72		244	219	306	328	373	545	951	1224	987	1193	980
Van Tassell								50	54	170	97	99	82	34	15	21	10	8
Veteran												400	63	35	39	35	50	100
Walcott							153	153				46		25	75	20	20	20
Wamsutter								125	76	320	174	202	169	103	110	139	681	240
Warren AFB																4527	3627	3627
West Laramie																700	2000	2000
Westvaco														400				
Wheatland						327	1315	796	810	1336	1281	1997	2110	2286	2350	2498	5816	3271
Wilson								50		213		200	107	200	250	200	300	500
Winton/Megeath											774	150	327	665				
Worland								265	454	1225	1265	1461	2710	4202	5806	5055	6391	5742
Wright																	1117	1236
Yellowstone					117	131		131		165		200	200	200		162	350	400
Yoder										1105	170	266	201	128	83	101	110	136

1884: Colorado, New Mexico, Utah, and Arizona Gazetteer and Business Directory. Chicago: R.L. Polk, 1884.
1905: Wyoming. State Department. Census of Wyoming, 1905. Cheyenne: S.A. Bristol, 1905.
1915: Wyoming. Secretary of State. The Census of the State of Wyoming, 1915. Cheyenne: Wyoming Labor Journal Publishing Company, 1915.
1925: Wyoming. Secretary of State. Wyoming State Census, 1925. Cheyenne: 1926.

ABOUT THE AUTHOR

Riley Moffat is currently the Head of Reference at the Brigham Young University-Hawaii Library in Laie, Hawaii. He was formerly the Geography and Map Librarian at the Brigham Young University Library in Provo, Utah. He has a Master of Library Science degree from the University of Hawaii and a Master of Science in Geography and Cartography from Brigham Young University.

Mr. Moffat is the author of *Printed Maps of Utah to 1900*, *Map Index to Topographic Quadrangles of the United States, 1882-1940* and *Population History of Easter U.S. Cities and Towns: 1790-1870* along with several journal articles. With Gary Fitzpatrick, he is the author of *Early Mapping of Hawaii*, for which they received the S. M. Kamakau Award from the Hawaii Book Publishers Association and *Surveying the Mahele: Mapping Hawaii's Land Revolution*.

He also teaches geography at BYU-Hawaii, serves as an assistant editor of the *Journal Pacific Studies* and surfs the North Shore regularly.